DEEP HEALING

A Practical Outline of Past-Life Therapy

Hans TenDam

DEEP HEALING

A Practical Outline of Past-Life Therapy

Tasso Publishing
Amsterdam, Netherlands, 1996

CONTENTS

FOREWORD
by Trisha Caetano

In the fall of 1992, at a convention in the United States, it was my good fortune to sit next to Hans TenDam at the speaker's table. I was impressed by his innovative and grounded approach to past-life regression therapy. When I started coming to the Netherlands regularly, our acquaintance developed into friendship and now our conversations explore the unlimited possibilities of the universe - and beyond. With an impressive background, vast experience, dialectic reasoning and wry humor, Hans brings his creative, inquisitive and open mind into the text of *Deep Healing, A Practical Outline of Past-Life Therapy*.

Much more than an outline for therapy, this book provides a paradigm for the entire application of past-life work to modern therapy. It includes philosophy, theory, a priory evidence, solid techniques, new language, case histories, examples, traditional and alternative methods, healing techniques, soul work and Hans' unique brand of humor.

A multidimensional man, Hans TenDam owns a management consulting business, has a private therapy practice and continues to offer a two-year Past Life Regression Therapy training program. Hans and his former students trained most of the past-life therapists in Holland, and he trained approximately one-third of the past-life therapists in Brazil.

His writing ranges across the spectrum of literature. He has published everything from management help to exploring intuitions and inspirations, from children's books to professional business analysis, from the practical to the subjective to the mystical. His beautiful book, *The Rose Window* is a modern equivalent to the *I Ching*. *Politics, Civilization and Humanity*, with unique insight gives a long-term view on the social, political and economic dynamics of today's world. This eclectic background gives comprehensive scope to *Deep Healing*.

In the past, the concept of rebirth was primarily limited to religious and mystical experience, and today it remains a fundamental aspect of most Easternreligions. Hermes Trismegistus describes reincarnation in the Egyptian Hermetic Fragments:

The Soul passes from form to form
And the mansions of her pilgrimage are manifold.
Thou puttest off thy bodies as raiment;
And as vesture dost thou fold them up.
Thou art from old, O Soul of man,
Yeah, thou art from everlasting.

For centuries there have been heated debates on whether reincarnation was fact or fantasy. It was most often agreed that it was a belief with no empirical evidence to support it. It remained intangible.

My purpose here is not to discuss whether reincarnation is a reality, or if rebirth is a sound hypothesis. Copious books are written on this subject and are available for those who seek debate or deeper exploration. *Deep Healing* does not use the reader's time discussing the theoretical possibilities. It simply gives background information and research findings; then it informs, giving the when, where, how and with whom to use the past-life techniques in the therapeutic setting, imparting deep healing to the individual doing the work.

I became interested in past life work as a therapeutic possibility and began doing past life regression therapy in 1970. Then I had no particular belief in past lives as a fact and to this day I have not invested in this belief one way or the other. I have also found that past life regression therapy is not a panacea for all life's issues or problems. Still, many clients have returned to the past to reclaim the present life. I have worked with clients who tried all the conventional and alternative medical practices available to find relief from devastating migraine headaches. As a last resort, they tried the unconventional technique of past life regression and found permanent cessation of the migraines. Patients have resolved illogical relationships, freed themselves from addiction, depression, compulsion and obsession. They have returned to positive lifetimes learning the truth of power, the essence of life and the magnitude of the soul.

Therefore, the question whether or not past lives are real is moot and irrelevant. The internal experience of awareness and the external expression of freedom become the reality. In my experience, past life regression therapy remains one of the most powerful healing tools available in the therapeutic process today.

8

A precedent to new and innovative therapy has been proposed. In the introduction of his book, *Memories, Dreams, Reflections*, the psychiatrist Carl G. Jung states, *Only what is interior has proved to have substance and a determining value*. Later in the same book he writes,

> *Prejudice cripples and injures the full phenomenon of psychic life. . . . Rationalism and doctrinairism are the diseases of our time; they pretend to have all the answers. But a great deal will yet be discovered which our present limited view would have ruled out as impossible. Our concepts of space and time have only approximate validity, and there is therefore a wide field for minor and major deviations. In view of all this, I lend an attentive ear to the strange myths of the psyche, and take a careful look at the varied events that come my way, regardless of whether or not they fit in with my theoretical postulates.*

Recently Thomas Moore wrote in his book *Care of the Soul*,

> *Psychology and spirituality need to be seen as one. In my view, this new paradigm suggests the end of psychology as we have known it altogether because it is essentially modern, secular and ego-centered. A new idea, a new language and new traditions must be developed on which to base our theory and practice.*

Hans TenDam develops new ideas, new language, a new paradigm and he lends "an attentive ear to the strange myths of the psyche." His book realizes this precedent with his innovative therapeutic techniques.

More and more psychotherapists are using past life regression as a therapeutic tool. With curious synchronicity, several psychotherapists in the early 1980's found themselves working with clients who were presenting material that obviously was not related to a present-life time frame. Was it archetypal material or from the collective unconscious, symbolic representation or psychodrama, or was it possible that these experiences were actual past life memories?

Realizing that this phenomena must also be occurring with other therapists, a support group was formed that has now evolved into a large, international organization. The Association for Past-Life Research and Therapies, Inc., has members in countries all over the world, provides the *Journal of Regression Therapy*, a quarterly newsletter, national conferences and an international information and networking system. It is presently based in Riverside, California, USA.

On his own, having already researched and used past life concepts in a therapeutic context for several years, Hans TenDam published his first book on the subject in 1983, *Exploring Reincarnation*. At the same time he was conducting his first past-life regression training program with Dutch students. Hans is a pioneer in establishing practical, specific tools for using past-life regression as a viable, therapeutic method in the healing process. The rationale and application of these tools are the foundation of *Deep Healing*.

Throughout the book, Hans compares his work with that of his contemporaries. He gives them credit where due, at times amalgamating their methods with his own to present comprehensive and effective ways of doing the process. Into past life therapy, Hans blends subpersonalities, family systems, archetypes, roles we play, Transactional Analysis and Gestalt. He explains how to integrate alternative methods such as Touch for Health and simple acupressure. Vast in scope, the reader explores everything from being an effective therapist to working with the soul.

Hans makes therapy simple by showing how to take what the client gives and working with it directly. He suggests minimal inductions where possible and stresses cathartic reliving followed by deep healing. His respect for the individuality of the client and his specific methods for staying with the client are impressive. He stays open-minded and objective. Many sentences begin with phrases such as, "My experience with past-life therapy indicates . . .," "Personally, I never . . .," "Make careful note of . . . ," I do not recommend . . . "

A new science must have a new language. Hans creates and defines words that clarify and make more efficient the communication between himself and the reader. He addresses areas of working with the human psyche often neglected by other therapeutic models. For example, many conventional therapies address trauma, as does Hans, but in addition he provides us with the word "hangover." He proposes that repeated abuse in the form of rejection, lack of affection, coldness, repression, etc., results in feelings of hopelessness and heaviness, exaggerating the "false self" and diminishing the psyche. He shows us how to recognize and work with these debilitating feelings.

Of great value is his client-centered approach to therapy, his way of showing unconditional client regard. "If people do not tell the truth right away, they have reasons for that choice. We are not prosecutors, but therapists." Hans says that therapy is based not on sympathy but on trust and staying with the client. At one point he writes,

The beginning of each session is trust.
The end of each session is catharsis.
The process of each session is musical.

This book invites into the mind and methods of the man. Hans' grounded, practical techniques are simply and clearly defined. His humor, veracity and wisdom thread through the book. In whatever language or however it is said, truth is universal and at the same time deeply internal. *Deep Healing* expresses internal truth. It encompasses all levels of past life work, but most of all, it is a practical "how to" guide for using the past life model.

PREFACE

In 1983 I published *Exploring Reincarnation*, a general study of the subject of reincarnation. Originally published in Dutch, it appeared in English in 1990. Following this general work I wanted to elaborate further on the methodology used in regression and past-life therapy, so that this therapy might become more widely accepted.

I had discovered past-life therapy by accident, in weekend sessions that were meant to help people remember past lives. Soon the exploration of past lives in therapy appeared more important and more interesting than exploration done simply out of curiosity. A colleague told me about the recently published works of Netherton (1978) and Fiore (1978).

Since then I have developed my own methods, working first in informal sessions with relatives and friends and later in weekend seminars and with individual patients. This book is based on my seminars for therapists, given from 1984 to 1993.

I have also practiced and shared these methods in Brazil, and they are as effective and efficient there as they are in Western Europe.

I thank Rob Bontenbal for his extensive notes, Dirk van den Brink and Jan Valk for their tape recordings, and Agar Rombout and Ineke Valk for transcribing the recorded sessions and lectures. I have included some material about dissociation and renovation from Rob Bontenbal, and about working with children from Tineke Noordegraaf.

Further thanks to the other students who, with their questions and observations, enlivened the seminars and so this book. Naturally, I omitted names from the sample sessions and sometimes changed details to preserve privacy. I have streamlined and shortened the session records, but have not embellished them.

Hanna VanBoeschoten helped me in translating the original text into English and Joanne Garland edited the English text and made it into a better book. Thanks.

CHAPTER 1. A MAP OF THE AREA

Regression therapy is simple. Most psychological and psycho-somatic problems arise from causes that began in the past. Discovering, reliving and understanding those causes may produce lasting relief.

Many problems result from traumatic experiences that occurred in the past. Those experiences, never having been assimilated, become repressed and can later be restimulated by weaker but similar experiences. Also, natural reactions to difficult past circumstances can persist, even when these reactions are no longer adequate. Such reactions may become compulsive programs: falsifications, distortions and unjustified generalizations.

The approach. The field.
A past-life therapist is a regression therapist who accepts that when patients return to the causes of their problems, experiences from apparent past lives emerge, as well as experiences from between lives and before birth. This phenomenon may sound unbelievable to lay people, but it happens. More importantly, this process heals people.

For many problems, regression therapy is much more effective and efficient than other forms of psychotherapy. Further, reincarnation therapy is often more effective than a mere regression therapy that would reject experiences of past lives and memories from between lives and before birth.

In regression therapy as it is approached in this book, the goal of each intervention is *catharsis*: cleansing, liberation, purification. Each session is directed toward catharsis. Nearly every successful catharsis produces, besides emotional purification and physical release, a growth of understanding. In psychotherapy, insight is the intellectual aspect of catharsis. Effective regression and reincarnation therapy with lasting results is insight-oriented therapy, rather than behavioural therapy. My psychoanalytical approach is based more on the work of Alfred Adler than on that of Sigmund Freud or Carl Jung, though the work of all of them is relevant. An Adlerian approach better supports regression and reincarnation therapy than a Freudian or Jungian approach. A Freudian interpretation help sone to understand traumas and emotional hangovers, at least without the nonsense that all problems have sexual causes. Adlerian ideas such as self-assertion, the quest for power, inferiority and superiority feelings, are more relevant to character postulates. Hans VonSassen produced an excellent survey (1967) of the similarities and differences between Freudian and Adlerian views. An excerpt from his work appears in the introduction to the Ansbachers' compilation (1982) of Adler's work.

Undoubtedly, a Jungian background helps us to accept regression and especially reincarnation regression, but saddles us with several ideas that explain little and in fact hinder open-minded guidance. Reincarnation therapists such as Denys Kelsey and Glenn Williston see respectively a Freudian and an Adlerian theme - the quest for love and the quest for power - as prime themes through lives. I would add a Jungian theme: the quest for self-realization. Still, for the practice of therapy, Adler's approach remains the most useful. I will return to themes of Individual Psychology when dealing with character postulates.

The next issue that arises with regression therapy is whether or not to use hypnosis. Do regression therapists use hypnosis? Many do so explicitly, while others hardly do at all. The approach that is described here does not use hypnotic induction, though a hypnotic state is unavoidable in any process of becoming absorbed in inner realities.

In practice *hypnosis* has three meanings. In the broadest meaning, hypnosis is a special state of mind, and thus of body. More especially, it is a state of mind induced by a hypnotist in a subject or patient. Technically, hypnosis is an induction method involving instructions that make the patient or subject sleepy, forgetful and dependent. Stage hypnosis shows this phenomenon dramatically, and this aspect of hypnosis has given the practice its spectacular and doubtful ring.

Generally, in a hypnotic state our brain rhythm is slower, our skin resistance is greater, our muscular tension is reduced, our breath is deeper and calmer, and sometimes our body temperature falls. We feel relaxed and peaceful, perceive less of our surroundings, and perceive our body either less clearly or more acutely.

Also, time perception changes. Hypnotized subjects often think that only a quarter of an hour has elapsed, while it has been an hour or longer. Sometimes the reverse occurs: after half an hour they think that a few hours have passed.

In daily life, hypnosis as a mental and physical state occurs spontaneously when we become absorbed in some experience. We can become absorbed by a film or a book, by making love, or by indulging in daydreams or memories. The perception of everything outside our focus of attention decreases, and our sense of time changes. Suddenly someone pulls our arm and says she has already called three times to tell us that coffee is ready. We had been so engrossed in our book that we did not hear it. Or we are deeply engaged in some job, and only during an interruption or afterward we notice that we have cut our hand. And only then it begins to hurt.

We often lack concentration and calm. So, methods abound that may increase our calm and concentration. Think about yoga, meditation, alpha training, and so on. Those methods are employed to relax us, to calm us, to enhance our concentration, our self-control, our peace of mind. They all involve some sort of self-hypnosis, but we had better limit our definition of "self-hypnosis" to classical hypnotic methods, such as listening to our own voice or to a recorded tape with suggestive instructions. Besides spontaneous and self-induced hypnotic trance, hypnosis may be induced by another person, probably a professional hypnotist or hypnotherapist.

In our therapy we have patients absorb themselves in their problem and its causes. Absorption and confrontation become more intense in this altered state. By contrast, classic hypnotherapy uses trance to make positive suggestions more effective rather than to explore and understand issues and causes. Such hypnotherapy induces hypnosis by instruction or by music, by sounds and visual impressions. Instructions first tell subjects to go to sleep, and then bind them to the hypnotist, often until these subjects lose their own ability to make choices.

In a second approach the hypnotist gives instructions to dream or "visualize," rather than to sleep. The hypnotist may then suggest that the subject be more oneself. Respecting the free will of the patient, such a hypnotist will remain as simply a guide.

I view the hypnotic state not as the product of a specific intervention, but as a natural by-product of good work. When we enter the right theme in the right way, patients will automatically become absorbed in their reliving, just as people become absorbed in a book or a movie. That process - indeed provoked, but also spontaneous - is often so strong that usual hypnotic instructions seem artificial and superfluous by contrast.

In regression therapy we say that we move back to the past. This is just a figure of speech, as we can move only to the future and we continuously remain in the present. With regression to the past, we mean contacting the past that we still carry with us now. We do not move back to past experiences and to past lives, but to the retained past that we carry now. We are not time travelers, but are detectives and surgeons in our own videotape library.

When we go back during therapy, we move to things of the past that continue to interfere with us. The only reason to move back to age three in therapy is that something of the three-year old child is in us right now, stuck in a traumatic experience with all its feelings and thoughts. We carry the problematic past with us as unresolved shadows and undigested residue. A therapeutic regression assimilates such episodes by discerning, reliving and integrating them, and thus releasing them so that they haunt us no longer. All those years, something had not been assimilated in our psyche, while it had often precipitated changes in our body. We are, after all, psychosomatic beings. Now we can assimilate and resolve things that happened in the past.

We all carry a great portion of past with us, in the end everything we have ever experienced. Much of this past is, in the mathematical sense, "integrated." But not everything is alive now. Only a part of our past is connected to the present personality who thinks and feels and intends and acts today. When the present makes us ill, we may need medicine, physiotherapy, simple advice or a change of conditions. But when the past makes us ill, psychotherapy is necessary.

Patients visit us for things they carry with them - problems of yesterday, of last month, of last year, or of five lifetimes ago - but carried now. In our present personality, shadows and echoes of the past haunt us, mostly unconsciously, with remnants of voices and feelings and impressions of long ago. We do not want simply to lift the unconscious contents into the conscious, but we want liberation, cleansing, catharsis.

Catharsis is an emotional release that leads to emotional peace. It is also intellectual purification that leads to intellectual peace, to that state we call understanding. Acceptance means both emotional peace and understanding, or "peace of mind." Such peace is not passivity but vitality; it means being in harmony with our surroundings and with ourselves. This vital peace, this "peace of mind and emotion," is equivalent to the Chinese idea of *Tao*, the perfection within the accepted imperfect, being congruent with oneself in the simple, provisional perfection of the here-and-now.

We have to gain access to our past, to its shadows, its knots, its ulcers, its loads, its poisons. We can also access the joy and the radiance and the power of our past, and sometimes that aspect is more important. But if you drive a car with one foot on the brake, you should not accelerate until you remove your foot from the brake. In the same way, removing loads helps us more than does simply increasing energy.

After explaining catharsis, this book continues with induction methods that locate and discover the charges and structures of the unassimilated past. The "bridges" to the past that exists within us are the *emotional bridge*, the *verbal bridge*, the *imaginative bridge* and the *physical* or *somatic bridge*. Then we deal with the essence of regression therapy: to guide a reliving that produces relief. After that reliving we introduce support methods that couple induction and catharsis directly. These methods include *acupressure, egostate therapy, aura exploration* and *postulate analysis*.

The basic therapeutic intervention is resolution of fear. We will use this intervention to explain the core ideas of the therapeutic session: the *prism*, the *arc*, and the identification and processing of *charges*. Resolution of fear provides a prime example of how to deal with traumas. Only later will we discuss other repercussion types such as *hangovers, postulates* and *pseudo-obsessions*. We broach on *obsessions* only as far as necessary. Then we address the problem of *alienation* and its special treatment, *homing*.

Finally, we try to explain how repercussions of past lives are recorded, and how catharsis works. Our data are limited, our models are awkward, but we can at least approximate a deeper understanding.

The research base.
The current research base in the field of past-life therapy is limited. The effectiveness of regression therapy has hardly been researched at all. Johannes Cladder has published interesting

material on the effectiveness of past-life therapy in phobias (1986); Helen Wambach did a survey of 26 past-life therapists (1986); and Ney Peres in 1983 evaluated the results of initial efforts of reincarnation therapy in Brazil.

In the Brazilian study, of 43 patients, 35 recollected a past life and eight did not. After an average of 17 sessions, 13 treatments were successful, three treatments were finished without result after an average of six sessions, 11 patients interrupted treatment after an average of three sessions, and 13 were still in treatment at the time of research. An analysis of interrelationships provided only one significant and interesting result. There was no correlation between believing or not believing in reincarnation and recollecting or not recollecting a past life (more than 95% validity).

The most important research to date has been done by Winafred Lucas, who showed that during effective past-life therapy both patient and therapist exhibit a brain-wave pattern that is simultaneously high on beta and delta, and low on alpha and theta.

Hazel Denning, Executive Director of the Association for Past-Life Research and Therapies, studied the results achieved by eight therapists with nearly 1000 patients between 1985 and 1992. Many patients had sought regression therapy after having pursued other therapies that proved ineffectual. Results of regression therapy were measured just after the therapy, after six months, one year, two years and five years. About 450 patients could still be tracked after five years. The rating of "symptoms gone completely" increased over the years, while other positive ratings declined. Denning found that after five years: 24% reported symptoms completely gone; 23% reported considerable or dramatic improvement; 17% reported noticeable improvement; and 36% reported no improvement.

Recently, Ronald VanderMaessen from NVRT, the Dutch association for past-life therapy, conducted another sizeable research program. He investigated the results of regression therapy with 401 clients of 32 therapists (1994). Six months after the end of this therapy, more than 50% reported that their problems had largely or completely been solved. This percentage was somewhat higher than what had been reported immediately following the therapy. About 25% showed some improvement, while about 20% did not improve. These results were reached, on the average, with 15 hours of therapy conducted during a total of six sessions. Also, this group included many difficult cases. Most patients had tried everything else before they sought regression therapy.

In 1994 I analyzed the results of 80 therapies from my own practice. Of these 80, nine had been canceled prematurely. Of 40 completed appraisal forms (three months after the therapy), 20% reported being very satisfied, 40% satisfied, 15% rather satisfied, and 20% ambivalent.

Patients mentioned mental results most often (65%), emotional results less (40%) and physical results the least (25%). These results were reached with an average of two sessions (five hours of therapy). Continuing therapy through more than two sessions corresponded with increased mental results. Emotional results increased when present-life regression was used in addition to the past-life regression work.

CHAPTER 2. PROBLEMATIC
REPERCUSSIONS

Regression is the process of going back to origins of the repercussions of unassimilated experiences. The repercussions that
we still carry with us may manifest as:
- *traumas*
- *hangovers*
- *postulates, or heavier: character neuroses*
- *pseudo-obsessions*
- *obsessions*
- *alienation*

The treatment of each kind of repercussion is different. For example, egostate therapy - using dissociation of subpersonalities
- is often useful, but for pseudo-obsessions such a dissociation
is essential.

Wilhelm Reich and later L. Ron Hubbard used the term
engram to describe the residue of an unassimilated experience.
Hubbard said that a traumatic experience weakens the "ana-
lytical mind," so that impressions enter the more mechanical,
instinctive, "reactive mind" without selection or interpretation.
He viewed engrams as the only source of aberration and disease. Many engrams originate in moments of unconsciousness
or relative unconsciousness, such as shock. This chapters re-
fines the concept of *engram*.

Karma and dharma.
Popular esoteric opinion uses the term *karma* for all problematic repercussions. About karma there are many thoughts, but I
believe that most are imprecise or wrong. In the end, the words
of Adler remain valid: "Not what we have got, is important,
but what we do with it."

During therapy, some of the ideas that patients may hold
about karma may actually hinder them, especially when they
see karma as a universal and immutable law. That view of karma
reduces a person's choices and responsibilities, and promotes
speculation about objective interrelationships. It avoids confront-

ing the concrete, subjective regression experience. People speculate, for example, about the spiritual, karmic bond that they have with others. Such reflections may expand to include society and the development of humanity.

Special bonds do exist. Personal relationships and groups indeed continue through several lifetimes. Groups of souls may even engage in joint "projects." From the evidence, I believe in group karma, but we may not assume that group karma is at work in any collective event. Mass events may have nothing to do with karma. The fact that thousands or millions of people died in concentration camps or at Hiroshima does not imply common karma, and surely it *creates* no common karma between them. No karmic bond was created between the crew of the Enola Gay and the population of Hiroshima. Likewise, victims of the sinking of the Titanic may have no common karma.

Karma and its associated term, *dharma*, derive from personal deeds and personal interactions. Companionship between any two people creates a tie only when that companionship becomes a factor in a personal encounter. Before that encounter, we remain subject to general evolutionary dynamics; events and encounters are not planned and meant as schooling, but they school by accumulation of experience.

Concentration camp experiences produce ties only between people who interacted personally, as companions or as brutes and victims. What people personally think of each other, what they feel for each other, what they do and fail to do to each other, create the liabilities of karma and the assets of dharma.

When ten thousand people die in a famine in Africa, or two thousand drown in Bangladesh, we cannot explain these events by karma. Such disasters provide experience and thus learning, but they are not planned so that they create learning. Their meaning comes after the fact, as when we learn how to avoid such disasters, or how to forecast them, or how to improve warning systems, or how to increase people's protection from them. All of this response is part of evolution, not karma. *Good judgment is the result of experience. Experience is the result of bad judgment.*

But if we in the West simply accept these disasters, if we don't help, don't we burden ourselves with karma? Hardly, as we are not in charge over there. The Ethiopian or Sudanese government have a greater responsibility for what happens in their countries than do we. Ethiopia, for example, had only one health care worker serving its people for every 122 in its military, when the world average is 1 to 2.3. Could we influence the Ethiopian government? No. With our thoughts maybe? I think not. We are not responsible for what happens in Ethiopia. We can help, but only modestly. Of course, nobody stops any of us from becoming a politician or official in an international organization. In that sense we have responsibility, but our first responsibility is for what is right in front of us. Many people feel burdened by not doing enough for Africa. Worry and guilt may seem noble, but these feelings may simply provide us with comfort, as preoccupation with such important things may excuse us from making something of our personal life. I do not suggest that all of us should turn inward and stop worrying about the world, but blaming ourselves or others contributes nothing. I do not think that we improve the world - or ourselves - in this way.

Many people who are interested in past-life therapy view life in an opposite way: they are fatalists, even in their own life. They see themselves as victims of circumstance. They do not feel responsible for themselves. They view everything that happens as their karma; it all happened *to* them.

Changing such an attitude is difficult, and regression alone will not be enough. I write in *Exploring Reincarnation* that in this respect being Christian or believing in reincarnation do not make any difference. A fatalist Christian can say, *Jesus bled at the cross and took away our sins.* A fatalist believer in reincarnation can say, *If I don't make it today, I may make it tomorrow.*

In regression, we often uncover our victim experiences first. Only afterward do we come across aggressor experiences. Memories of ourselves as aggressors tend to be more repressed. Full exploration of a karmic theme often includes *aggressor lives*, *victim lives* and *observer lives*. People who had several aggressive lives, but then changed their mind, do not necessarily have to experience victim lives. Conversion of attitude can be enough to make victim lives unnecessary. And victim experiences do not automatically make us aggressors. We may seek revenge, but vindictiveness is a decision, not a mere emotional reaction. Remaining a victim may also be a decision, usually with the presence of a character postulate such as, *Poor me, everybody always takes it out on me,* or *They are great and I am small, and that is not fair.*

Such postulates are something like a switch stuck in one position. We may even fear our own aggression, especially if our aggression once got out of hand. Such fear may also be a way to opt out: *I am a victim, so I do not need to develop.* Below that you may imply, *I am better, more gentle; I do not belong on this rude, primitive planet.*

Inferiority feelings and superiority feelings are all character problems. People may relive a series of traumatic experiences to no avail, because their own behavior and attitude got them into or kept them in situations of suffering. Character is destiny.

Self-pity is something that is easy to spot in regressions. Self-pity and patient mentality (*I am weak and suffering and others need to help me.*) are attitudes that clog the process of a person's own resolution; such attitudes are *recursive*. Their attitude may be, *Poor me, everybody always takes it out on me. This session will just confirm that again*, or *I need you, I am dependent on you; I cannot do it, please you do it for me.* Beware of self-pity, also in yourself. Patients may suffer under wrong, incompetent or even evil therapists, and therapists may suffer under unresponsive patients.

Don't play the game of blame, either. It is no use to blame yourself for every useless session, but neither is it of use to blame the patient for every useless session. Do the best you can, try to be sensible in your choice of patients, and know that you can't win them all. Your batting average is what counts.

Pity toward others is no better than self-pity. It directs attention to others, but it smothers perception with feeling. A therapist who is full of pity feels more, but sees less. She also may trigger the self-pity of the patient. There is a place and time for everything, even for sobbing together, but don't make a living out of that. Our job is to heal, not to co-suffer.

Empathy, perception and trust are jewels in the crown of professional attitude. Pity does not belong there. Compassion does, as a visitor that drops in at unsought moments, but not as a permanent guest. Therapy is about the feelings of the patient, not about our own feelings. Therapy works best when the therapist is happily married and leads a life that is also rewarding outside of the therapy practice, so that the therapist's own emotional needs do not contaminate the sessions.

Therapy is about the patient. When a woman wants to talk about her husband, keep the discussion focused on the woman. If she thinks her husband should change, he should visit you himself. Long stories about other people are useless; long discussions about other people are gossip. Gossip in a professional vocabulary lacks even the only grace that ordinary gossip may have: being juicy and saucy. In a therapy session don't dwell on other people.

Character is about attitudes that endure. The following example is about such persistence. A woman could not stand her recurrent illnesses. She wanted to know why she had them. The therapist used verbal exploration (see Chapter 4), starting from the sentences *I don't accept it* and *I do not want to remain in bed*. These statements triggered a memory of her life as a paralyzed girl, rebellious about having to remain in bed forever. Her anger and rebellion ran deep and had persisted to the present day. Using a higher-self intervention (see Chapter 6), the therapist asked her the reason for this life.

Before being a paralyzed girl she had been a farmer who had a paralyzed and deformed child. The farmer considered this child a *horrible chunk of flesh*, and despised it. After the farmer's death he remained hovering about his small farm, to see if his other sons did all right. This led to the next part of the session, in which the patient perceived communication from a radiant presence:

T: *Do you think once in a while about your deformed child?*
P: *No. I don't want to think about it.*
T: *So you don't think about your lack of love then?*
P: *That other one also keeps harping about that.*
T: *Which other one?*
P: *I do not know who it is. I rather feel its presence.*
T: *What does it try to convey to you?*
P: *That I have to come along with it.*
T: *Why don't you go?*
P: *It badgers the life out of me about lack of love for my first child.*
T: *You don't accept that?*
P: *No! If a cow gives birth to a deformed calf, you also don't keep whining about it.*

The radiant presence could not convince him of the rigidity and impropriety of his attitude. He stubbornly stuck with the analogy of the deformed calf: *Such a beast you simply remove, don't you?*

Then the radiant presence used the principle of *They that will not be taught, must suffer*, leading to the well-known experience of involuntary birth. This man was then sucked into a new womb, becoming the paralyzed girl. As he had refused to learn during the period between lives, he began a hard lesson on earth. This lesson continued into the present life. After a long session, for the first time this patient fully accepted that she had to remain in bed for a few days.

Character is also about positive traits. But some positive traits, some talents, are hidden. In addition to *karmic* charges and structures, there are *dharmic* (positive) charges and structures to discover. Those dharmic charges arise from assimilated experiences, integrated issues that for some reason have remained submerged. Therapy usually does not deal directly with dharma, but if our inhibitions fall away and we assimilate the not-yet-integrated, everything runs better and dharmic issues surface.

Sometimes we do have to intervene to liberate those energies and capacities. Such an intervention may be small, but its effects may be great. Sometimes recognition by another is enough to free the dharma. Sometimes the remark of a sensitive about a past life may trigger recognition and release energies.

A quality or a capacity may emerge suddenly. For instance, you are preparing a lecture and suddenly something in you starts to whir and you can do everything without paper. That experience is a kind of positive pseudo-obsession. A powerful part of you puts the worrisome preparations aside and says, *Girl, let me do that.* The more such subpersonalities you have, the better, as long as they are adequate and do not push one another aside.

As another example, a girl of 16 meets a rapist. Suddenly she knows precisely what she has to say and do, and she makes the guy slink off.

In a regression she appears to have once been a prominent courtesan. Well, that woman knew how to deal with men. On the brink of that rape, "Madame" emerges: *Now this brat, not even decently clean, should just not try to fool around with my girl!*

"Madame" has never emerged before. She does not fit in the person of a young girl. But right now she is needed, and arrives to help. After that time, "Madame" may begin to integrate with all her capacities, and the girl will make a leap into adulthood.

A dharmic structure, a subpersonality who as such is positive, joins the girl. As Madame interfered easily and successfully, probably Madame's life carried no heavy problems, hangovers or traumas. She was effective, and she remained herself, even in a difficult position.

Dharmic capacities emerge when a person mobilizes a positive past-life personality or releases a negative past-life personality or pseudo-obsessor. Often, one's capacities are not blocked by a pseudo-obsessor but rather by a negative subpersonality of the present life.

Some people even display a front personality that is the great inhibitor. These people are their own pseudo-obsessors. They have built, for example, a façade full of problems and worries, full of postulates, often full of hangovers. Their ordinary consciousness is like a "dirt-skirt" that covers many positive things. Sometimes great pressure tears away that dirt-skirt, just as war makes many things possible. Instead of the inner ego collapsing, the artificial outer ego collapses and a more capable personality emerges.

Talents are dharmic structures. Rarely do we have to hunt for them. By removing and resolving problems, by integrating the not-yet-integrated, we wake up our hidden assets. That is also true with traumas. A trauma from a past life may still sleep, if it has not yet been restimulated. A person may appear to have no problem at all, then something restimulates the trauma and it wakes up. Positive things awake in the same way, but not always by restimulation.

Wouldn't it be better to integrate all positive subpersonalities, so that we can always respond adequately, not only when we are in need? No. Such integration may actually be counterproductive. That "Madame" with all her admirable qualities really does not fit in the life of a young girl. It is better for the time being that she emerges only when necessary. If a subpersonality has qualities that it can express less than one percent of the time, integration of that subpersonality would simply be an exercise in frustration. It is better to allow this subpersonality to remain sleeping or dreaming in the background.

When our subpersonalities know, accept and like one another, and when they can enter and leave at will, we have attained the best integration possible. However, subpersonalities that are completely merged can prevent our adaptation to the different conditions of different lives, and to those that occur within each life. The best option is to be able to use each subpersonality when appropriate. Interaction between subpersonalities provides development and flexibility, whereas complete integration of all personalities discourages development. Feeling whole is near to feeling perfect. Beware of premature completion.

Also, treatment of pseudo-obsessions, interfering past personalities, does not always result in integration. Ask each subpersonality, "What do you want? What should we do?" A subpersonality may crawl inside us, may enter a discarnate realm, or may remain close and only sometimes enter us. Absorption of a subpersonality into the present personality is not a requirement. Always ask the subpersonality, "What do you want, what should be done right now?"

Some subpersonalities are so negative, so virulent, that they appear to be hostile, alien. They are not pseudo-obsessors, but obsessors. Edelstien exorcised one, the "Avenger."

Edelstien treats ego states as states of our present self that have started at specific moments in our life history as response patterns, and have never divorced from our main personality, unless, like Sybil, we have different parts that are more or less cut off from one another. When we are conscious in one personality, we may have forgotten about the others. I will return to this subject when dealing with pseudo-obsessions.

Restimulation of repercussions.
Not everything that happens to us is amusing. When I come home from work, I am tired. Maybe I need half an hour or an hour to restore myself, maybe with slippers, a newspaper, the cat on my lap, a pipe in my mouth, a cup of coffee or a book. In other words, I feel the repercussion of weariness and irritation of that day and slowly I recuperate from all that.

This weariness and irritation may result from many different things: the chatter in my office, my uncomfortable chair, the smell in the corridor, an unpleasant task, a tiresome colleague, or any combination of these factors. It may come purely from boredom and wear and tear. Or the work may no longer appeal to me; I may dislike it. The repercussion of such a situation I call a *hangover*.

Hangovers lack specific, well-defined occasions. They grow more gradually and are less definite. They have chronic causes, not acute ones, as if mist or grit or dust or dirt, or even something sticky or slimy, has entered the soul. If people are so listless that they no longer regenerate or recuperate, the process worsens itself. This listlessness is like a *dirt-skirt* that sticks on and takes time and effort to dissolve. With a so-called hangover, maybe a person dreams of it. That person wakes up in the morning and feels heavy. He may dislike his work more every day. The dirt-skirt thickens, the hangover grows.

Usually hangovers include some compulsion, so they imply avoidance or the impossibility of a liberating decision. If I, for example, decide to quit my job, that decision will probably cheer me up. I may feel liberated. On my last days in that job I go whistling to my office. Precisely because I don't care any longer, everything goes fine.

We may resolve hangovers by relaxing, or doing some jogging, or engaging in something else that we really like. We prevent hangovers by doing things we love, or things that are challenging and meaningful. If we function smoothly, we have *Funktionlust*. Smooth running of the human machine, especially at peak performance, drains away "psychic waste" during the process. The hangovers that interest us as therapists, however, are hangovers that are not cured in daily life. Usually they are hangovers from a tedious childhood. Often they are from a tedious past life.

A hangover is the result of long frustration, the accumulation of small miseries. Children may by the age of six have hangovers from their parents, even without traumatic incidents. A mother who treats her child roughly, using a hard brush with soft soap, does not inflict trauma, but if she goes on like that for a couple of years, the child can incur a hangover.

Sleeping and dreaming help provide restoration. We may wake up refreshed the next morning. Sleep is the small regenerator. The afterlife, the period between lives, is the great regenerator. Few things refreshes like a good sleep, and nothing refreshes us like a good death. But sometimes, as when we wake up in the morning feeling broken, we enter our new life with a burden.

People with low energy often appear to have such hangovers. The central charge of many hangovers is impotence, and their main clutch is usually rancor, intense ill will. By fostering rancor, we remain victims, so that we may indulge in self-pity and do not need to change our behavior. In this way, character postulates freeze hangovers into our system.

Hangovers are engrams, as are traumas, but hangovers are a different type of engram. A hangover is a burden, a dirt-skirt. A trauma, on the other hand, is a wound. The quintessential trauma is that of the sudden death of someone near to you: your child, your husband, your wife, or when you are young, your father or mother.

For example, let's say that you are six years old. You whined until your mother allowed you to play at the home of a friend. Mother didn't like it, but she gave in. Your mother would usually come to fetch you, but this time she does not come. Later a neighbor arrives, all confused, saying only that you have to come with him. You are perplexed. The first thing that you hear when you arrive home is your father shouting, "Mummy died in an accident when she went to fetch you."

Then the ego collapses, not gradually but suddenly, as if someone has thrust a knife into you or a bomb has exploded. Your ego may be so shocked that your mind is no longer protected. Everything just enters, no longer controlled. Only later, as the trauma is repressed or worn down, life takes its normal course again. Although the ego has returned, it carries a wound that may fester.

On specific occasions the trauma re-emerges. Being called away suddenly, or shouted at, may drive you crazy. Someone with a green sweater gives you the creeps, because that neighbor wore a green sweater. Your father yelled at you with a haggard look, and if you see someone with a haggard look you feel terrible. This trauma happened just as you took off your jacket. When someone now says something to you as you take off your jacket, you feel frightened.

Traumas are locked in a layer of the psyche that reacts mechanically. What if something similar happens? Then the psyche interprets this new event as the same as the old. Any sensory, emotional or verbal component of an experience may, through association, restimulate the charges of the traumatic experience. Restimulation provides association, but with an emotional charge, and so each restimulation may swell the original charge.

A typical example of restimulation is sexual fetishism. Some men become excited by a pair of high heels or even by an open window. Regression is fit for such cases. During regression, people may find themselves in situations with women who are wearing such shoes or standing behind open windows or open shutters.

Pregnancy and birth.
Much restimulation occurs during pregnancy and at the moment of birth. Events that happen later in life then restimulate the traumatic experiences of pregnancy and birth. Pregnancy and birth so often link traumas of past lifetimes with problems that occur in the present life, that regression therapists such as Morris Netherton suspect that this link is necessary. They think that without restimulation during pregnancy or birth, nothing could enter from a past life. I think that this conclusion is premature, but I do not want to diminish the importance of pregnancy and birth.

Lee Salk, a child psychologist of Cornell University Medical College in New York, compared 52 teenagers who committed suicide with 104 who did not. Salk found that the teens who killed themselves had suffered more medical problems during birth, and their mothers had been ill more often during pregnancy. Problems that occur before or during birth increase one's susceptibility for stress. Among those teenagers who committed suicide, three to four times more often (Findlay 1985):

- *they had mothers who, during pregnancy, suffered a chronic illness or handicap such as anaemia, arthritis, high blood pressure, kidney problems, asthma, hepatitis or obesity*
- *they had breathing problems during the hours directly after birth (Modern means save newborns who used to die)*
- *they had mothers who received no prenatal care in the first twenty weeks of pregnancy, suggesting an unwanted pregnancy and so probably an unwanted child*

Netherton found that people who feel isolated or have autistic traits were often born to mothers who had been unconscious during birth, or were taken rapidly to an incubator. Regressions to the prenatal period often uncover a mixture of the experiences of the mother and of the fetus. Netherton finishes each prenatal regression with a verbal confirmation, directed to the patient *and* his or her mother, that the problem is over. The following example comes from one of my student therapists:

A young student distrusts people. She has difficulty in relating to people and feels unhappy. She thinks that this distrust may derive from her conviction that her parents rejected her as a baby. She hates her father for this.

After several childhood memories that gradually move her back in time, she finds herself in the womb. She is confused until the therapist anchors her. Then she realizes that her father is unhappy with the pregnancy and wants his wife to have an abortion.

When her mother considered this option, the child-to-be became so angry that she tried to poison her mother. The mother dropped the idea of abortion, despite increasing phenomena of pregnancy poisoning. Yet the girl continued to make her mother ill. Only when she realized that by harming her mother she also affected herself, she stopped.

Catharsis came when the therapist asked her why her father wanted her mother to have an abortion. Then she saw that her father felt insecure as head of the family. He considered himself too young for the responsibility and thought that he didn't earn enough money to support a family. When she perceived that right after birth her father expressed his emotions with difficulty, but surely was happy with her, she felt filled with joy. Understanding had replaced hate.

Does this change her character? Yes and no. It straightens her out. She loses a persistent emotion and reassumes her underlying attitudes. This process is one of integration, healing, therapy. But it doesn't mean she becomes soft, weak or naive. Getting rid of a heavy piece of armor is getting rid of a handicap - that is, in times of peace.

Regression is not about universal forgiveness or unconditional love. It is about understanding, acceptance and growth; it is about balance and full strength. It is not about becoming able-bodied, but about becoming able-souled and able-spirited. Real character is freedom.

CHAPTER 3. A TYPOLOGY OF KARMIC REPERCUSSIONS

This chapter deals with five types of karmic repercussions, five types of engrams: *traumas* (the classic type), *hangovers*, *character postulates*, *pseudo-obsessions* and *alienation*.

Traumas.
Traumas originate from concrete episodes, each of which had a definite beginning and end. During regression to a traumatic situation we can find the exact beginning and end of the trauma. The list below includes probably 95% of the traumatic situations that we encounter during regressions to past lives.

TRAUMATIC SITUATIONS

Abandonment	Inquistion
Accident	Loss
Asphyxiation	Murder
Assault	Mutilation
Attack	Persecution
Burning	Rape
Drowning	Starvation
Execution	Suicide
Fire	Surgery
Humiliation	Terror
Imprisonment	Tortur
Injury	War

Traumatic periods are strings of such traumatic situations. A traumatic period may begin, for example, with persecution and continue with imprisonment, inquisition, torture, and in the end, execution. Perhaps a person was surrounded at the marketplace, ridiculed, humiliated, finally raped and then abandoned. Or maybe someone has lost his way in the forest. He stumbles along, alone and dirty, then he is injured, and in the end he starves.

The basic *emotional charges* that we encounter most in traumas are: disgust, fear, loneliness, hate, jealousy, envy, shame, guilt, repulsion, despair, anger. These emotional charges are not mutually exclusive and can appear in almost any combination. Disgust and repulsion, for example, may blend into each other.

In addition to these basic emotional charges, the *somatic charges* of traumas are thirst, heat, hunger, cold, cramp, pain, filth, stench, exhaustion, paralysis.

Finally, the *mental charges* in traumas can be loss of consciousness, confusion, mesmerization, feeling beside oneself, freaking out, using drugs, fascination, hallucination, hypnosis, trance, exteriorization, infatuation, perplexity, anaesthesia. The significance of these mental charges is that they damage the assimilation mechanism. They also act as *complicators* when a person attempts to relive a particular past-life memory.

Some other emotions may also act as complicators. Craving, shame, guilt and lust complicate primary emotions, either by covering up those primary emotions, or by exhibiting ambivalence. For example, when I feel ashamed of my jealousy, the shame covers the jealousy. Then I can feel disgust about my shame. Such combinations are like what I refer to as emotional onions or knots.

Clusters of emotions that reinforce one another are something that I call *boosters*. For example, fear and desperation reinforce each other and form panic. Desperation increases fear, and fear desperation. The emotional state of anger, when combined with the mental state of feeling beside oneself, form rage. The frame next page offers a survey of typical trauma charges.

Other such clusters are more complex. Emotional complicators are of two kinds: *lockers* that cover up other emotions, and *twisters* that knot opposing emotions. The most common locker is guilt. Other lockers are shame, perplexity and absence. The ultimate absence is exteriorization, which occurs when the perceiving mind leaves the body.

An anger-grief cluster is a twister, because the two emotions work in different directions without neutralizing each other. Lust is a common twister when it is connected to emotions that by themselves are unlustful: pain, shame, impotence, envy, disgust. Lust is a positive emotion, but so primitive that it easily clusters with negative emotions. For example, people watch horror movies and engage in sadomasochism (SM) for pleasure. Probably such pastimes provide a measure of relief for people who have many twisted tensions.

TRAUMA CHARGES

Primary emotions:
Despair
Disgust
Dislike
Envy
Fear
Grief
Guilt
Hate
Impotence
Jealousy
Loneliness
Rage
Rancor
Repulsion
Shame

Physical charges:
Cold
Cramp
Discomfort
Exhaustion
Filth
Heat
Hunger
Pain
Paralysis
Stench
Thirst

Mental complicators:
Anaesthesia
Confusion
Desperation
Exteriorization
Fascination
Feeling beside oneself
Hallucination
Hypnosis
Incomprehension
Infatuation
Loss of consciousness
(etc.)
Mesmerization
Perplexity
Trance

Emotional complicators:
Craving
Guilt
Lust
Shame

Knots:
Anger + grief clod
Panic
(= fear + desperation)
Rage
(= anger + feeling beside onself)

This clustering may also happen with desire. Let's say that a girl is anxious about a nightly encounter. She trembles from excitement, about the expected lust, as well as about fear and even disgust. Besides *guilt* and *punishment*, the most common complicators are:
- *shame*
- *a negative emotion tied to delight*
- *a positive emotion tied to anguish*
- *narcissism: the postulate has become part of the self-image, so having the problem is tied to self-esteem*
- *secondary gain: the problem is the lesser of two evils; it draws attention from other people, it avoids self-judgment, or it avoids demands, etc.*

During a trauma we lose ourselves. The ego leaks; it goes to pieces. A trauma begins with a piercing experience, and then the ego collapses. When we are traumatized, suddenly we are no longer thinking, or self-conscious. We may be reduced to feeling like a frightened animal or a dazed robot.

Similarly, if other people wound us we may regard their action as "psychic rape." Gradations of psychic rape are (in increasing order): keeping people small, making people small, badgering people, hurting people, making people ill, making people crazy, destroying people.

Why do we retain our traumas, even into our future lifetimes? After a trauma we go on living. Usually we have repressed the memory of the awful experience. Then we die, and maybe we look back on our life from a clear-headed perspective.

Assume that you have had an excellent death experience. You have reviewed and understood your life, including a traumatic situation, and maybe you have forgiven other people and yourself. If the trauma had been purely emotional or mental, you could probably have assimilated it in the afterlife. But most traumas carry somatic (physical) charges. If during your lifetime you despaired, you may release that despair after death. You may wish to relive it, but from a different perspective, and then dissolve it. But if that despair is connected with coldness and weariness, you cannot completely dissolve such a cluster.

We seem to need a physical body before we can release somatic charges. More precisely, in the afterlife we are dealing with the etheric body or vehicle of vitality (see Chapter 8). Thus, in therapy it is wise always to look for the somatic charges of a trauma, because any traumatic cluster is anchored in its heaviest, most dense charges. Be suspicious of any catharsis of a traumatic experience if that catharsis does not include somatic agony and somatic relief. Without such agony and relief, the catharsis may still be incomplete.

One example of a locked cluster is an anger-guilt complex. Perhaps you feel guilty about what you once did when you were angry. Thus, you repress your violent outbursts; your guilt has locked in the anger. Guilt is a persistent and nasty emotion. It shouts all over you, *I am there and I will never go away!* while smothering this shout with the whisper of, *For God's sake, forget all about me!*

Persistent guilt feelings are really generalized guilt experiences. Generalization is always anchored in character postulates. Questions you may pose with guilt, as well as with other persistent charges:
- *What are the actual consequences of that guilt?*
- *What do you gain by holding onto it?*
- *Do other people have something to gain if you hold onto it?*
- *What do you do with that guilt in a positive sense?*
- *What do you want to do with it?*

Unlike such lockers, which may cover up emotions, twisters usually combine an expansive emotion and a contracting emotion. The most common twister is grief clustered with anger. Let's say you have been abandoned. You are sad, but also angry. Your anger prevents you from indulging in your grief. Your grief prevents you from expressing your anger. Anger is explosive, and grief is implosive. If the grief is inside and the anger is outside, you can express your anger only little by little and always in a tempered way, because your grief prevents you from exploding. But keeping anger inside and grief outside hinders any form of release. In general, traumas are wounds. What is the first thing we need if we are going to treat a physical wound? We need to know where it is. To treat a psychological wound we must also learn where it is - in place and time, in the situation where it originated.

Within therapy, we locate the psychological wound by surveying a traumatic period to find a string of situations similar to the ones I listed. Any one of these situations may carry its own charge, and the entire wound is anchored in one or more basic emotions. Look for these basic emotions by asking how a feeling feels: *I feel as if I have to withstand the whole world.* How does that feel? *Exhausting.* How does it feel to be exhausted? *Then I dislike myself for allowing it to have developed so far.* What kind of feeling does that dislike give? *Shame.*

When people mention items from the list of traumatic charges, and cite these items as reasons for therapy, we can use those mental and emotional charges - when they are actually present - as bridges into the regression. The same is true when these charges emerge at the beginning of a regression session. In addition to these traumatic charges, the mentioned somatic charges can also be used as bridges. The next list illustrates characteristic somatics that may lead into traumatic experiences.

SOMATIC BRIDGES TO TRAUMAS

1. Sharp headache
2. Lump in throat
3. Stings or cramps near the heart
4. Pressure on the chest
5. Stomach cramp
6. Belly pain
7. Tense muscles
8. Stabs
9. Spasms or tremors
10. Clearly located cold or warm spots
11. Involuntary posture changes. Shocks.
12. Sudden sweating
13. Dizziness, nausea
14. Titillation

No real catharsis will occur without agony first, agony in the form of intense pain, grief, impotence. But locate the agony. Don't search for cosmic, boundless moods and emotions. Locate the trauma where it occurred in time, but also where it may now manifest in the body or around the body (in the aura). Guide the catharsis to that double location - in time and place. Everything happened there and then, but reliving is here and now.

During regression you experience a trauma again, but now your ego stands up. It stands up because now you relive it out of free choice, because it happened in another time, place and body, and because a therapist is now available to help you. Now you can endure it and assimilate it.

Some therapists may hamper their clients, even prevent them from experiencing a catharsis. Such therapists are afraid of the agony. They avoid rebirth like the plague, because they cannot stand the pain, even the sight of pain, the smell of pain. If that is you, close this book and go for any kind of jigsaw puzzle that strikes your fancy. Conversely, if you actually like the sight and the sound and the smell of pain, you don't belong in the delivery room either.

Agony is the narrow gate through which we have to pass. It is the eye of the needle. Our job is not to induce agony; we work with the agony that is there, though often this agony is half suppressed. We need to liberate the agony. As with childbirth, once it is happening for real, never try to stop the pains!

Also, karmic charges that are stirred but are not liberated and assimilated become worse. These charges may produce all kinds of unpleasant psychological and somatic phenomena such as chronic mustiness.

Clusters of emotions need to be handled methodically. For instance, if someone appears to be carrying an anger-grief cluster, separate the two emotions by having the patient locate these emotions at different points in the body, and anchor them in different bodily sensations. If the patient's emotions appear to be dormant, use aura exploration (see Chapter 7). Then find out which emotion is the more accessible. With most patients, grief is more accessible, while with some it is anger. It all depends on energy level (grief is a lower energy response than anger), and on gender roles (crying is less masculine than swearing). But the best way to find out is to ask.

A higher-self intervention may help to answer those questions. Also, aura exploration is effective: "Where is it located? What do you want to do with it? How does it work out for you?" From the higher self you can often move in time to a point just prior to the present lifetime to consult someone's lifeplan.

When you don't know what to go for first, dampen the secondary charge: "Forget that grief in your throat just for now. Let it be. We will leave that grief for the moment, and we move instead to the anger in your head." While you work with the anger, the grief may suddenly erupt in great waves. Sometimes people simultaneously kick when in anger and cry when in grief. That is all right; such catharsis releases the cluster.

But lockers and twisters block such reliving and catharsis. In a prior lifetime a woman was kidnapped and raped by labourers. Then during each day they imprisoned her in the bower of the thick wall of an old, ramshackle building. She lay alone in the hay all day. In that awful setting she sometimes had lustful experiences in which rats played a role. Revulsion and lust therefore became knotted together with shame and incomprehension. A difficult session.

Hangovers.
If we feel tired and empty for a long time, our capacity for deep emotions, even our ability to feel wounded, decreases. We become mechanical and dull. Even a successful regression to a traumatic situation will produce no direct catharsis for a dulled mind, because that trauma is embedded in a thick, tedious "dirtskirt." Such heavy, amorphous residues are what I call hangovers instead of traumas.

A trauma begins and ends at specific moments. It is a precise episode of negative emotions, such as fear, in which the ego collapsed. Fear is fierce. Fear emerges and stops at a given moment, although it can remain as a shadow. Anger may continue hidden, and at a specific time it explodes. But how do we deal with boredom or depression?

Just as trauma is a wound, a hangover is either a callous or an overly sensitive piece of skin. With a hangover the injury has grown gradually. We do not collapse, but we go to the wall. A hangover makes us smaller and more wearied, slower and heavier and gloomier.

The basic emotion that underlies many traumas is fear. In contrast, basic feelings that are present in most hangovers are repulsion and weariness. Hangovers are less specific than traumas. The number of examples is great, as the lists of verbal, emotional and somatic bridges to hangovers will show.

Coldness may be a traumatic charge. For example, if in a prior life you were assaulted and left behind injured in the woods, you had pain, you were cold and you felt lonely. Coldness also may be a hangover charge, from a life or a marriage that had always been cold. Dying from hunger is different from having been hungry all your life.

Helen Wambach found people who looked back with revulsion on lifetimes that had been full of superstition and suppression. Such lifetimes leave hangovers. To give one example, in 13th century Germany the pregnancy of a woman was discovered by neighbors. She was beaten with sticks. Clearly this was a traumatic situation for her. Yet she remained numb. For her that beating was merely a culmination of something that had always been present. People always lived under pressure, always got beaten, always were threatened with punishment, by other people or by the church. Life was crushing, with repression and toil until death. Reliving all this repression can be tedious, dulling both patient and therapist.

Hangovers are the repercussions that stem from not being ourselves for a long time. How many women carry hangovers from their marital lives? Fetch and carry, the endless cycle of domestic chores, and experiencing again and again, just as tiring and unpleasant, your lawful wedded husband on top of you. All that produces not trauma, but a hangover.

Many hangovers result from perpetual battering of our ego. Perhaps a challenge has been too strong for us to respond. Our capacity to react in an aware and humane manner may wear down and wither in brutal enslavement. Even escape opportunities may pass unnoticed. We lack the energy to escape, or even to consider it. We can no longer think independently.

HANGOVER CHARGES

Mental charges:	*Emotional charges:*	*Somatic charges:*
Cynicism	Being fed up	Deformity
Distrust	Boredom	Discomfort
Doubt	Depression	Listlessness
Ignorance	Disappointment	Ugliness
Incomprehension	Dissatisfaction	Weariness
Insecurity	Indifference	
Obstinacy	Irritation	
Rebelliousness	Melancholy	
Suspicion	Passivity	
Timidity	Repulsion	
Vacuity	Unhappiness	

What are the charges that are present in hangovers? They may be emotional: repulsion. They may be somatic: weariness. They may be mental: rebelliousness. They may be all of the above. The list on the previous page illustrates typical hangover charges.

Other hangovers may result from losing ourselves gradually because of lack of stimulation. Boredom and cynicism are examples. A cynical attitude often results from a life in which we were intelligent and had power. In an imperfect world, intelligence and power can be such burdens that cynicism becomes a defence against being crushed by imperfect conditions and imperfect people. If we can learn to look at our cynicism with some sense of irony, our emotional hardness may soften.

SITUATIONS THAT PRODUCE HANGOVERS

Domination	Narrow-mindedness
Duty	Obstruction
Exhaustion	Poverty
Harshness	Pressure
Imprisonment	Prostitution
Isolation	Rejection
Loneliness	Repression
Monotony	Slavery

Hangovers are like heavy mortgages. Czar Nicholas II of Russia will have acquired a heavy hangover from his life. His last years surely had traumatic moments, but his life as a whole carried more of a hangover: a continuously overwhelming situation. What are typical situations that produce hangovers?

Hangovers result from situations that make us miserable, but which do so without the sudden collapse of our ego. We bend, but we do not break. Our ego does not go to pieces. Instead it is diminished, pinched off, almost stagnated, from long weariness, long depression, long pressure, long despondency: like a *bonsai* ego.

The facts alone are not what determine if we will acquire a hangover. Rather, what matters is how we experience those facts. Often our experience depends on why we lived a life. A freely chosen life of toil does not necessarily leave behind a hangover, because most likely we assimilated all of our life experiences right after death, except for any remaining somatic charges.

Releasing traumas is something that belongs to the easier things in therapy. If we just remain well-focused and we do not divert attention and energy in our preamble, and if we make no detours, healing from traumas occurs almost automatically. Dealing with a hangover, especially one with a postulate on top, is tougher. Just as with traumas, hangovers may carry positive side effects:

> *A woman with few specific problems did relive her past life as a Jewish girl who succumbed in Bergen-Belsen during the last winter of the war. In her present life she carried the feeling that she never could enjoy things; she always saw the ugly side. In an aura exploration session (see Chapter 7) she saw that she wore before her eyes a sheet of transparent plastic that carried the image of the concentration camp: "I look at everything through that plastic sheet."*
>
> *In her present life she had grown up in a family of nature lovers, but she had difficulty enjoying things in free nature. During the session she understood that she associated fallen trees, etc., with the lack of care of that last winter in Bergen-Belsen. She now understood why she preferred well-trimmed parks and gardens, while her family considered parks to be artificial, unnatural.*
>
> *Interestingly, she felt no need to remove this hangover aspect: "Now I can enjoy parks the more." While feeding her children, by breast or bottle, she always had the strange feeling that there was gold in the food. Now she understood that she compared the warm baby food with the cold and hunger of Bergen-Belsen, and therefore she felt the richness so deeply. She felt no need to take away that plastic sheet. "We all have a right to our own memories."*
>
> *Catharsis brought comprehension, liberating insight. She saw her present life now in a soft golden glow. It was important that she had incurred few personal traumas, despite the terrible experience of Bergen-Belsen, and that she had died well.*

Somatic charges of hangovers may also manifest themselves during therapy, and these charges can be used as tools for induction.

In therapy, we find hangovers from lives of poverty, serfdom, or prostitution. Merely resolving the traumatic moments of revulsion, pain or humiliation from those lifetimes does not liberate, because when a hangover is present, those moments are embedded in a general mass of negative experiences. Apathy and weariness dull any emotional release. Sometimes we can release the traumatic charge only after we have cleaned up this inert mass first. Then, with emotional vitality restored, we can focus on individual traumas and resolve them.

SOMATIC BRIDGES TO HANGOVERS

1. Vague, shifting, unpleasant sensations
2. Feeling stiff
3. General heaviness
4. Weariness and exhaustion
5. Feeling cold
6. Feeling numb, feeling empty
7. Slow changes in posture
8. Slow rolling of the head
9. Slow facial expressions of repulsion
10. Curling up slowly.

The problem with hangovers is their tedious, tenacious, amorphous character. I discovered hangovers while working with patients that did not respond well to the use of normal trauma techniques. Reliving a trauma involves so much action that the process is often, as it were, self-lubricating. In reliving a hangover, however, catharsis goes more slowly and people often get stuck. As therapists, we have to dredge more.

Analyze the somatic, emotional and mental charges and guide the patient to find situations that each illustrate one charge: "Go to the moment of the worst weariness. Go to the last moment you felt weary. What else do you feel? Revulsion? Okay, go to the most revolting moment."

In treating hangovers it is important to have the patient view the life panorama after death: "How? What? Why? Why not?" Afterward ask, "What still remains of that problem today?" Often a person's answer reveals the most pertinent charge, be it weariness, victimization or self-pity.

The beginning of each charge, as well as its long duration,

must be understood. Moments of choice are important. An essential question is, "What prevented you from changing your life?" If the patient finds it difficult to locate decisive moments, then move first through the death experience to the *panorama platform*, the place of overview, and locate such moments from there.

Character postulates.

We learn from experience. Bad experiences teach us to avoid them. But when bad experiences repeat themselves, when similar traumas and hangovers recur through lifetimes, they are anchored in a *character postulate*. A postulate reveals a disturbed adaptation mechanism. All neuroses and many psychoses carry postulates. Pride is often anchored in postulates, but often so is humility.

A postulate is something that we register, that we program into our unconscious computer, and this program runs whenever it is triggered. Postulates structure how we feel, think, act, under certain conditions (or even always), how we react to things, how we see ourselves.

Each engraved decision, such as *I never want to go through this again*, is a postulate. Many postulates block release; they cause the most blocks. A postulate remains undigested, not by an overwhelming emotional charge on the experience, but by judgments or decisions that we engraved on it. Let me give some illustrations.

A man shouts at us and calls us names. One way to deal with such an action is to declare the man to be a son-of-a-bitch. That label is understandable, but it blocks understanding of why the man acted the way he did, and how we may have triggered his reaction. If, when reliving the episode, we see and accept that the man acted for a reason, our own intolerance may suddenly melt. If we can understand how in this case we were part of the cause, we will feel freer in similar situations. Without such understanding, however, our interpretations remain fixed, and our responses unmanageable.

You are a boy of seventeen. You haven't had much success with girls and you are a lousy dancer. With beating heart, after three songs have played, you approach a girl and ask her to dance. She looks critically at you, whispers with her girlfriend, looks

47

at you again, whispers again, and then says, "No." That is a
small trauma, at least if your self-esteem is already sensitive.
Now you may react in anger: "Damn those untrustworthy
bitches." That reaction may lead to a postulate: "Women to
whom I feel attracted are untrustworthy." This postulate will
hamper part of your life. An alternative reaction would be to
say to yourself: "That will never happen to me again, being
rejected in such a fashion. Who do they think they are, any-
way?" That response may result in a postulate such as, "I have
to be asked." This postulate may contribute to character neuro-
ses such as inferiority and superiority complexes. A program is
neurotic if it works against our will and is maladjusted to the
actual circumstances. In a sense, we have robotized a part of
ourselves.
You may hold the postulate, "I can trust no one." Now let's say
that you have an intimate relationship and you would like to
trust the other. You simply can't. The other is asking: "Why
don't you trust me?" You may want to, but you can't. Postu-
lates vary in scope and intensity. If, each time if you fail at
something, the sentence emerges, "Never again!" you have a
neurosis already. "You can't trust women" has a broader scope
than "You can't trust attractive women." "You can't trust at-
tractive blondes" is again more specific. And if such a postulate
is true only at night, it is still more specific.

A fixed program is an unfree reaction, a fixed response that
became a part of our identity, such as *I am a failure* or *Nobody
loves me*. With such a fixed program in place we react mechanically and therefore seldom adequately. Postulates are registered
opinions, persistent attitudes, decisions we made about ourselves. They often appear in core sentences such as:
- *I am hemmed in.*
- *I feel helpless in life.*
- *People scare me.*
The heaviest and most important programs are *character neuroses*. Character postulates are their building blocks. A character
neurosis is a rigid program; character postulates are the program's lines. Character is a huge topic, involving a major seg-
ment of psychology, with projection, repression and numerous
other aspects. We deal here with traits that continue through
lifetimes. Such lasting traits are based on interlocking, mutually reinforcing postulates.

Postulates describe how the world is or how other people are. For example, *Men are mean,* or even worse, *Men are mean and women deserve just that.* This last statement is what we call a "totalitarian" postulate, because for someone who believes such a statement, nothing is funny anymore. A postulate about the entire world might be, *Nothing is real.*

Many postulates include the words *I am . . . , People are . . .* or *They are . . .* and absolute terms such as *never, always, nowhere, everywhere, nobody, everybody, completely, all.* Postulates define ourselves, other people, or the world, but in the end they all state something about ourselves.

Postulates may also be registered in our thinking, when other people said them to us and we believed these people. If, in the presence of others, parents always say to one of their children, "You will end on the gallow," such a statement threatens to become a self-fulfilling prophecy: *I will end on the gallow.*

A *shutoff command* may be given by others or even by ourselves. Perhaps someone spoke against a third person, and we assumed that person's statement to be about ourselves. Girls are often weak in math because they have been told, or have heard other girls being told, or have simply heard people state that this is true. *Math is not feminine, is it? As a girl, you are weird if you are good in math.*

Maybe exact and technical talents are more common in men than in women, but that does not mean that it is unnatural when a woman has such abilities. Her talent may be locked away in a box that reads, *If I am good at math, I am not a girl.*

Most postulates originate as standard explanations, standard defenses against particular wounding circumstances or experiences. Other postulates are reactions to situations where we failed or overshot, or where we behaved inhumanely: as a robot, as an animal, as a demon, or as an inaccessible angel. Those individual postulates are about ourselves. A postulate such as *Being cheerful makes me feel guilty,* says something about how we see ourselves.

Many postulates are defenses against disappointment, and prevention of failure. For example: *I am too good for this. I do not want to become involved,* may signal a superiority complex. Similar postulates might be: *This audience is not what I like,* or *I do play the piano, but only a white piano,* or *I could be a good painter, if I just didn't have these headaches,* or *I am so talented that I could succeed in anything, but alas, I am lazy and that is a shame.*

Induration, or hardening of attitude, occurs when we stick by some postulate. The jacket has seemingly grown into our flesh. Consider a statement such as *I am not involved*. At some point you decided this, probably with good reason, but now you cannot do otherwise, at least in similar instances. Induration comes from, in astrological terms, a *saturnine* or sullen judgment. We cast it in lead or cast iron or, as some say nowadays, in concrete.

A judgment indures or hardens because we are insecure and repress our insecurity. A right, balanced judgment liberates us from perplexity, but a saturnine or sullen judgment gives us a bad deal - driving out the devil of doubt and perplexity by using the even worse devil of rigidity.

Maybe we have turned our experience around. Perhaps, for instance, we choose to believe that being considered naughty enhances our self-esteem. Still, this is a victory won at excessive cost, because we can emancipate ourselves from such a belief only by accepting a statement from our parents.

A postulate is a magical formula; it requires a mind of some concentration. A sleepy soul that has just entered the big game of human development may do stupid things, but yet it lacks postulates. Postulates presuppose intellect; a postulate is a folly that only rational people have.

Let's look at a postulate regarding failure.

> *With your little sister you sneak into the kitchen to steal candies, but you fail, because you cannot reach the candy box. Your sister whines, "You can't reach it, you can't reach it, serves you right, you can't reach it." If her words eat into you, maybe you forget the experience and find that regression is difficult, because while you try to retrieve the engram, the reactive mind reads, "You can't reach it," and decides that this event cannot be reached.*

If I have had a bad experience with a fire, then any fire may restimulate that bad experience. If I have translated and generalized the experience into the statement *I fail*, then opportunities for restimulation of the failure message are boundless, and the charge of failure will spread like wildfire, till I know *I am a failure*.

Let's say that in an earlier life a house caught fire and a child died. I felt guilty, I had failed. Personally that is traumatic enough. If I register, *I always make the wrong decision*, or *I am always late*, then the charge of that trauma will be connected to this postulate of being wrong or late, and it will eat in more deeply. The postulate ties in with the trauma or the hangover. One reinforces the other. Maybe I see my small child about to cross a busy street, and suddenly it flashes, *My God, I will be late again!* That belief will paralyze me for a moment and so I may indeed be too late. The postulate eats in more deeply again.

Habits are present not only in what we do, but in our attitudes, how we think and feel. In particular, our response pattern to frustration, ambivalence and conflict defines our emotional character. Frustration results in two basic reactions: self-pity and aggression. Two fundamental character postulates are self-pity and aggression programs on frustrations, and choice programs - oscillation, delay or blind choice - on ambivalences.

Character is structure, and character postulates are verbal representations of elements of our character. Therapists are usually interested only in the problematic elements. But people also talk about a good or bad character, about a strong or weak character. Character is the totality of habits in thinking, feeling and doing with which we identify, and which form part of our self-image.

A good character has effective but humane habits; a bad character has ineffective or inhumane habits. Habits are valuable, but the price we usually pay for them is rigidity. Therefore, an essential ingredient of character is the willingness and the capacity to remain open, to learn and to change.

Our character contains programs that are dysfunctional, but are part of our self-image, and so determine our self-esteem. We may temporarily lose our identity when these habits are thrown into disorder. Generalizations are mind-closers, experience-stoppers: *All men are the same.* Does that work well or does it not? Insofar as men differ, it does not work. And men do differ. (Cross my heart, ladies!)

Postulates about people in general may often backfire on us. Let's take the case of a patient who relives that he is judged by people who, according to him, cannot judge him. "How do you feel about that?" the therapist may ask. The patient replies, "That seems to me characteristic of human judgment in general."

This statement is a generalization, and a hidden comparison with non-human, i.e., divine, judgment. So it seems that we have got ourselves a priest here, and we have to proceed cautiously. He says that this society is wrong, that people judge one another, without being competent to do so, and no good can come of that. At the same time the patient judges himself. He puts himself in a *double bind* with the postulate, *People are not competent to judge others*, because now he is a judge himself, and in the second degree - judging the judges.

Postulates often repeat themselves through successive lifetimes and even reveal a pendulum phenomenon. Sometimes a poor life is followed by a rich life, then a poor life, then a rich life. In such a case, somewhere there is a postulate about property. Such swings come by *antithetic* postulates.

The most simple antithetic postulate is, *Never that again!* Perhaps we bled to death during childbirth, the child died too, and our husband went crazy and drowned himself. *Never that again!* What does such a pronouncement mean? Maybe next time we will choose to be a man, or to be infertile, or to grow a tumor in our womb, or to be gay. Anything is possible, depending on our other traits and programs. The antithetic postulate as such gives no direction. It only says, *Not this*, or *I don't want this to happen*. But what *do* we want?

Such negative, unspecified reactions often induce hurry, even in being reborn. Perhaps someone is killed, does not accept being dead, and so takes the first body around. If you do *not* want something very badly, stop and think what you *do* want. Don't register anything in your computer before you know what you want.

One character trait may be irascibility, or a tendency to be angered easily. Is that trait really okay? The usual thought is, *Not quite; an ideal person is composed.* Yet an ideal person is also lively. Liveliness is a good quality, isn't it? An ideal person makes decisions quickly, but is also thorough and deliberate. Vance Packard gives an example of the ideal car that consumers want: spacious inside and yet easy to park; economical but capable of rapid acceleration; exclusive, but with service around the corner.

So, whatever a character trait you are looking at, do not judge it morally, but pragmatically: *How does it work out?* Some people are irascible. Okay. Maybe a quick temper is justified and works out nicely where they live. Irascibility is an unfree reaction only if a person cannot remain calm when necessary. Again, a character trait is unfree only if it works against our will or against the circumstances.

Character postulates that we encounter in therapy are usually fixed generalizations that provide apparent security and therefore apparent character. Most character postulates are negative. Some are positive, although always at a price. *Despite everything, I am convinced that life is meaningful.* Such a conviction works well, while a deep conviction that we are guilty, and that God punishes us for our guilt, works poorly.

We do pay a price for positive convictions. That price is hidden in the words *despite everything.* Such a qualifier stops learning, is a mind-closer. Postulates are programs that don't account enough for the circumstances. A postulate generalizes, equalizes: *A is B,* or *If A, then B. If it is that, I will do so.*

Character neuroses are phenomena that are just as easy to locate as they are difficult to treat. A character neurosis is made up of character postulates, which often are more delicate than traumas. Character postulates are about someone's "psychic bones" and that is pretty intimate, even if it is hogwash. Traits that may be involved: submissiveness, aggressiveness, self-hate, inferiority feelings, vanity. Such themes, which involve the structure of the ego, may play through many lives.

If we relive a traumatic experience that is connected to a postulate, we have to find that postulate and treat it as such. We have to understand how that postulate originated and how it grew. The origin, the first root may seem small and innocent, but only after reliving and understanding this root experience do we resolve the subsequent string of experiences.

Regressions may discover postulates, but a postulate may also be used as a verbal bridge to move a patient into a regression. Sentences that are repeated, or pronounced with intensity, often suggest postulates. The list on the next page is an arbitrary selection.

A woman, for example, finds herself in lifetimes in which she has a dull husband and an exciting lover. This pattern expresses, in the end, two sides of her character that are not integrated; or even more simply, it expresses her response to her own dullness. Such unresolved character neuroses grow through lifetime after lifetime. Insight-oriented therapy is necessary in these cases. How did this woman's pattern originate? In which lifetime? Why? We do not want merely to remove idiosyncrasies, but if possible, we want to produce liberating insight into problematic character traits.

SENTENCES THAT SUGGEST POSTULATES

I belong nowhere.
People are jealous of me.
I am all alone.
They can all go to hell
I trust nobody.
That always happens to me.
I can't help it, but that's how I am.
I want to be left in peace.
Nobody loves me.
They drive me crazy.
I am always on my own.
Nobody notices me.
I simply love people.
I do not accept people's shit.
I keep my mouth shut.

A therapist's search for the source of a pattern involves "long-distance surgery." It often becomes difficult to find the core from which the coral began to grow. First we want to expose a patient's basic pattern or mechanism. We do not directly attempt catharsis. Clients have to think about their own mechanism or pattern to decide if they want to undo that mechanism. The free will of the client is sacred. Supporting people in their movement through an unpleasant experience is okay. But convincing people that they have to be, feel, think or do differently is a job we leave for our competitors: gospel preachers who try to nudge people along.

Recurring sentences with *I am* often suggest a character postulate. A strong character postulate does make related traumas and hangovers repeat. Problems keep returning, not by being locked in immutable conditions, but through a fixed program that is ever again triggered by thoughts such as: *They always take it out on me*, or *I am not a lucky bird*, or *I have two left hands*.

Sentences with *always, never, nobody*, or *everybody* are usually keys to hangovers or to character postulates. Super-generalizations may have originated in the length of the source experience, as in hangovers, or in having programmed ourselves.

How do we know if a recurring sentence is a postulate, is really charged? By repetition, by completion, or by modification. Modification of postulates triggers resistance. Somebody may say repeatedly, *I have no time.* Change that to *I make no time,* and have the new statement repeated. That simple alteration may shock the patient into a new awareness, or it may trigger anger that we can use as a bridge into regression.

A sentence is a postulate only if it carries a great charge. Verbal repetition of a postulate sentence always triggers responses, including somatic ones. If such repetition results in no images or emotions or somatics, that sentence is not a postulate.

If someone is often unhappy, but the unhappiness is not there at the moment, you may try repetition of *I feel unhappy.* If this repetition does not succeed, then completion of the statement *I am unhappy because . . .* may lead to recovery of one or more traumatic experiences. If completion does not produce results, then try *I always feel unhappy.* This statement will lead to a hangover, a postulate or a pseudoobsession.

The difference is sometimes in *I always feel . . .* and *I am . . . .* The first sentence probably will reveal a hangover, and the second sentence a character postulate. *I always feel . . .* is a sentence structure that shows that you do not identify with it. *I always feel unhappy* implies that something makes you unhappy. But, *I am always unhappy* shows that unhappiness has become internalized, a part of your ego.

Such an identification is especially problematic when strong suggestions from other people are made when a hangover is already present. For instance, let's say that you are a poor, dirty slave and the supervisors shout continuously at you, "Hey, trash!" "Hey, dog!" One way to reduce the pain in a verdict is to accept it. Acceptance may result in the belief, *I am a dog,* or *I am nothing.* This acceptance makes life bearable, but it drains a person of energy. If that spot is touched, even in a later life, it drags you down. You cannot resist it, because it has become part of your ego.

Someone says, *I always feel like crying.* He feels it right now, but a regression to the source of that feeling fails. Perhaps there are different sources of that feeling, like different rivers flowing into the same lake. Then we have to separate those sources. We let him complete several times: *I want to cry, because . . . ,* producing maybe eight responses. Those responses we explore separately, and probably we will find two or more different past lives during regression.

When searching for and processing character postulates, remember that they are not idle appendices to be removed, but that they fulfil functions. Character postulates are survival mechanisms, protection mechanisms. People are not born lazy, nor are they lazy by whim. They became lazy because laziness seemed a good way to make life easier and still to assert themselves. Laziness avoids action, and avoids the risk of failure, and so protects their self-esteem. Also, guilt complexes avoid the need to become active and self-responsible. Aborting the effort is less painful than the birth of new failures.

Similarly, guilt postulates inhibit or prevent catharsis from traumas and hangovers. Typical guilt postulates are: *I ought not be happy* or *I am not allowed to become free* or *I have to atone*. People who hold such postulates cannot find release.

Other postulates that hinder people, are shutoff commands such as, *Sleep restores everything*, or *I forget everything*, or *Don't look back!* It is difficult to help someone regress to the source of such postulates, because the charge of the postulates closes off the road to their own origin. The content of the bottle becomes the label. Those postulates are *recursive*.

Conversely, mediumistic people often carry a postulate by which they cannot close themselves, because of some life of indoctrination to remain open, to guarantee sensitivity (and obedience): "The more you remain open, girls, the better for your work, and the sooner you will wear the priestess robe," or ". . . the sooner you get a chevron on your sleeve, boys."

Postulates may also be triggered by the therapy situation itself. In the relationship between patient and therapist the two prime themes of character postulates - power and love - may appear recursively. The therapist has to have power as well as love, but both must be tempered, diluted in trust: power absorbed in self-confidence, and love absorbed in trust in the patient.

Denys Kelsey poses it as either-or: *power and love exclude each other*. Williston keeps the possibility of and-and open: *sovereign action beside unconditional love*. Personally, I opt for the vision of Williston. However we look at it, this relationship between power and love remains a core theme through lifetimes. As therapists we will encounter it again and again in sessions, and in our relationship with clients.

If people have trouble with a regression, notice how they express that difficulty: *I cannot reach it*, or *I cannot enter*, or *I get stuck, I cannot relax, I feel nothing, I see nothing, I understand nothing about all this*. Such "stupidity postulates" do impair our intelligence, and rather betray the reasons. Often a shortcut instruction such as, "Go back to a situation in which you understand nothing about what is going on. Where are you and what is happening?" may produce instant regression.

When a postulate resulted in induration of an experience, reliving the episode is not enough, because the postulate itself perpetuates the charge. Each character trait is a perpetuation. We have extricated the response from the original circumstances in which that response was natural. But such an attempt is dangerous. Everything temporal and local that we perpetuate and generalize works wrongly in the end.

The natural bridge for postulates, to ease a patient into a regression, is the verbal bridge. Use direct, simple phrases. Don't have the patient repeat *I think that men are nasty*, but rather, *Men are nasty*.

I talk about "postulates" because with postulates we can reduce character traits to sentences. Sentences can be spoken aloud, can be completed by a patient, used as verbal bridges, as verbal explorations, or as renovations. Once we have resolved a problem and changed the switches, repetition of a reversed sentence reinforces the cure: *I arrive in time*, not *I always arrive in time!* (Why not?)

There are other reversion techniques. A patient once said, *People are cold, ugly and dumb*. I let her repeat instead, *I am warm, beautiful and intelligent*. She exploded, blushing, hyperventilating, legs kicking in the air, *I can't say it!* This was the breakthrough.

Persist when you notice such strong somatic responses. Perhaps say to the patient, "You will not leave this session before you have said it. Next time, when you come back, the first thing you will say is, *Hello, here I am again: warm, beautiful and intelligent*."

When do you use a postulate as an entry point? First, when the intake reveals generalizations or absolutes that are intense or repeated or both. Someone said, even before he came through the door, *Now you see what became of me!* That one sentence later appeared to carry the heaviest charge and served as the key to the session.

During regression sessions, repetitions of the same problem in different settings, even different lifetimes, suggests a program, and thus a postulate. Someone, for example, once arrived late somewhere, with traumatic consequences. That particular experience can be assimilated well in the regression. Perhaps its assimilation does not produce real catharsis, but it results in noticeable relief. We move to another regression, and again something emerges related to being late. Or perhaps someone is tortured to death in three different lifetimes. Such repetitions usually suggest a postulate. Much difficult work will be required before we pierce the postulate. There is one other explanation for such repetitions: *attachment strings* maybe present. But we will deal with that topic later.

When a regression is slow and tedious, usually it is because we have to unravel complex issues. For example, we may have to cleanse contradictory charges, such as anger and grief. We can use *egostates* or *aura exploration* (see Chapter 7) to disentangle such charges. Perhaps trauma is present, but also a postulate, and to that postulate a second trauma is connected. Maybe on top of that is guilt. Guilt often leads to postulates.

If we have found a postulate, we ask the patient to repeat that postulate until its emotional and somatic charges emerge. Then we should use E + S (Emotion + Somatic) to move back to some situations that formed and reinforced the postulate, and to some other situations that demonstrate the consequences of that postulate - how it produces problems. Often these are the same situations. Postulates reinforce themselves.

If we ask a patient, "When was this postulate registered within you?" we may find situations that occurred in this life. Probing further, we may suggest, "Let us go back to where this was true. Okay, now to an other situation, in which this was true, and now to a third situation." Uncovering about three such examples will illustrate sufficiently how the postulate works.

Next, ask patients if they want to release the postulate. If so, continue with, "Okay, go back to the situation where this postulate was registered for the first time." Guide the patient back to this origin and ascertain precisely which charges are present there. *I always feel guilty* may be connected with fear and coldness. You also may find character charges such as condescension, submissiveness, idolatry or contempt.

Release character charges by using egostates, aura exploration, or repetition of positively reversed sentences. If these methods do not succeed, suggest that the patient renounce the postulate consciously here and now. Suitable approaches are rational emotive therapy (RET) and standard forms of counselling. In such cases, regression therapy has merely done an important piece of preparation efficiently, no more and no less.

Resistance to releasing a postulate may be present because that postulate is anchored in a more general one. For example, perhaps someone has the feeling, *I always have to hold on.* In therapy it appears that behind that feeling lies, *I am afraid to lose face.* This fear may be related to a more general charge, such as a perfection or superiority complex. Such complexes prevent acknowledgment of rash or wrong decisions.

A character postulate often locks in right after a traumatic experience that a weak or distorted mind interprets, concludes and generalizes. In such cases, explicit questions work: "Which conclusion did you draw then?"

We encounter character problems at the start of a therapy when we recognize charged sentences, and we encounter them later when themes persist through several lifetimes. Repetition of a plot, even several times within one life, suggests a fixed program. Normally, people do not like to be rejected, so they try to avoid rejection next time. If rejection has become embedded in a character postulate, then again and again that postulate places a person in rejection situations. A trauma returns because it is connected to a postulate.

Character postulates are not corrected, but rather reinforced by experience. That is why simple reliving as such does not help. We can help patients to perceive and understand an issue, but they have to decide if they want this issue to change, and they must act from there. Character problems are by their nature tenacious. Recursive postulates may especially inhibit the solution of traumas and pseudo-obsessions.

With character postulates, first we must clarify the pattern by exploring illustrative regressions. Then we have patients understand why a particular pattern always happened to them. Nothing falls out of the blue, except meteorites, and those are incredibly rare. There is always a reason, and therefore always the possibility of understanding.

When you find a repetitive theme, such as one of being raped, say, "Let us find out why that happens every time." Have the patient go back to similar situations and concentrate on what happened, why it happened and what decisions were involved.

Especially notice decisions when they are made for the very first time. An alternative approach would be aura exploration: "You carry something that makes it happen every time. Look at it. What do you see?"

Keep asking until you reach the original engraving of the program. Then find out how it is anchored now. When Edith Fiore finds clients who keep returning to misery without improvement, she sends them to the source of a character neurosis, the *karmic event*, which is usually a personal decision rather than a chance event.

Each conviction stems from a root experience. Regression has to move back to that root. With postulates, reliving is not done to produce relief as it is with traumas. Rather, it is done to learn and to understand. The decision to release a postulate is always a conscious one in the here and now.

LeCron addresses phantom pains asking the next questions. Most of these questions apply to postulates as well:

1. *Is it the consequence of a trauma?*
2. *Is it an expression of feeling guilty, a punishment that you inflict on yourself?*
3. *Is it symbolic body language?*
4. *Is it a conflict between wanting something and not being able?*
5. *Is it a conflict between wanting something and being forbidden?*
6. *Does this problem have a goal? Something to accomplish? Something to avoid?*
7. *Is it the consequence of an indoctrination?*
8. *Do you identify with someone? Is it a symptom that you have copied from someone?*

LeCron has patients respond by using the hypnotic method of finger signals, but instead of finger signals I use spontaneous somatics. For example, if someone has a sore throat, let the throat respond. When a particular question increases the physical sensation, it means yes. When that sensation decreases or remains the same, it means no.

A final step in the healing of character postulates is *postulate reversion*, which is repetition, after catharsis, of a new, opposite sentence. Postulate reversion is effective, but risky, because we may fix the reversed sentence as a new postulate. *Women are worthless* may become *Women are great*. This reversal is an improvement, especially if it is said with joy and relief, without any heavy conviction, but since it is a new generalization, it is no solution. However, the new sentence could be *Many women are great*. Even repetition of *Some women are sometimes worthless* will produce interesting reactions, because such a sentence forces one to think, *What kind of women? When? Why?* But repetition of a comparative is always unlocking. If it is done with joy and relief, such repetition substantiates the cure.

One patient held the postulate, *What will people think of me?* Regression revealed that her mother used to say to her, "What will people think of me having such a child?" Suddenly the woman laughed, "Oh, that mother of mine, I can see her now - in a shop, shouting to people, pushing us forward to get priority with her children." Then the therapist had this patient repeat, *What will people think of her?* This new repetition reinforced the liberation of her problem.

Use your common sense and your creativity. Never reverse a negative sentence in a mirror image. *Men are all different* is better than *Men are all the same*, but the new statement remains exaggerated, as men also resemble one another. Someone who says *I am an asshole* may after the regression say *I am not an asshole*, but real liberation will produce a positive sentence, such as, *I am pretty competent*, or *I am okay*.

To check and to reinforce a catharsis, you may have the patient repeat the original postulate sentence to see if it is still charged. You may even ask the patient to repeat a reverse sentence. If a catharsis is complete, there should be full relief, joy, enthusiasm.

How intense will the relief be? That depends on the intensity of the catharsis, but also on the patient's own temperament. If the session worked, but the result appears to be so-so, then use egostates (see Chapter 7). Dullness often results from mixed charges. Often one subpersonality is cynical and distant. In regression we de-generalize and de-mix such mixed charges into separate charges; in aura exploration into separate spots with separate things or energies, in egostates into separate subpersonalities.

Pseudo-obsessions.
In a Swedish children's film, *Dunderklumpen* is a troll who lives alone but, as he explains, never completely alone, because he has his previous ages with him. "If I suck on my finger, I am one year; if I whistle, I am eight years; if I shout, *Hey, you there, stop that*, I am 35 years. I am one person for each year of my

life."

If a past age is triggered, all emotions of that time emerge. For instance, when a man is rejected at a meeting he sinks back to the age of 17, the age at which he felt rejected most strongly. He can almost feel the acne sprouting on his face, and may hum the songs from that season. Sinking back can be annoying, but it can also be pleasant to sink back into your childhood - when playing with your own children, for example. We should carry all our past ages in harmony with one another and accessible to one another, while accepting the guidance of our present age.

Real subpersonalities are usually splits caused by traumatic experiences, often with strong postulates. Rarely are they due to hangovers. A subpersonality usually starts if someone is about to collapse in some way. If the active personality withdraws, the soul mobilizes an other part that takes over. Some subpersonalities seem to be gone for a part of our life. They may hibernate and then return suddenly.

Past-life personalities that we left behind at birth, have traumas too. Few lives are completely clean. As for emotional traumas with somatic charges, we can never completely clean these charges while discarnate. Traumas from so-called "sleeping" lives are restimulated more slowly, but if they are, the pertaining life wakes up, or at least begins to dream. If we resolve one trauma, the past personality may be integrated as an extra feeding personality, but it also may return to sleep.

Many people choose among their past personalities in preparing for this life. They select these feeding personalities for what they want to do or whom they want to meet. Women who want to make a social career often have as a feeding personality a man who was socially prominent, because that experience is one that they can use well. If you want to become a composer and you were once a flutist in ancient Greece, you will take that earlier life with you.

When people plan their next lifetime, the feeding personality that has most to offer for the coming life usually gets the leading role and becomes the root personality. That personality usually has the same sex as in the current life. When people don't plan, their immediate past life serves as the root life.

When we incarnate, we get parents who carry a certain heredity. That heredity may include genetic characteristics that we do not want but must accept. We may overlook unwanted characteristic, or downplay it. We choose our parents mainly because we have karmic business to finish together, or because we recognize them as old friends. Whatever the reason, that choice arouses memories of the lifetimes in which we knew them, possibly including lives we did not want to include in the first place.

Pseudo-obsessions are previous personalities that live around or inside us, as if they were other people. They are an extreme form of subpersonality. A pseudo-obsessor is not a partial residue from a past life, but is the full personality of that past life. That personality is conscious, but is contained within a mood, interfering rather than contributing. Sometimes we have chosen this personality, but sometimes it has attached itself to us, like a forgotten brother or sister whom we did not invite. The personality may have been a village fool who followed us into this incarnation by instinct. Once we perceive its presence, we may think that it is an attachment and we want to get rid of it. Or we consciously brought it with us, to drag it out of its mood.

A pseudo-obsessor, then, is a previous personality that hinders us and at the same time is difficult to access. Reincarnation therapists do not deal with pseudo-obsessions of a past age, but of a complete, unassimilated past life - roaming within, interfering, and sometimes even taking over. Many pseudo-obsessors are past lives that brought about heavy repercussions of traumas, hangovers and character postulates together.

There are many reasons for a previous personality to remain outside. A frequent type of pseudo-obsessor are the worldly cynics. They are aware, but they may dislike childhood, their present female sex, or the present personality. A girl may have this kind of a withdrawn pseudo-obsession sleeping until she begins her first responsible job. Then the sleeping personality feels that out there something familiar happens; it comes looking, and it just can't resist becoming involved, without necessarily integrating well.

Many women carry this kind of cynical fellow next to a strong female lead. With such complex persons it becomes difficult to build a straightforward, stable relationship. If you build a relationship with one side, the other begins to sputter, and if you are acceptable for the other, the one sputters again.

Sometimes, such cynical subpersonalities are more intelligent than the therapist. They try to overpower and trap you, but if you avoid discussion with them, they hold you in contempt. The first thing you have to do is win their respect; it helps if you also respect them.

Often these subpersonalities were active in politics or business. Originally they were more sensitive than indifferent, but then they experienced something that froze them. If they trust you enough, they will be willing to address that experience, and their coldness will begin to melt. Their exasperation may then relent while their intellect remains. They may remain forceful personalities, but now they have empathy.

Allergies, as all psychosomatic phenomena, often suggest pseudo-obsession. I rarely had people who sought therapy specifically for allergies, but I often had people whose symptoms included allergies. I suspect that many allergies originated in earlier lifetimes. They may sometimes be part of a pseudo-obsession, often with an unassimilated traumatic experience, especially a traumatic death experience. With allergies, do not begin with subpersonalities, but rather with aura exploration.

A patient may have had asthma from childhood. But when the asthma disappears or is suppressed, a skin rash appears. This kind of shift suggests a pseudo-obsession. A jamming station sends negative energy, and if the usual channel is muted, this energy has to find another outlet. Such a substitution does not prove the presence of a pseudo-obsessor, but does offer strong indication of one.

How do we discover the difference between a pseudo-obsession and an obsession? With egostates (see Chapter 7) a negative personality enters our room. Questions that discriminate between the two are, *Since when are you with me? Why did you come? What do you want?* You rarely know the answers beforehand, although suicide tendencies usually suggest obsessors.

Paranoia may be an obsessor that is after us, pushes us on, usually piggybacking on a past life in which we were persecuted. This obsessor tunes in on that weak spot and enters there. Paranoia may be also a pseudo-obsession, someone who is still in a panic.

Alcoholics and junkies are their own obsessors. They let themselves be taken over, not by another soul, but by a self-created program, which in this case is physical. Alcoholics may attract several discarnate alcoholics who want to go on boozing. People may feel beside themselves to such an extent that they acquire real obsessors.

Our souls have reflected themselves in many bodies, in many

lifetimes, producing many personalities. All those personalities form a growing network. Some are stronger, some are more communicative, and some remain isolated, in the dark. In the end, each soul seems to strive to develop itself to the utmost, to become well rounded. Well rounded means feeling complete, not like everyone else.

A pseudo-obsession is a past life that is not integrated and roams about in the present as a disturbing subpersonality. The cause of insufficient integration is always incomplete dying, resulting in a life that is not assimilated. This lack of assimilation may come from character postulates, or from dying as a child. Perhaps the life was too painful, had too many traumas and hangovers. The pseudo-obsession may be caused by anything, but the central issue is that there has been no catharsis after death, and the personality has remained stuck. *Thus, the coping-stone of treating a pseudo-obsession is renovation of the dying experience.*

If we die well, even after a mentally handicapped life, we may return to normal after death, certainly if we chose or accepted the life that just ended. No pseudo-obsession then.

Repressed or rejected subpersonalities of our present life also function like pseudo-obsessors. We simply may have ignored our inner voice, and adapted ourselves to circumstances in which we don't fit. If we remain passive, our active part may withdraw in despair or repulsion. Then we stay behind, duller, with less energy. Such passivity becomes a loop, a trap.

With a trauma only the charge in question emerges, but with a pseudo-obsession there emerges the total personality of the earlier time period, with all it has. If the former personality was a bear of a man who walked through life with great strides, who behaved as a glutton and womanizer and who at the end of his life felt guilty about people dying in a fire, then a fire may wake him up while until then he had been wrapped up in his shame. Then his eating patterns may suddenly change to habits of gluttony, and the present person may become coarse and rude and begin to chase women.

Another example may be a man who sits in a corner without eating, because he thinks his wife will poison him. That lasts about three months and then it is over. This could be a pseudo-obsession. Why would an obsessor stop? He may have become saturated or, because he is divided inside himself, he may feel guilty because of what he does to himself. If we saw the same pattern in his daughter, this pattern might instead be an obsessor. Or, possibly, a past personality of the father is her obsessor. Obviously this latter situation would be karmic in nature.

I will go one step further, making the subject still more complicated. People may be their own pseudo-obsession. Some people may have built a fake personality and identified with it. To resolve such a situation we use dissociation. Then the present fake personality has to recognize the other, because the other is the real one.

An artificial personality will exhibit a strong Superego, a dominant Parent with strong norms. As a subpersonality, a worthy citizen (someone who has not lived through the Sixties) may enter. The newcomer may be an artificial personality. Or a friendly guy enters: *Boy, what have you done to me? You have expelled me.* He is the real personality, and the patient is the robot. The patient may have been too successful in adapting to circumstances.

We can adapt ourselves away. We can make ourselves so small, so repressed, that our personality packs its bags and withdraws. Surgery having succeeded, the patient has died.

As children we may identify with the examples we see, but we also may reject these examples and go our own way. Often we lack the strength to do that; sometimes we don't. With some of us, dominance by other people eats in more deeply, and with others less deeply.

If parents trample a child, they are fully responsible. But how strongly that trampling will affect the child depends on the child. We may not cancel our own responsibility: *Poor me, if I hadn't had such a weak and worthless stepfather I would have been different.*

Pseudo-obsessions always produce emotional instability, but not everyone who is emotionally unstable has a pseudo-obsessor. Pseudo-obsession manifests itself rather in being divided against yourself. Therefore, look for identity problems. Work with egostates (see Chapter 7). Often a subpersonality appears that is an unassimilated past life. You will soon recognize this situation if the person who enters is from another time.

There are no special restimulations that will wake up pseudo-obsessors, but a pseudo-obsessor who has a sexual fixation (e.g., lasciviousness or fear of it) will not usually emerge before sexual maturity. Likewise, in the case of anorexia, sexual maturity is usually the trigger.

Some pseudo-obsessors may emerge during an illness. If the

energy level sinks, a past personality with low energy is able to connect and emerge. Other situations depend on the charges that lock in the pseudo-obsessor. If we restimulate those charges, the pseudo-obsessor wakes up.

What happens to a pseudo-obsessor without intervention? Maybe it separates, maybe it assimilates or, more probably, maybe it wakes up and forces its way into the current life. Often it continues in the actual person and invades during an illness or any other difficult period. But such isolated previous personalities may also remain for centuries in the same twilight state, as they have died incompletely. Most likely, pseudo-obsessions do not heal spontaneously.

In exceptional cases a pseudo-obsessor could be ejected and become an obsessor of another person. We tend to seek out other people because we have unfinished business with them (30% of obsessing situations are karmic), or out of general hate.

A pseudo-obsessor has not died properly, did not find release after death. Therefore, it interferes, it decreases our energy, it draws us into negative emotions. If we try to work on those emotions without addressing the personality involved, we may revive the mess instead of resolving it. *Trauma techniques worsen cases of pseudo-obsession.*

Treatment of pseudo-obsessions is efficient: you help two for the price of one, at the pleasure of four. Just as when you go somewhere with your partner because you have a difficult time together, and you both come out radiant and happy, you feel your happiness and that of the other, and vice versa.

We may recognize a pseudo-obsession by peculiar behavior changes during the intake, or by a history of shifting psychosomatic complaints. Someone finally gets rid of headaches, and now is troubled by itching elbows, skin rashes, or emotional crying fits.

Begin to treat a pseudo-obsession as you would a subpersonality. If you make contact via the somatic bridge, start to localize that personality in the body, but also then instruct patients to see someone standing opposite themselves, as when using an egostate. Have patients imagine a place where they feel good, and have them evoke the subpersonality there.

The first question is always, "What does this figure project? How does it feel? What is its mood?" Concentrate on how the eyes are. What do they express? Ask further about what impressions the face and the posture give.

We approach the problem this way because we want to find the charges, the basic emotions. Have the patient speak with that pseudo-obsessor, or you speak with it through the patient. After listing the charges that the pseudo-obsessor feels, we seek that pseudo-obsessor in its after-death environment: *She remained stuck, perpetually staring into a dark pool.*

As with hangovers, relive episodes that illustrate the life history. Usually, an unassimilated life has both a hangover and traumas. A child grows up unloved, misunderstood, lonely, and during a bombing dies in perplexity and shock. That child leaves its body in isolation and incomprehension, and without orientation. Telling the life history then means regression to particular episodes. The difference between this situation and a common hangover is that in this case you harvest catharsis only upon renovation of the dying experience.

First move back to episodes that explain the life path. The pseudo-obsessor may carry grief as the main charge. You may instruct the patient, "Go back to a situation that explains her grief." As a follow-up, ask, "Are there more situations that made her sad?" With a normal cathartic reliving we use the present tense, and we want identification: the patient says *I* instead of *he* or *she*. If someone says, *Then he did this*, or *He thought that*, we change the statement to *I do this*, or *I think that*.

With pseudo-obsessions, however, reliving is dissociated, not associated. The patient describes what the other then experienced, in terms of *he* or *she* and *then this happened with her*. If someone continues in the I-form, thus identifying with it, this is not wrong, but still we need dissociation and renovation in the dying experience to cure the pseudo-obsessor.

If a patient has relived several episodes, and has gained a certain understanding and acceptance, then go back to the after-death environment - for example, that dark pool:

T: Do you see her sitting near that pool?
P: Yes, she is still there, but she feels less attached now; she wants to leave.

If simple renovation does not help, and it usually doesn't, dissociation is necessary. The patient, the present personality, enters the after-life environment of the past personality to help it. Such a step is always necessary with roving children and deranged people.

Sometimes people stay bound to their dead body. They keep staring at that injured body. The renovation may consist of the present personality helping the other to care for the body, to cure it and sometimes to wake it up to life. If the other personality is unable to do that, the present person must do it, while the other observes. This approach forms a triangle: the injured body, the former personality who is watching, and the present personality who cares for the body and heals it. Anything may happen, but the thing to do usually suggests itself.

For example, a deceased child who remains in panic sits huddled in the corner of a ruin. You seek this child in its own environment. It may take time to approach and to calm that child, to embrace it, and bring it to a better environment, for example to a pet farm, where it cares for animals and is left in peace. More often the child stays close to or crawls inside the patient. Often it grows later, and then either leaves or integrates with the present personality.

Renovation often means that the personality simply leaves the darkness and isolation and gloom, to go to a place of light with other people. The most common approach is to lead such people to "the light." I prefer to lead them to people they have loved.

The second most common response after renovation is that the present and the previous personality embrace each other and even may blend into each other. The patient feels the previous personality entering the present body. The most usual location is the breast, and the second most usual location is the belly. Any other body part may be involved, including the head, the hands or the feet.

If renovation is blocked, there is still a charge undiscovered or forgotten in the regressions done, or there is still some regression undone. Ask, "What keeps you tied to that life?" Locate any remaining charges. Regress to these charges and have that personality relive them to achieve a catharsis if possible. With a pseudo-obsession, always confirm and complete such catharsis in the afterlife.

You can't win them all. Once I had a discussion with a bishop who had burned heretics (see the example sessions). He didn't repent. If religion and guilt come into play, healing can be tough.

With deceased adults, you look first to see if they can go on their own strength to where they want to be. And where they want to be differs. They blend with the patient, or go to the light, or go to sleep peacefully, or remain a subpersonality, but they are harmoniously connected. Do not force blending, but ask them what they want. If a response does not come, ask the present person, "What impression do you get? What do you want to do with him or her? What has to happen?"

If people first imagined subpersonalities entering their room, as with egostates, then you finish back there again. Is that subpersonality satisfied, happy? Check the processed charges, just as with a trauma. If someone gets stuck while traversing the charges, you may help, but not too much, except with children. With adults, do not enter the after-life like some spirit guide or guardian angel. People must do their own work. If your intervention as therapist does not help directly, then you have to work on postulates. Sometimes souls are locked in by shutoff commands from others.

In addition to addressing subpersonalities and implementing cathartic reliving, for treatment of pseudo-obsessions you thus need renovation and dissociation methods. Those methods are easy, imaginative ones. Even if you are clumsy, such still work. A crude, general and inefficient instruction such as "Go to the light" usually works.

Renovate either by using elements that emerged during the session, or their reverse. If a child cries *I never had a doll*, then give it a doll. If the child had a doll that was lost, taken away, trampled by horses, run over, etc., that doll will have become a symbol of the child itself. The child feels lost, trampled, or run over in the mud: "Where is your doll? Look for your doll. There is your doll, in the mud." We pick up and renovate that doll, then work from the doll to the child itself.

Use dolls for children who died in perplexity, especially girls. A lost girl will project herself in a doll. Holding that doll close to herself, the child mobilizes her own positive energy and becomes accessible.

In another example, a couple of drunken mercenaries rape a girl of twelve while they beat her mother to death, and afterward kill the girl as well. That dead child is locked in terror, does not grow, because adulthood is terror; being a man, being a woman, is terror. Therefore she recoils and remains small.

Give that girl a doll, a sweet doll, a pitiful doll, a doll that should be cared for, protected. To that doll we let her do everything that should have happened to the girl herself. If the girl's throat was cut, that doll will have a head half severed. We are going to repair, to mend, to heal that doll. Sometimes it takes a couple of days, sometimes a couple of minutes, and then suddenly the healing is there.

If children are so perplexed that they refuse any contact with menacing and fearful people, including us, the pet farm may help. Somewhere is a barn with goats and lambs and little chickens. "Go and care for them." Or a friendly "aunt" is there to help. Those animals and those people may be thought forms, not necessarily real presences.

In this way, the soul of a lost child returns into the *oecumene*, the inhabited world. Use dolls, sometimes animals, and sometimes newborns: "Look, there lies a foundling baby, crying." The child projects on that foundling its own congealed and coagulated self-pity, so the child's own feelings start to flow again, and later blend with the grown baby.

Alienation.
Another type of problem is a general feeling of not being at home, of remaining a stranger, an outsider. Such a feeling may come from the family in which we grew up. Often that feeling is already present prenatally - not feeling safe and sheltered in the womb. Sometimes it is a feeling of being lost on this planet. The basic prescription for such feeling of alienation is *homing*, sending patients back to people and places where they were truly at home, to a world where they felt at home.

Reliving home is such a strong experience that it means real homecoming. Therefore, in homing sessions it becomes especially important to return to the here and now. Usually people don't want that. The solution is as simple as it is revolutionary: have them feel there and here at the same time. Such an experience most often results in feeling an indestructible link with home - in the back, in the neck and shoulders or at the top of the head. Sometimes it may even be felt between the eyes; then we really feel like citizens of two worlds.

Homing is seductive for people who would prefer to keep unfinished business unfinished. If you are not completely grounded as a therapist, don't do it, unless you want to become a second-rate priest instead of a first-rate healer.

As long as people prefer over there to down here, they will hang onto problems - a general hangover from being here, anchored in a basic character neurosis, usually a superiority complex.

A simple homing session may produce a breakthrough that changes the life of a patient. However, it may also reinforce his basic problem. I am so wary of this possibility that I do not give general homing instructions in writing. For further background, read Chapter 8.

Resuming.
A trauma rips a hole in the ego. A hangover is a mortgage on the ego. A pseudo-obsession means a distributed ego. A character postulate is a problem in the structure of the ego, an identification with a particular response pattern. Alienation is an illness that has eaten into the soul itself.

Unless a patient is ready to clear attachments first, and the therapist knows how to do this, we should start with traumas, preferably with debilitating fears. The most natural order of treatment is: *traumas, pseudo-obsessions, hangovers, character postulates*. Sometimes we must first remove the tough *dirt-skirts* of hangovers before traumas can be resolved. But in the end, patients themselves decide the sequence and the pace. If any problem is clearly on top, start with that problem. The golden rule is to find the order that wins energy on the way.

The basic reaction to frustration is, according to most psychological theories, aggression. I think that the basic reaction to frustration is first self-pity, and only secondly aggression. First there is the collapsing reaction of *poor me*, and only then the erupting reaction of *that damned other*.

Self-pity and anger are the basic reactions to frustration. With slow, tough, long frustrations, self-pity always wins because it requires less energy than anger. Sudden frustrations often produce irritation in which aggression dominates, but endless frustration exhausts our anger, and self-pity remains.

Emotional clusters may grow and complicate a number of emotions. Ultimately, we may have a volcano of anger, smothered in a lake of grief, packaged in layers of guilt feelings. Then envy hitches to it and the whole is armored, defended by postulates such as, *That always happens to me*, or *People can't be trusted*, or *People are indifferent*. An array of anger-grief-guilt-envy, surrounded by postulates, is a typical composition of a malignant karmic ulcer. Often this combination is topped by an *autopsychodrama*, a self-pity complex, like a shoddy gray mass of whipped cream, making an unpalatable, disgusting dessert.

In most humanistic psychologies, fear is overrated. It is even seen as the antipode of love. Rubbish. Fear is not a negative experience, but is an anticipation of a negative experience. The negative experience itself is frustration if it is weak, and pain if it is strong. Raw, intense, seemingly unending pain, both spiritual and physical at the same time, is the rock bottom of suffering.

The reverse of pain is joy, and the reverse of love is hate. The ultimate twister is to feel joy in pain. Therefore, in sadism and in masochism, simple reliving does not release, but rather it reinforces.

What about the pathology of daily life, in the form of habits, smoking, nail biting and such? Tenacious habits do not arise from traumas, but from hangovers or pseudo-obsessors. If habits occur periodically, think of pseudo-obsessors. But if they are continuous, think of hangovers. Use egostates. Call up the "Nailbiter" or the "Sufferer" or the "Man-in-a-Hurry" or "Don Quixote." Have the smoker and the non-smoker talk with each other. Don't forget to call up a third one, who doesn't care either way. Voice Dialogue techniques are effective to follow up egostates.

Another way to deal with a habit is to catch that habit in a sentence and see which charge that sentence carries: *I bite nails because* . . . . If clear responses emerge, the habit may include postulates.

Some addictions, such as drinking, often stem from previous lives. Others, such as smoking, rarely originated in previous lives. According to Bruce Goldberg, it is rare to find causes of smoking in past lives. Netherton finds causes of alcoholism and other addictions in prehistoric times. According to him, an addiction always begins with situations of mortal danger. He has a patient go back to " . . . the first moment when an alien substance that relieved the pain entered your body." Often that substance is snake poison, while sometimes it is poisoned arrows or poisoned food. With alcoholics, Netherton uses five sessions of four or five hours. He always begins the treatment with a regression to birth and then has his patient enter the prenatal time: "What are the first words that your mother thought or heard or said, that suggested drink?"

Netherton is very effective and very efficient, but he generalizes quickly. Once a therapist knows what is the problem, the session belongs to the therapist, not to the patient.

Beware of that. Keep following, keep learning, keep going.

CHAPTER 4. NATURAL DIGESTION AND INDUCED ASSIMILATION

How do people assimilate experiences? Why do some experiences remain unassimilated? How do those experiences linger on? What, in the end, happens to them?

Slowly growing out of something, and getting over something, provides a natural catharsis. When our life partner dies, our healing will take years. We may mourn for the rest of our life. Assimilation of that kind of experience is something that we can hardly speed up. Such healing carries its own time constants. Only the repressed charges are the ones that we can handle through therapy. The other charges have their own clocks. Some tick slowly and are difficult to speed up. Other charges are impossible to digest gradually and have to be assimilated in one piece.

For example, it takes a long time to grow accustomed to the fact that someone no longer comes home. Slowly that wound will heal, more or less. A person will still have a scar there, but sometimes by restimulation or by a partial charge, that scar starts bleeding again. *I would have liked so much to say goodbye, but I never got the chance.* When in a session we allow someone to take leave from the deceased, in ten minutes a deep catharsis can be achieved.

Let's look at a different kind of problem now. A friend does something very annoying behind your back, and you feel so betrayed that you remain ill for weeks. You understand why you are upset, but not why you are so deeply upset, or why you are upset for so long. The answer is restimulation.

Within you there was a forgotten feeling of being betrayed. The actual smaller experience restimulated the previous greater experience. Each time someone's emotional reaction to a situation is stronger than the actual conditions would justify, similar repressed emotions are emerging.

Regression therapists know the mechanism of restimulation, but they usually interpret it as something that makes life more difficult. They then ignore the essence: old feelings emerge because those feelings want to become assimilated!

In the case in point, during our illness we process some or all of the old repressed feelings of being betrayed. We use this opportunity to reduce these feelings to at least reasonable proportions. We become better instead of worse. What appears to be the disease is in fact the cure. When such repressed feelings emerge and temporarily swamp us, we think that we have fallen back, while in fact we are assimilating old feelings.

This brings us to the concept of *abreaction*, which is a well-known manner of releasing tension, both inside and outside therapy. Abreaction involves expressing one's grief, one's anger, one's frustration. It works, but it has its limits and is not always necessary. When this release is not directed to the right people, when the original issues are not confronted, when people do not understand their own tensions, such a release is merely a blowing off of steam. This kind of release is sensible only as a prelude to real work. Palliatives work, but they don't cure.

The best assimilation is one that occurs right after the event. Such prompt response takes guts. Being courageous and realistic, using common sense and keeping self-pity at bay is always good, even better than seeking regression therapy later. What is the main reason for delaying assimilation and instead repressing emotions? People delay and repress because they still carry earlier repressed experiences and feelings. Undigested experiences have the nasty habit of accumulating.

Therefore, most people heal slowly, even with the help of wonderful therapists. Worse still, many forms of psychotherapy are inefficient. Still more importantly, many therapists are not very effective. But much inertia is present inside the patient, and a person's seemingly positive attitudes can mask a stubborn resistance.

People who believe in reincarnation speak readily about karma when progress of the patient is very slow. However, as Edith Fiore points out, when nothing much happens with the client for a long time, there is usually unconscious guilt, not karma as some kind of spiritual punishment. Guilt aborts action, and thus avoids the risk of tasting the forbidden fruits of success.

An additional consideration is that people assimilate information differently, as we also find during regressions. Some people observe horrible and traumatic events from the past and view these events dispassionately and without emotion. They describe every detail of what is happening, saying for example, *I know that I am that person to whom this happens, but I feel nothing.* Afterward they analyze the events and connect those events to their actual problems. The session may free them from their symptoms, even if no emotional release has occurred.

Other people relive all physical and mental agony with a vengeance when they are regressed. We may have to suggest to those patients that they release their pain and explore the meaning of the experience. Most patients succeed in this effort, but some remain in agony until they have relived the entire episode. Very often, generalized feelings of guilt or grief or mourning worsen the pain.

The basic rule for efficiency in therapy is to follow the right order when treating issues. We can find that right order by psychological understanding, but most of all by careful listening and observation.

Sometimes healing occurs without new insights having been won, and even without conscious processing. For example, a woman comes for past-life therapy to rid herself of a persistent mental bonding with her ex-husband. Everything goes fine. Soon she notices that her always scant menstruation, never mentioned during the sessions, becomes more "adult" every month. Though this change may be painful, it gives her great satisfaction.

Another woman may have serious menstruation problems. After many sessions dealing with these problems and her corresponding emotions, the problems are almost gone. Then, sometime after her final session, the patient discovers by accident that her fear of dogs is also gone. A later analysis of the sessions shows that this unexpected healing may be related to a regression that involved a deadly encounter with a bear. Before that encounter, she had witnessed wolves mangling her husband. Even in therapy there is serendipity. But the better we work, the luckier we get.

Neurotic reactions.
Reincarnation therapy often attracts the more spiritual and altruistic types of patients. These patients are not necessarily sane; they have their own problems. Their search for enlightenment may mask inferiority or superiority feelings. Compassion, pity, altruism and emotional involvement in misery are often connected with repressed aggression. Even therapists who very

much like to help people may uncover power abuse and violence in regressions to their own past lifetimes. People who want to play helper or savior have often been victims, but nearly as often they have been perpetrators.

As Adler has already said, people who feel that they live in a hostile world, that they are too good for this world, just think about themselves and their own problems and not about what they could give. A person's quest for completion, perfection and victory may involve neurotic reactions to his or her own imperfections. Without realistic acceptance of one's own limitations, such aims will include neurotic elements.

Neurotic people have strong ideals and measure real people against those ideals, because in this way they may devalue everyone. *All or nothing* is a typical neurotic life motto to explain why someone did or accomplished so little.

Sane people are willing to lay their plans and opinions aside and deal as open-mindedly as possible with reality. Neurotics prefer their fiction, whatever the price. Neurotics suffer, but they prefer to endure this suffering rather than risk the greater suffering that would result from failing to solve their problems, and thus appearing worthless. We all want to get rid of our problems, but the fear of losing precious and vulnerable self-esteem is often greater than problems we may already have. Neurotics have less of a sense of humor, especially about themselves.

Neurotics are anxious about losing their money, psychotics believe that they have already lost their money, and sane people take care not to lose their money. Normal people realize that symbols are symbols, while neurotic people take symbols for truth, and psychotic people turn symbols into reality. This reminds me of Pol Pot in Cambodia, who rigorously applied the theories of his Sorbonne professors, but cost the deaths of millions of people and brought on a medieval darkness. Instead, normal people like us know that professors should only be parroted, or at most commented upon wisely.

In each neurosis, look for the person who suffers most from the condition of the patient. Usually this is a member of the family. Perhaps the patient may feel that other people in general are to blame, or society, or something even more vague - the system, the structure. When we keep asking, we find that the patient's rejection is especially directed at the "establishment." For spiritual people, this "establishment" includes all superficial and materialistic people - in other words, successful people. At the receiving end we find the noble, spiritual sufferers.

The most common root of neurosis is discouragement. Many people complain about problems that their parents or other family members have caused. Often there is truth in this complaint. Four types of children lack courage:

- *weak, deformed or defective children*
- *spoiled children*
- *rejected or hated children*
- *frightened children (who are treated unpredictably, usually by psychotic parents)*

Whatever the life history, whatever childhood, whatever previous lives, what matters is not what we have, but what we do with it. The past may provide explanations, explanations may offer understanding, but excuses are produced here and now. Humans can always act differently.

Patients may avoid solving their own problems because then they will have nobody left to blame. Conversely, by not solving their problems they can go on blaming their parents or family members or "other people."

Character may be destiny, but such destiny is the consequence of choice. In the past we chose to define ourselves in a certain way, and now we have the choice to remain ourselves in a certain way. These are fateful choices indeed, especially the choice to refrain from choosing, and to continue business as usual. Adults of normal intelligence are not destined to have problems, but they may let themselves be seduced into their problems (Adler) and they may become addicted to their problems.

Reliving does have its limits. It may show addiction, it may explain addiction, it may help to accept the fact of addiction. Yet the next step is up to the person behind the switchboard. Conversions happen every day. Conversion may never happen.

We are in the healing business, not in the conversion business, and even less in the proselytizing business. We help the horse to get to water and we encourage it to drink.

In our capacity as healers we must also pay attention to the roles that people tend to play. Neurotics often assume standard roles: *Victim, Perpetrator, Witness, Prosecutor* and *Helper* or *Savior*. The triangle of Prosecutor, Victim and Savior comes from Transactional Analysis of Eric Berne. In *Games People Play* we always encounter these three roles in an ever-changing cast. The other two roles, those of Perpetrator and Helper, come mainly from Netherton. He showed that Helpers have often been Perpetrators. The Witness is also a role that offers a way to avoid responsibility. *It is all my fault* (guilt), or *I'll get them anyhow* (anger or resentment) are Perpetrator statements, and *It is not my fault, I just happened to see it* (disowning responsibility) is an Observer statement. Finding any of these five neurotic roles during therapy should always ring a bell.

Complaints (Victim), simple blame or moral indignation (Prosecutor), guilt or anger (Perpetrator), unsolicited help (Savior or Boy Scout) and studied non-intervention (Observer) are all useless roles. They enable a person to avoid responsibility and action, and thus avoid learning. Real responsibility lies between avoiding responsibility on one side, and guilt, shame and regret on the other.

The most common neurotic role is that of Victim. We begin life as children, and thus we start our lives being small, weak and ignorant, compared to the adults who call the shots. Feeling victimized is a reaction to feeling inferior; an inferiority complex focuses itself in the end to exaggerated feelings of being left behind, usually compensated by what Adler called "Cinderella fantasies."

The Victim role provides an ideal basis for imagining being a beautiful princess in a past life in which we already suffered and were wronged. In both cases we tend either to upgrade (*Look how good I was*) or to downgrade (*Poor me*) the experience, and we want the therapist to help rectify a present unfairness.

The Prosecutor blames others. That can be an excuse: *It is not my fault, I can't help it, society has been wrong, the government does nothing, my father was dominant*, etc. However, if a woman furiously blames her father for her incest experiences, she does not assume the neurotic role of Prosecutor. If her accusations are true, her behavior is sane; if they are not true, then her behavior is insane but she is no Prosecutor.

Once we assume a neurotic role, we slip easily into a complementary role. If we are the Victim, but we are angry, we easily turn into the Prosecutor. From there we can become the Perpetrator. Perpetrators can blame their victims, because victims are so terribly annoying and weak, so rabbit-like. In the Perpetrator's mind, victims don't deserve better. Most people change roles all the time, while some remain in only one of them.

The most simple role is that of Victim, because we happen to start life helplessly. We need the smallest amount of energy for that role. The basic reaction to any form of frustration is self-pity. In psychotherapy this response has been named the *autopsychodrama* or self-pity complex. Such a complex is almost the same as *patient mentality*.

People can become victims of circumstances. Let's say that a good friend of ours is run over by a car, or our own child dies from an error in medical treatment. We are then, factually, victims. The question is whether we declare ourselves Victim and remain like that.

Victims look for Helpers. When they find such helpers they become Enthusiasts, and after disillusionment with Helpers they turn into Prosecutors. A patient may announce, *My former therapists have not discovered what you have discovered with me.* In this case the patient prosecutes the former therapist and defines us as Savior. Idolization paves the way for prosecution. A Prosecutor is very often a disillusioned Enthusiast.

Prosecutors may often employ a *pedestal*, a device that can be offered and then withdrawn: *Please accept this beautiful rug so I can pull it from under your feet later.*

Therapist, beware! Avoid pedestals and rugs. Just look for mutual trust and afterward mutual appreciation of a fruitful and interesting episode.

I remember a client who carried the postulate, *Men have ruined my life.* As a male therapist I had to avoid the Savior position at all costs, though I declined the possibility of operative sex change.

Behind the roles of Helper or Savior one can often find suppressed aggression. Saviors choose superiority: *I am better than others; I am more then others; I come from a higher planet; I am only here to help people.* Usually this attitude is a projection. Even if true, it is neurotic. In this case a superiority complex is a reaction to an inferiority complex.

Inside we know that we are special, but the outside situation that we perceive does not bear that out. We feel caught. Now we assume the role of Helper - mother, teacher, priest, elder brother or guru. We gain satisfaction from helping others. Nothing good comes out of this, because of a lack of equality.

Likewise, the Savior role is false, as this role requires that we put ourselves in a superior position. If we assume a higher point of view, then others are smaller. *Just listen to me, darling; just wear your red skirt tonight and everybody will adore you* - a parent-child transaction.

Being superior feels good, and it nicely avoids the vulnerability of being equal or feeling inferior. I would not be surprised if many of those people who feel such a great need to help others (and therefore attend seminars in past-life therapy), steamrollered others in former lives.

If we feel we are better than others, we encounter situations where others irritate us. That contrast could make us aggressive, so we may switch to the role of Perpetrator. Or we may react by asking, *Why did they refuse to listen to me again?* Then we assume the role of Victim.

We may find ourselves changing roles in subsequent lives. Perpetrators can become Victims, and Victims can become Perpetrators. Woolger gives an example in his book (1987, 301):

> *We're riding on horses, we're starting to cut them down. They're poorly armed. My men behead some of them. I cut down some women. They're herding others into houses and setting them on fire. Now I'm with this woman. I'm raping her. It's wonderful. Now I cut her throat. It makes me feel strong and masterful to have another's life and pleasure at my command. . . Such an image of omnipotence is the very obverse of the vulnerability that Milton felt in earlier lives; the victim has now reversed into persecutor.*

If I am a Helper and I succeed, I can write it on my account. If I fail, I write it on the account of another. Helpers can feel comfortable because they use their good intention to excuse their failures. Many people don't want to be judged on their results, but rather on their intentions.

Neurotic roles can trigger complementary neurotic roles, and it becomes difficult to break through such a game. Parents suffered to pay tuition for their children, and then those children aren't grateful. The parents become Victims, they Prosecute the child, the child feels like a Perpetrator and may be a Victim itself. Then such parents say that the child should not feel that guilty. This statement makes the child feel even more guilty, etc. Being a Witness can also be a traumatic role. Somebody has to watch how her favorite son is tortured to death, to break her will. Seeing it happen is almost more traumatic than being tortured herself. If she suffers such a fate, she has a couple of demonic hours that may seem like an eternity. But if that woman lives for twenty years more, her experience becomes engraved. She cannot flee into the Victim role, because her son already assumed that position. She thus freezes in the Witness role.

In the case of father-daughter incest, mother serves as Witness: "I couldn't do anything. Caroline never talked to me about it, and neither did John. Wasn't it terrible?" *Wir haben es nicht gewusst.*

Presence and absence. Karmic transactions. Untrue identities. Presence and absence are important for therapy. I discovered this issue in my training programs for managers. The first condition for leadership appeared to be presence. Nowadays, managers who participate in my seminars have to list under which circumstances they are more present, and under which circumstances less.

People always complain about their bosses, often rightly so. Common complaints are that the boss is not there, has too many external commitments, lacks interest, shields himself. Leadership means being present physically and mainly mentally, giving continuous attention and interest.

Bureaucracy is often the opposite. Counters, procedures and formalities create distance. People write memos to others, as if those others were on Mars instead of at the opposite end of the corridor. Bureaucrats avoid taking phone calls, or even meeting and talking directly.

A common reason for absence is a personal preoccupation that interferes with our work, a preoccupation that drains our attention away from where we are and what we do. That preoccupation can be negative, but also positive. Perhaps we are thinking about our coming vacation or about the lottery prize that we hope to win, or we may dream away in love. In fact, we don't really want to be here, but would rather be somewhere else.

There is also something like *seeming presence.* We are there, but we are not ourselves. We might act forcefully, copying behavior of our boss or of our father. It looks as if we are present, but we are acting. Superiority feelings gives us a seeming presence, and inferiority feelings provide insufficient presence.

Both repression and inflation of our egos make us vulnerable. People who display inflated egos provide a walking invitation to pierce those egos. Why do we want to enlarge ourselves? Because we feel small. Why do we feel small? Because somewhere we lost a part of ourselves. Or we compare ourselves to the wrong people, and that we would not do if we would simply be ourselves. If we are ourselves, we cannot feel ourselves as great or small. Size problems, superiority and inferiority, are a form of presence problems.

A common problem is that of maintaining order in a classroom. This problem relates also to presence, absence or seeming presence. Students react instinctively to presence or lack of it. They tackle fake behavior. Their response certainly has to do with the teacher's grounding. To be present means to be here and now, to be centered, to be grounded, to accept ourselves and our situation.

Feeling incompletely present is not always a problem. We cannot show everything simultaneously. I can present my female side with greater difficulty than I can present my male side. But if I accept my feminine side, then that can be present, although in the background. There is always more to people than meets the eye.

Problems of not wanting to be present often stem from birth and even pregnancy. Rejection can begin in the womb - if the child doesn't like it there, it wants to be out. Birth may be a painful experience. Disappointment may set in at the first moments of life. Both before and during birth, withdrawal reactions may already have started.

Morris Netherton says that during the prenatal stage no conscious mind is present. Helen Wambach found that almost 90% of incarnating souls are not really in their body before the sixth month. Other therapists always find experiences that occurred as early as conception. I find that many people are fully and personally aware of how they felt inside, and sometimes outside, the womb.

After reading Karl Schlotterbeck's book I concluded that three different registers are available to the unborn, and the existence of all three explains the different views that therapists hold regarding the prenatal phase. Those three registers are:
- *our psychic register as incarnating human*
- *an etheric register that our mother advances us*
- *the physical register of the embryo, depending on the growing nervous system*

My experience with past-life therapy indicates that most souls enter the embryo only if it is at least six months old. Often they are connected with the embryo earlier, but they stay outside of the mother and perhaps enter the embryo only now and then. Although a soul may choose to enter only at the seventh month, it arrives in an environment where tapes already run. These include an etheric tape that has been running since conception, and a physical tape that has run from the fourth month or so.

Once experiences are registered on the physical or on the mother-tape, our own sensitivities or traumas tie in, causing restimulation. Attachments work the same way. An attachment enters on a similar emotion, a similar thought or similar "vibration." We can be outside of the embryo during pregnancy, while the other two tapes keep running. Only with the definite entry of the soul into the embryo do all three registers connect.

We contact the physical world through an etheric link. Probably the growing embryo starts with an etheric body that is a specialization of the etheric body of the mother. At the connection we revitalize our own etheric body, with its etheric burdens and holes from former lives (karma) and its etheric harvest from former lives (dharma).

How does a child become fully present? By wishing to grow up, and simultaneously enjoying being a child. A child who is always busy with the future, either anxious over it or desirous for it, is less present in the now. To be present is also to feel at home. We may feel connection to a home elsewhere, or we may carry our home within ourselves. Not feeling at home means that we would rather go somewhere else.

We can extend the notion of feeling at home to include feeling well in this body, feeling well in this world, being incarnated. If we are not incarnated, we are at least in a psychic environment. If we feel depressed we are in a depressive environment, and if we feel glad, we are in a glad environment. If I think strongly about you then I am with you, if I can find you, and vice versa. If we are incarnated we cannot always do that physically, as our spirit is tied to our body. But our spirit may still want to be somewhere else.

In past-life therapy we often deal with people who don't want to be in this world, or don't like being in their body. They may feel too good for this world, and that feeling can express itself as *Society is wrong*, or *I am lonely and I feel rejected around here*. If such people are regressed to an earlier period of their present life, we may find a problem with their parents.

In the past, children dreamed that their parents were not their real parents. Such people dreamed that they were actually foundlings of royal birth. Nowadays, people relive that they came from higher planets to help the people here. Behind that attitude could be a problem with a person's first incarnation on Earth, or first incarnation in a physical body. Each time we are born, our birth restimulates emotions from our first incarnation here, and if we have ever lived elsewhere, our first time in a physical body.

It also may be the other way around. A difficulty with feeling present can be projected back from a difficult birth or from the shock of the first lifetime here. Some stories of the primal trauma seem to me to be dramatizations of the birth experience in this life.

Between feelings of presence or absence there may be a sense of alternating or ambivalent presence. I call this state *wavering presence*. Why do we waver? Because of an unstable balance between emotions that make us want to be here, and others that make us want to be elsewhere. Or stronger still, some of our emotions make us want to be present and other emotions make us want to be absent. Freud spoke metaphysically, but correctly, about the life wish and the death wish.

Wavering that makes us vacillate between wanting to be here and wanting to be elsewhere comes from conflicting desires or conflicting fears. Wavering that makes us vacillate between wanting to be more present and wanting to extinguish ourselves comes from lust-pain ambivalence (*I hate you! - Please go on!*), from hope-despair ambivalence (*It will never happen! - It still might happen!*) or from me-you ambivalence (*I want to do my own thing! - I want to be with you!*). Wavering presence is irritating, becomes exhausting and in the end is maddening, both for ourselves and for others.

In aura exploration (see Chapter 7), absence manifests itself as seeing or feeling holes in our aura. If we experience a hole, we know that there has been some loss or trauma in our past. We are created without holes. We feel a hole only if something is lacking. We thus can search for whatever we once lost, whatever left a hole behind. We realize that there had been something, but we just forgot what it was. We can experience this loss as an empty hole, as a hole with something inside, or as a hole in which something is hidden.

If a hole looks empty, we let the patient either shine light in there with a silvery white beam, or move down into it themselves. Sometimes the hole appears to be bottomless, but as the patient descends into it he or she arrives at the original situation. A suggestion that the patient enter that hole sometimes does not work, because moving down into that emptiness may restimulate the empty feeling. What we can do then, is: "Search outside yourself what belongs in there. Somewhere, wherever, is something that belongs in there." If we make such a suggestion at the right moment, this kind of search gives power to the patient, and we thus avoid any paralysis that the hole may stimulate.

With an empty hole the instruction is: "Imagine that opposite that hole something else is with you that doesn't belong to you, something that is too much." The three possibilities are:
1. *Look at what is in that hole.*
2. *Search for what had originally been at that spot.*
3. *Release something that is opposite the hole, something that is too much.*

The answer might lie the other way around - we have lost something because we took over something, have absorbed something that was not ours. If we take over something from another, we lose ourselves. If we betray ourselves, we take something from others. There is always balance.

Opposite our bigger and smaller holes are all kinds of bigger and smaller inserts and quasi-presences of others, as satellites. There is much around us and in us. Swarming all around us is exactly as much as what we are not, or what we have lost of ourselves. Each time we lose something and simultaneously gain something, a *karmic transaction* has occurred.

We may feel that we have lost something, have been robbed, have bartered away something, have had something forced from us or forced on us, or have received something that we have not wanted. If we feel that we have lost something, then we believe that it happened by accident or by negligence, but without us realizing it. To be robbed or deceived, however, implies that a thief, an opponent or an enemy has been at work.

Perhaps, by contrast, we let something come inside, and simultaneously we lose something of ourselves. When we take something of another, we drop something else. The soul has a limited capability. Unless the soul grows, there is no way to win or lose without compensation.

Let's say that something has been stolen. How come? Maybe we were not paying attention. The therapist may ask: "What do you still carry with you of that thief?" The answer can be surprising. If the answer is *Nothing*, then ask, "Look and see if you had something with you that wasn't yours and, as long as you had it, prevented you from holding onto what you have lost." We may have walked around with belongings of another that we had not yet returned, and therefore something could again be stolen from us.

We can also give something out of compassion. We may pray before going to sleep: *Please give my little sister something of my keenness and intelligence.* We lose something, but simultaneously we get something back - her lack of concentration, her asthma or her weak feet.

With a real karmic transaction, two parties exchange what they have. Such transactions happen half-consciously. They do not go through the front door, but through the back door or the side door.

If a woman worked as oracle in a temple, carrying the postulate, *I am here for others*, her attitude will draw a hole. Why did they use her in that temple? Because she had certain abilities. From where? She had developed them. At one time those abilities had been a part of herself. Now she is exploited by people who are too lazy or too unfit or too important to develop those abilities themselves. She is no longer present in her abilities. She has disowned them.

If in a regression session we instruct her to go back to the situation that caused the hole, and see what she lost then and what she gained in return, a surprising inner shift may occur. The session may then lead to a confrontation with the then high priest. If she accepts and wins that confrontation, she suddenly perceives still an earlier life where she stands in her full glory, in full state. That is the catharsis. That is what she gets back in her life now.

Within us are scattered holes, and around us is an inner crowd or inner swarm. The swarmed human is a powerful image. The idea that we are swarmed suggests all kinds of fellow travelers, outside our own control, half or wholly in the shadow. Some parts always draw attention, while others hide themselves and still others rise or set at unsuspected moments.

What swarms around us in our aura? Suppressed desires, guilt about unfinished business, all kinds of impressions that we have picked up during the day or the night and not digested. But also present is everything we have willingly or unwillingly picked up from others and have not yet returned. There is buzzing and whispering and groaning going on. We could also speak of the whispered-about or buzzed-about human.

The swarmed human is lively, unpredictable, creative, but also clouding, preventing us from coming into focus. Swarmed means not in focus, fragmented, not grounded, not concentrated, not complete, not quiet. If we were wholly ourselves, wholly in focus, then we would assume our true form and appear in state, brilliant and alive.

Perhaps we should avoid appearing that way. Imagine if each of our looks, each of our thoughts, were laser-like! This could prove fatal, having so much power with so much immaturity! Staying swarmed also provides self-protection.

However, patients are not themselves enough. They have emotional problems, programming problems, etc. Their swarm is heavy and difficult. An extreme example is that of Sybil, a sparrow swarmed by sixteen firm birds of subpersonalities. More power is present in that swarm than in herself. Her swarm also contained helping fragments, but she had to draw all those fragments back into herself.

What is the difference between improper, deformed or disfigured presence, and seeming presence? *Seeming presence* is the kind of presence that we display when a visitor tells us something and we are not interested. "Gee, nice what you say, very interesting," we may reply, but we are with our thoughts elsewhere.

Disfigured presence is forced presence, the kind of presence that we show when we are playing a role that ill fits us. Perhaps we play the self-assured man of the world, when in fact we feel unhappy and tense. Or maybe we assume the wrong age.

Real presence is the kind of presence that we show when we have all our former ages assimilated. What shows at the forefront is our present age, but behind that are all our previous ages. Usually we don't behave as a four-year-old, but we can switch into that age if we want or need to do so, perhaps when in contact with our own young children, or when floundering deliciously for a moment in the waves. But a person of fifty who always behaves like one of twenty does not accept his true age, or has a disfigured presence. This kind of presence is not

unreal, but it is twisted, artificial, forced. To sharpen the difference:
- In a seeming presence, people do as if they are present, but they are elsewhere in their mind.
- In a deformed presence, a 60-year-old acts like a 25-year-old, or the other way around, or assumes a neurotic role.
- In an improper presence, somebody is a copy of her mother or someone else.

We can assume non-human roles, too. I have learned to recognize seven such non-human identities. Some of them may come in pairs.

NON-HUMAN IDENTITIES

Angel   Devil

(Human)

Plant   Animal

Stone   Thing   Robot

These identifications are not present in the aura, but are images that we made for ourselves. They are inhuman self-images. The five former roles (Victim, Perpetrator, Witness, Prosecutor, Helper/Savior) are neurotic, and these seven inhuman identities (Angel, Devil, Plant, Animal, Stone, Thing, and Robot) ultimately are psychotic.

If we think of ourselves as a service hatch, the way that mediums or channels want to do, we declare ourselves to be inanimate, a thing. Serving as a channel is a beautiful role. *I may talk, but I'm not talking really - it talks through me.* Normal people are responsible for what they do and what they say. The Channel is not. The Channel can be even more attractive than Victim, Witness or Helper. You can be the Prosecutor without becoming angry. You are the Helper, erased by a superhuman spiritual eraser.

If we see ourselves as a Stone, we are just there, released of human emotions and human frailties; apathy is the ultimate in contemplation. If we view ourselves as a Robot, we live according to program. The robotized human is one that we encounter often when we work with character postulates. The table lists a few typical Robot statements.

ROBOT STATEMENTS

This is the way I am.
Chance doesn't exist.
Everything is destined.
I know my duty.
I do everything according to plan.
I follow my inner voice.
I live according to the law.
Time doesn't exist.
I do what I have promised.

If we have a religious experience or a sacred mood without a will of our own, but we still feel alive, then we get either the Angel or the Plant identity. We are pure, we only do things that Our Sweet Lord wants. *Thy will be done.* We are without will, and thus we make no mistakes. Many people in churches and spiritual movements seek this kind of identity. Dogmatic people are either Angels or Plants.

Playing the role of Angel frees us from many burdens - of criticism, of insecurity, of failure, of responsibility: operation succeeded, patient deceased. It is easier to love the world than to love our neighbor. Many people who want to be absorbed in universal love play this role. With Angel people we often encounter statements about transformed emotions, mainly transformed love.

Angels also have no itch. They have redesigned their identity - if successful, almost fatally - almost, because life always presents us with experiences by which we drop out of our role. Ultimately, Angels are confronted with their animal nature. Sex is an interesting one for would-be Angels. They may then see sex as imperfection and seduction, and before they know it, they regard themselves as Animals or as Devils.

ANGEL STATEMENTS

I do not stray from the straight path.
Nobody understands me.
This is my last life on earth.
Virtue is its own reward.
I always look for the good in people.
I do not feel at home anywhere here.
I seek enlightenment.
With positive thoughts we help the world along.
I seek purity in all things.

You might say that if I push my presence artificially in a certain direction, then the rest becomes orphaned, runs wild. A monk who tries to free himself from the lust of the flesh, who in vain prays and flogs himself, may not be as bad as someone who succeeded and turned himself into an Angel. A failed identification is painful and confusing, but at least experience goes on.

One response to situations we cannot handle is to become perfect. We pull a shield around ourselves, as a cylinder or cube in our aura. Pay close attention to metallic colors in the aura! Such colors suggest that these people were already old hands before they became human, or may suggest a perfection postulate. Metallic Angels are Robots.

Believers and mystics tend toward the Angel identity. Instead of doing good, they avoid doing wrong. So they desire nothing, and dampen their selfawareness so that it becomes as low as possible. They may feel like Angels, but they look like Plants.

In contrast, if we just do as we like, we rather identify with an Animal. This role can be nice as a vacation, but if we spend too long at it, we run wild. Few patients who come to us are Animals or Devils. We encounter mostly Angels in our trade. Sometimes we wish they were a bit more Animal or Devil.

One difference between the Devil and the Angel is that the Devil has the courage to see ugly aspects of itself. The Devil is the inhuman Perpetrator. *For me no more rules, no more bonds, no embarrassment, no inhibitions, I am Bad.*

Each one-sidedness is a sign of weakness, because when we see ourselves as one-sided we reject our humanity. If I drive to the next town by car, for 95% of the trip I act as a Robot. But I don't identify with the Robot. Assume that I never want to be a Robot, that I want to do everything consciously - I would never arrive in one piece.

As for the overall therapy session, the way I begin and end a session is all about presence here and now. I take whatever there is at that moment. That's the point, not soap operas or ritual case histories. What do patients want *now*? What do they feel *now* in their body?

I reject long intakes. An intake is rarely essential. The main function of the intake is to build trust, while the second function is to discover postulates. The rest is silence. The pure situation of beginning here and now contains as an oracle the actual problem and even the actual solution. In that sense the whole session is about making explicit the implicit, developing previous envelopment, elaborating and completing what is there.

If at the beginning of a session we are still elsewhere mentally, perhaps with another client on our minds, or an invoice, our vacation, or thoughts about the situation in Eastern Europe, then an intake helps us to kick off from that other concern and come back to the here and now. Once we are here, further talk is superfluous.

Avoid letting people become engrossed in telling their stories. When that happens, patients are no longer in the here and now, but in their story. Do not say unnecessary things in an intake. A long intake is usually a flight, for the patient or for the therapist. In principle we can do without all of that. What truly matters is, "What do you want to work at? Okay, say when you are ready." Go.

If an intake is necessary to bring the patient to the here and now, then do it. If it isn't necessary, don't! If the intake anchors the patient in the there and then, shame on you! That error is in two respects a typical beginner's mistake.

In that here and now, almost all subjective problems are *repercussions* of the past, and thus these problems manifest themselves in a lessened or unreal presence. The seven kinds of repercussions that I have distinguished, we can redefine in terms of presence and absence:
- *trauma: temporary absence, draws a hole*
- *hangover: gradually becoming pushed away or sucked away, thinner, vaguer or smaller presence*

- *pseudo-obsession: presence of former personality*
- *obsession: foreign presence (intruder, hiker or guest)*
- *character postulate: robotized presence*
- *alienation: feeling absent; not being grounded, having lost contact with home*
- *attachments: smaller, lighter, passing obsessions*

The ideas of presence and absence provide another way of looking at therapeutic processes and skills. The only point methodically new is the strict connection between holes in the aura, lost possessions and presence of foreign things, and thus karmic transactions.

Another aspect of therapy that should be considered is our attention to our own presence as therapist, but not as Helper, Witness, Angel or Robot. We need not be impersonal, but we must be professional and humanly, firmly present: *I am with you.*

The most common seductions that therapists encounter are overinvolvement and underinvolvement - becoming either Helper or Witness. For warm people (as are most readers of this text), the Helper role comes most naturally. Taking on this role is almost an occupational disease.

Morris Netherton and Thorwald Dethlefsen have grown tired of doing seminars. They found that their students easily identified with victim experiences, but became moralists when they uncovered aggressor lives. These students became Helpers to Victims and Prosecutors to Perpetrators; they did not understand therapy.

We are not in the justice business, but in the healing business. We help people to understand and to feel humanly responsible, not too little, not too much. This kind of therapy is about empathy, acceptance and insight.

A related mistake is to get into the forgiveness business. Understanding is incomparably more helpful than forgiveness. Hazel Denning assumes that each trauma contains guilt and that guilt needs forgiveness. She describes guilt is a basic charge of traumas. I disagree. The first reactions to traumas are fear and pain. I view guilt as a secondary reaction, a complicator.

Mainly the priests, with their superegos and models and examples, have engraved upon people the idea of guilt and forgiveness. We are forgiven that we are not yet angels. I say let's forgive the angels for not yet being human.

Does an Angel want to understand? No, it knows already

the answers. Does a Devil want to understand? No again. Only a human can be surprised, wondered, curious, exploring, seeking. And naughty. If superior beings exist out there, they are more than human, not less than human.

By the way, why would Dethlefsen and Netherton be tired? Also because of wrong transactions. Students copy teachers, and if teachers are not careful they may lose parts of themselves and acquire parts from students in return - nothing important, but enough to make the teacher feel tired. This tiredness is rather a compliment of Dethlefsen and Netherton. If they had assumed the guru role, they would have become energetic with energy they would have drawn from their followers.

I think that a seminar went well only when I learned as much as the students. When I feel that I have to transmit something, it all goes wrong. During each session we can learn something. We are on the road, making progress. A seminar does not make me bigger or smaller than I am. So I became a teacher, getting the students I deserve. I am not tired.

When are we functioning without roles? Not when we are perfect, but when we are truly present; when we also carry and accept our less human aspects as animal companions; when we know we have cynical, hard, sarcastic sides; when we know we can't be everything, can't control everything; when we know we are never ready; when we can play.

Nietzsche said that the first human is like a camel, strong-shouldered, carrying everything. The second human is like a lion, who always follows his own will, even against his creator. The third human though is like a child, "a wheel rolling from itself, a first movement." The truly human includes the child.

We are human when we suppress nothing, not even our suppressions; when we accept the facts, even that we cannot or will not accept some facts; when we can handle insecurity and imperfection; when we can identify with everything and everybody, without losing ourselves; when we are responsible without losing our freedom; and when we are free without losing our responsibility. In short, we are human when we are children and sovereigns both.

The start. The entry point.
A good therapy session is musical, like a perfect jam session. Usually, therapists divide sessions into intake (especially the first time), induction, the proper therapy, closure, and often

evaluation. Intake is generally overrated. Induction is overrated by hypnotherapists and underrated by the rest.

There is something that occurs between intake and induction that is underrated and even mostly forgotten, and that is *identification and confirmation of the entry point*, the precise, actual topic that will be the focus and aim of the session, or of our contract with the patient. Some therapists may even have no inkling of what I am talking about.

Closure is also underrated. Some therapists may simply say that time is up. Those therapists should be branded as time-uppers and given a special entry in the Yellow Pages. (Look under T - don't ever go there.) Closure is reverse induction. It is the confirmation and consolidation of the session, the return to the present, and the framing and anchoring of gained results.

People who are interested in past lives may absorb themselves in a plethora of previous lives, almost drowning in the confusion among all those personages in themselves, forgetting that they live here and now. These people are especially in need of closure. Often such patients have no clear aim or real need to do regressions. They are digging like amateur archaeologists. *Look Ma, what I have found this time.* They dig the peat off, and some dead bodies emerge. They play Youngest Day. Anything may emerge. They get quite a chatter and rattle, sure. But why did they dig in the first place? What were the reasons behind all this exploration?

Curiosity is a virtue, a motor of evolution. Being curious about your past lives is not wrong. Such curiosity is understandable when you discover that such a thing is possible. But always return to the here-and-now coordinates. Closure does that.

Newcomers to the field of past-life therapy are amazed when they see for the first time that people may enter straight into full and detailed regressions to past lives within less than a minute. These newcomers associate leaving a room with breaking a wall instead of simply turning the doorknob.

Now if we start looking for doorknobs, we might find walls full of them. But which doorknob belongs to the unlocked door leading to the next room? Don't worry, the patient knows, even without knowing. People have a knack of going for the right thing with the surety of a sleepwalker. People are basically self-curing, but often they need catalysts. Intake is not done simply to create a file for the therapist. It is done to connect, create trust and watch the flow. The whole secret of doing effective therapy is being a fully aware sleepwalker. If you don't believe that, read the research of Winafred Lucas (1989).

You may have heard some horror stories, that someone suffered heart failure during a regression with a psychiatrist. Maybe the psychiatrist was scared to death and began applying heart massage. Maybe you heard that some students in America (story in the Netherlands - it is always in a faraway country) did a regression and couldn't come back. Wow! Scary!

Such stories are simply newer versions of the old fear of people put in trance by a hypnotist and getting stuck in the hypnotic suggestion. *A good neighbor of Auntie Trudy was 15 years ago hypnotized and believed that she was a chicken. They could never bring her back to her normal self.* All this is rubbish (unless the hypnotist by accident triggered the real identity of Auntie Trudy).

The only real thing in these stories is that hypnotic states may linger on if sessions are not closed well. Waking up from a trance is quite natural. Some sleep works wonders. Only with hypnotists who have personally bonded their deep-trance subjects may trance be persistent. But the body, however involved in reliving, never gets stuck in the past. It gets cold, tired, and hungry in the present.

Getting stuck can and does happen, but only with an incredibly incompetent hypnotherapist, and only temporarily. With a heart patient I would not do an emotional regression, or I would give instructions to temper the emotions. The worst that I ever experienced was someone who relived dying slowly in a swamp. He was coughing and dying graphically, but he still lives and got the better of it.

Trust the process, go with the flow. The only exception is when there is a "repetitor" in the agony itself, and patients cry several times, *This will never stop.* Then bring them back. If necessary, slap them on their solar plexus with a flat hand. Return is guaranteed. Then go back to the same experience and have the patient traverse it in a less agonizing form. Any dissociation technique works.

Above all, remember that time is limited, and energy is limited. Take the road offered. Do not take roads based on a diagnosis, or before you know it you will get stuck. Don't start to roam about, taking whatever seems interesting. Swamps may be very interesting places, but they don't have exit signs.

Also, a regression is the patient's trip, not ours. Self-gratification is okay, but don't try to get paid for it.

If we do have a topic in mind, we check whether this topic is what the patient wants to work on. If so, follow with an open instruction: "Go back to the situation where that problem began." Never mind where and when - before birth, in the womb, in a past life or the day before yesterday. That part is for the patient to decide.

We never have a patient regress specifically to a past life, or even to a past age. We have patients move to where the problem lies, at whatever level the patient offers. Take seriously whatever a patient says, but listen between the lines. Even if you suspect rightly that a past life is interfering in the background, do not instruct the patient to go to a past life. *We do not go to past lives; patients go to past experiences* wherever and whenever those experiences occurred. Beware of the danger of digging simply because of your own interests.

The best start for a session is mutual trust that is based on the previous session. Therefore I recommend that therapy begins with the second session. Every good session improves trust and tuning. When you have already had a good session with someone, you have become tuned in to each other, and you will proceed more smoothly and precisely every time.

Begin as a therapist in as concrete a way as possible, and as simply as possible. Good beginnings are simple. Also, when many things emerge, treat only one thing at a time! Never instruct a patient to search for something, or to look for something. Use only the charges that are already there, charges to which the patient needs only to connect.

Everyone has more than one remnant from the past, more than one traumatic episode, more than one character problem. So the question always becomes, "Which do we take?" Fortunately there is a surprisingly simple solution - we leave that to the patient. We simply begin with a sound sense of "here and now" at the start of the session.

The submerged past that we are looking for is already there, waiting, within the patient. If that were not the case there would be no problem, so why bother to look further? The past is like a slowly convoluting iceberg or mountain range below sea level. With restimulation, a small volcano with its ugly little crater rises just above sea level and smokes or belches fire. Gotcha!

Work on only one thing at a time. At any moment, only one piece of the submerged, unassimilated past is the most active.

Only one underwater mountain is the highest. Just lower the sea level slowly, and you'll see. Sometimes an entire archipelago shows itself. Go for the highest top. Go for whatever is most awake, most present, most active within the patient. And remember that the patient's voice may be louder than the actual words, and the patient's body may speak louder than the voice.

Finding the entry point, the not-assimilated, the "undead," is maybe the most important aspect of a regression. If a seemingly insignificant point arises, for example some anger from the last few days, then process that anger in maybe twenty minutes until you achieve a mini-catharsis. After a pause, you again take the top that is highest at that moment. Once you have processed a problem, the pattern may change. What seemed the second-highest top at first, may now have dwindled in significance, and another top has risen. The question, "What do you want to work at?" needs to be asked after each cycle.

Even when someone comes to you and appears to be unfocused, one top is always the highest. Always one thing emerges first, though the patient can push it away or distort it. Therapists need to become sensitive in this respect. Watch, listen, smell. Trust your nose, your instinct. Effective healers are shamans; they have animal spirits that can sense on many levels.

The life retrospect that occurs after death, and the assimilation of a lifetime, is the catharsis of that lifetime. It is the great restorer. It helps a person to find peace after all the toil, all the limitation, all the misunderstanding, all the friction, all the imperfection, all the unaccomplished things, all the things that went wrong, all the seemingly endless burdens of that lifetime.

Now, however, somewhere within the patient lies something that is undead, unassimilated. In therapy we bring that undead part through a death experience. That means digestion, or letting go, and also integration, absorption. It means internalizing and letting go at the same time, as is done with each catharsis and each death. So entry into regression makes contact with that something that is undead.

At the beginning of a session ask patients if they want to lie down or sit. When they are comfortable, ask them to tell you when they are ready. When they are ready, ask what they want to work at. Only in the first session do we reverse the order: we first ask what they want to work at, and then if they are ready to begin.

I repeat: always take a clear entry point. We are not in the endless-analysis business. The patient comes to a therapy session to resolve something specific. We can use our time better if we focus on this entry point than if we allow ourselves to be pulled along in a towboat that we - if we are not careful - in the end pull by ourselves. We want results. That has nothing to do with impatience. You can cross the ocean calmly in a jumbo jet or you can do it tensely and hurriedly in a small ship.

So, at what does the patient want to work, here and now? When patients lack a clear entry point and have several complaints, ask then what they want to accomplish with the therapy. Or be a good fairy and let them have three wishes. This approach will move the issue into focus. Discover the patient's priorities, or ask for them. Specify and elaborate upon the first wishes to be fulfilled, if necessary with a short verbal exploration.

Often people already carry an idea of the subject on which they want to work, but the moment they lie down, the subject changes. *I realize suddenly that through the last two days the words "feeling responsible" have been running through my head.* Take those words. Probably the words *feeling responsible* provide the entry.

Ask if they want to work on that issue. Okay, feeling responsible, there we will dig. There we drill and we'll see what comes up. The entry never begins with the therapist, but with the patient.

If the patient blocks right away, before any contract has been made, suggest that the patient take the block itself as the entry point.

P: *I am afraid that nothing will come (or) I cannot relax.*
T: *Why not?*
P: *Too many people around me. (In a group session.)*

Then suggest starting with these statements of the patient as an entry point. You can't lose.

Someone says, *The lights are annoying me.* If you cannot turn off the lights and there are no curtains to shut, take the patient's statement as the entry point; it is more specific than it seems. In other cases a patient may be annoyed by background noise or by the people around, and the same suggestion applies:

T: You are annoyed by the light? Okay, concentrate on this: "I am annoyed by the light." Say it aloud five times, "I am annoyed by the light, I am annoyed by the light, I am annoyed by the light . . ."

We have to gain entry to the past and reach the shadows from the past, the ulcers from the past, the knots from the past, the burdens and poisons from the past. And we want to gain entry to the joy and the light and the strength from the past. This joy and strength may be more relevant than old shadows, but removing burdens usually helps more than simply boosting energy. When we use the accelerator and the brake simultaneously, the best way to move forward is not to accelerate more, but to take our foot from the brake. Start with the bad things; the good things usually follow by themselves.

Begin also with where you are yourself, with how you feel, and in whom you have confidence. Mutual confidence is the womb of a session, and that one entry point of the patient is the egg that we are going to fertilize. Often you will find something essential in just a few seconds, not because you did complex things, but precisely because you did not, and you accepted what came. You were all eyes and ears, calm and open as a lake.

Induction.
Induction is the process of contacting the past that is already present. With our patients their past is troubling them now. Strictly speaking, this is true for all mental, emotional and psychosomatic problems (except for problems caused by the therapist). Patients enter therapy for what they carry with them - problems from yesterday, from the day before yesterday, from last year, and maybe from five lifetimes ago.

Most of those problems remain subconscious. From the symptoms that emerge we can rarely infer what the submerged parts look like. The consequences of those problems are always conscious; otherwise people wouldn't visit a therapist. The causes are subconscious. We want to contact subconscious charges, and through the consciousness release these charges, by way of catharsis.

The word *induction* comes from magnetism and hypnotism, and means the process of bringing the subject into *trance*. The idea behind induction is that patients first need to be aided into the state in which they can move into the past. That idea is a half-truth.

101

If we enter at the right point, if trust reigns, trance comes naturally. We don't need the chef in the restaurant whispering soothingly into our ears that the food will be delicious. We don't need the writer to tell us in the preface that this story will enthrall us. Good food will delight us, as a good story will enthrall us. A good session will bring its own trance.

Induction has to be minimal: "Enjoy your meal, madam. Chapter 1 - The Years of Innocence. Go back to the first time you ever felt this fear, with throbbing temples and sweating hands."

So, keep the beginning of a session simple. We can treat only one problem at a time, and usually the subconscious of the patient already knows which problem is the right one. When there is trust, we need only to look at a patient and ask, "Shall we begin?" and there they go. That simplicity may sound exaggerated, but it is the rule, not the exception.

People sometimes have trouble lying down and relaxing, because the emotional charge that they will uncover is already emerging. A good beginning is simple. Make it simple and keep it simple. Not all beginnings are difficult; only complex beginnings are. Ask someone to lie down. "Just tell me when you are ready." What does "being ready" mean exactly? Somehow the patient defines that.

Regression itself consists of a series of images (including other sensory qualities such as sound) that are embedded in emotional impressions, bodily impressions, and intellectual impressions: thoughts, insights, understandings and misunderstandings. The entry point always lies in one of these four realms. An induction also has four faces.

Someone says, *I came because of a guilt feeling, but now I see something. Once I had this dream. I am standing in a strange landscape. The sun shines and I am standing before a well.* Since in this case the beginning is an image, we will use the *imaginative bridge*.

Or the beginning may be a feeling.

P: *I feel unhappy. On the way here, that feeling became stronger. It doesn't bother me too much now, but still I notice that I am unhappy.*
T: *Can you feel that right now?*
P: *Yes.*

In this case an emotion is the beginning, and we use the *emotional bridge*. The beginning can also be a persistent sentence.

When we have such a mental beginning, we employ the *verbal bridge*. Likewise, a beginning can be a bodily experience:
P: *I am ready.*
T: *Okay. What do you notice?*
P: *My feet are tingling, and my heart is pounding.*

In this case we have somatics and we use them as a *somatic bridge*. Begin with whatever comes. Begin with whatever has already begun.

We don't simply send people to the past. We send people to what they carry with them now. Patients rewind their own videotape. The recording was made in the past, but they carry the recording with them and it is troubling them now.

People may come to a therapy session with a certain theme in mind, but when they lie down another theme emerges. Usually this new theme is the truly relevant one. The present dominates the past, even the immediate past. Even if strings of past lives are waiting, the royal moment is now.

When we sit opposite someone with whom we want to work, and who wants to work with us, that part of the past on which we are about to work is already present. We do not need to elicit that past, we have only to contact it. We have to contact only that layer. Karma and dharma are "nearer than hands and feet."

With karma as it is used in this respect, I mean all repercussions from unassimilated experiences, whether those experiences occurred in a prior lifetime or in the present one. Induction is the process of making contact with karmic charges or structures.

In a group session, one person reported that he experienced nothing. Upon further questioning, it appeared that he had an impression of some black space, a hole that he entered: *I sank and came up again more or less.* That was all.

His use of the term "more or less" implied that he was still in it. So I knew we couldn't fail. First I tried the sentence *I am sinking.* Nothing happened. Then, *It is dark around me.* He could not manage to speak that sentence aloud for the second time, his response was so emotional. So it appeared that we were ready for regression. In fact, we were moving right into it.

When we already know the issue that needs to be addressed, the simplest induction is, "Go back to the situation in which that problem was caused." Sometimes this approach works. The fundamental instruction to the computer of the subconscious is, "Go back to . . ." Sentences such as, "Remember that . . . ," "Try to remember how it was . . ." work less well. The basic instruction is, "Go back to . . ." Then we link up the actual issue.

People may have fears, may have seen a therapist about those fears, but may have had just a couple of frustrating experiences and may remain angry about them. As they start to think about themselves, that anger emerges and for the moment suppresses those fears. Or once in the therapist's office, people no longer suffer from their problem, just as some toothaches mysteriously disappear on the way to the dentist.

The reason that a patient sought therapy can be pushed aside at the very moment that the therapist asks for the entry point. For example, a young woman is excessively timid and wants to do something about this. When she lies down and we ask what problem she wants to address, she says that she is thinking strongly about her father.

Likewise, some people are confused and have to be helped to choose what they want to work at first. Why is this selection so important for the therapist? Because the therapist does not want merely to talk about problems, but wants to solve them. And we solve them one at a time. Induction becomes almost superfluous once we zoom in, when we focus on only one thing, when we want to work at only one thing at a time.

Let's look at a different case. Someone had difficulty in visualizing. Because of that difficulty the therapist chose the technique of the *Christos Experiment*, a form of imaging and massage that may give one the sense of moving out-of-body and seeing past lifetimes. In this case the patient perceived an out-of-body experience as roaming soul. Since this particular induction technique visualizes an out-of-the-body experience, it may trigger such a memory more quickly then some other induction would have done. The induction could have identified this sense of roaming, but maybe the feeling of being a roaming soul had been waiting on top. People who carry a roaming-soul disposition (a pseudo-obsession), often have concentration difficulties. With a different induction technique we might have found the same thing. Still, most people regress to memories of a previous lifetime with this technique.

Relaxation is necessary only when a patient exhibits confused turbulence that we first have to still before we find the right entry point. Following the analogy of mountain peaks poking above sea level, we pull the sea level even. But when a sea mountain is already poking out, we come straight to the point.

All the past that still affects us is now present, sleeping or dreaming. We move toward the dream that is about to wake up. If someone comes to us with a confused look, then in that look the past already "dreams upward." Should we first relax? Emphatically not. "How do you feel? Nervous? Where in your body? Does that trouble you often? Shall we just begin with that?" All of the past is present, but some past is even more present and one past is particularly present.

A patient says that she often feels timid. Even while she says that, she feels timid. So the past already lies in the present. Say simply:

T: *Okay, lie down (and do not add: and relax). You feel timid, don't you?*
P: *Yes, I feel especially timid when I lie down.*

Avoid relaxation, because then the timidity sinks away. Instead, intensify the timidity. Could we say, "Go back to the moment when you felt this timidity for the first time," and count backward? We could, but usually we need two other steps.

These two other steps are best illustrated in the following example. Someone has a phobia for dogs. Just before she came to you, she encountered such an animal. She still feels it strongly. Can we count backward after saying, "Go back to the situation in which you felt this fear for dogs the first time"? No, before doing that we should have the patient recall her memory of the most recent experience. Then we have her recall her most frightening experience ever. Third, we go for her very first such experience.

The more intense her fear of dogs at the time of therapy, the better. The only actual emotion that may be counterproductive in such case is a *recursive emotion*, an emotion that will tie this fear with the therapy situation itself. In this case, that possibility is unlikely, unless the therapist has a dog lying next to the couch or has a face like a dog. But in fear for men, fear may become recursive when the therapist is male. Then the problem clogs its own solution channel. In such a situation we need to establish enough trust, despite our being male.

105

If that woman who is afraid of dogs already knows us, or our reputation or her first impression produces trust, she can move into regression with a simple induction. She will find herself in her youth or in a past life before she knows it, usually in a matter of seconds.

With that timid girl we need to establish more trust, as most therapists will be more likely to cause timidity than to resemble dogs. Timidity may be present especially toward men and particularly with male authorities. The chance that a therapeutic situation itself may restimulate a problem and thus become recursive is greater with timidity than with a phobia. Such restimulation is okay because it awakens the past, as long as the patient trusts the therapist sufficiently to counteract this restimulation.

Once an induction is initiated, a block or barrier that appears to emerge at the beginning is often neither block nor barrier. Perhaps the therapist asks the patient to imagine a fountain, but instead this patient sees a coffin floating in the pond. He tries in vain to forget that coffin and to imagine the fountain. Is this interference a block? Emphatically not! The therapist gave a wrong instruction. Each such superfluous instruction produces loss of energy and weakens a therapist's the relationship with a patient. The coffin *is* the entry point.

Do not be afraid if patients say that they feel they cannot do something. Lack of ability is often lack of willingness. If someone says, *I cannot close my eyes*, ask "Why don't you want to close your eyes?"

Magnetic passes, like in laying on hands, may be effective in removing blocks, but reconsider three times before using this technique, as blocks are present for a reason. Sometimes the problem is so complex that it becomes very difficult for a patient, despite serious efforts, to dissolve a block. Then we can help, but ask first, "Why do you need to solve that problem?" The situation is different with patients with whom communication is difficult: people in shock, psychotic people, slow people, very ill or very young or very old people. Then such healing interventions are allowed.

But for ordinary people, remember that we give them *knowledge*, *attention* and *trust*, three really royal gifts for any rebirth. Do not underestimate those gifts when you notice that someone proceeds with difficulty or keeps applying the brakes. Making use of body contact and energy transmission may provide extra channels for those gifts, but it never substitutes for knowledge, attention and trust.

Knowledge is what this book is about. *Attention* is something that I assume the therapist will give. But what about, the third gift, *trust*?

Trust.

How do we know that our entry point involves the right iceberg or volcano? Because a patient's problem, the issue that brought him or her into therapy, is already present in the form of a homeopathically diluted catharsis. There is already a Tao, or philosophy of life; there is already "peace of mind." Catharsis and "peace of mind" result only from catharsis and peace of mind. The peace of mind that produces a good entry is what I refer to as the "square of trust."

That trust means four things: the self-confidence of the patient, the self-confidence of the therapist, the trust of the patient in the therapist and the trust of the therapist in the patient. These four sides form a square, and on this basis we can begin to build. Trust is the basic condition that must be present for a cathartic session to occur. Looking at catharsis as the apex of a pyramid, when a session constructs this pyramid, the square of trust is its foundation. The four sides of this foundation are, again:

1. *Trust of the therapist in herself or himself*
2. *Trust of the patient in the therapist*
3. *Trust of the patient in himself or herself*
4. *Trust of the therapist in the patient*

Healing is based not on sympathy, but on trust. When this square of trust is solid, the therapist and patient can go through hell together.

In therapy, the first issue must be the therapist's own self-confidence, then that of the patient. After that the patient's trust in the therapist becomes important, and finally the therapist's trust in the patient. In a good session all four kinds of trust will grow, but the most important aim is, of course, that the *self-confidence of the patient will grow*.

At first the trust relationship between patient and therapist may be based on hearsay, or on first impressions, but not yet on the experience of working together. A successful session reinforces all four kinds of trust.

Essential for the therapist's trust in the patient is the therapist's belief that the patient is self-regulating. Some people believe that patients who enter a regression enter a dangerous emotional adventure that we might not be able to handle. This belief is nonsense. Patients enter regression with us only when we can handle it. Patients feel unconsciously or half-consciously that a regression is okay with us; otherwise they simply do not get to where they need to be. Nobody ever enters regression with a therapist who cannot handle it, unless the therapist is forcing things, as in classic hypnosis.

I view the use of hypnosis to induce regression as a testimony of poverty, an example of incompetence. We may not know how to regress people otherwise, or we lack self-confidence. I have the impression that therapists usually start with relaxation, mainly to relax themselves, and that the hypnosis of a patient is mainly self-hypnosis for the therapist. When trust is present, artificial hypnosis or self-hypnosis become superfluous, while natural hypnosis follows.

A successful session makes the ambiance of trust grow, or "shine out." At the beginning of a session the therapist's self-confidence is the most fundamental. After the session the patient's self-confidence has to be the most fundamental. Mutual trust between therapist and patient is only a scaffold, a temporary womb.

Patients who have faith in themselves and in the therapist, and who have a problem that is "awake" at the moment of entry, regress naturally as soon as they lie down. The simpler, the more direct and shorter the induction, the more chance for success. Lengthy searches for problems, and long detours, seldom lead to Rome. The right, simple way suggests itself.

If you want to complicate things, choose another trade or at least a different approach. Our kind of regression therapy is for rich but simple minds. The longer I am involved in regression therapy, the simpler it appears to be. But to make it feel simple for you, you have to have self-confidence. That has to grow.

In Chapter 9 we look at sources of self-confidence and of lack of self-confidence. You will notice that you have faith in some kinds of patients while with others you do not. You must become sensitive to that difference. What do we do when we don't trust the patient? I recommend a short trial session. Make it a mutual test. If doubt remains or grows, refer the patient elsewhere.

L. Ron Hubbard checked the perception, the memory and

the imagination of the patient, beforehand. He posed questions such as, "What did we talk about in the beginning of our conversation?" and "What was on the cover of the book that I just showed you?" The patient either forgot or remembered, or may have distorted or exaggerated. Hubbard talked about "lie factories" that might produce false and useless material during sessions.

That is all fine, when such distortions do not occur because of the therapist's distrust of the patient or because of the therapist's lack of self-confidence. Do not start therapy with cross-examination. If you like cross-examination, go into criminal investigation, but stay out of the therapy room.

Be aware also that a common type of fake self-confidence of therapists leads to patronizing and knowing it better than the patient. Trisha Caetano states it nicely (1985):

> *One of the greatest offenses in therapy is telling people what their problem is, where it began and what they need to do to be rid of the problem. Second to that is bludgeoning the person into the area the therapist thinks the problem is in. The basic truth is that the individual knows exactly what the problem is because he or she experienced the cause. Because the client knows the cause he or she also knows the solution. It is our responsibility to get the client to this subconscious information so the problem can be resolved. Asking questions and hearing the answers with no value judgments until the "interview" is finished is a cornerstone of this technique. The cardinal rule is: don't evaluate, invalidate, judge, give opinions, hint, tell or bludgeon. Ask.*

Amen.

Catharsis.

Regression is the process of contacting some unresolved, interfering past, some jamming station within us. That contact should produce release and assimilation. What should happen in a session if release and assimilation are to occur?

First, a patient needs to experience *emotional purification*, or emotional catharsis, taking leave from negative emotions and welcoming positive ones. For example, if a patient carries an envy that eats at him, and from which he suffers, then that envy has complicated his relationships. If he works toward *catharsis*, that means he is here to resolve that envy. Resolution does not mean neutrality, but rather an emotional reverse. Calm, peace and acceptance replace the negative feelings. Paradoxically, a patient can get rid of a problem such as envy when he accepts it as a fact and understands how it came about.

That brings us to the second component of catharsis: *liberating insight* or intellectual catharsis. A session may relieve certain emotions, but without permanent resolution of the problem, because emotional relief without understanding, without overview, remains floating. Probably this relief evaporates in time. A patient may be free from feelings of envy now, but the mechanism that created this envy remains. To stop the envy altogether, a patient needs insight, at least a beginning of understanding.

Relief without understanding is vulnerable and usually short-lived. A person can take leave of a problem only when he accepts it, and he can accept it only when he understands how it came about. Acceptance without understanding is a second-rate commodity. It is sentiment. It has no roots, and the first wind will blow it away.

Intellectual catharsis results in peace of mind. People have heads, too; we are thinking beings. People not only want to feel good, but they also want to understand the why and how. Most people feel restless until they know, until they understand. Things have to fit, to form a pattern. Configuration is transfiguration.

The third component is *physical catharsis*, tied closely to emotional catharsis. Someone who "touches bottom" experiences, beside feelings, physical sensations. A muscle cramp may relax, a distorted face may become peaceful again, cold hands and feet may become warm again, a skin rash may disappear, a lump in the throat may dissolve.

In *Exploring Reincarnation* I gave the example of the man who feared barbers. Barbers in many countries display red and blue twisted poles. In regression, this man found himself working as a Venetian gondolier:

> *It was early in the morning, misty. He punted to an appointment and when he reached the quay, some fellow came out of the mist and rammed him in the chest with a red-and-blue painted punting pole. The man collapsed into the water, wounded, hit his head against the quay and drowned. Only when he recognized the as-*

sailant as being the husband of the woman with whom he had had an affair did he understand why the assault had occurred. Suddenly his fear of barbers resolved itself.

The soul of catharsis is emotional release. That release should be rooted in the body as well in the mind. Sometimes the emotional catharsis is dominant, sometimes the mind speaks louder, and sometimes the body speaks louder. But always they should speak in unison.

Death is the great catharsis of life. We leave our body and rise, we undergo a life retrospect, we gain an overview, we understand, we acknowledge and take our leave. We accept and let go of the misery, the heaviness and inertia, the misunderstandings, the weariness, the incomprehension. If we die well, we leave those imperfections behind.

The life retrospect with its assimilation of a completed lifetime is the great catharsis. That catharsis sometimes remains undone, as already shown with hangovers and pseudo-obsessions. Just as dying well provides a great catharsis, therapeutic catharsis resembles a small death and a small rebirth. In this sense, I feel that "reincarnation therapy" is a better term than "past-life therapy."

If someone undergoes a regression that reveals a good death experience, and he sees other people waiting for him as he enters the light, he probably feels liberated of everything. And yet charges may remain. With his arms and legs he may have been chained to a wall, no longer wanting to eat or drink, and so he slowly died. He exited that life well, and he experienced a reasonable catharsis after dying.

In reliving his time in that body that now hangs there endlessly, all of the weariness and pain and misery of that experience comes out. Somatic charges apparently can be released and assimilated only in a body. But dying does not clean all emotions, because the bond between emotional and somatic charges may be too strong for a quick release.

When we carry with us a remnant of the past, it appears that we did not die well with that remnant. Therapy may help to transform an experience of incomplete dying into one of complete dying. In therapy, catharsis is a small dying; it is an acceptance of things while letting them go.

Besides the relinquishment of a worn out, affected body and often the letting go of limiting life conditions, the main function of dying is catharsis. In death we gain an overview of what until now remained incomprehensible. Feelings of insufficiency disappear, and we gain peace.

Catharsis is a natural process. Sleep can be somatically cathartic, and dreams can be emotionally cathartic. Liberating experiences also occur in daily life, without therapy (think of conversions and evangelists). As many therapists may tend to block rather than facilitate emotional release, such release may happen without a therapist - except for a well-trained regression therapist, of course.

In principle, each regression session is a complete cathartic cycle, a small death experience. Sometimes a session includes two or three of those cycles, but in principle a session is one complete process that results in a three-fold catharsis: *physical*, *emotional* and *intellectual*.

There is a beautiful expression from Goethe, *stirb und werde* (die-and-become). Each therapeutic session is a *stirb und werde*. Something of us dies, and after that death we are more ourselves.

I discern four kinds of *emotional catharsis*. After a catharsis the patient's emotional tone may be *cheerful* (spring), *satisfied* (summer), *gentle* (autumn) or *intimate* (winter). These are the four basic moods of a free, untrammelled soul, within or without a body.

First let's look at a *spring catharsis*. When patients have relived a trauma, have moved through the death experience, have awakened, have become themselves and felt revitalized and cheerful, the saps start flowing again. They want to enjoy life. They want to laugh, to sing and dance, or however they like to express themselves. They may feel as if everything has been cleansed by rain, and now the sun shines and everything smells fresh.

We recognize a *summer catharsis* when patients curl up contentedly, purr like a cat, and appear satisfied. They may stare at the ceiling with a placid smile on their face. They are drowsy, relaxed, warm, perhaps just smiling, sometimes grinning.

An *autumn catharsis* provides gentleness, a beautiful, deep melancholy. Patients feel moved, are pensive, calm and wide and wise.

For outsiders, a *winter catharsis* is the most difficult to perceive, because its essence is intimacy. Patients are turned inward. The winter landscape is cold and lonely, but their home feels warm and cosy. There may be warmth, the flame of candles, looking at another person without words. People feel close.

These four types of catharsis correspond to the four classic temperaments. Spring is sanguine, summer choleric, autumn phlegmatic and winter melancholic. Only do not assume that people with a certain temperament will always experience the corresponding type of catharsis. That depends on the nature of the wound and so the nature of the cure.

Take the case of someone who has had a painful experience of being abandoned, with a long and lonely lifetime afterward. What kind of catharsis might that abandonment produce? When we take leave of loneliness, do we feel fresh and new? Maybe, but a winter catharsis would be more probable. Likewise, as there is light at the end of the tunnel, so there is intimacy at the end of loneliness. By contrast, getting over the death of a loved one may result in an autumn catharsis.

Dying is often seen as going into the light. That image is right, but it is also superficial and general. One death may be more like spring, another more like summer, autumn or winter. When a wrung-out slave or a worn-out prostitute dies well, will she feel like spring? Some dame who through half her life had to sing and dance for gentlemen she patently disliked will not become cheerful, but may find rest, and may come to herself. She probably experiences a winter catharsis. She finds herself in a psychic body that is hers alone, and is dressed in a robe of snow and pearls.

A catharsis can be also like the coming of the rainy season, for example, for people who had lost their emotions. Imagine that all has been dry and dusty, and then the first drops fall, and the drops become torrents and finally a roar in the planes or in the forest. *The day that the rain came down.* Rain is cathartic, especially when we had forgotten what it was like.

Ultimately, we therapists always want our patients to experience catharsis - emotional peace, peace of mind, including understanding and acceptance. Acceptance is never just emotional, but always intellectual as well. And finally, we want them to know "peace of body," relaxation, feeling at home in the body, and in this world. We want them to have calm, deep breathing; a calm, steady heartbeat; a firm and warm skin.

FULL CATHARSIS

Peace of mind:
understanding

Peace of soul:
intimacy (winter peace), or
cheerfulness (spring peace), or
satisfaction (summer peace), or
gentleness (autumn peace)

Peace of body:
relaxation, vitality and health

Peace is not idleness or emptiness. Peace is fullness, acceptance. Full peace is what Lao-Tze calls *Tao*, perfection within the accepted imperfection of the here-and-now.

An imminent catharsis is something that we have to learn to smell. We have to know the signs of the "dilation." We become calm, because somebody is going to be reborn in some manner. The mood, the smell of the winter, or of spring, summer or autumn, we can already pick up. Catharsis is a rejuvenation of the emotional tissue.

The fountain of eternal youth is easy to find; it lies in being reborn, sometimes intensely, dramatically, more often calmly and in a friendly way, as a habit, as the tides of the soul.

What do we do after catharsis? What do we do after drinking from the life elixir, from the fountain of eternal youth? We go on living.

When we have resolved the problems that had plagued us, we lie back for a while. Our next step is to look for what is still lacking in our daily life. With many of the spiritual types who seek our couch, this next step is about assertiveness.

Dick Sutphen, in his *Master of Life Manual*, says that all people have a right to their own body, their own time, their own money, and their own opinion. Check these items, or use the checklist of the ten forms of assertive behavior:
1. *Think and talk positively about yourself.*
2. *Feel at ease when giving well-meant compliments.*
3. *Accept compliments without becoming confused.*

4. *Express yourself directly and spontaneously.*
5. *Ask for what you want.*
6. *State calmly when you don't agree with something.*
7. *Be capable of saying no.*
8. *Demand honest treatment.*
9. *Maintain contact with friends.*
10. *Take the first step in establishing new friendships.*

Look with this checklist to see what is still lacking, and identify the inhibiting charges by verbal exploration. Use egostates when you encounter ambivalences. Now we leave the area of proper regression therapy, and we enter the area of counseling and workshops.

The entire process.
In true psychotherapy, healing means catharsis, peace of mind and soul, restored presence, restored integrity. Healing means sanity; sanity means that the roads for further growth and evolution lie open. How do we identify those roads? Session by session. How do we succeed in this effort? We keep in mind the following:

1. *The end of each session is catharsis.*
2. *The beginning of each session is trust.*
3. *The process of each session is musical.*

The basic composition of a session is symmetrical, and it has seven stages. The core of the session is the cathartic regression. The first stage is one of *connecting*, establishing rapport and trust. The second stage is one of *contracting*, defining the objective and the entry point.

The first two stages are usually called intake. Classic intakes may be helpful, but may also be very unhelpful. Usually therapists use the intake for making a case history. During a classic intake, patients describe what is wrong with them and what they have tried before. Forget it. We are in the healing business, not in the filing business. Usually such information is superfluous, even counterproductive. What do patients need so that they can trust you enough to give it a try? Then what do they come for? What do they expect? Keep it simple: short and business-like. Often a few sentences will do.

These first two stages and the last two stages mirror each other. *Contracting* mirrors *discharge*: a check to see if the mission has been accomplished. *Connecting* mirrors *disconnecting*: clearing any enmeshment between therapist and patient, any transference, having the patient connect the session and its result to his daily life, making appointments for homework, giving some parting suggestions as a counselor, taking leave and, if you are into that, visualizing that you and the room are cleaned, ready for the next session with the next patient.

The third stage is *induction*; and the fifth stage, *closure*, mirrors the induction. Closure is, so to speak, "e-duction", guiding people to the exit. Induction leads from the entry point into the proper regression. Induction takes the emotional or somatic charge that is there, outlines it, anchors it and strengthens it to use it as the door to the past. If a charge is not actually present, the induction elicits a charge by a verbal or visual bridge. The induction ends with some instruction to move back to a place and time when this charge started or was reinforced. We never ever mention past lives, because experiences from the present life can be essential, too. We may uncover birth experiences, prenatal experiences, discarnate experiences, even experiences from other people. Leave the instruction open, always.

In exploration there is no contract, no entry point. Therefore we start always with verbal exploration or introductory visualizations. The same is true for group sessions. Often, charges emerge, but these charges are not part of the contract. There may also be a negative contract, in which no charges should be touched.

When someone gets a choked voice, a lump in the throat, and grief emerges, it does not matter if these reactions were induced or came spontaneously. Just outline them, confirm them, and say, "Go back to the situation that caused this grief," or, "Go back to the first time you ever felt *this* grief and *this* lump in your throat."

These suggestions are often sufficient. It is careless to untie an emotion from the past and say that you can feel it only now. We say, "Go back to . . ." Once we have touched a real charge, we usually find ourselves at the main root, and that root usually lies in a past life. The proper regression begins with a patient's first impressions.

The golden rule for a regression is to follow the patient but stick to the contract, the entry point. When a patient rambles, roams or springs toward a new topic, we ask, "How does this relate to . . . (the entry point)?"

If induction is the hors d'oeuvre, regression is the main dish and closure is the dessert of a therapy session. The induction has few degrees of freedom, and is more patterned. The closure has more options. In closure we use therapeutic imagination the most. Sometimes personal empathy is important, but in principle the important thing is that we follow someone as well as possible.

If people have been troubled by jealousy, after the regression we may have them repeat *I am jealous* a few times. Then they may realize that this statement is no longer true. They may exclaim, *I am not jealous anymore. I no longer feel it!* Then we let them repeat *I am no longer jealous* until they burst into tears of joy. That is closure.

Closure is part of therapy. It does not deal with the problem, but rather with the newfound solution, the newfound freedom or happiness. If catharsis resembles birth, then closure is receiving the child, cutting the cord, washing it, dressing it and cuddling it. Closure often resembles name-giving. Closure is confirmation. Closure is baptism.

One session began, for example, with fear of water. Water is deep and dark. In the deep, dark water are scary monsters. The session is worked through, and during closure we have the patient repeat *I am afraid of water.*

P: *My fear is gone!*
T: *Okay, you stand on the beach, with a beautiful white sand, the water is transparent and beautifully blue-green. You walk into the blue-green water. It becomes deeper and deeper, until it reaches your chest. It rises above your head, and you swim splendidly. The water becomes deeper and darker until you touch the bottom and everything is dark and beautiful. There is deep peace here, deep and slow and hidden life.*

Then we let the patient rise from the deep, from the bottom, to the surface. How we do all that, we resolve on the spot. It is an imaginative trip that can stand somewhat apart from the content of the regression, but it confirms the catharsis. We use the patient's material, his words, his images, his feelings, his somatics. We use them, we may turn them around, we may combine opposites, we may clothe the catharsis in delightful paradoxes, we may invoke the loved ones of the patient, we may invoke his favorite spots.

Creatively, almost artistically, we reframe, but always using material from the session itself. Closure is the most creative stage of therapy. The other stages are more methodical, more technical.

When we consider a therapy session as resembling a musical composition, here at the end is a cadence that we as soloist can fill ourselves. Our play has to include the emerged motives and make liberating variations on them. That form can work superbly.

Being stuck in the past is always an isolating experience, a drawing inside, and the liberation from this state is radiant. Accompanying this liberation is the most creative part of therapy. The first person who stands there after the trip is the therapist. Therapists then have the same function as the people who take care of us after death. Closure brings the patient back among people, in the inhabited world.

When a crowd has killed somebody, will liberation then mean getting away from people? Not necessarily. Many traumas are caused by people who were inhuman. That crowd was inhuman. The fact that we want to be left alone after such an experience is understandable. But we have only been liberated when we again encounter people. What happened in a Roman arena was inhuman. Returning to people means returning to human people, in a human world.

Closure implies a return to the present, so that the repercussions of the past are removed consciously. Closure is the moment of definitive cleaning, of realization and confirmation that the charge has indeed disappeared. Closure recreates trust in the *oecumene*, in the world of humanity, and it liberates us from the loneliness of being stuck in the past.

When you still feel awkward with closure, use the instruction of Louise Ireland-Frey: "Now silently relive this entire session and find everything else that is significant to your present life." Or ask the patient if there is anything else they need to do or to see. "I'll count softly to ten as you do this and at ten, tell me what you have found."

My preferred instruction for exit, at the end of the closure, is "Come back in your own way and at your own speed." When someone cannot come back (rare), then simply ask, "What is holding you back?" Often we had ignored something.

Sometimes an image or a memory or a sentence or a thought emerges that at first may appear to have no bearing on the session. Ask then, "Can this wait until the next session?" When there is nothing that holds someone back, or there is no response at that first question, ask then, "Why don't you want to return?" If people want to keep on pondering, tell them how much time we still have, and after that time pull them back with the positive instruction used after a hypnotic session.

So, the composition of a session is symmetric. We deepen it in stages and we come out again in stages. *Connection, contract* and *induction* at first; *closure, discharge* and *disconnection* at the end; the proper *regression* in between. A therapy session is a duet in seven moves. Play and hear and wonder.

CHAPTER 5. INDUCING A REGRESSION

The word "induction" comes from the field of magnetism and hypnotism, and suggests that we guide the patient into a "trance." The idea behind induction is that we must first guide patients into a state in which they can move back in time.

Work with a minimal induction. If you find the right entry point, inducing that "trance" goes naturally. Natural induction begins with the natural choice of bridge. Bridge methods tune in directly to the problem at hand. In therapy, previous relaxation is a detour. There is no use in taking the tension away only to evoke it again so as to locate the source of the problem.

There is one common exception to this rule. People who know very few boundaries get enmeshed with other people; they get enmeshed with their therapist. Those people need a safe space and progressive relaxation at the beginning. In serious cases use hypnosis to construct boundaries. Usually, relaxation flows easily into the imaginative bridge or the somatic bridge. Hypnotic induction may continue in any bridge, though the verbal bridge may be the most natural.

Bridges do gradually emerge in a patient's first impressions. This phenomenon prevents unnecessary deep trance, and is advantageous when patient and therapist are working at insight. Netherton has advised that a therapist connect the subconscious without disconnecting the conscious. This "elliptical consciousness" enables the patient more easily to perceive links between present and past. The research of Winafred Lucas has confirmed the possibility and the effectiveness of this combination.

Bridges are more than roads to a deeper state. They lead straight to the goal of the session: to reach and enter a specific karmic charge, to relive the experience that caused the charge, to liberate the charge and to assimilate the experience now.

A torture relived, no matter how painful, is incomparably less painful than was the real torture. The new experience is homeopathically diluted and gives insight and overview, precisely because of that dilution. What we did not understand then, if only by pain and grief, hunger and cold, we now do understand.

Again: the process.
Traversing a past experience means reliving it in diluted form, but also in concentrated form, because we experience in a quarter or half an hour the lowest points of some event that may have taken a week in reality. But we now experience it free from the despair and misery of that earlier time. The grief and the perplexity come up, but without the pain. We now traverse it with intact ego and we achieve catharsis, the liberating realization that we have digested, resolved, processed that experience. Entering that reliving from free will almost guarantees that we will come out right.

The process of liberating reliving is "prismatic." The content of that prism is a series of memories, images and perceptions: what we saw, heard, possibly smelled, what we tasted, how our body felt. The more concrete and varied our sensory impressions, the richer and the more valuable the reliving.

To get through the karmic mass, this series of images should be anchored in and fed by three things: *emotions, insights* and *somatics*. Memories are usually images with thoughts. The emotional, mental and bodily intensification of the regression give flesh to the experience, and decide how deeply we traverse it and how thoroughly we cleanse it.

How thoroughly should we cleanse? Until we have removed the obstruction and restored the flow. We experience that cleansing as catharsis. If the experience had been unassimilated only because of lack of understanding, insight alone is enough. Take the example of that Venetian gondolier. Why did understanding the reason for his death liberate him? Why didn't he know and digest that information after death? Did he leave his body in rage or in panic? Possibly he did know why he died, but repressed that knowledge out of shame. It was too much for him, he withdrew into his shell, he did not want to see it.

Digestion does not happen in the imagery of the regression, but in its concomitant intellectual, emotional and physical sensations. We traverse a triangular prism - the threefold processing of those memories that in the end are sensory - especially images, but also sounds, smells and body sensations. We often feel the somatic precipitation not in the experienced body of our past life, but in our present body. These three aspects we try to keep integrated.

One of my students once had a client who saw no image, but felt the impression of a knife at his throat. He saw nothing, thought nothing, felt nothing and could say nothing, but physically an intense catharsis took place. He sweated all over his body. After that 10-minute session a load had been lifted. Apparently, that misery from the past had still carried only somatic charges. His mood and his energy level changed. He began to see everything differently; he changed from pessimism to optimism; he became another person - much to his wife's liking. If such basic moods change, a real catharsis has taken place. Normally, though, we try to touch all three of those aspects. If one aspect is lacking, part of the misery may linger on and we achieve only half results.

The emotions and the somatics form the keel of the regression experience. Anchoring enriches the sensory stream and couples that stream to emotions and somatics. The stronger these emotions and somatics are, the less we need to worry about noncommittal thoughts and images. Thoughts are part of the experience, but thoughts lead easily to other thoughts and before we know it, people are speculating instead of experiencing.

The emotional bridge. The somatic bridge.

Catharsis is four-fold, so regressions are four-fold, and bridges are four-fold:
- *verbal statements*
- *imaginations*
- *feelings*
- *somatic sensations*

Each of these four -a sentence, an imagination, an emotion, a physical sensation- we can use as a starting point. Usually we connect these sensations, as we want full experiences in which all four are present. We repeat a sentence until feelings, bodily sensations or images come up. We tie an emotion in with a somatic. Each bridge can lead to each problem, but with traumas the *emotional bridge* is the most natural. With pseudo-obsessions it is the *somatic bridge,* and with character postulates the *verbal bridge.* The *visual bridge* is the most gradual, the verbal bridge the most versatile.

The emotional bridge is best known in the literature on hypnotherapy, for example in Gerald Edelstein's *Trauma, Trance, and Transformation* (1981). Edelstein first does a hypnotic induction, but practice has shown that approach to be superfluous. Netherton has been a champion of the verbal bridge.

To enter into a forgotten or repressed experience, we need *images, thoughts, emotions* and *physical sensations*. If we have elicited all four of these aspects, the patient enters regression.

Instructions to strengthen an emotion without first locating it in the body can be compared to turning on the volume before tuning the radio. First locate, and only then strengthen!

In practice usually E + S is enough: an *emotion* is then felt *somatically.* For example, in the case of timidity:

T: *Do you feel that timidity now?*
P: *Yes.*
T: *Is that timidity strong?*
P: *Yes.*
T: *Where and how do you feel that timidity in your body? Describe and locate it as precisely as possible.*
T: *My cheeks are warm. I hunch up my shoulders. I breathe with difficulty.*
P: *Okay, you feel timid, your breathing is difficult, your cheeks are warm, you hunch up your shoulders. When I count back from five to one, you move back in time, and when I say one, you have arrived at the moment when you felt all this for the first time; five . . . , four . . . , three . . . , two . . . , one . . . , what comes up?*

In another case, the patient lies down. He wants to work on his relationship with his father:

T: *Just say when you are ready. If you are ready, say "Yes."*
P: *Yes.*
T: *Are you experiencing anything?*

In other words, do we go to a bridge or does the bridge come to us?

P: *I feel a cramp in my calf.*

The patient begins with a somatic. E plus S works the most quickly, so we try to couple an emotion.

T: With what kind of emotion do you associate that cramp in your calf?

Sometimes an imagination emerges first.

P: As if I had sat in a wrong posture for some time.
T: Is any feeling connected to that?
P: Yes. Being forced.
T: Concentrate on that spot in your leg. You feel forced, more and more strongly. If you feel that, say "Yes."
P: Yes.
T: Okay, we go back to a situation in which you had a cramp in your calf and you felt forced. I count back and at one you are in the situation that caused this feeling.

Again, the simplest, the purest induction is E + S, *Emotion + Somatic.*

T: That emotion, where is it in your body? Feel it right now. Now we go back to the beginning of this feeling, when you felt this feeling for the first time, or when this feeling that you now have originated.

When we have an emotion and a somatic together, the combination is usually enough to go back: "Five, four, three, two, one." If we have only an E with a S, all other starting points are superfluous.

T: That guilt feeling, do you feel that right now? Where?

Begin with locating it, not strengthening it.

P: It is here, it hurts.
T: What kind of pain is it?
P: Cramp, a sting. It stings and it presses.
T: Okay, feel it right. We go back to the origin of this feeling. I count back from five to one, and at one you are in a situation that caused this feeling. At one you come somewhere where you feel a pressure on your chest, You feel pressure on your chest, it stings and it is cold, five . . . , four . . . , three . . . , two . . . , one.

125

Go. The worst that can happen is that it fails, but it happens so quickly that no energy is lost. Sometimes the trigger is a body condition that carries a strong emotional charge. Not always is it the obvious emotion that provides the entry. Netherton:

> *There was this guy with a paralyzed arm. I asked what was his greatest fear connected to this arm. He responded that he feared knowing that he could never use it again. I then asked: "If you could use your arm, what would then be your greatest fear?"*

The *somatic bridge* uses bodily sensations at the beginning of a session. Someone says, *I feel cold.* Where? *Not my skin. It seems if it is in my bones. I feel it inside.* Then we have got a somatic. Deepen that somatic before you elicit emotions or images or thoughts. The body is spatial, so you ask, "Where do you feel it the strongest? In your feet? Okay."

Then we switch to emotions, images or thoughts. Use a simple and open question to go there: "What do you associate with it?" or, "What does it mean to you?" Someone responds, *As if I am a smooth water surface, something like that.* Or if the word "fear" comes up, "Can you feel that fear?" *Now that you ask it, my heart begins to pound.* Then we catch a second somatic.

If we have different somatics, we must avoid confusing or switching them. We may ask, "If you feel your heart pounding, do you still feel your cold feet?" Someone may respond that the coldness becomes stronger or the same or less. Explore that difference.

Someone has cold feet, then his heart pounds, and that makes his feet less cold. Something shifts around in his body. Then we start at the heart. If we are already at the heart, we go back to the feet. Possibly that coldness is already resolved. Retain symmetry. What we encountered last, we check first. At the end we reverse the order of the beginning, unless the patient spontaneously chooses another sequence. If someone first gets palpitations and then cold feet, we work first with those cold feet, and when that is resolved, ask, "How do your feet feel?" *They feel warm.* "Then we go to your heart. Do you still feel those palpitations?"

Compose your session, construct it like a symphony. Symmetry is the simplest construction. Imagine at the beginning where you may end, and check at the end whatever you began with.

Again, use the *somatic bridge* when the patient has clear somatics. With the somatic bridge we do not work from E to S, but from S to E. For example:

P: *I have had terrible headaches, for months now.*
T: *Now too?*
P: *Yes, although right now it is bearable.*
T: *Right, just concentrate on that headache.*
P: *Yes, but then it will get stronger.*
T: *If you want to discover where that pain comes from, you have to go through that pain to some extent. Do you want to try that?*
P: *Yes. (Sighs.)*
T: *Great. Go with your attention to that pain in your head. What kind of pain is it?*
P: *Heavily pressing, as if I were wearing a helmet. (An image (I) emerges.)*
T: *Heavily pressing as if you were wearing a helmet. Remain conscious of that feeling and find out which emotion is connected with it.*
P: *Especially fear, I believe.*
T: *Especially fear, you say. Any other emotions?*
P: *Also grief, I believe, but mainly fear.*
T: *Mainly fear, but also grief. Where do you feel that fear in your body?*
P: *Only that pain in my head.*
T: *And that grief, where is that?*
P: *(Pause.) I get a thick throat.*
T: *You are scared and you have pressing headaches as if you were wearing a heavy helmet. You have a thick throat and you feel grief there. Go back to the time . . . (There we go.)*

The imaginative bridge.

A somewhat less frequently used bridge is the *visual* or *imagination bridge*. The imagination bridge is the most logical entry when someone already carries an image. For example, someone might carry the image of a child who had been run over before her eyes, or animage from a dream that is strongly retained. The imagination bridge is also fit for auditive or kinesthetic people, as long as the memories or visualizations are directed to body impressions. The imagination bridge as such is not enough. We need thoughts and emotions as well:

127

P: *I believe I am sitting cross-legged before a heap of mud or clay, and I am doing something with my hands.*
T: *Can you see that?*
P: *Yes.*
T: *What do you feel right there?*
P: *I don't know, it's vague.*
T: *You have a vague feeling. (Repeat and confirm what someone says.) What feeling is attached to that feeling, or what thought or what word?*
P: *Exertion.*
T: *Okay, exertion. There is exertion in that experience. Can you feel where that exertion is in that experience?*
P: *I don't know.*
T: *Does is have to do with you hands? Imagine that you are busy with your hands in that clay.*
P: *No, it is not tiring, rather dirty, but not unpleasant.*
T: *Where is that exertion then? Feel your body.*
P: *I have the feeling as if I am stuck in some posture from which I cannot free myself.*

Thus we discover the emotions and somatics of that image.

The best way to a somatic is by way of an emotion: "Can you feel that fear now? Yes? Where is that fear? Where do you feel that fear?" If we have the emotion, we can always arrive at the somatic by locating the emotion.

A strong dream, especially when it repeats itself, is often an excellent imaginative bridge, although when we use it as a bridge we may land in a psychodrama. The next three examples are childhood dreams of adult patients. In each of these nightmares the patients were children. In all three cases, the dream image that pushed itself most strongly to the foreground was used as an imaginative bridge. Immediately, somatics came up.

Patient A: *I lie in a stable behind cows and I feel very uneasy.*
Patient B: *I am running in a beautiful meadow full with flowers. Yet I am scared; they want to destroy me.*
Patient C: *There are lots of adults around me who look at me coldly and want to hurt me. I am afraid and suspicious. I can't trust them.*

The first dream image led to the life of an old farmer who dies of a bleeding stomach in the cow stable. His devotion to the animals is strong, and the promise to his father to look after the beasts weighs heavily. So after his death he hangs on in the stable. Because his farm is remote, his animals die afterward. There plays the postulate *I have been negligent,* because he thought he did not look after the animals well enough. He does not dare to face his father after his death.

The second case is that of an attractive Polish Jewish girl of fourteen who is forced to be a camp prostitute in Auschwitz. She is raped by the guards, sometimes secretly in a washroom or shed, sometimes openly during drinking parties. Every time she is raped, she imagines herself not being there and instead sees herself in a sunny meadow with lots of flowers. She is fifteen when a commander beats her to death with his belt after sexual experiments in which pain and lust were intertwined. The image she uses to escape becomes the essence of the childhood dream. The regression released her great fear of persecution. The third case is a young go-between in the French resistance, who is betrayed by someone from her group and dies after severe torture.

The imaginative bridge works well with *phobias*: fear of heights, fear of speaking in public, fear of streets, fear of animals, etc. Patients who have such fears often have trouble feeling those fears at the beginning of a session. Remembering the last time they had this fear often evokes the E (fear). Once the E is there, we can find the S. Take that fear of dogs.

P: *No, I can hardly feel it. Only when a dog is nearby, it bothers me.*
T: *When was the last time you felt this fear of dogs?*
P: *The day before yesterday. I walked across a bridge and there lay a dog. It scared me stiff.*
T: *Try to relive that moment. You go across that bridge. What happens?*
P: *Oh God, that dog! A big one, too.*
T: *What kind of feeling does that give you?*
P: *It scares me stiff!*
T: *Where do you feel that fear in your body?*
P: *In my stomach and I start to tremble. (Trembles.)*
T: *What else happens? (The patient's trembling gets worse.)*
P: *Nothing. I stand there frozen. I am so scared it will bite me.*
T: *You have fear (E) in your stomach (S) and you tremble (S). Now you are scared that the dog will bite you and you are standing there frozen. That fear, where do you feel it especially?*
P: *Everywhere! I freeze completely, especially my legs.*

129

Later we instruct this woman to go back to the first time she felt this same fear in her body in the same way, etc.

In another example, someone has examination fright. The *emotional bridge* means, "Can you feel that now?" If patients don't feel it right now, they may imagine it, and their imagination triggers the emotion.

Avoid instructions and questions to which people have to say *No*, especially people with examination fright. If people feel they are well on their way into regression, they may submit to us without disconnecting themselves. Then there is trust.

In a case of examination fright or fear of water, we simply say, "Imagine the first time you had that feeling. When you think of it now, can you feel that fear again? Where do you feel that fear then?" So then we have: imagination (I), emotion (E) and somatic (S).

With fear of heights, we would have to have a high sofa for people to remember fear of heights when they lie down. So, "Imagine the last time you felt fear of heights." If that suggestion is not enough, we let them return to the strongest experience they remember, and thirdly, if necessary, to the first time. The most certain procedure is from imagination (memory) to emotion to somatic. The best choices to elicit an emotion are the last time, the strongest time and the first time.

The Christos Technique uses a special imaginative bridge. It simulates an out-of-body experience by manipulating body awareness through having a person feel elongated and swelling up, then visualizing being at their front door and going up in the air, until that person sees that the horizon is curved. I suspect that the curvature of the earth is necessary for a person to enter another time when that person comes back down. If people see no curvature, they may return either into the present life, or at most into a preceding life that is strongly merged with their present life, but they never go back further.

This is a safe method. It is gradual, slowly paced, it goes step by step with repetitions, and has many "fuses." To start with, not everyone feels elongation, not everyone feels swelling up, not everyone goes up in the air. Visualizing your own front door is a powerful but familiar image. We force nothing, as in counting from five to one to move back in time. The final test is whether people feel a shock under their feet when they land again.

I find this going up high in the air and coming down on your feet so important that I usually use it in group sessions. When we cannot personally accompany people, any individual blocks in the visualization process provide important entry points for individual sessions. Some typical blocks might be *I remained locked in my body*, or *My feet became longer, but my head could not get out*, or *I got too stuck in my head*. Also, creating images of day and night provides a built-in fuse against fear of darkness.

The Christos Technique guides a person to where they see the horizon curved. In group instructions I always say, "Go higher until you think it's enough." Some see Earth become a dime or a point, or just disappear. Sometimes, people leave Earth altogether in going as high as they want. Often we then find an old extraterrestrial lifetime.

The verbal bridge.
The most versatile bridge and the last resort if feelings, thoughts and images do not emerge, is the *verbal bridge*. The simplest form is to recognize charged core sentences of your patients and let them repeat those statements. Surprisingly often, simple repetition leads to a strong E or S. Often a patient moves straight into the regression.

I take the example of *I am stuck*, to show the identification of E+S. (Postulate sentences often begin with "I.")

T: *Just tell me when we can start.*
P: *Now is fine with me.*
T: *Repeat with full attention and calmly, five times, the sentence: "I am stuck."*
P: *I am stuck. I am stuck. I am stuck. I am stuck. I am stuck.*

Often after five or fewer times patients say or show that they feel something:

T: *What are you experiencing now?*
P: *I become anxious! (The first E.)*
T: *You become anxious. Let this anxious feeling become clearer.*
P: *Pfff.*
T: *Where do you feel that anxious feeling especially?*
P: *In my chest. (S)*

T: *You feel anxious, especially in your chest. Let it become as clear as possible.*

P: *I feel the difference clearly enough. Good heavens, just as if something lies on top of me, something heavy. (I + S)*

T: *And how does that make you feel?*

P: *I am furious (E), but also scared (E).*

When the regression does not emerge naturally, we say:

T: *Something heavy lies on your chest. You are furious, but also scared. Go back to the first time you felt this. I count from five to one, and at one you experience the situation where you had such a feeling for the first time.*

P: *Oh my God! Something has fallen or been thrown on top of me. I can't move, I am stuck. (Etc.)*

With a different type of problem, in an exercise session someone once talked about brooding and later about worry. Then came responsibility and then again brooding. (A pity really when these things are coupled.) When such feelings arise, ask if that brooding feeling is present, where it is and how it feels. Only if the feeling remains vague do we let the patient repeat five times, *I am brooding.*

If the feeling remains elusive we may ask, "Do you feel that worry now?" *No. Right now I feel good.* Our aim is to bring that brooding feeling into the here and now. We ask about the last time the patient felt brooding, and we let the patient express these feelings. If the feelings remain weak, we say, "I will count back from five to one. At one you move to the moment in your life when you felt this brooding the most." We normally begin with the most recent experience and then we move to the most intense experience, and if necessary to the first experience.

If the patient still does not feel that brooding feeling, switch to peel-downs: *I am brooding because . . .* or *If I feel brooding, then . . .* or *I am especially brooding if . . .* or *Brooding is . . .* If that exercise leads to nothing, we make another contract. *In a different situation, a patient enters the room and says, I don't know what is the matter with me, but I am stuck. I can't move in any direction. I am trapped in my work. The relationship with my wife is locked, I am closed off from my children, even my friends I don't meet anymore. I don't know how I can ever get out of this situation.*

Mind the expressions: *stuck, trapped, locked, can't get out*. Such words could indicate old imprisonment. The regression methodology of Netherton takes such core sentences or postulates and uses them as a bridge into regression. Netherton discerns five crucial elements in this method:

1. *Identification of core sentences during the intake or later during the therapy.*
2. *Repetition of these core sentences, so that the subconscious reacts, while the consciousness remains connected.*
3. *Careful reconstruction of pain and emotional trauma. This reconstruction is vital, as the only way to release grief and other emotions is to relive them.*
4. *Liberation of the trauma by repeating the core sentences. This last repetition leads a patient to see experiences in their proper perspective and make links between present and past.*
5. *Working through the prenatal period, birth experiences and early youth to find and release restimulations of the core charge.*

Netherton has almost certainly (if indirectly) derived his method from L. Ron Hubbard, the father of Scientology. In his best known book, *Dianetics*, Hubbard spoke about postulates and engrams, registers of episodes of decreased consciousness and physical or emotional pain.

Hubbard probably learned of the idea of *engram* from Wilhelm Reich's *The Function of the Orgasm*. Originally, the word came from Richard Semon. Engrams or postulates can be recognized in characteristic sentences. Location and repeated reliving of the postulates results in discharge, and in the end disappearance of the problem.

Hubbard's methods are rigid and inefficient, but effective. Hubbard reminds us of Columbus: obstinate misconceptions, but pioneering results. Netherton is, to begin with, a practicing therapist. He limits himself to helping solve the problem that someone presents. In Netherton's method we find nothing of Hubbard's theoretical pretension and ideological rigidity.

Personally, I only search for restimulations when the patient did not achieve a complete catharsis. If the patient feels excellent, I do not recommend further poking around, whatever Netherton or others may think of birth or prenatal restimulation. If the patient does not go there during regression, we don't try to go there later.

Netherton's summary of crucial elements lacks a careful going-through of the death experience and a checking or taking care that the personality of the earlier time is healed. Often this process is needed, but with pseudo-obsessions it is essential.

Make careful note of repetitions! Be it words or dreams or whatever, what repeats itself is waiting for liberation. In one of my cases, a patient twice dropped the sentence, *I am becoming more and more practical.* Those words were charged so heavily that he could not say them aloud as an opening sentence, not even once.

By contrast, whenever you encounter a patient's confusion, and especially emotional hardness or falsification of memories, switch to a postulate analysis. Make this switch not to release the charges, but to understand them and get the regression back on track. You may note falsification when you see that people have difficulty in continuing. You may not have noticed that the patient already changed his memories, representing the events as better or maybe worse than they really were. If a topic is ready to be addressed, the patient always gives a sign that something is wrong - a word that sticks out or a phrase we can note.

If images, emotions or somatics continue to be elusive, and if repeating a core sentence or postulate five times does not give one E or S, and variations on that sentence produce nothing, then work out the most promising sentences with *peel-down chains*:
- the *return* series, *"because . . ."*
- the *forward* series, *"if . . . , then . . ."* or *"if . . . , then I feel . . ."*
- the *specification* series, *"is especially . . ."*
- the *equalization* series, *"is . . ."* or *"means . . ."*

These peel-down chains make the postulate bridge effective and flexible.

Working with chains is difficult at first. The *because* chain is the simplest. "Because" deepens what is behind, what is next or what is before (in time), or what is underneath. NLP (Neurolinguistic Programming) discourages the use of *why* questions, because those questions are associated with interviews and examinations, and they easily lead to rationalization. I never found this problem with completing *because* statements. The second chain is: *if-then*, or *if-then I feel. If this happens, I feel that way.* With *if-then*, we ask for reactions, for consequences. Here is an example:

I am scared because: I am alone. I am alone because: I am abandoned. I am abandoned by: my friends. My friends have abandoned me because: they no longer trusted me. They no longer trusted me because: they thought that I had betrayed them. They thought that I betrayed them because: someone told them that. Someone told them that because: he wanted to cause trouble. He wanted to trouble me because: I once let him drop. I once let him drop because: I did not trust him. I did not trust him because: he always looked at me in such a creepy way.

Now we can proceed in two ways: *He looked at me in a creepy way, because* . . . Then there is a chance that we get, *Because I didn't trust him.* Therefore, we take, *If he looks at me in that way I feel: foolish. When I feel foolish: I start trembling.* Then comes a somatic charge in the realm of the consequences.

The first two chains, the *return* series and the *forward* series, are two directions of implication: backward and forward. I especially use *If . . . , then I feel . . .* to get at the basic emotions, the basic charges. After *If I feel scared then: I tend to run away,* there is no sense in saying, *I tend to run away, because . . .* Then we get . . . *. because I am scared,* and that we knew already. Often we find that if one chain gets us stuck, another chain will get us moving again.

The third chain is *specification.* If someone says: *all* or *much* or *a lot,* we ask, "What especially?" *It makes everything so ugly.* "What especially makes it ugly is . . ." *I am always so sad.* "I am especially sad when . . ."

The forth chain, the *equalization* chain, works in ways that are similar to the specification chain. *Anger is: dangerous. Danger is: wounding. Wounds are: painful. Pain is: maddening.* At completions that are superficial, repeat the sentence but insert the word "really": "I *really* find that . . . " etc.

When do we stop peeling down? When we get an emotional or somatic charge that is close to an imagination. If the chain starts to produce more general or abstract material, then stop. Otherwise we go on until it halts, or until we can enter regression, or until we find ourselves in a paradox or a circle.

The sentence *I am locked in because I am locked out* is a postulate because it touches a fundamental issue and because it is an inner contradiction. Paradoxes are always postulates. *I am scared for a crowd because they are no longer themselves* can refer to a real situation, but *People become beside themselves when they are themselves* is a postulate. *I get cold from warmth* is a psychotic postulate. Or a more horrible one I encountered once, *Everything is nothing.*

A circle is, *I dislike men because they are brutes. Men are brutes because I dislike them,* or, *I feel scared because I am alone. I feel alone because nobody can console me. I seek no consolation because I am scared.* Those are loops.

Sometimes it helps to recognize the course of the loops. We may thus be able to map out the problem without actual regression. That mapping out can be easy: *I am dissatisfied with my job, because* . . . We let the patient complete this sentence a few times, and four or five things come out. Some patients may enter a regression, and others may perceive a cycle. What to us is the prewash is the main wash in rational therapy.

Netherton, when he has identified a postulate from the intake, repeats it loudly himself. I have patients say it, because the manner in which they say it provides much information. In one such case a woman lay down and thought of her youngest son, who always gave her problems and exhausted her. I let her repeat and complete the sentence, *My youngest son is* . . . The sixteenth completion was, *My youngest son makes me powerless.* Then she experienced a deep emotion, felt a burning in her head and a hole in one eye, as if a spear or lance had been rammed into her eye and right through her skull.

She found herself experiencing a traumatic death, with charge on the statement, *I cannot move at all.* She was literally nailed to the ground at the moment of death. She appeared to be a man who had tried in vain to get to his family to warn them or protect them. The powerless feeling about her son triggered this past experience of powerlessness, which was also related to family and carried heavy somatic charges. After three quarters of an hour the problem with her son was still there, but the exhaustion he triggered and her feeling of intense, maddening helplessness had lifted.

In a different type of case, when people come for therapy because of physical complaints but lack an actual somatic, use the verbal bridge. There are two points of departure, *I have belly complaints because* . . . and *My belly is* . . . .

When someone has frequent problems with a body part, the second option works best. *My breasts are* . . . Then we encounter charges from many lives. *My eyes are* . . . Then we also encounter important and divergent dharmic charges. Imagine what may happen with, *My hands are . .* What have we done in all our lives with our hands? *My hands are . . .* we have the patient repeat and complete until nothing more comes.

On such lists we may get between five and a hundred responses. This method provides an excellent way to map a person's past lives. We may end up with a hundred statements about our hands; twenty may be from this life with eight different charges, and the rest from thirteen different past lives.

If we do that for different body parts, we'll find interconnections and we can map charges and lives. Only, this is not therapy but exploration, though more concrete and less pretentious than, *Who have I been before?* or *Why am I interested in Morocco?*

Taking the body as point of departure is one of the best ways to explore past lives systematically. Our body is more than our present body, it is also the mental body image with which we identify. It is the self-image that carries all those charges.

One patient had trouble with his legs: *My legs are: dead; of wood; strong; wasted; the most important I have.* Those different responses will be about different charges. Dead and wasted may carry the same charge.

I usually elaborate on these statements in the given order. Thus we identify patterns that may repeat through lifetimes, often with character postulates. If we are to follow this approach, we have to begin with a good level right at the start. People who take this exploration seriously are able to enter deeply into regression. Sometimes people cannot repeat a sentence for a second or third time because of the emotions that that statement triggers. Yet, the weakness of the verbal exploration is that when we start superficially, we may remain on a superficial level. Then the harvest remains thin.

Combining bridges.
If people wish to lie down for a therapy session, the simplest start is, "Just say when you are ready." When they're ready, we can start. When they're not ready, we suggest that they take as the entry point whatever problem is interfering with their readiness.

I am not comfortable. Something keeps bothering me. I feel cold. "Where?" *Somewhere inside.* "Where do you feel that the strongest? In your feet? Okay." Go then to emotions, by images or thoughts if necessary.

A simple and open question is, "With what do you associate that?" or, "What does that mean to you?" *A feeling as if I am drifting in cold water*, or, *The word "fear" comes to my mind.* "Can you feel that fear? *"Now that you ask, my heart starts pounding.* Thus we catch, in addition to the emotion, a second somatic in the form of a pounding heart.

When the patient is ready to begin with the regression, simply ask, "Are you experiencing that emotion, that feeling, now?" If so, then we have hit the E already and may seek the corresponding S: "Where do you feel that in you body?" When the E and the S are clear, we can enter regression.

The imagination bridge uses memories or fantasies to recollect forgotten experiences. The meadow with flowers, the heaving raft, the ascent higher into the atmosphere, are imaginative inductions. If we already have an image, what do we want then? Emotion! Then again we seek a somatic along with the emotion, and the simplest question for finding a somatic is, "Where do you feel it in your body?"

If we say, "Go back to where and when you felt that sensation before" (Edelstien), then the somatic, the physical sensation, helps by serving as an actual, physical anchor. The past is also in the present, and if we know where, we easily awaken that past.

Again, the simplest approach is through the emotional and somatic bridges. If we don't get an emotion, then we use imagination. If we don't get an image, then we use the verbal bridge. If we find clear postulates, then we may take the verbal bridge right away. In that case the complete line would be: *verbal bridge, imagination bridge, emotional bridge* and *somatic bridge*: *V-I-E-S*.

Working with bridges is similar to seeking a sender on the radio. First we tune until we find the frequency, and only afterward do we turn up the volume. The search for E + S is similar: first get the E + S straight, and only then go for regression.

An interesting way to deepen a memory into emotional reliving is to place or lie someone in the body posture of the original situation. This will provoke the emotional charge.

Then we have the verbal bridge of repeating and completing core sentences: *I feel confused* (repeat), or *I feel confused because . . . I never get time. I never get time of . . . that stinker.* That is the verbal bridge.

The most promising sentences that may be used in the verbal bridge contain the words "I" or "me" and express a feeling or imply an event. For example, They *hunt me down.* Keep the sentences in the present tense. That is important, because we want to uncover that part of the past that is present now. Also, in your choice of questions never ask, "What happened?" but rather, "What happens?"

The verbal bridge is most powerful with a postulate. The statement *I feel confused* does not necessarily carry a heavy charge, but the statement *I am branded* certainly is a postulate. Another postulate is, *Nobody loves me.*

If we get a postulate, we take the verbal bridge, letting the patient repeat the postulate until an emotion, somatic or imagination emerges. Sometimes we continue verbally in a full verbal exploration (see Chapter 7).

How do we choose between bridges? In first place we do not choose, we take whatever emerges. Often the patient shows the choice already by verbal and nonverbal signals.
- *If the patient displays a clear emotion, take the emotional bridge.*
- *If the patient has a physical complaint, take the somatic bridge.*
- *If the patient sees a clear image, or if emotions emerge under specific conditions, take the imagination bridge.*
- *If the patient makes striking statements, take the postulate bridge.*
I often have fears. "Can you feel these fears right now?" *I feel restless, but not frightened. My body is okay.* The emotional bridge is closed, as is the physical bridge, so we work with the imagination bridge or the postulate bridge. We don't know the postulates here, so we search for them. Or we have the patient say five times loudly, with increasing attention: *I am scared, I am scared, I am scared, I am scared, I am scared.* Often their eyes close and flutter while they repeat this statement.

If people say they can't do that, we know that we have hit something. Everyone can repeat an unimportant sentence, but may feel blocked when asked to repeat an important one. That block translates itself easily into emotions or somatics. The breath halts, for example, or the throat becomes thick. Often we see that someone can not say that sentence a second time.

You can use a verbal bridge with a somatic, but go for the emotion before you move into regression. For example, let's say that someone has always had problems with her legs. We let her lie down. "How do your legs feel right now?" *Like rubber.* Taking this statement as a cue we have her repeat five times: *My legs feel like rubber.* Some people may enter regression naturally by only the second repetition, or we may continue with:

My legs feel like rubber because . . .

Often this somatic is enough if the somatic itself is incisive, if it triggers a strong titillating feeling, a deep chill, or a smarting feeling. Someone may say: *I feel a stab in my throat and my eyes are filling with tears.* Then we can understand what charge has begun to emerge: grief.

Using a verbal bridge to uncover an emotion is also possible, if that verbal bridge is specific enough. But an attempt to strengthen a vague signal makes no sense. A sentence such as *I feel sad* is too general. Have the patient complete this statement first, to make it more concrete. For example: *I find it sad that . . . it rains. I find it sad that it rains because . . . I feel lost.* Let this new sentence, which is more concrete and emotional, be repeated five times. If there is an emotion or a somatic we may ask, "If this feeling could speak, what would it say?" In this way we complete an E or S with a V. Patients who have trouble expressing feelings may need gently prodding.

T: *You just told me that you feel sad now and then. Can you experience that sad feeling now?*
P: *A little.*
T: *Great. Just experience that sad feeling. Just let it emerge.*
P: *It becomes stronger. I . . . (Cries.)*
T: *Right. Let it just come, let that sadness just emerge, just feel it. Where do you feel that sadness especially?*
P: *I don't know for sure. (Still crying.) Everywhere, I believe.*
T: *How do you know that you are sad?*
P: *I - my eyes. I have to cry.*
T: *Your eyes. Are there other places where this sadness is present also?*
P: *In my belly, I believe, and in my eyes.*
T: *How does that sadness feel in your belly?*
P: *As if there is a stone inside.*
T: *You feel sadness in your eyes, and a stone in your belly. Go back to the first time you experienced this sadness in your eyes, and this stone in your belly.*

People may appear to wander in vague spaces in which they feel fuzzy, without a body. We do not explore such discarnate states through somatics, but through emotions or thoughts. Use the verbal bridge, "If I feel vague, then I feel: *lost.* If I feel lost, then I feel: *lonely.* If I feel lonely, then I feel: *wide.* If I feel wide, then I feel: *lost.*"

If use of a verbal bridge leads right back to the starting point, then some part of the patient is trapped in that circle. The circular argument is the rational counterpart of a trapped, frozen emotion. Kelsey speaks of "the spirit of the event," a piece of our mind, that is trapped.

If it appears that "feeling vague" carries an important charge, we specify it by seeking examples: *I feel especially vague when:*
- *I have just eaten.*
- *I am about to make an important decision.*
- *I feel awkward. (Etc.)*

Sometimes a patient's statements may yield more than one potential entry point. For instance, someone may complain: *Almost daily my mother is on the telephone asking when I will come home next time. But if I go, I feel very bad. I am broken when I come home again.* Which bridge should we use then? Move first toward the emotion: "Imagine the last time that happened. That feeling of being broken, can you feel that now?" If a patient's memories are not enough to get at the emotion, use the verbal bridge, *I feel broken on account of my mother because . . .* until we touch the emotion.

What if a patient begins a session with the following kind of complaint: *Through the last few years I have noticed something strange. If I am to be honest, I always feel unhappy. I have a good job, an attractive wife, lovely children. We do nicely together, but in fact I am unhappy.*

Beware of a statement like that, because it can be a soap-opera of "poor me." If someone makes such a statement in wonder and has not the faintest idea why he feels unhappy, what do we do then? Do we begin with the emotional bridge? Probably not, because the patient's stated feeling is amorphous, protracted. It looks almost like a hangover. With such a vague but pervasive theme, the verbal bridge may work best.

Take "I feel unhappy" and have the patient repeat it five times. "Pay attention to your body. How do you feel now?" *My feet are cold.* Thus, by starting with the verbal bridge we got a somatic. "That coldness in your feet, where is that precisely? What kind of cold is it? Vague or sharp? With what can you compare it?" *As if my toes have been severed.* "Shall we look and see if there is something there? I will count back from five to one, and you go back to a situation in which you are unhappy and your toes have been severed." *I see a railroad switchyard.* Continue from there.

141

If nothing comes, but he still has feeling in his toes, a brief silence is all right. Never try something different merely out of nervousness. Usually, patients will see something, have some impression, but they repress it. They may see a railroad switchyard, but they think it is weird or nonsense.

Often people have expectations about a regression. Or they may see something obscene that, at least at first sight, is unrelated to cold toes. If they do not want to talk, they do not want to talk; then it stops. Do not ignore this pause, because in that apparent silence something is always happening. There is no empty space in human consciousness. There is always something.

If people hardly know on what problem they want to work, or they display ambivalent or confused points of entry, the method used by Kelsey may be a good bet. Ask the patient to draw a blank and let one thing emerge. Without a specific question, from zero, zoom in on one point. Be curious as to where that point leads. What emerges, what surfaces, depends on an unconscious evaluation of the inner situation, but also on the situation with the therapist. The soul seems to ask itself what is now the most fertile problem on which to work.

If someone, for example, talks about feelings that are *wrapped up*, then an imagination bridge may be indicated. You might try: "Imagine this room being empty. If I snap my fingers you will see several boxes that contain your emotions. How many are there? Just unpack them one by one." Thus take literally a word or phrase such as *wrapped up*. "Where are these emotions? Where have you taken them?" *They are in the attic.* Continue from that point.

When something specific is thrown into your lap, please do not try to make it abstract. Keep it concrete! For example, during an exercise session one patient saw the image of a calloused hand. Something like that image we should never ignore.

People may describe their pain as *choking* or *horrible*, verbal labels of a somatic. We can use these sensations as a verbal bridge when we let the words repeat, or when we use them to make peel-downs: *It is choking because . . .* or *I feel choked* or *I am choked*. A verbal bridge uses repetitions of phrases, and completions of sentences, to get at deeper charges.

But merely eliciting a patient's emotion may prove to be not enough. Abstract thinkers often hide emotions in such labels. Therefore ask, "That choking feeling, can you feel it?" If someone says, *No, I don't feel that,* we use the word *choking* in a sentence that we let them repeat. Ask what people feel in their body when they say those sentences. Continue with the sentence that gives the strongest somatic charge. Take for example, *I am choked,* or *I choke,* or *They choke me,* or *It feels choking here.* That last sentence may elicit the strongest somatics. Let that sentence be repeated five times. If that is not enough, then continue with, *It feels choking here because . . .*

Examples.
Let's say that someone comes to us with fear of water. He wants to get rid of that fear. What kind of bridge should we use? How do we get to that fear of water?

When we begin with the emotional bridge we touch that feeling immediately, at least if we succeed. To understand the principle involved, just try comparing a fear of water to a fear of spiders. Which of these two fears do we evoke most easily? Usually fear of spiders. Someone who is frightened of spiders can easily imagine a spider. Then the imagination bridge works quickly. From the imagination to the feeling, from the feeling to its location in the body, one can move quickly into the regression.

Evoking a fear of water is somewhat more difficult. If I were lying on a couch I would find it easier to imagine a spider crawling toward me, than imagine being on the water.

The following are several examples. What kind of problem is each one, and what bridges would you use and in which order?

1. *Fear of walking the streets.*
2. *An unassimilated death of a close relative.*
3. *Shifting belly complaints.*
4. *Impotence or frigidity. (Limit yourself to the bridges you have learned in this book.)*
5. *Someone who always gets fired. The shop closes down or he becomes obsolete, or the department is eliminated or he is fired because of a misunderstanding, or he is being blamed for something.*
(*Note your answers before proceeding with the text.*)

Fear of walking the streets is not a fear that is specific enough. Merely *being on the streets* is vague. We still do not know what this fear is all about. A verbal bridge is possible: *I am scared to walk the streets, because* . . .. This option is possible, but it is an unhappy beginning. Something such as *I am scared of cats, because* . . . would be more specific. In such a case, the imagination bridge would produce a more concrete image and allow us to zoom in.

In this case, where a patient fears walking the streets, begin with the imagination bridge, at least after the question, "Can you feel that fear now?" doesn't produce a "yes." The fear of walking the streets, what is that probably? Might it be a trauma, a hangover, a character postulate, or a pseudoobsession? The most probable cause of a fear would be a trauma. Thus we may go from imagination (memory) to emotion to somatic. Ask for the last time the patient felt this fear, then if necessary to the strongest time, then if necessary to the first time, until we touch the emotion.

The second example, one of an unassimilated death, is clearly a trauma. Sometimes it may be an obsession of the deceased. We often encounter such an obsession involving deceased parents. This may especially be the case when growing up has been a painful business, with many things never having been resolved. Unresolved problems and ambivalent feelings then hang on.

In this case, if we elicit an imagination, the emotions may be overwhelming. It would be a mistake to suggest, "Imagine what he would look like, as if he were entering the room now." That would be a bad beginning. The emotion was there already.

In the case of an unassimilated death, it may be too early to use the verbal bridge. The results may prove to be too emotional. An unassimilated death is a wound. That wound may include guilt, shame and other imperfections. The wound may have restimulated earlier feelings of loneliness and abandonment. But the wound is concrete.

First go to the somatic in this case, and not to the imagination. Using imagination might boost the emotion, so anchor this emotion before boosting it. Aura exploration is probably unnecessary, but it does exist as an option. You can always use aura explanation with somatics.

In the third example, someone has shifting belly complaints. The somatic bridge would be the natural start: "What do you feel in your belly? How does your belly feel?" Sometimes these questions are enough, but even better would be to add the emotional charge: "How does that belly cramp feel? What emotion is connected to it?" Thus, ask how the feeling feels and how *that* feeling feel, etc. Using such a route, we always arrive in an emotion.

Asking for the *feeling* of a *feeling* is always the right way to get at basic charges. "How does that cramped feeling feel?" *As if I am under pressure.* "How does it feel to be under pressure?" *It makes me feel desperate.* Despair is a basic emotion. So we have despair within pressure within belly complaints.

But what should we do when we do not have an actual somatic? *I always have belly complaints, but right now I feel nothing in my belly. Nothing comes.* Typically a toothache stops when we finally get to the dentist. If fear of therapy (by association and restimulation) is not the culprit, this lack of feeling is usually a shut-off command. How do we solve that problem?

If what is involved is a trauma, and these belly complaints result in clear triggers, then the suggestion, "Go back to the last time you felt that" will help. But often the patient's complaint is amorphous. He or she may describe different kinds of complaints that come and go now and then under different conditions.

"With what do you associate that feeling? What does it evoke?" This question moves a patient from the somatic to the imagination. We can couple these feelings, but such a choice also can result in an imaginative experience instead of a regression.

If someone says, *Now and then I have pangs in my belly*, almost certainly a trauma is involved. But if someone says, *For weeks I have felt pressure on my belly, and that feeling comes and goes*, then we have a hangover. People may describe shifting complaints that involve their belly. For example: *And when the ailment was finally resolved and the doctor told me I could go home, two weeks later I fell down the stairs, landing on that scooter right on my belly.* When a person's belly gives them shifting complaints, they may have a pseudo-obsession. Some women continue to have belly complaints, like phantom pains, even after a D & C or surgery. Such a problem suggests a pseudo-obsession.

Problems such as impotence or frigidity, in our fourth example, can sometimes be cured in one session, although usually these ailments involve secondary complexes. With impotence or frigidity we use the imagination or memory bridge, asking, "When did you have it last time?" With an answer to that question, we evoke the feeling and we move through the emotion to the somatic. The surprising switch always comes when we ask, "Where do you feel that in your body?" Using the verbal bridge is possible, but do not ask for a description or history of that impotence, because then you get tear-jerkers and soap-operas. Usually someone who presents such a complaint has rd booklets and has been with many therapists already and is full of ideas. If you open that door, a library comes down on you. All of that is wearing, it consumes energy, and your first session is over before you can say, "Relive it."

Rather ask, "How does it feel to be impotent?" *As if I am nothing, no good.* "How does it feel to be nothing, no good?" *Real bad.* Such a response is still not a verbal bridge, but a preamble.

Impotence can be complex, and every thought or emotion can connect with it. On the other hand, sexual characteristics may say nothing about the person. So with which sentence should we begin? *If I make love, then . . .* assumes that impotence manifests itself only when making love. What about someone who fails during masturbation? Minimize any assumptions. Begin simply with the patient saying five times, *I am impotent.* That statement may already evoke emotions or somatics. If necessary, continue with, *I am impotent because . . .* or probably better, *If I am impotent, then I feel . . .*

Aura exploration will also work well. "Look at what makes you impotent." *Above my right shoulder is a crab.* "You had better take that away." We let it be taken away, and then we let the patient return to the moment when the crab first arrived. Then they may regress to a past lifetime or an earlier time in the present life.

After the verbal bridge move to the emotion. When a sentence contains emotion, ask if the patient feels that emotion now. If the voice becomes emotional, ask for that emotion, and from the emotion move to the somatic. Mind you, the somatic of an emotion that is related to sex will not necessarily be at the sex organs.

Sometimes an imagination comes up, and we go through the imagination to the emotion and to the somatic. Sometimes direct somatics come up. Then we seek the connected emotion. If someone says, *I feel like drifting away; it is deep,* we may say, "Pay attention to your sex organs. What is happening there?" or, "Say five times: *I am impotent,* and while you say that with increasing attention, you pay attention to any reaction in your body."

If that approach fails, you may try, *My penis is . . ..* After that comes, for example, *My penis is a plaything.* If someone makes such a statement, usually a feeling comes up. "Go back to a situation where you feel most deeply that your penis is a plaything." *I am a Roman slave boy and . . .* "What kind of feeling does that give you?"

If still no image has emerged, and we pursue the emotion by the verbal bridge, then use, "If I am impotent, then I feel . . ." *Then I feel awful.* "If I feel awful, then . . ." *Then I tend to crawl away in a corner.* "If I crawl away in a corner, then . . ." *Then I feel small.* "If I feel small, then . . ." *Then I want to crawl away in a corner.* "Okay, say three times: *I am small and I want to crawl away in a corner.* Let that feeling emerge." It is interesting where we land then. We may then ask, "Where is that emotion?" and through the somatic we continue.

Finally, with impotence or frigidity, what kind of problem is that usually? It is rarely a trauma. A traumatic experience as such does not lead to impotence. It can be a hangover, or it can be a pseudo-obsession, often connected to postulates. It is not specific. Impotence can be the cause of relationship problems, but also the consequence of relationship problems. Someone can avoid relationships if he is impotent. Impotence can also have symbolic value. Charges on parts of the body are often symbolic. The general feeling of being unable to perform at anything precipitated this symptom, for example.

If we suspect double meanings, we use a verbal exploration to identify expressions, programs that could be interpreted differently. The expression *I can't come* can refer to sexual problems, even without a sexual cause. Someone could, for example, not finish something right before a disaster. Something may have gone wrong, and the resulting postulate was interpreted sexually, although it was completely unrelated.

Finally, taking our fifth example, if someone is repeatedly fired, we use verbal exploration. Why would we not use the imagination bridge? Because a porridge of images is connected to situations of firing and being fired. This situation differs from fear of heights. With a verbal bridge we move easily to a specific situation. A verbal exploration is excellent for first zooming into to the relevant elements.

147

We could begin with, *I am always fired, because . . ..* We also can take, *If I am fired, I feel: awful, shaky, humiliated. Humiliated* is more concrete than *shaky* and *awful.* We try to identify a specific element before we enter regression.

"What kind of feeling do you get upon being fired?" *As if my knees are trembling. They feel cold.* "Okay, your knees are trembling, they feel cold." We move back to the cause of those physical sensations, for the time being without knowing how they are related to being fired. We work with a concrete charge: "Go back to this feeling at your knees. Your knees are trembling and they feel cold. Go back to when this feeling originated, emerged for the first time." We work through that regression, and then if necessary we go back to being fired.

We can always use each bridge, though the hit rate differs from one bridge to another. But there is always just one royal road.

Induction provides the prelude to a patient's reliving of a prior experience. In the reliving itself, we always follow the patient. Trust and induction are elements that help a therapist connect with the patient. First connect, then follow.

CHAPTER 6. METHODS OF
CATHARTIC RELIVING

Many beginning regression therapists, especially amateurs who have no professional schooling in psychotherapy, feel that success means getting people into a past-life memory. Getting into past lives is usually a piece of cake. What you do, once there, is a different story. Listening to tapes or reading transcripts from regressions, even published ones, often gives one the impression that the "therapists" involved have no clue as to what they should do once a patient is there. In regressions, therapy means catharsis from old charges - full catharsis where possible, otherwise partial catharsis in the sense of understanding, peace or strength gained. How do we go about achieving catharsis?

Let's take a look at a typical regression session. Induction is over. The first impressions of the past emerge. Where do we go from there? Usually the best thing to do is continue with exploration of any charges that may be present. We delve into the past, using emotional and somatic charges, and now we want to find out what other charges are there.

But why do we do this? Because each charge needs its own catharsis. Each charge is tied to specific aspects of the experience, and shows the experience in a different color. Each charge is anchored differently and should be released differently. Charges may complicate or even block each other and so should be attended one after another, not together.

Therefore, first we skip through the experiences that had caused problems, to identify whatever other charges a person may carry in addition to the initial charge. We may find further guilt, grief, helplessness, despair, shame. We literally make note of those charges; they become our shopping list. Skipping through them means gaining a general understanding of the string of events, and always asking what people feel about something and what else they may feel about that same thing. "What else is in it?" may seem a strange technical question, but people respond to it.

We go shopping with a very short list of items, just enough to take us to the right shop. Once there, we start looking around to find what else we need. We complete our shopping list while shopping. Once we seem to have completed our shopping list, we are set to do real business.

Exploration can easily slip into an aimless wandering about. For effective exploration, keep two things well in mind. They are absolute conditions for success in therapy:

1. *FOLLOW THE PATIENT. Always tie into where people are and what people say.*
2. *STICK TO THE ENTRY POINT. What was all this about? What was the work to be done? What was your contract with the patient? We want a symmetrical process: where we begin we have to return. The catharsis must also be directed to that goal.*

These two criteria may seem to conflict. If so, then simply check by relating what the patient just said, to what this patient had said at the start: "How does that feeling of loneliness (the feeling that has just emerged) relate to your fear of water (the feeling with which we started)?" Usually patients know how the two feelings are related. If they do not know, then suggest that they let go of the more recent impression: "We can return to that loneliness at another time if you want. Now go back to . . . (the last item that still was connected to fear of water). " If the patient does not want to return to the start, then stop the session. The patient may want to renegotiate the contract. If this option feels right for you, accept it - once. If the patient changes the second contract, end the session and refer him to some colleague you respect but don't like.

Patients who change the contract during a session often do so to wrench initiative from the therapist. They may have a lack of trust in the therapist, a lack of self-confidence, or even a need to remain in control. Whatever its true cause, a repeated wish to change the contract means that something was wrong at the start. As a game this contract-shifting is okay, but as therapy it is a waste of time. Shifting the contract may be the most frequent problem of beginning therapists who are unsure of their skills and need to prove themselves.

Be serious and attentive when making a contract, and stick to it. This is the first test of your professional integrity. The flip side of not letting the patient fool around with the contract is clear: you don't fool around with the contract, either. Once you start, you follow up to the best of your ability. Patients instinctively perceive that.

Wandering aimlessly also may result from the dynamics of the experience itself. Expansive emotions are like rivers - they need beds. Contracting emotions are like mud pools - they tend to choke themselves. Fear is a contractive emotion. When we want to treat fear, the emerging fear may choke any further emergence of it. To avoid this fear, the patient starts to wander. If we are going to be successful in evoking fear, we need some trust. This trust should not suppress the fear, but rather it should support the process of allowing the fear to surface.

By contrast, anger boosts its own expression. When we want to treat anger, we can evoke that anger. If the anger is not pointed toward us, this anger comes out by the energy of the anger itself. Anger may come out, but it needs to be directed. We call up anger when we are in a state of calm. Yet when we are in a state of joy we do not evoke sadness. Sadness comes up when a person is in a melancholy mood, but that sadness needs to start flowing. It is often stopped, lumped, kept stuck, or stored somewhere. As therapists we must be gentle with sadness.

Examples of trauma regressions and the other types of regressions that follow, are in Chapter 11.

Trauma regressions.
A full, methodical regression of a traumatic episode includes the next steps:
1. *A general impression of the traumatic trajectory as a string of traumatic situations (as listed in Chapter 3).*
2. *Location of the precise start of the trauma with all its charges. Skip through each episode and identify any new charges. Find the precise end of the trauma (often the moment of death), with its charges.*
3. *Precise reliving, step by step, of the charges of each situation. This reliving is done so that the patient can experience, understand, accept and release the emotional and somatic charges: "How did that charge begin? Then go to the moment when this charge was strongest. Feel how it was. Absorb it and then release it completely. Move through it. Move through all other experiences that hold this charge. Leave nothing behind. Move through them completely. Can you now release that charge?"*

If an important sentence was uttered during the traumatic situation, have the patient speak that sentence aloud with all charges. Then take the next charge: "Now we go to . . . Feel how it was," and so on. If no emotional charges emerge, then go back to an earlier moment where this feeling had still been present.

If a charge remains stuck, despite instructions to move through it, then aura exploration of the moment of getting stuck usually works: "What entered at that moment, and where did it enter?" Then to the present: "Is it still with you?" Have it removed, and then return to the original situation to continue the session. Or: "What did you lose then? Why and how did you lose it? Find it now, retrieve it, take it back, ask that it be given back. "

4. *If the traumatic situation included death, then move carefully through the death experience. Include the life evaluation that occurs at the place of overview. Check to see if any charges remain, and if understanding is complete.*

During this entire process, be attentive to:
- CONNECTIONS: *moments at which statements, images, emotions, and physical sensations elicit one another. Especially important are moments when emotional and somatic misery trigger the formation of postulates. A standard question at each episode is therefore: "Have you made a decision or formed an opinion that has remained with you since?"*
- PRECIPITATIONS: *moments at which people contact emotions, as their body shows by change of breath or voice or other expressed or manifested somatics.*
- MUTATIONS: *sudden acceptance or sudden rejection, sudden insights, sudden strong reactions of the present personality.*

A cathartic reliving is the discharge of the sensory feelings and the emotional experience string of the traumatic episode. For such a catharsis to occur, a correction is often necessary, especially if the intellectual experience string includes confusion, hardened attitudes or falsification by postulates. That correction means analyzing postulates and removing mental complicators. No liberation without acceptance, no acceptance without understanding.

Hangover regressions.
A patient relives a lifetime as a female slave who has been abused sexually for many years. She becomes less attractive, her teeth fall out, and finally she is dumped on the rubbish heap. Then we can say, "Move through that experience completely. "

But moving through it will result in a great loss of energy and may simply wear the patient out. Therefore we never give that instruction when we find a hangover. Likewise we do not instruct the patient to relive or fully absorb such an experience. With hangovers, the steps of the cathartic reliving are:

1. *A general impression of the hangover trajectory as a succession and combination of situations mentioned in Chapter 3.*
2. *Skipping these situations to note charges such as: helplessness, insecurity, submission, guilt, penance, revenge, etc.*
3. *Going to the beginning of each charge: "Precisely what did you experience then?" "Precisely how did that come about?"*

It matters if a slave grew up in a slave family, or if a rich man was convicted for murder, or if a farmer became trapped in a war. We want to know how it came about. *I am playing between the huts, and, oh God, slave dealers talking to mummy!* Why is that important? Because the cluster of charges related to slavery then contains betrayal, wherein one could not even trust one's own mother. We need to know where and why and how that inner "dirt-skirt" has grown.

4. *Take each charge separately and follow it to its worst moment. For example, if you have collected coldness, monotony, and weariness: "Go to the moment when you were coldest. Traverse this moment completely. Feel it right now. Go to the moment when you felt the most monotony. Go to the moment at which you felt the most tired." So you limit a trauma-like reliving to the worst moments, no more, no less.*
5. *Move to the end of each charge, which often is death. Then you have a total image of the situation: how it went, and what its negative impact was. Always move carefully through the death experience if that experience is part of the hangover.*
6. *One typical characteristic of a hangover is compulsion. In this case, catharsis is based upon finding the moment of choice. Therefore, we have patients move to the place of overview and ask, from this vantage point, "Which moments of choice did you have?" I tried to escape but they found me and beat me up. "Why did they find you? Could you have done anything to prevent that?" Again look for decisive moments and for the patient's own responsibility for what may have occurred.*
7. *Link to the present life. Garrett Oppenheim had people move to the place of overview and see their past lives extending to the left and the present life to the right, to find connections between the two.*

This is one approach that may be useful. In any event, let patients check to see if each charge may still be present today. Aura exploration may help to strengthen a patient's freedom from old charges.

Many people carry unconscious programs that may help one escape attempt to fail and the other to succeed. Good luck and bad luck exist, but much luck is something that we attract. The goddess Fortuna favors the bold. Insight into past moments of choice and responsibility may liberate a person from passive suffering. In a certain sense this insight completes the life retrospect that occurs after death. Patients now see what they could not see or did not want to see back then.

What if those moments of choice do not emerge? Thorwald Dethlefsen says that we have to take distortions into account. Truth can remain obscure. I am not at all interested in distortions, yet I am very interested in these. When patients represent things as being better or worse than they actually were, they aren't liberated completely, but instead they remain in a halfway house.

A patient sees himself in a lifetime as a farmer. He had a father who worked in the mines, but now he is proud because he is the only one in the neighborhood who ever bought land. His whole life is cows, cows, cows, and children, children, children. He cannot list the names of his children, but he knows how many cows he has. One-half of his children die young, the other half run away.

While he lies dying alone, he hears the mooing of the cows that he no longer can help. Looking back he stresses that it was a good life, especially because he had bought that land. But catharsis? Forget it.

He keeps repeating that he had bought land. An uncle had died and left him money. In a second or third rerun of his story, we discover how he really got the money. As a young man he had unseated an unknown rider by letting the horse stumble. The stranger broke his neck and appeared to have much money on him. Even in this version the man disclaims that he was a robber - it happened by accident.

So I agree with Dethlefsen that distortions occur, but the admonition "Don't trust the patient" also gets under my skin. If people do not tell the truth right away, they have reasons for that choice. We are not prosecutors, but therapists. We assume that patients speak the truth, and if they do not speak the truth, they have a reason. We have to find that reason whenever results of the session tell us - and the patient confirms - that the end is unsatisfactory, that "there is something rotten in the state of Denmark. " For example:

> *A woman who has been raped and abused is locked into a crevice. From her sketchy description we may infer either that she had played a dirty game with cheese, rats and her vagina, or that she had been daydreaming about such a game. She does not fully describe this part of the story during the regression, but she hints at it and is revolted by it. Her experience includes imprisonment and isolation, revulsion, but also lust. This last aspect is difficult to acknowledge, not because she wants to play falsely or present the story more favorably, but she feels confusion and guilt, and therefore she suppresses the experience.*

Masochism also produces such a double feeling: something is painful and therefore lustful. Releasing the pain means losing the lust. Such a knot is difficult to remove. If such knots and swirls emerge, we prefer to simplify, to avoid confusion. On the other hand, if patients reveal a knot during a regression, they apparently trust us.

If the moment of choice and personal responsibility cannot be found either within the life or in the retrospect after death, then move to the time before birth. People may exclaim: *Oh God, I don't want to. This will be a horrible life. I don't want to.* "So why did you go anyway?" *I have to, because of that man with those horrible eyes. He forces me.*

Do not respond, "Ah, poor girl, come here, I will now shower you with light and you will be all right. That man will leave and you will never more be forced. " Instead ask, "Why did you let yourself be forced?" *I cannot help it.* "Why can't you help it? Why does that man have power over you?" The patient accepted that power or could not resist it for some reason. "Go back to the origin of that acceptance, or that impotence. " People can always return to a moment of choice. But don't force them.

If people find no moment where they could have changed something, do not say, "But of course there has been such a moment. " Such a remark shows only lack of self-confidence.

People may remain stuck because they hide events related to their responsibility for something that was annoying, or because of duplications, complications, conflicting feelings. But sometimes there was no such moment. If there wasn't, catharsis will come, without any real trouble.

Treatment of character postulates.
Reasons to deal with character postulates are:
- Patients repeat strong and typical sentences about themselves or people in general during the intake.
- A trauma or hangover regression leads to some relief, but not to catharsis. During the session, or afterward, we find a blocking program.
- A theme persists, with or without inversions, through several lifetimes. As a more specific example, similar victim experiences recur in several lifetimes.

1. Use short regressions to collect examples of the characteristic behavior patterns. Note charges such as punishment, guilt, penance, revenge, contempt, submission, lack of self-confidence, etc.
2. Go to the moment that the charge in question or the sentence in question was registered for the first time. "What happened inside you at that precise moment?" "Precisely how did that come about?"
   Aura exploration of the registration moment can confirm these feelings. Afterward connect these feelings to the present: "Is something of that experience still present?" "Does it still work?"
3. If the original anchoring happened as part of an emotional impulse:
   - Let that anchoring be understood and accepted cathartically.
   - Resolve any remnants of that anchor in the present.
   - Release the anchor by aura therapy or postulate change.
   If the original anchoring had been a conscious choice:
   - Let the choice that was made in that situation be understood and accepted.
   - Check to see to what extent this behavior pattern has been generalized.
   - If necessary explore the problem using egostates: "Which part of yourself thinks so?"

- Check to see if the client wants to change this behavior pattern by using a new conscious choice.
  With impulsive decisions the therapy is primarily emotional; with conscious decisions it is primarily rational.
4. If the postulate remains stuck, first check to see if there have been separate moments of registering and of engraving. Registering is like noting in pencil, engraving is like noting in indelible ink. Sometimes a secondary confirmation occurs that turns a previously recorded and provisionally accepted postulate into a permanent fixture. In such a case, working with the first moment that a decision was made is not enough. If you find such separate moments, start with when the decision became engraved and then continue back to the first recording.
5. If the postulate still remains stuck, then look for complicators. The original postulate may have collected new charges or related postulates later, or it may have been generalized beyond recognition. Start with the most recent complicator or addition or generalization and work backward. The more complex this process, the more important it becomes to anchor the postulate well in the body.
6. If you do not find complicators and still the postulate remains stuck, then switch positions, move to situations in which the postulate was true for others. Or dissociate to find the block by using aura exploration or egostates.
7. At the end of the session, always release the anchor by using a postulate change, if necessary preceded by aura exploration, and if necessary superseded by "collapsing anchors. "

Aura therapy and postulate change (often postulate inversion), anchor a catharsis that had been more intellectual than emotional. Inversion works especially well when the postulate was instilled by others. For example, *I am only a stupid woman* becomes *I am a woman, and so I see and understand much.*

Double inversion works well with negative postulates about other people: *People are stupid, cold and conventional* becomes *I am intelligent, warm and unconventional.* At the beginning of sessions, inversions may also shock any sense of dependence and self-deprecation that may be present: *People are great and colorful* becomes *I am small and pale.*

Simple inversion sentences such as *I am great and colorful* usually do not work, because they lie within the line of expectation held by many patients. Most patients expect their therapists to offer only uplifting words; do not walk into that trap! We go for healing, not for comfort.

Frequent themes that recur in character postulates are definitions of one of the five standard roles: Victim, Perpetrator, Prosecutor, Helper or Savior, and Witness. The Perpetrator often expresses anger and resentment and creates resentment and guilt. Also, the role of Witness often produces guilt by sins of omission: a person continues to observe without intervening while something horrible happens. Such guilt feelings become anchored and later restimulate paralysis.

Netherton considers that the basic emotions carried by Witness, Victim and Aggressor are respectively grief, fear and anger. But a Victim can also have grief, and an Aggressor can act from pleasure instead of anger. Still, grief, fear and anger seem to form a triangle. Fear, grief and impotent anger, together with revulsion, are the most common responses to traumas. An angry person elicits anger, fear or grief in others. Fear and grief can through powerlessness generate anger. And through self-pity we easily arrive at a feeling of grief. Always relate a postulate to one of these five roles and find the basic emotion that belongs to it.

Curing pseudo-obsessions.
Treating pseudo-obsessions means renovating the death experience. Death serves as a maxi-catharsis. It also rids us of a worn-out body. All of us carry some hangovers from our life. Life in a body is often heavy from disease, hunger, weariness, limits, or pain. Sometimes a body feels like a prison. It puts a callus on our soul, gives weight to our life.

The body gives us much, but without it many of us feel better. If we have been underwater in an old fashioned diving suit for a long time, it feels delicious to surface, to throw off that diving suit and stretch.

The hangover of the incarnate state can be especially strong after lifelong toil. If relaxation and catharsis remain elusive after death, the past personality may not be rightly integrated with the next incarnation and may remain fluttering about. Then we have a subpersonality, as a special egostate. The presence of subpersonalities makes dissociation and renovation methods necessary.

How do we identify pseudo-obsessions? During the intake, the main symptom that suggests a pseudo obsession is a history of shifting psychosomatic complaints, with a persistent or recurrent specific depressive mood. During the regression session, the main symptoms that suggest pseudo-obsession are as follows:

- Easy contact is made with depressive charges, but the patient has no definite impressions of concrete situations. Instead, the patient may see shifting images and feel a weak sense of presence.
- Over and over the same vague image recurs.
- Somatics start to wander around the body.
- The patient feels disoriented and wandering about.
- After treatment of a trauma or hangover the patient gets stuck in the after-death experience.

A general imaginative bridge that is useful in identifying pseudo-obsession is to imagine a house where some people are left outside or remain wandering outside. Chapter 10 provides an example. A similar visualization, but one tailored to the specific situation, can be used with an individual patient.

Once we suspect that we have a pseudo-obsession, we follow the next procedure:

1. We use egostates. (See next chapter.) We have the patient imagine a part of themselves that exhibits these particular mental, emotional or somatic charges as someone who is entering the bedroom, the living room or any other area that the patient feels as his own.
2. We establish how that subpersonality itself looks and feels, and when its charges first entered the life of the patient.
3. We move with that former personality to the place where it usually stays. That place is usually an afterdeath state. It may be a dream-like environment, or it may be the situation in which that personality died. In such a case, the former personality may not realize it is dead.
4. We relive the death experience and we note carefully the charges involved. Are there any last conclusions or decisions?
5. We move back to the beginning of each of those charges in the previous lifetime, and then to the strongest moment of each charge. We do not need to go to the last moment, be-

cause there is no last moment. Because of incomplete dying, the charges have never been released.

6. We instruct the patient to release the charges now. Release means straight renovation of the incomplete dying that occurred before, into a complete dying that occurs now. If this renovation succeeds, the personality moves to the place of overview to understand its entire life and reasons for that life. Then we go on to integration, but integration differs.

   People may feel that this past lifetime has entered them harmoniously, and has settled itself next to them or inside of them. Or the liberated past person may suddenly disappear into the light, as a long-overdue good death experience. In the osophic terms, the past person integrates with the higher self, and remains as a parallel personality in the circle above. See what happens spontaneously, and otherwise let patients choose for themselves.

7. If release is impossible, we try a deeper renovation by having personalities think back to people they loved, and meet those people again. Then we move to the place of overview. If the personality is a perplexed and fearful child, this process may be handled more indirectly and may include the introduction of pet animals or dolls.

8. If those renovations still do not succeed, the ultimate renovation is having the present personality enter the after-death situation or intervene at the beginning of the traumatic situation that ultimately led to the death. The present personality takes the past personality to his own present surroundings, and helps the previous personality until a cathartic peace is reached. Then we go to the place of overview.

Why do we use the present personality? Many therapists invoke guides or helpers or the higher self of the patient. Some therapists enter personally as helpers. All of these options are helpful at the moment, but unhelpful afterward because they reinforce the idea that the patient is a victim who needs help. If the present personality of the patient is the main actor, the intervention's success is anchored in the present personality. Therapy is about strengthening the patient, not about demonstrating our own valor or entering joint ventures with spiritual entities. Such manipulations merely make us feel special. If you want to be a noble priest, hit the streets, but leave the therapy room. Therapy is the patient's game, not ours. I will return to this topic when discussing the higher-self intervention. Let us consider some specific situations:

> *A boy of seventeen was hurled from his body during a bombing, and immediately sought another body. He was present in the whole body of the patient, but especially in the hands. He thought he had chosen wrongly. What do we do with that?*

Seventeen is old enough to know if he wants to work on his problem. We check what drove him to get a new body so quickly. What charges were present, and what charges does the present life carry? There may be rejection or even revulsion from the new personality, because that new personality continuously reminds the previous one that its decision was a rash one.

Here the main charge was impatience. Impatience drove the boy into the new incarnation, impatience drove him during his present life, and now he feels impatient with himself. Understanding and acceptance come only if three things are understood and accepted:
- *why he was impatient, and how this impatience came about*
- *why he landed in this particularly body and life*
- *how he is now*

A pseudo-obsessor can be friendly, but unbalanced, wounded or confused. Isolation after death can come by a curse, or by whatever nonsense others had hooted in its ear.

> *A group of men capture, rape and abuse a girl. All the time she is hearing that she is just a nice stupid plaything. If that abuse continues long enough, if her personality has been smashed enough, after her death she no longer dares to enter the light and meet proper company, because she is only a stupid plaything, isn't she? Such a girl is going to be a pseudo-obsessor the next life, hanging around the patient as an inferiority complex, especially if the present life is female.*

Pseudo-obsession is common with girls who suffer from anorexia, sometimes complicated by postulates. Often the symptoms emerge around sexual maturity. Such girls do nearly everything to keep from growing breasts and assuming sumptuous female forms, because heavy negative charges are connected with those features. The main past-life reason for anorexia is sexual abuse with persistent allusions to a full body and the persistent neglect of a full mind.

Emotional vulnerability, perhaps from divorced parents, increases the chance of someone carrying any repercussion from the past, but this vulnerability is a condition, not a real cause. The fear expressed by many anorexia patients is: *Eating makes me sumptuous.* Sumptuousness is associated with brute randy fellows who are continuously making remarks about and abusing it.

Anorexics are often intelligent girls who in a past life were also far from stupid, but were looked upon and used as sex dolls. Intelligence and independence make everything worse. If such a woman loses mentally, she may become a dumb blonde in her next life, she has fled into dumbness. If such a woman survives mentally, she will retain intelligence and independence, but may trim and starve her body.

Bulimia, the habit of overeating, may also be a pseudo-obsession, but it seems more difficult to treat. It may alternate with anorexia. Then several lifetimes may be involved. Very overweight people often use their flesh to smother old pains, especially pain-guilt complexes. They have seen people butchered and they have felt either responsible or helpless. They want to embrace, to encompass those poor people or they try to envelop a poor, mauled body that has been starved and tortured to death.

Treat subpersonalities as real people. Respect them. Give them time. Make appointments to talk with them next time. In the meantime, such past personalities may change. They may grow, become older. They got stuck along the road, because they could not resolve their past life. Often these subpersonalities carry postulates of their own.

Sometimes they get younger. The age of a discarnate person is a mental age, and this mental age depends on self-image. They got stuck in a self-image, or they chose it. The right age is the age at which you feel best. For discarnates, becoming older or younger is not a consequence of the passing of time, but of the change of their self-consciousness, their basic feelings about themselves.

Dissociation techniques.
Dissociation is the opposite of association in that it is separation, divorce of what had been together before. Spontaneous dissociation, which is a patient's viewing of events from the

outside or from a distance, can prejudice the regression because this distance keeps the patient from touching the charges. When patients report that they see their body from the outside, have them enter that body. If they are unable to do so, then ask them which part of the body holds the most attraction for them. Often they can enter or become absorbed in the body at that location.

However, some patients may carry strong associations or identifications with charges from the past. Sometimes these charges are so strong that the induction itself halts. When overinvolvement, or fear of overinvolvement, is present, dissociation is an appropriate option. We can also use dissociation when we encounter a patient's ambivalence and inner conflicts. With ambivalence we dissociate to create distance from menacing or confusing charges; with inner conflicts we use dissociation to unravel the problem before we enter the proper regression.

Emotional catharsis implies association: identification with the charge of the past. Intellectual catharsis often presupposes dissociation. Insight usually requires overview, and overview requires distance. There are several dissociation methods:
- *then and there*
- *film picture and similar visualizations*
- *bird's-eye view*
- *higher-self intervention*
- *egostate therapy*
- *aura exploration*

The simplest dissociation is achieved by continuing the session in *then and there*, in the past tense and in terms of *him* or *her* rather than *I* or *me*.

P: *I am so afraid. I don't dare to look.*
T: *She was afraid, okay. What was she afraid of?*

Do switch when such switching appears to be necessary, but not too soon and not too often.

The *film picture* offers another simple dissociation technique. We take patients out of their personal reliving and let them look at the events as if they are watching a film:

163

P: Oh, I feel such a pain in my legs, such a terrible pain.
T: You feel a terrible pain in your legs. What is happening?
P: I see no more. I feel only pain.
T: Take more distance. You are no longer in the situation with that pain in your legs. You are only a spectator, looking at it as if it were a film. You remain involved in what happens, but you see it now from the outside.
P: My legs are severed!

Once the flow of the story resumes, we associate again and we let the patient move through the personal experience.

Some patients see only film pictures, and do not enter real reliving. Often they are afraid of losing control, becoming involved or accepting responsibility. They would rather watch than become involved. The film picture dissociation may offer them a way to start a regression experience, but it is never a way to end.

When our aim, for the time being, is merely insight, or when a strong fear prevents real reliving, film pictures or other dissociations are acceptable as a first step. With fear, we need to have the patient move through the experience a second time more personally, to find emotional and somatic charges and to release them. Rarely do film pictures alone produce catharsis. Similar visualization techniques for dissociation are as follows:

- Let patients imagine that they are standing in front of a mirror. Their mirror image shows them what happened, what this was all about.
- "Imagine that rapist as an aggressive lion. At first he is powerful, but now you see him grow older and older. He is now a pitiful old lion. Keep this image of that pitiful lion with you, while you move through the experience."
- Especially with children: "You surely must have a pet animal. Your cat? Fine. Imagine that your cat experiences everything that you have experienced."
- With children as well as with adults: "Imagine that you have a twin brother (or sister), and that this twin experiences everything that you have experienced."
- "Hum a sound (visual people may imagine a color). While you hum, you can see what happens, and the more you feel, the more loudly you hum."

I discourage use of most of those techniques as being artificial and superfluous.

The *bird's-eye view* goes a small step further. If patients encounter blocks in a confusing situation, we may suggest that they watch the situation from above, from a sufficient distance to see and understand what is going on:

T: *What is happening now?*
P: *I don't know. It is so confusing. There are people, but I can't see them properly. I don't understand anything!*
T: *Take distance. See it from above, as if you see it the way a bird would.*
P: *Oh, I see it now. There is fighting. I am fighting, too.*

This intervention also helps when strong emotions halt the reliving.

P: *Oh, this is terrible!*
T: *What is happening? What do you see, feel, hear?*
P: *Oh!*

The emotions become so strong that the patient says nothing more but shows nonverbal signs of intense fear and grief.

T: *Take more distance, until you can handle the grief and the fear. Take enough distance. You hover over it and now you see what is happening. You remain involved in what happens, but the fear and the grief are now at a level that you can handle.*
P: *I'm being beaten up! Oh, I'm being beaten up!*

We later let the patient relive that situation personally with all its charges. Don't go too far. Gaining overview and insight is sometimes more important than squeezing out the last drops of emotion.

A *higher-self intervention* elicits still further insight, not only into what happened to us, but also why and how we landed in that situation, and what were the consequences. We suggest that the patient move to a "panoramic place of overview where you are completely yourself. " This move simulates the life retrospect that occurs after death. The higher-self intervention works, especially if the past person had died well and had integrated that lifetime into the total personality. It is not a method to use just anytime.

An alternative that is frequently used by therapists is to address the higher self directly and ask it what and how and why and when, and what to do. Usually, answers will come quickly and easily and will be on target. This is the ultimate in efficiency.

Still, I believe that higher-self consultations are unprofessional because they violate the square of trust. They imply that the ordinary self of the patient, guided by the ordinary skills of the therapist, do not suffice. When we use higher-self interventions we give the patient and ourselves spiritual candies instead of strengthening the patient's ego. Resolution that is achieved by this method is not anchored in the ordinary consciousness of the patient, but at some spot above.

The term "higher self" implies that the normal, conscious self is the lower self. Never vest authority in the subconscious. Let people learn to listen to the many voices of their subconscious, let them learn to respect those voices, but never let them abdicate their own responsibility.

Sometimes in seeking contact with the higher self, a complacent quasi-spiritual subpersonality takes over and we find ourselves jumping out of the frying pan and into the fire.

If people see nothing and get stuck, however, we may be tempted to switch to the higher self that does see. But if the patient sees nothing, so what? When people see nothing, that failure to see has a reason. As I have already said many times before, "Nothing comes out of the blue except meteorites, and those are very rare indeed. " Instead, ask, "Why don't you see?" *I am confused, I feel scared, I am stuck.* "What makes you confused and scared, why are you stuck?"

If I find dissociation necessary, I prefer to work with the present person. If the patient gets stuck in a terrible situation, I will ask that patient what should be done: "What comes to mind?" This question resembles a higher-self technique, but without having projected it to the higher self.

If you handle the problem well, higher-self intervention is rarely necessary. It is necessary only with experiences that carry mental complicators, for example because in a past life the patient was drugged. It is important to see how that situation came about, and to be able to clean it. Regression to an experience of drunkenness or anaesthesia clarifies little, because the patient will become groggy again. Seeing that situation from above is then justified.

Let the higher self work subconsciously, unless you work with psychotic people. Then classic hypnosis, followed by a higher-self consultation, may be the only road to sanity. Once sanity is restored, the locus of responsibility and action should shift to the ego of here and now, despite all its limitations.

Many therapists like to work with the higher self for the same reason that they like to work with guides. This method makes them feel special, even esoteric; it caresses their ego and it makes them appear special in the eyes of the patient. But we are not in the business of feeling special. We are not even in the fast-problem-detecting business. We are in the business of helping clients to work, feel, and think better in the reality of daily life. Therapy is all about the patient, not the therapist, remember?

There is one great exception to my reservations against healing, higher-self guides, etc. , and that is if these guides manifest themselves spontaneously with patients who had never heard of such things. Such sessions are satisfying and impressive, but there is no reason to seek them. Do not confuse the dessert with the main dish; do not confuse the dressing with the salad.

An example of a higher-self intervention is that of a patient who after death, although returning into the light, retains strong guilt feelings. Then higher-self intervention is a valid and effective intervention, though some of my reservations remain:

T: *What do you want to do with these guilt feelings? Are they useful for something? Can you use them in your life now?*
P: *No, of course not! But I can't let go of them. Those feelings remain.*
T: *The sphere, the light surroundings you are in, make it easy to contact that part of yourself that has overview over all your lives and all the self-knowledge which you are able to access. Ask that higher self within you to advise you about that guilt feeling.*
P: *(After some silence) I am told that my guilt has been settled already, that I have already worked too long, and wrongly, trying to correct what I did wrong in that life as tyrant.*
T: *What do you think of that?*
P: *That I can let it go!*
T: *Excellent! Why did you hang onto it until now? See and understand that.*

P: *Strange. I see that it gave me an excuse to avoid really making something of my life, as if I have to crawl from an unpleasant but sheltered hole and have to stand up to the wind. I am also ashamed of myself, as if everybody sees that I was foolishly withdrawn in the earth.*

T: *And what do you want to do now?*

P: *(After some time) I can no longer go back.*

T: *What do you want to do now?*

P: *I don't want to go back anymore, but I am trembling. I feel cold.*

T: *Feel the warm sunlight on you, as if you are standing in a great sunny space. There is a fresh wind that blows gently. There is a beautiful pond. You already remove your old and dirty clothes and enter the warm sunny water until you are again warm and clean. Feel that warm, clear water rinse through your whole body. How do you feel now?*

P: *Excellent!*

T: *And what are you going to do now in your life with that excellent feeling?*

This intervention is acceptable because it leads back to the personal judgment and actual situation of the patient. Still, these results could have been achieved without involving the higher self. My preferred alternative is to send the patient to the place of overview: "There you can see why you retain those guilt feelings."

If you really feel the need to have someone contact his higher self, then use the method of Robert Shubow, who asks the higher self to enter the body for a short time. This presence seems to heal and helps to diagnose unresolved business. It seems to be an alternative to aura exploration. Still, it violates the principles of simplicity and full confidence in the patient-as-he-is.

Aura exploration (next chapter) works well when patients remain stuck in a trauma or hangover. Through aura exploration they may gain insight into their weariness. But a part, for example a stiff back, remains. Other applications are traumas with mental complications, confused death experiences and clustered somatic charges. Egostates (next chapter) dissociate by separating subpersonalities. Especially with fear of fear, with the fear of losing control, and with other complex or recursive disturbances, we separately address the part that does not dare, does not want or cannot yet enable the reliving of the undigested. For example, *I see nothing. I want to, but I am terribly scared.* "Imagine opposite you the part of you that is scared, and let us talk with it. "

Renovation.
Renovation means renewal; each successful therapy session restores. An effective session restores the ego that had collapsed in a traumatic experience, or had almost collapsed under the mortgage of a hangover, or had been tied off by incomplete dying, or had gotten stuck in a program with a character postulate, or had become consumed by nostalgia for a better world. That "making new" we can call restoration.

Renovation goes even further than restoration. It rewrites history, which is an essentially wrong practice, but one that is already widely practiced outside of therapy. Renovation involves acting as if things had gone differently from the way they actually went, that we behaved differently from the way that we actually behaved.

Renovation is our last resort to remove a vicious knot. Justified for after-death experiences and pseudo-obsessions, and even for all events that happened physically, it is an expedient, a sometimes necessary but indirect route to facing the facts. Renovate only when this option becomes necessary, but forget it when it is unnecessary. Renovation is a preliminary to the only acceptable form of rescripting: facing the facts, but with a new interpretation, especially of our own role.

After the cathartic assimilation of a traumatic life, often the quality of that life changes. In a subsequent regression the grief or the emptiness of that life may have disappeared. Clients describe more interesting or joyous experiences of that lifetime.

This rescripting is the reverse of hitting screen memories. In screen memories we have to cut through masking covers until we discover the true course of events. Guilt is probably the greatest mask of the truth. But after acceptance and insight a patient can see a positive change in the quality and mentality of that earlier life.

As an intervention technique we use renovation especially with pseudo-obsessions, to complete a death experience. When stress had been present, especially when related to incomplete dying, renovation may contribute to an intense cathartic experience. Several examples:

- *Someone feels guilty because he resisted too little when his family was assaulted. Renovation is the experiencing of what would have*

*happened if he had resisted. He soon learns that resistance would
not have worked, either.*

- *A woman, alone in a hut, dies in childbirth. The experience of a
successful birth, with its aftermath, renovates the experience. She
welcomes and recognizes the baby she never had.*
- *A man is tortured to death on a marketplace. After death he remains looking in horror at his terribly mauled body. In renovation
the present personality takes care of the body, cleans it, heals it and
gives it a good resting place. Only then can the past personality
release itself from that earlier situation.*

In the first two examples the essential question is, "Which qualities would you have needed to meet this challenge more successfully?" Move to a situation (in this or another lifetime),
where patients had those needed qualities. If they do not discover those qualities within themselves, ask, "Do you know
people who do have those qualities? Imagine that you are able
to borrow these qualities. " Or use progression: "Experience
yourself in a future in which this problem is resolved. Which
conditions are satisfied? What made the problem go away? What
did you need for that?"

The example of the murdered man is a renovation in which
we involve the present personality. When the body is cared for
and has a last resting place, the present person can now, in principle, cooperate in two ways to integrate the past personality.

Anchors and future paces.

In NLP, anchoring is the conscious, almost hypnotic association of a patient's positive or negative charge with a spot in the
body or with an act of the therapist, so that this charge can be
evoked at the right moment. We anchor just before or at the
moment that the charge is the strongest. We do not anchor lukewarm reactions.

This NLP process involves choosing an anchor that is repeat-
able exactly. To touch that charge, you would select an accessible spot that you can touch precisely: a knuckle, a kneecap, a
mole, etc. Repeat the pressure of your touch as precisely as possible. When you anchor with a word or a phrase, you repeat as
precisely as possible the intonation, sound, rhythm and accent
of that word or phrase.

Anchors should be specific, not simply a handshake or a pat
on the shoulder. Key words that a patient uses to describe a
feeling or express an internal state can form strong anchors.

Simultaneous verbal and nonverbal anchoring is even stronger.

The concept of anchoring is powerful, but I regard its application in NLP as artificial, often superfluous and usually therapeutically wrong. Therapists should not play God unless it becomes absolutely necessary. Why create something artificial when something natural is available? Why connect solutions to acts of therapists instead to acts of patients?

The basic act of anchoring is that of connecting an emotion to a somatic: a bodily feeling at a particular spot in the body. This anchor can be strengthened by visualizing or by touching. Have patients touch themselves. Above all, do not create an artificial spot if we can simply ask for one instead, or if a natural spot offers itself: "Where is that feeling in your body?" Why do tricks? Keep it simple.

I can imagine the use of artificial anchors in complicated and confused cases such as those of drug addicts. If the patient is seriously committed, but the somatics jump around like fleas, such anchors will indeed work.

Artificial anchors such as touching arms or knees, or uttering key words or key phrases, are hypnotically constructed buttons. If you forget to neutralize them, they can act as posthypnotic suggestions. Your patients might later knock their knees or hear some words and find that some specific positive or negative reactions are triggered.

To confirm the resolution of a negative emotion after a cathartic regression, we can use what are called *collapsing anchors*. This NLP technique is simple and powerful. We trigger an anchor of a negative charge simultaneously with an anchor of a positive charge. This combination results in strong physical reactions: trembling, laughing, crying, grimacing. Sometimes the patient moves more deeply into trance. Often one-half of the face shows one reaction, and the other half another. Both of these reactions mix for one moment, and then the face relaxes with fresh color and remarkably clear eyes. With collapsing anchors, artificial creation of anchors becomes less of a problem, because these anchors are neutralized in the process anyway.

The following is an example of collapsing anchors, and is one that I use frequently. It has the advantage that it can also be done by the patient alone. A problem has been worked through. It has become clear, it has been solved, but no catharsis has yet come. Have the patient imagine that one side of his body has the problem and the other side has the solution. If no natural immediate choice becomes evident, suggest that the right side of the body has the problem and the left side the solution.

If the problem is loneliness and coldness and darkness, have one side of the body imagined as lonely, dark and cold, and the other half as light and warm and embracing. Ask the patient to imagine and to feel the two halves as strongly as possible.

Anchor the problem by pressing hard at the open palm of the patient's hand. When you do it yourself, press the thumb of one hand into the palm of the other. Have the patient feel that the pressure remains after you have withdrawn your thumb. That pressure is translated into the feeling of a pillar of energy weighing heavily on the outstretched hand. Have the hand go up and down a bit so that the patient experiences the enormous weight of all the negative energy involved. Do the same with the solution energy on the other hand.

The patient now feels two pillars of energy in his outstretched hands. The hands turn inward, until the two rods of energy lock into each other, making one massive rod between the patient's two palms. Ask the patient to strengthen this impression by imagining that the rod is glued to one hand and is bumped a few times into the other hand. When the patient feels this sensation, have the other rod glued to the other hand, bumping a few times the other way round.

When this rod of energy is a firm reality, imagine that the rod is shoved slowly with the non-dominant hand (usually left) into the dominant hand. Inside the hand you imagine an intense glow that burns away or an intense mill that grinds away the massive energy of the rod. The rod shortens until the hands touch each other. Then the two body halves shortcircuit, resulting in a strong turbulence that slowly fades away.

Confirm the cure by using progression, or a *future pace* as it is called in NLP. We send patients to a future situation that they will almost certainly encounter, and that would normally trigger their problem: "Imagine yourself in that situation and observe how you react and in what ways that new reaction differs from your past reaction. " They perceive and feel how they can react, and this perception increases the chance that they will react this way.

We can take up to three future situations in different areas of life, for example: work, family, friends, sport and play, etc. We check to see if the intervention has had the desired result, and if undesirable side effects manifest themselves in another area of life. Summarized, the use of collapsing anchors combined with future paces is:

1. *Evoke the charge of the undesirable situation and ask for a somatic. The somatic may be strengthened by visualizing or by touching.*
2. *Seek with the patient an opposite, positive charged reaction pattern. Evoke that charge and anchor it also in the body.*
3. *Check each anchor separately. Are they about equally powerful? If not, then strengthen the weaker anchor.*
4. *Trigger both anchors simultaneously, until the charges no longer intermingle but become integrated in one new reaction.*
5. *Let the patient make three future explorations. When undesirable side effects show, have them corrected or start again.*
6. *Trigger both of the old anchors one after another to see if they still result in any reaction. If that happens (rarely), probably your positive anchor was not powerful enough. Strengthen that positive anchor and make a new short circuit.*

Deadlocks and glitches.
What do we do when we encounter deadlocks? First we check to see if the patients experience nothing, or if they find it difficult to talk about something. Netherton uses some clever questions here:
- *"If you could see, what would you see?"*
- *"If you could feel, what would you feel?"*
- *"If you could talk, what would you say?"*
- *Or else, "Just move right into it. "*

When we encounter a deadlock we may switch to egostates. Sometimes the previous personality wants to be left in peace. That personality is not happy, but has bought peace. Such a person hesitates to appear and talk with us. We also can use aura exploration to discover the reason for the deadlock, though this method is less direct. Through aura exploration we often arrive at an egostate anyway.

When we feel that patients are beating around the bush, we can let them open their eyes and sit up straight, and then we confront them directly. "There is something you are holding back. What is it?"

Resistance can be intelligent, and can change while we're busy with it. This is true with obsessions, with pseudo-obsessions and with people who don't really want to be cured. We may suggest relaxation and the patient replies: *It's hard for me to relax. Can you let me visualize something?* Of course, we aren't put off that easily. We offer a visualization, for instance a meadow with flowers. Afterward they say, *It was difficult, for I happen to dislike flowers.*

When patients are divided against themselves - one part says yes, the other no - we separate the two by using egostates. But when doubts are directed toward the therapist, we have a problem. When people say, *I liked to come here, and I am glad that I am here, but still I felt doubts on my way to your office,* then a subpersonality is bothering them. When they say, *I don't know. I wonder whether you (so not "I"!) will succeed,* then answer, "I also wonder whether *you* will succeed. "

Recursion is the ultimate complicator. The product blocks the process, and thus the problem blocks its own solution. According to Hubbard (1950), five kinds of recursive sentences, when they keep occurring, complicate therapy:
- BOUNCERS: "Out!" "Never come back!" "I have to stay away."
- HOLDERS: "Stay here." "Stay and sit there and think about it." "I may not leave."
- DENIERS: "I am not here." "This is going nowhere." "I am not to talk about it." "I cannot remember." "I don't know."
- GROUPERS: "I'm mixed up." "Everything is happening at once." "It all comes together now."
- MISDIRECTORS: "At this point you cannot go back." "Turn around." "I don't want to go through this again."

When at an early age people hear their mother moaning in a depressed period, "I'm fed up with it all," their unconscious becomes fed up with this memory. Another example is *I cannot reach it.* Such a postulate can be the result of an experience in which people tried to reach something in vain and failed miserably.

Always note how patients phrase their block. Regard the phrasing as a postulate, and use that postulate as a verbal bridge. Usually the patient will then simply enter the regression. With recursive postulates we can also ask, "How does that feel?" or "What do you feel about that?" A good additional question is, "What would happen if you could reach it?" (Netherton)

Important recursive postulates are shut off commands: *Woe betide you if you talk about this! Mind, you saw nothing!* Character postulates, too, can block. For example, *I won't let myself down!* Use the postulate bridge here as well, or switch to using an egostate. A part of the patient wants to solve the problem, but another part obviously doesn't. Call the person who does not want to solve it, the one who shrinks back, who doesn't want to show itself.

Emotional charges may be recursive once in a while, but mental complicators are always recursive. Reliving a confusing episode confuses the patient. When recursion appears, we need dissociation. If people have died well, we may have them move through the death experience to look back. This viewpoint gives them oversight.

Then we have them move back to the *results* of the confusing episodes, instead of asking them to relive the processes. Aura exploration works best for examining results. We remove the negative results, and only then do we ask the patients to go back to see how these results had originated. After that we bring the patient to the place of overview, so that they gain complete understanding: "What happened exactly and why did you retain it as you did?" We have broken the loop of recursion and have set the patient free.

First we fly over the recursive charges, later we defuse them from below, as it were, and finally we return to the overview. Straight reliving is then possible, but often it is no longer necessary. This approach I learned by experience through tedious, laborious sessions that exhausted me.

Fear may be recursive, especially fear of losing control. Fear may also be a defense against what might come up. When fear appears, try dissociation by aura exploration or egostate. Use hypnotherapy as a last resort. But don't try too much. Without the square of trust in place, there will be no catharsis. Patients with whom we can't build up trust, for instance through recursive fear, are not suitable for regression.

When people do not relax, use their tension as a starting point. When they don't even want to close their eyes, accept that. The only real contraindication for regression is a patient's lack of trust in the therapist. Any lack of trust stops us from being able to start such a session. Sometimes the real problem is general stress, general tension and worry, the hangover of daily life. In such case preparatory relaxation or preparatory homework may be useful. Again hypnotherapy can be an effective last resort.

If people say they are afraid that regression won't work, we respond, "That happens often. What do you want now?" *I want to try anyway.* "Okay, let's try it. " Fear of failure is usually based on a trauma as well as on a character postulate. This fear occurs especially when patients have high expectations. They can be so afraid of disappointment that they abort their efforts beforehand. Similarly, some people turn down others merely out of fear of being turned down.

Such a self-fulfilling prophecy can also be present in a session. We suggest to a doubting patient that they do it another time. *Yes, but I would like to do it now.* "Well then, do we do it, yes or no?" *I think I'll do it.* "Thinking is okay, but not good enough. What do you want?" Break their ritual. They expect persuasion and encouragement. Once we as therapists are motivated by wanting to show our tricks, we enter a handicap race and our arms are already twisted.

Experiences with mental charges, such as those that had resulted during hypnosis, are the most difficult to relive, because reliving hypnosis or perplexity or loss of consciousness will confuse and slow down the mind, even the mind of the therapist. We lose contact with our clients when they traverse some period of relative unconsciousness. Keep talking, and stay in touch with the body. Even touching one finger will do.

If that does not work, use dissociation. Aura exploration is always possible: *I see a poisonous greenish gray that swirls through me like a blanket.* "Okay, pull it out through one spot. " But such a step is difficult, because it may make the patient feel dizzy. That is why we use dissociation. Have the patient split himself into one personality that is hypnotized or poisoned, and the present personality that helps from the outside.

Through what spot should we pull something like that poison out? Preferably through the spot where it had entered originally. If a mist had entered through the nose, we draw it out through the nose. If that effort fails, we ask, "Where would you rather draw it out?"

How do we resolve clustered charges, e.g. involving pain? We don't know beforehand if lust or guilt or grief is connected to that pain. The simplest question is, "What else is connected to it?" Curiously, people tend to give a specific response to such a general question.

If people seem to resist a possible charge such as lust, then we work with aura exploration, because that charge will emerge in symbolic form: "Describe it. With what do you associate it?" and then, "Move back to the first moment this entered you. "

176

Isolate each charge before you treat it. If you find no charge, you say, "Move back to an earlier situation in your life, a situation that will draw up something or say something about this block. Move back to a situation in your life that is connected to this block. "

Or have the block visualized, using aura exploration. Red dice appear. What those mean, we do not know - yet. "Move back to the moment when these red dice entered you for the first time. "

If we know the charges, but those charges conflict with one another or cluster together, where do we begin? "What do you experience right now? What feeling or what thought is the strongest?" "Go to the moment when you felt this thought most strongly. " Go back on the charge. If it is lust, go first to a pure lust experience, and after the patient has relived this experience ask, "When did the next charge connect with this lust?" Or ask, "What do you associate with lust?" Or let the sentence repeat and complete: "Lust is . . ." *Lust is sinful, lust is sweet, lust is dirty, lust is dangerous, lust is sky high,* and so on. So we analyze, we de-mix it. A complicator locks this lust experience, for example, because lust had been considered sinful. "Go back to the moment that . . ."

When images emerge, but no emotions accompany those images, when reliving remains flat, we have a number of options:
- *Ask patients what they like and let them enter that situation. Suggest afterward that this situation will be reversed now. This reversal may trigger the repressed negative emotion.*
- *Let patients listen to a dripping tap.*
- *Pull out the emotion by use of breathing. Suggest that with continued breathing the emotions come free, or that each inhalation brings up an emotion, and that with each exhalation that emotion comes out.*
- *Work with egostates. Let the most unemotional side enter first, then call up a moderate unemotional side, and finally let the emotional sides come in.*

People may say something like, *That feeling of being imprisoned I only meant metaphorically.* In such a case the anchoring was bad. It is not important what the patient meant, but how they felt and where they felt it. Or they may be working against us instead of with us. Then get another patient.

When people say they keep thinking, we ask what they mean by that. *Yes, well, I thought I shouldn't.* "Who said so?" *Well, I thought, I wouldn't come into regression properly.*

Another silencer that can ruin a regression is, *I cannot reach my emotions.* They sweat and sigh with pounding heart, but they cannot reach their emotions, meaning they don't express their emotions in an uninhibited way. They want to have at the beginning what they should have in the end.

Conversely, when emotions seem to be getting too strong, ask, "Can you cope with it?" If they answer *No,* ask, "Why not? What stops you?" When someone doesn't know, "Why don't you know? What stops you?"

Only if the answer for a second time in successionis *I don't know,* we say, "Okay, take distance, see it from above, go up until you can manage to see it. " When we take people up to a dissociative state too quickly, we show that we don't take them seriously, that we don't trust them. When what is happening is not therapy but exploration, always ask if people can handle it.

When patients experience something that conflicts with their present personality, ask what they think about it. A health freak relives a previous life as a fat person, and to his amazement enjoys being fat. When this memory blocks him, then analyze his urge to be healthy: "What does health mean to you? When did it start?" Find the charges, positive or negative. He may recall a religious life with an awful bland diet and regular starvation exercises. Then the urge to be healthy may lose a secondary charge, since he sees no need to suffer. Now he may accept having been fat. He doesn't intend to become fat now, but he accepts fat people.

When many entry points offer themselves, then focus on one: "What bothers you most?" or "What do you want to get rid of most?" or "What in particular is troubling you?" *That I never do it right.* "Do you feel that now? Where especially?" When they can identify where they feel that feeling, we are ready for regression.

When you have forgotten an element in the session, one specific charge for example, deal with that charge the next time. You may even complete a half-finished session by telephone. You may call or they may call. *I do still have this pain in my throat.* "We can leave that until next week or the following week, but let's see if we can take it away now. Have you got a minute?" When patients say they want to stop, listen carefully to their phrasing. Do they use the magic word *stop*? Let me summarize some common deadlocks and what to do about them:

VAGUE STARTING POINT, FUZZY CONTRACT:
Don't accept vague starting points. Focus or stop: "Good beginnings are simple. " List possible topics and let them choose one. When they have difficulty in choosing, keep specifying. "What do you want to get rid of most?" or "What is especially bothering you?" Limit yourself strictly to the chosen topic until the patient achieves a catharsis. Never lose track.

When patients wonder about details or reasons or consequences, ask, "Shall we first go on with the main problem, or do you want to do this first?" or, "We have about three quarters of an hour left, so let's use it to finish this part. Next time we may continue with that other point. " Sometimes it is not necessary to come back to it, because meanwhile the patient has already discovered the answer to his question.

BLOCKS TO GET INTO REGRESSION:
- *Insufficient E+S*. Often we have turned the radio louder before we have tuned in to the right channel. Either the emotion was too weak, or the somatic was too weak. Complete the E+S before continuing.
- *A recursive postulate*. Overdo it. Explode it by repetition, by verbal exploration or by reversal.
- *Mental complicators*. Dissociate. Use a bird's-eye view, higher-self intervention, aura exploration or egostate.
- *Fear of losing control*. Often this block carries elements of the previous two blocks. It may be fear of surrender, of trance, of the therapist, or even of lying on one's back and closing one's eyes. Diverse situations may have caused this fear: bad experiences with anesthetics, with therapists or physicians; abuse of hypnotism; rape; a moment of inattentiveness that led to a disaster. "Always stay with the fear!" Use egostates. Address the blocking fear as a subpersonality.
- *Confusion, induration or falsification*. Simple confusion occurs when too much happens at once, or when everything moves too quickly. Specify the problem and anchor it; dissociate only if necessary; simplify. For example, "You see only the things that are important to you. " Use a bird's-eye view or freeze the image and carefully analyze its charges.

179

Induration is an experience of getting stuck in a judgment, and induration is recognized when a patient makes a generalization. For example, a vulnerable boy got his ears boxed by a dominant elder person and accepted the expressed negative views on him as if they were absolute truths. In this kind of case, shift the attention to the other person (the ear boxer) and his motives and limitations.

Falsification is a wrong interpretation. Ask, "Was that remark meant for you?" Or the problem may be about an unjust punishment. A child does some small thing wrong and then a bomb drops, a fire breaks out, a volcano erupts, or a ship sinks. Make patients see that their action did not cause the accident.

DIGRESSIONS AND LEAKAGES:
Check to see if anchoring was done sufficiently, and if the right questions brought the patient well into the emotion and into the body feeling of the earlier time. If all these steps were taken properly and still you encounter digressions and leakages, then you have missed an essential detail in the reliving. The main thing to keep in mind with the following disturbances is reference to the entry point.
- *Avoiding* an episode. The patient may escape into insignificant details, into the broader surroundings, into episodes that occurred before and after, or into life in general. Ask, "What does this have to do with (the starting point)?" or "Shall we go back to (the starting point)?" If the patient continues to digress, ask, "Is there something that stops you from experiencing the event that is related to (the starting point)?" Note charges that may come up, and use those charges to move through the experience.
- *Jumping* to other situations that have the same charge. The patient may jump to different situations or different lifetimes that hold the same charge, short-circuiting similar but unrelated experiences. "Fine. You seem to enter past experiences well. What you see now is important, but let's first finish what we were working at. You can always come back to this later. "

We may often find arbitrary shifts with psychotic and serious psychosomatic problems. With shifts that move the patient to similar situations, a postulate of unmanageability can be tied to an emotion: *When I'm scared I don't know anymore what I'm doing.* Constant shifting also can be the result of bouncers such as, *And now for something completely different!* or *Get out of this!* We may find such postulates during the intake or during a verbal exploration.

When the patient jumps from an image that has no relation to the entry point to another image that does relate to the entry point, continue with the new image. Check before closure the first image. Maybe then it makes sense.

Sometimes shifting expresses a patient's power struggle with the therapist. React then in the manner of, "You obviously get impressions very easily. Shall we continue to stick to the starting point?"

A patient relives that he is about to beat up someone and then he jumps to a situation in which he plays tenderly with a child. With such opposites, look for guilt and look for a postulate.

- *Overinvolving* with others. Ask, "Who of them contributed to your (starting point)? Can you feel that now?"
- *Metaphysical musing*, existential reflections, assumptions and cries for help. For example, "I ask you, sir, what else could you do as a man in that situation?" Neither confirm nor oppose such statements. The best answer: "Behave like a man! And how does it feel (not) to behave like a man?" Then take the session back to the starting point.
- *Associating* with recent situations. Such associations are fine after the regression. First move through the lifetime including the death and the place of overview, and only then move on to other lifetimes. When associations occur, ask, "Has this got to do with the starting point? Yes? Then we will come back to this later. "
- Personal *commentaries*. Fine too, if done after the regression. People who make comments during regression often do so from the idea, Don't let the therapist think that I need him. React in a slightly ironic fashion, and when that reaction doesn't help, then say that they obviously don't need us, and say goodbye.

CRISIS:
Don't panic. Speak calmly and clearly, touch the top of the patient's head, the solar plexus and sometimes the hands or feet.
- Getting *stuck in a negative charge*: a cramp, a paralysis, or a panic. The labor pains stop. Dissociate, and search for what the patient needs before he can relive it. Use collapsing an-

181

chors. If that approach doesn't work, bring the patient back. Say that you will return to that problem later, but for now this was enough. Check to be certain that it was not your own fear or emotion that made you break off the session.
- Being *stuck in a postulate* instilled by others. The worst kinds of postulates are curses or black magic. Give the suggestion, "Leave it behind. Go to a place where you can be yourself. " Mobilize help through regression or imagination. When the source of negative energy wakes up as an obsessor, give personal guidance, if necessary.
- Getting an *out-of-body experience*. Patients feel that they have lost themselves and are difficult to address. Say, "Though you have lost yourself, you will stay in contact with me, for I haven't lost you. However far you may go, I will stay with you. " Or the classic assurance, "You can go on hearing my voice. " If necessary, use somatics for communicating by physical contact.

RUSH:
Rush occurs with hasty or intellectual people. Rush manifests as a film with commentary rattling on, or as the patient giving up and going silent. When rush occurs in an otherwise good session, it usually has to do with a threatening experience that the patient needs to get over or avoid as quickly as possible. The remedy for rush is to stop the film, freeze it to a still, and then have the patient describe it meticulously. Without that halt, we lose track in no time.
- Impressions arrive so quickly that the patient cannot describe anything further. The therapist may lose track. Freeze the image and again connect the reliving to the starting point. After that, list all the charges and go through them one by one. When the patient appears to be observing all kinds of backgrounds and consequences simultaneously, we had better move along quickly. Have the patient see it as a great vista spreading out. Take in the entire situation. Then go through it step by step.
- Patients remain passive observers. Ask what makes them so passive. The answer can suggest hangover experiences, guilt feelings, fear of responsibility, avoidance of facing one's own mistakes. Go through it again with the patient, and focus on choices and decision moments. Where and when could they have acted otherwise? If necessary, mobilize strength first:

"What would you have needed then to make you feel less passive?"
- Impressions come quickly but emotions remain shallow. The patient remains emotionally involved, but as an onlooker. The regression looks like a sports commentary. Being an onlooker is safer. Freeze the image and ask, "Shall we quietly do this again? Event after event?" Check which moment carried the strongest feelings.

STANDOFFS:

The reliving falters and breaks off, or continues on the level of memories and storytelling. Standoffs are hard to remedy. Sometimes we simply have to stop.
- The patient is in a vague but obviously unpleasant situation, does not understand it, sees only a part and cannot move backward or forward. Dissociate with a higher-self intervention or focus on the block: "What's keeping you?" Then say, "Go to the element you overlooked. " Direct the patient toward insight and clarification, element by element if necessary.
- The patient suddenly refuses to talk. When the patient is obviously not having an out-of-body experience, we ask, "Are you experiencing something?" If they confirm, say, "You don't have to tell me, but experience everything connected with (the starting point). " The patient's experience may be about intimate or embarrassing things, or shut-off commands.
- The patient stops experiencing. Ask, "How do you feel now?" and "What is the last thing you experienced?" Netherton sometimes says, "Open your eyes. Look at me! What are you holding back? What stops you? Don't you know? Okay, close your eyes and let it surface. "
- The patient returns to the here and now. React as before. Both forms of stand-off are often caused by the negative influence of someone the patient knows. Use egostates: "Who halts the experience?"

STRESS:

Emotional reliving may be intense. It may trigger bodily tensions, sweat, heart palpitations, headache or physical restlessness. Go through the experience once more, calmly, and sug-

gest that this time the patient will understand and that pain and emotions will be restricted.
- The reliving is so slow that the patient's contact with karmic charges is exhausting. This problem is often a guidance failure. Go one charge at a time.
- Conflicting charges emerge or guilt feelings cover the emotions. Analyze the charges separately. Use guilt feelings to trace earlier guilt. Usually we bump into a character postulate.
- Actual opinions and attitudes conflict with some content of the experience. Get the patient back and ask, "What do you want now?" Or use the conflict as a new starting point.
- Difficult somatics come up, for example a migraine. Use aura exploration and resolve these somatics. When you doubt whether the headaches have something to do with the starting point, add, "Later it will become clear what the headache has to do with it. "

General hints.

The choice of when we touch patients and when we don't is a question of style. I use physical contact sparingly. Use your intuition, but avoid stroking and cuddling. Patients can become cuddly if they have regressed, for example, through a traumatic childhood experience. Then it is okay to be paternal or maternal. Somatic contact strengthens the sense of "I am with you. " A light touch is enough to provide that reassurance. Radiate trust (if you feel that), but do not become personal.

Patients may block: *I cannot say it because of that lump in my throat.* We can resolve such a block by aura exploration, if we feel that this is the right moment to resolve it. But if even aura exploration halts, we may help with our hands to remove the block or to help it flow. Do that only if patients fail to do it on their own. Trust the patients, and treat them as adults.

Establish physical contact when patients are mediumistic people, people leaving their body, people trembling all over or becoming cold or stiff, people making remarks such as, *I am drifting away* or *I can hardly talk anymore.*

The only form of physical contact that I use frequently, apart from touching the underarm or the hand, is holding cold feet. People are usually deeply involved mentally and it may be difficult to ground them, especially if cold feet are related to basic charges such as loneliness or coldness. Can't we send warmth to the feet? Yes, but people often are still engaged in their negative emotions. They may move through a catharsis with feelings of intense cold. Feet should *become* warm, not be made warm.

Bodily contact should anchor patients, not divert their attention. Therefore keep it limited and focused. When intense fears emerge, I may place my flat hand firmly on the solar plexus. With that touch I confirm the reassurance of "I am with you. I do not shirk from it. We go on. " Sometimes I keep my hand only lightly over the plexus. You can do a great deal with your hands, but do not make it too easy for the patient.

The importance of somatics in reincarnation therapy shows that this therapy is related to body work. Body work and bodily contact ease the somatic side, because physical touch mellows resistance. But always ask first if the patient can handle any physical discomfort without help.

Also, with aura exploration I might give something to patients, but I keep it as limited as possible. I may give them a tiny star, the smallest star they can imagine. I say, "This is a small, but very smart little star. " They themselves have to enlarge it. Or I give them a staff and ask later, "Whose staff was it, anyway?" Often they respond, *Gee whiz, it was mine!* That is right. I helped them by handing it over, but it was theirs, not mine.

Generally, spiritual healing is done too often and too quickly, especially by therapists who have more sensitivity than insight, therapists who love to help people. Healing is something like painting white a wall that has bubbles underneath, is dirty and greasy, and badly primed. At first sight the result is wonderful, but three days later the first cracks emerge.

Healing that is full of goodwill and empty of method is sentimental whitewashing. A therapist may think, "How wonderful, all that white light! Look at me working with this!" Feeling full of goodwill can work excellently, but it often hides a personal need. We tend to give patients what we need ourselves. Therefore tense beginners and insecure amateurs put a great deal of relaxation into their induction. To hypnotize patients is also to hypnotize ourselves.

Some hypnotherapists offer post-hypnotic suggestions that cover up problems instead of solving them. They plaster up cracks, while the layer below continues to warp. Leave any spraying of the aura - white or any other color - to spiritual house painters and wallpaper hangers.

Many therapists heal too much and too quickly because they themselves are not whole enough. Also, some therapists are more priest than craftsperson. Healing is a valuable instrument in the therapist's suitcase, but use it sparingly. Psychotherapy is a craft and an art in which the client has to do the real work. If we so much love to help people, we would do better to become a doctor, join the Red Cross or the Salvation Army. Then we really help. I try to train professionals, not alternative soothsayers or parsons.

In a good session, patients heal themselves naturally, especially from traumas. A trauma often provokes its own catharsis, and we need to accompany that catharsis only lightly. It grows under our hands. If we feel that we have to heal somebody, or that we have to transmit energy in any form, we probably missed the right approach. With complex issues we may blank out confusion by using healing methods to concentrate on one point. But some people always begin with healing: "Relax and imagine a beautiful light . . . ." all roundabout.

The general principle is simple: *If an associative procedure blocks, then dissociate; if a dissociative procedure blocks, then associate.* When blocks occur during a regression we usually resolve them with dissociation, employing: subpersonalities, bird's-eye view, higher-self intervention, or aura exploration.

If both association and dissociation are blocked, use ambivalence and paradox. Have sentences repeated such as *I waver, I keep switching.* Give paradoxical or ambivalent instructions, even during the induction, instructions such as, "You feel more free and more protected, more free and more protected," or "Go where you don't want to go. " Only if you must, suggest, "Become aware of what you should avoid at all cost," or "Concentrate on becoming wide and dispersed. "

Even unrelated, general paradoxes may break a deadlock: "Remember that you had to forget about this. " You can instruct the patient to follow an inner voice and not to listen to you anymore. Somatically, you can switch very quickly between anchors, or you can palpate them with your hands.

Ambivalent and paradoxical instructions are fun; they give us a sense of power. Use them sparingly. Simplicity, efficiency, effectiveness and elegance usually go together. A fast, simple, smooth approach provides the best chance for permanent results. With a proper start and enough trust, one session may be enough, certainly with traumas. With sexual deviations, especially the aggressive ones, a patient may need one session to resolve the problem and one session to understand where it came from, to satisfy the mind. With pseudo-obsessions (and real obsessions) it is often the same. With hangovers it often goes more slowly because of the likelihood of recursiveness.

Character neuroses or "personality disorders" are a different chapter altogether. They involve, almost without exception, many sessions.

Something more should be noted about restimulation. When we resolve the origin of a problem, the chain of possible restimulations is not immediately gone but the problem's basic anchor has been removed. The consequence of this removal is often that secondary charges emerge in the form of chaotic feelings. That is a good sign, but prepare the patient for some weeks of afterbirth: mental, emotional or somatic unrest.

Netherton always looks for restimulations: in the prenatal phase, during and immediately after the birth. He might have learned to do this from Hubbard. In my experience it isn't necessary to search for all restimulations. We go nowhere that the patient doesn't go.

Let me summarize. There are three main points of attention in cathartic reliving. *First: the start.* If it is worry, it is worry and it remains worry. *Second: the simplest induction is E + S, emotion plus somatic. Third: always connect to whatever surfaces.* Follow the patient!

If the patient gets lost, connect with the starting point. If trust is present, following and reconnecting are easy moves in the dance that is called therapy.

CHAPTER 7. SUPPLEMENTARY METHODS

This chapter is about methods that may precede, support, follow or substitute for regression. These methods include: *verbal exploration, aura exploration, egostates, acupressure* and *arm test*. We end with an overview of these methods and how to choose among them.

Verbal exploration.
A complete inventory and analysis of a topic through words and statements, prior to entering regression, is a *verbal exploration*. During the intake, some patients remain vague about why they have sought therapy. Such people may be intellectuals with general problems of orientation and self-knowledge. Also, when patients arrive with many different complaints, or during the intake show many different postulates or emotions, it is useful first to map the problem field.

A general verbal exploration will map as many postulates and emotional or physical charges as possible. From that inventory we later choose a topic for regression. The broad comprehensive coverage of verbal exploration is this method's main strength but also its main weakness, as we will see.

The technique of verbal exploration has already been discussed in part, with discussion of the verbal bridge. We explore the completed sentences by using listings and peel-downs, while we note emerging postulates, emotions, somatics and images. Verbal explorations produce excellent material for regressions, but such explorations can also have value as eye-openers, and sometimes even lead directly to catharsis.

As a guide, refer to the list that appears on the next page. The same list, when expressed in the past tense, works well for searching a past life. This list is intended for people who are curious about their past lives. Previous relaxation and induction are then desirable. We let the patient complete all sentences, and afterward if necessary we explore them further by using peel-downs. Exploration is not therapy, but sessions with people who are curious often get a therapeutic twist, so this topic would belong in a chapter on acquisition of clients.

GENERAL VERBAL EXPLORATION

1. I see . . .
2. I feel . . .
3. I hear . . .
4. I don't like . . .
5. I like . . .
6. I don't accept . . .
7. I accept . . .
8. I don't hope that . . .
9. I hope that . . .
10. I am not afraid of . . .
11. I am afraid of . . .
12. I don't trust . . .
13. I trust . . .
14. I make . . .
15. I seek . . .
16. I find . . .
17. I think . . .
18. I expect . . .
19. I doubt . . .
20. I believe in . . .
21. I have to . . .
22. I am not allowed to . . .
23. I am allowed to . . .
24. I cannot . . .
25. I can . . .
26. I don't want to . . .
27. I want to . . .
28. I dream of . . .
29. I go . . .
30. I will . . .
31. I am not . . .
32. I am . . .
33. I . . .

The simplest example of a more specific verbal exploration would be a "fear listing." Someone says: *I am often scared.* He doesn't feel it now, so you say, "Just lie down. Are you ready? Okay. At what do you want to work?" *On these fears.* "Can you feel these right now?" *No, not now; I feel good.* "Do you feel them anywhere in your body?" *No.*

Then ask the patient to repeat five times: *I am scared.* If this still evokes no emotion, images or physical sensations, let the patient complete: *I am scared of . . .* Then you may get: *I am scared of water, I am scared of snakes, I am scared of something white.* So you get a list of, for example, seven or thirteen or eighteen phrases. This is your shopping list.

You begin at the top with *I am scared of water,* and let the patient repeat this statement five times: "Say with increasing intensity: *I am scared of water.*" Observe the patient carefully. "Something comes up?" Usually images, emotions or somatics emerge. If this repetition deepens the patient's mental state, but there is still no contact, you elaborate further upon these sentences with the "because" chain, the "if-then" chain, the "specification" chain or the "equalization" chain.

You continue with this approach until an image emerges or a charge (E or S) is hit, or until you encounter a literal repetition or a loop: *I am scared because I run away. I run away because they are angry with me. They are angry with me because I am scared.* We are back at square one.

With a loop you seek the most remarkable sentence within the loop. You let that sentence be repeated until an image, emotion or somatic emerges. In the loop above, the last sentence is the most remarkable.

The elaboration has three levels. For example: *I am afraid of water, because . . . it is so deep. Water is so deep because . . . it is full of beasts!* So sooner or later you hit the charge, making contact with the past that is in the present. With that contact come emotions, somatics, images; someone becomes absorbed, and enters a spontaneous self-hypnosis.

Then begin the induction with: "Okay, we move back to a place and time where there was deep water full of beasts." You add, if necessary: "I will count back from five to one." But if someone has already entered an altered state, you don't need to say that anymore. You can add suggestions such as: "Five . . ., we go further and further back, four . . . , you are getting closer now, three . . . , always nearer, two . . . , you now get contact, one

191

. . . , what do you notice?" Then the regression begins.

You touch first the *level of expression*, the *I am scared*; then the *level of specification*, the *I am afraid of water*; and finally the *level of concreteness*, the *I am afraid of deep water with beasts*. This technique is similar to that used in NLP, but is simpler.

A special application of the verbal exploration is exploration of parts of the body. You list, and elaborate afterward:

T: *My feet are . . .*
P: *My feet are . . . cold.*
T: *Repeat and complete: My feet are . . .*
P: *My feet are . . . ugly.*

This continues until nothing further comes, or until a literal repetition follows. Afterward you elaborate again:

T: *Repeat and complete: My legs are cold because . . .*

For a general exploration of the body, before we know where we have to be, aura exploration works more quickly. If an aura exploration produces material about a local problem, for example a painful hot spot on a shoulder, but the patient gets stuck in that exploration, then switch to a verbal exploration: *My shoulder is . . . .*

The most existential verbal explorations are based on completing: "I am . . . ," "My body is . . . ," "My soul is . . . ," and "My spirit is . . ." Be sure to reach a deep level with the patient before engaging such general issues. Avoid philosophical chatter.

Aura exploration.
Aura exploration is a technique that I have developed myself. It is, in addition to a dissociation technique, also an induction technique and a cathartic technique, just as is egostate. Aura exploration is a way to search as well as to treat charges. This method is especially effective as a dissociation technique for physical charges that remain stuck.

As an induction technique, aura exploration is a combination of the imaginative and the somatic bridges. My experience with the following preamble is such that I have never had the tendency to change it. As it stands now, it seems to work perfectly:

T: *Imagine that you are lying down at a place you know well, where you feel completely at home. Imagine that place. Where are you? You are lying there as you are lying here, precisely the same.*
Imagine that you are there alone. It is late in the afternoon, with twilight already beginning, and you are lying relaxed, precisely as you are lying now. If you can imagine that, say yes.
You feel yourself calm, relaxed, slow. You feel no urge to rise. You are lying nicely and it becomes slowly dark. The twilight darkens and you feel yourself become calmer and slower. You see the twilight darkening until you hardly can see anything anymore. If you can see that, say yes.
Now you fall asleep. You fall asleep and the next thing you notice, is that somehow you are outside your body, and you vaguely see your body lying in the dark. If you can see that, say yes.
In that dark you see now coming some light, a soft glow around your lying body. If you can see that, tell me what kind of color it has.
P: *Yellowish. (For example.)*
T: *Excellent. You see a yellowish glow around your lying body. Now that light grows stronger, especially at one spot. Your attention is drawn toward that particular spot at your body. Your attention is drawn to a spot where the light is strongest. Where is that spot?*
P: *At my head, especially at my temples.*
T: *Now you will see something in the yellow light that is related to . . . [the start]. You are observing intently, with full attention, like a doctor or a nurse. What shows itself in that light?*

What patients see can be very diverse: a dark spot, a hole, a wound or injury, a deviating color, a symbol, a thing, a stone or a metal object, a person or a complete image. The standard questions are similar as those used with egostates.

T: *Does it belong to you? Does it have to remain there? When did it arrive there? How did it arrive there? Why did it arrive there? How does it make you feel?*

In responding to these questions - one by one, of course - the patient usually enters naturally into regression. Otherwise, we need to ask for the accompanying emotion and then do a common regression induction: "Go back to the moment that this came there and you felt this way."
If what is seen is painful or threatening in any way, first have

them remove it, clean and heal any remaining wound or scar, and only then have them go to the moment when this thing or energy or whatever it is, entered them. Be careful with anything living: rarely plants, often animals or vermin, sometimes people.

Don't use the word "aura" during the induction. Never say "aura," but talk about a vague light or a glow. I think that this glow has something to do with the etheric body, but that is of no importance. People see what they see. The glow is an effective visualization.

Aura exploration is first an induction technique, a way to get at charges. It is also a way to find solutions, even without regression. You can combine this method perfectly with regression. It is an excellent technique if you are in a hurry.

I call it aura exploration because at first it has this element similar to an aura. But it is independent of a vision or knowledge about the aura as an extrasensory body with chakras, and so on. Indeed, people often see something at classic chakra spots. Sometimes people even perceive structures that resemble chakras, but usually nothing of the kind shows.

Remain strictly within the personal, immediate experience. Never suggest which colors a patient is going to see, but do ask for colors. People may see symbolic objects. Some may feel that they have to remove a church tower from their belly. Others may see a hole, may come closer, look into it and then have the impression that they are tiny and are looking into a huge hole in the ground. Changes of magnitude happen often.

A man who had a sexual deviation and was afraid of being caught by the police needed only one session with aura exploration to resolve his problem. Later he wanted only one more regression so that he could understand where his problem had originated. A regression then provides the insight that aura exploration itself sometimes does not give.

Regression itself is a return to the past, but that is only an expression, because regression is actually the act of reading from the library we carry around with us. In therapy we work on undigested charges that we carry with us. Aura exploration shortcuts these charges.

Aura exploration is an I+S bridge (image + somatic). When an emotion joins these charges, then we have I+E+S, and we can regress on that. If no emotion emerges, but insight does, that insight may still be therapeutic, sometimes even cathartic.

Aura exploration is an enrichment, but can, if you apply it too often and too easily, keep the therapy superficial by neglecting the emotions.

Aura exploration is especially suitable for psychosomatic problems and even for a person's curiosity about the reason for somatic features. Someone has been born, for example, with a red skin spot and wants to know if that birthmark has a reason. Aura exploration is an excellent method to explore that question.

If people can see the glow, but they see nothing particular within that light, then we did not focus well. What was the entry point of the session? If the start is a physical complaint, such as a problem in the back, we let the patient if necessary turn the sleeping body on its belly. Before zooming in, we need a description and location of the physical sensation.

"Look to the spot where that smarting pain in your back is. What do you see there?" Do not ask merely, "Look and see if you see anything." You have to follow patients in regression, but they have to follow you also, as they are working in a way that for them is strange and new. You may lead them, if you lead them only to the points that they have indicated already.

If at the body or in the body the patient sees something that looks sticky or dirty or dangerous, especially when they see some parasite or vermin, then I let them imagine that a silvery white light radiates from their hands. With the right hand (if they are right-handed) that light forms itself into a silvery white metallic glove that protects the hand and the underarm. At the other hand that light forms itself into a thin ray that they can shine into a hole, can use to clean tissues, to disengage something stuck and let everything that does not belong in the body work itself to the outside. They can even focus that light and transform into a laser beam.

If they see a hole, have them shine their ray into the hole. If they see something at the bottom of that hole, they can loosen it with their light and wash it or force it out. If no bottom appears, they have to imagine that they have become very small and enter the dark space themselves, but they can take their lights with them. Once they arrive at some bottom, they usually find themselves in the original traumatic or fateful situation.

If they encounter stones or balls or clods, we let them remove these objects and then cut through them with their laser beam to find out if something is hidden inside. Sometimes there is: treasure, babies, fetuses, pure water, pure energy.

Vermin are destroyed by imagining a kind of furnace, without fire but with the same intense, silvery white energy that now consumes everything. "If there is anything of value in these vermin, it will be released in its original form. All else will be reduced to pure energy."

When we encounter animals or birds or fish, we ask the patients what they want to do with these creatures. Often the best solution is to imagine the natural surroundings of these living things, and return the animals there. Sometimes an animal hides a human intelligence, sometimes an almost demonic energy. We first have to separate the animal from what is inside it, to treat the inside separately.

Aura exploration is very effective and efficient if it is combined with regression, with reliving and understanding causes that lie in the past. Its main drawback is that we may encounter myriads of things, beings and presences, some of which extremely repulsive or frightening. The more psychotic the patient, the more extreme the items that we may encounter. The first challenge is to learn to discriminate between thought forms and real energies; the second is to disentangle clusters and to expose layered realities. The third is to learn how to deal with the discovered and exposed charges.

A terribly disfigured lion may be fearful and almost demonic, but inside may be a frightened boy, a previous life of the patient, who was once eaten by a lion and has surrounded himself by this thought form made from the terror of that situation. Likewise, a salamander may hide the presence of an ancient priest who once bossed a patient so thoroughly that the patient is still dependent on him. When we try to reason with this priest, his eyes may look frightening and he may appear to have been or still be obsessed.

Convince yourself that by the time the session ends, objects or parasites will indeed be gone. Use images that confirm this result, for example by having the patient see and hear that an item really falls away. A metal object rattles along a rock precipice or splashes into a body of water.

Working with aura exploration is an art that can be learned only by practice in actually doing it. Be careful when you enter this field and be certain that you are still doing your own work on your own issues. This warning is not to discourage you, but aura exploration may wake up evil, and you should either avoid that or be prepared for it.

Aura exploration is especially suitable for hangovers, because with common bridges you often have difficulty in getting at the most pressing charges. Aura exploration locates and contours any vague charges that are present. For traumas, aura exploration may be superfluous, because we can usually reach traumas more directly. We can also use aura exploration effectively to tap hidden or half-sleeping talents and to learn what covers these talents.

Aura exploration also works well with physical pain, especially with local pain, and if the pain is not so intense that the patient will need to dissociate during the session. Some have found that aura exploration works well with cancer patients.

Do aura exploration if a regression has resulted in partial relief but no catharsis. People may have had tiring lives. Perhaps they have gained insight into those lives and much of their old weariness has gone, but they may report: *Only my pelvis is still stiff.* Use aura exploration to go to the pelvis, look at what is there and remove that drabness or hardness from the past. This approach is not renovation, because you project the problem not into the past, but into the present: "It is now in your body, and we are going to remove it now."

If the preceding session has been conducted appropriately, this remaining problem will be easy to remove. Insight and liberation occurred already, but that etheric drag or knot remained. This remainder is what you clean. After cleaning, we let the patient again look back at the earlier lifetime to discover new things.

Someone may have experienced a suffocating, monotonous lifetime. The remnants of that lifetime are resolved by using aura exploration, and the patient looks back once more at that earlier life. "What do you note now?" *I had a pet horse*, or *I never realized that my mother loved me. But she didn't dare to show it, I see now, because she already knew that daddy wanted to sell me.* Then tears may begin to flow and the session gets an afterbirth.

Use aura exploration with traumatic situations that contain confusion and misunderstanding, mental pressure or loss of consciousness. If during a regression someone enters an episode of confusion, ask about that confusion's consequences "that still are with you today." You remove these consequences with an aura exploration, element after element. After the aura exploration you follow up with a general regression so that the patient understands the how and why. Move back once more to oversee everything calmly, to bring the patient's mind to rest.

An alternative is to do an aura exploration of the traumatic moment, or of a moment when a regression got stuck. Stop the action and let everything become completely dark until a glow surrounds the patient's body and, if necessary, a glow also surrounds the body of the main adversary. Then have the patient look into that glow to see what happens mentally and emotionally. This process offers instant clairvoyance to the patient, and that is three times better (and cheaper) than chronic clairvoyance of the therapist.

During a regression we can always switch to aura exploration if there is only an E+S, as we need a somatic for aura exploration, and an emotion to maintain contact with the experience, so we can switch between the present mode of the aura exploration (locating charges spatially in or at the body) and the past mode of the regression.

Egostates.
The basic technique for working with egostates starts with letting patients imagine a pleasant spot where they feel at home. Once they have settled in that spot, have them imagine that another person arrives. That other person exemplifies the problem that is in question, or causes the problem, or can solve the problem. The person who arrives has to be imagined concretely.

Have the patient get a first impression: a man or a woman, young or old, strong or weak, dark or light. The important element is eye contact and an impression of the mood of that person. Then communication begins.

The patient's first question should be, *When did you come to me?* The second question is, *Why have you come to me?* Often a third question is, *What do you want?* If the arriving person had ever been inside the patient's body, where particularly? We accompany the conversation. Sometimes we may address the arriving person, this subpersonality, directly. Always address the subpersonality as a real person!

We may evoke other subpersonalities. We may ask if there is someone "over there" with the same problem, or someone who can solve the problem.

Egostates provide a forceful disentanglement technique. We may use this technique when people experience some inner conflict or ambivalence. People may see something horrible that at the same time fascinates; they may feel guilty doing something that they like to do; they simply feel blocked. This kind of conflict shows ambivalence. If people talk hesitatingly about their problem, or seem divided within themselves, such ambivalence is already a reason to work with egostates.

Addictions are also suitable for egostates, although sometimes aura exploration is more effective. Have the most addicted part arrive. You may continue with the part that most resists the addiction, the part that is afraid of the addiction, and the part that doesn't care about the addiction. Finally, there may be a part that can help to solve the addiction.

If people feel inferior, using egostates helps them to take some distance, but the real application of egostates is for problems of conflict and ambivalence. In the first case, egostate provides a technique for creating distance. In the second case it offers a response to ambivalence and conflict. After using egostates to resolve ambivalence and conflict, it is necessary to integrate again.

Dissociation is a powerful principle, so egostate therapy is a great and important technique, and for the same reason aura exploration is usually very effective. First we dissociate, then we address each personality as a responsible and respectable complete person. Never ask for good and bad egostates.
Avoid morally defined subpersonalities. Avoid superior and inferior subpersonalities. If we label them, their labels should be respectable. They all belong, they all are part of our integrity. People who carry a strong inner "Parent," with a strong ideal of how they should be, tend to repress whatever inclinations conflict with the ideal. That response sometimes works paradoxically, for example with the strong norm: *I need to be more integrated.* Then one tends to repress the parts that block integration.

The examples of Edelstien show that a part that interferes always does so for a reason, with good intentions, despite any maladjusted elaboration. We see the same with the subpersonalities of Sybil, who became evident when the main personality collapsed.

We may push parts of ourselves away into the subconscious. They may be parts of which we are ashamed, or parts that had been too sensitive to cope with some situation. By contrast, they may be active parts that withdrew because we gave up. Such

199

parts remain hidden in the body or in the aura, or may hang around somewhere else.

Our use of egostates is one stage more complex or fundamental, because we include subpersonalities who are not parts of our present personality, but were personalities of past lives.

If, for example, we are dealing with rebelliousness, we invite the most rebellious part to arrive. A woman enters. The patient associates her with "the whore of Babylon." She is rebellious, she is energetic. What energy that person has! *She looks fierce.* "Okay, but what is her basic feeling?" *Revenge!* So she is rebellious from revenge.

Egostate is one of the most powerful therapies imaginable, but we have to realize that we hardly know what we are doing. When we deal with inner realities of the mind, what happens in reality? What happens etherically? Treat each subpersonality as a real person. Egostates are never constructs. We do not label them as the Smoker, the Rebel, the Coward, the Pleasing Child. Whatever the trigger, whoever enters is treated as a full person, unless that person itself says otherwise. Play it safe.

Working precisely and carefully with the material of the patient is not only necessary, but it's enough. Theoretical constructs do not cure patients; they merely satisfy therapists, and they may contribute to general psychological understanding. But they do not belong in the therapy session. Patients who have knowledge of such constructs may get more trouble than benefit from them.

What if a crowd of subpersonalities appears? In such case we have forgotten to define the entry point, which should be a well-defined topic. When the patient experiences the arrival of several subpersonalities that hinder or prejudice one another, address them one after the other, and ask them if they want to talk directly with one another. If they want to, but don't succeed, we may ask them, "Do you want to talk with someone else?" Sometimes a more inclusive personality enters.

Sometimes we may encounter an intruder such as the "Avenger" that Edelstien described. Even if what arrives are attachments, my first choice is not to unseat anyone, but to treat all of them with consideration. If we learn that one who arrives is a hiker or squatter, we can remove him or her. But people should not be removed, they should remove themselves. Our first responsibility is to the patients who come to us, and we stick to that responsibility. More about this subject appears in the chapter on attachments and obsessors. Luckily, humanity is not the enemy of effectiveness. There is nothing as effective as treating people like people.

Again, use egostate as you would use aura exploration. Use it when associative methods don't work because there is no charge with which to work, or when one of the charges is a complicator. Especially with mental charges, dissociative techniques work more effectively. Use egostates particularly with ambivalences.

With people who tend to intellectualize, find the "controller" and ask how and why it operates. Convince this controller that we accept its good intentions, but we think that its modus operandi is counterproductive. Or we may find that the patient has an ardently jealous part, but that part has an origin, a reason. When and how was it born? "Jealous Minny" may say, for example, *I felt that if I did not intervene, that son-of-a-bitch would take advantage of her.* Jealousy is an emotion. Like all emotions, it is dangerous. It may get the better of us. But any emotion is a sign of life. It may be a twisted sign of life. But twists are invitations to be de-twisted.

Although a particular reaction may be premature or ill-considered or negative, any reaction is at least understandable. Never disqualify subpersonalities. Subpersonalities are just like people. When we attempt to disqualify people, they hedge themselves against change.

Any attempt at dissociation from these subpersonalities, and then repression of them, will only worsen the problem. Instead, help subpersonalities to make their repertory constructive, for example by using better timing or a more differentiated judgment. Begin to make clear that these subpersonalities once started with good intentions. Be curious, show interest: "How did you come about?" After acceptance we can do business.

Typical for Sybil was that many of her subpersonalities were stronger than Sybil herself, but Sybil remained the real, the root personality. Each time Sybil collapsed, from the reservoir of her soul emerged a part to help: *Look what they are doing to my little one! I have to interfere.* Sybil shrunk ever more, because parts from her became independent. But she remained the center to which everyone had to return.

Many subpersonalities are born from a character postulate as reaction to a trauma. Many are mobilizations. I gave the example of that girl of sixteen who is about to be raped. Suddenly there emerges a businesslike madame who makes that fellow slink off. In this case a past person suddenly takes over. Why was that past person not present before? Because she could not yet work, there was no employment for her.

Complete integration of all personalities is a delusion. When we are incarnate, not everything is simultaneously relevant. Integration is an ideal in the sense that when integrated, everything is accessible and open, and that there is harmony and communication. To be complete in the here and now may be possible for poor souls, but it is deadly for rich souls. The appropriate holistic approach is to accept that at any one time, some parts are awake while others dream and still others sleep. We may have moments of total awakening, but not too many and not too often. Don't stop your evolution by relying on marvellous short circuits.

Whatever is present within us, some day there might be more. Whoever we are, some day we will be more than we are now. The imperfect is the womb of the perfect. There is no other womb.

Simple acupressure: back pressing.
Undigested charges can be found in tensions in our muscles, especially of the back. We look for psychologically caused, local muscle tensions. We seek points of tension by pressing with our fingers or thumbs. Then those undigested charges emerge in the form of feelings and images. Back pressing is especially suitable for hangovers that carry somatic charges. Possibly other parts of the body are also fit for acupressure, although only with medical and physiological knowledge would I press on soft parts. Of course, avoid doing this with patients who have back problems.

The harvest from a back-pressing session vitalizes the patient. When we remove tenacious charges, however, the effort itself may be tiring. I think that acupressure may also be used for immediate hangovers in daily life. If you come home exhausted you can, by back-pressing find the right button. It hurts for a moment, but then the weariness is gone.

We seek such a spot with the tops of our index fingers. Keep your fingernails short! I use pressure only on the back, although we sometimes have to move to the buttocks. That is annoying, because on the buttocks we have to press hard to hit the sensitive spot. The side and front of the chest may also work well, however.

Begin in the neck. Slowly move the fingers down along both sides of the spine, and then up again somewhat further from the spine. Continue until the patient reports that you have touched a sensitive spot. Move your fingertips in the immediate surroundings until you have found the most sensitive point, the real hot spot. I do not reckon with any standard meaning of a spot. I am only interested in the content of the experience. When we have found the pain point, it may feel like a pea or a ridge. When we press firmly, much physical energy is released. We ask for the patient's emotions and images and thoughts during this release. The patient enters a mini-regression, anchored by our pressing of the sensitive spot. For pressing hard I use my thumbs, and if the spot is great, an elbow. You can do it on yourself with your thumbs, although that is more difficult and you can reach only few spots.

When we press, we ask the patient what kind of feeling that pressure gives. The feeling is usually annoying, but with what specifically does the patient associate that annoyance? Emotion may emerge after the association *I get angry*. We have created a somatic and we seek the corresponding emotion and preferably an imagination or a word. The association may suggest an imagination: *a dark forest* or a postulate *I hate those bitch*es. That is enough for regression.

While we press firmly, we count back and the patient begins to perceive a situation that caused this tension or pain. Once the original trauma becomes clear, the patient has to breathe consciously and deeply against all pressure. The least tiring technique for the therapist is to keep the arm straight during pressing. An alternative is to press with the point of your elbow, although then you may miss the sensitivity of the thumb.

Using this technique to deal with problems from the present life, we may especially resolve residue of hangovers, problems with which the patient had lived for a long time; traumas emerge less easily. The same is true for past lives, especially tenacious, slow, prolonged situations. For example, slavery or prolonged sexual abuse are often found low in the back. With acupressure we harvest things other than what emerges with common regressions.

Sometimes the patient's consciousness diminishes when we press. People may nearly faint because we restimulate an experience that had involved unconsciousness, hypnosis, or drug use. Don't then pull someone back to the present, as this loss of consciousness is part of the regression. In some ways it resembles a simple yawning during regression. We call that a "boil-off," the evaporation of pieces of unconsciousness. Remain talking during a boil-off: "Let it just go through you. You do not know precisely what happens, but move right through it."

Often I help releasing the last tensions by tapping very quickly or by pressing rhythmically on the spot. When the catharsis has been appropriate, the pain disappears. You can press as hard as you want, and the patient only smiles. I finish by softly rubbing the red spot. The patient should feel all right now.

Homing.
Homing is a simple technique. In homing, we do not ask someone to move to the cause of a problem, but to the prime cause of feeling good, to home. If feelings of alienation, abandonment and isolation are the point of departure, we evoke those negative feelings. We ask where in particular these feelings remain in the body. Then we evoke the thought of "home."

"Now you move back to a situation in which you really completely felt at home. You move back to an environment with others with whom you feel deeply familiar. You move back to a situation of understanding and contact. You move back, always further back, until you reach a situation in which you felt completely at home."

We explore and anchor the resulting experience. Finally, we let the patient be there and here at the same time. They will feel or re-establish the link. They feel that link in their own body. A successful homing may be emotionally calm, but is always energetically intense.

A homing usually belongs in a series of sessions. Sometimes it is a crowning, sometimes an intermezzo that mobilizes energy to enter a new problem area. When feelings of alienation and isolation are uppermost, homing is a real hit: an explosive regeneration. The crux always consists of bringing the experience back to the here and now, and elaborating its practical consequences; otherwise the experience remains a moving revelry.

A similar approach is to let the patient contact other experiences of happiness and strength. On our long journey we sometimes succeed in creating new homes, often around us, but always within us.

Netherton sends people to happy lives. He begins usually with: "What is the first word of happiness that comes to mind?" If he sends someone to a happy life and he finds a mixed life, then he considers that the level of mixture suggests how far the therapy has progressed. In exploring happy lives we have to go through the full range of emotion and actions. We go through the death experience to check dramatic material, and because a pleasant death may lessen any remaining fear of death that the patient may have.

Netherton sends them back to a situation in which they were very happy, and asks them what they said to others when they were happy. After this, he lets patients open their eyes and sit right up, and asks them if they ever said the same things to the persons they love now. An excellent closure.

Arm test.

The arm test provides a way to check material: *Is it real? Is it mine? Is my impression right? Is the location in place and time right?*

Patients lie relaxed on their back and we ask them to raise their left arm (a left-handed person would raise the right arm). They concentrate on the image, emotion or thought in question, and state aloud three times the statement to be tested. We press their arm down with our stretched hand at their wrist, while they have to resist our pressure. Their arm going down shows an energy leak related to the question or situation on which the patient concentrated himself. Ask what the patient felt during or immediately after the downward movement of the arm. Pain is often a signal of deep charges. Stop using this method before any weariness sets in. The arm test is part of the Touch for Health method. It is an alternative to finger signals, but is more intense and more conscious. Errol Schubot offers a good variant on the arm test that he somewhat inflatedly calls Creative Source Therapy.

The arm test is especially good for solving identity problems and to strengthening identity. Patients who come to reincarnation therapy often are somewhat more sensitive, and sometimes they even have a measure of clairvoyance. Because of this sensitivity, they may absorb experiences from others. Sometimes they doubt if some experience was theirs. With group regressions the chance for mix-ups is greater still. In such confusion the arm test can bring clarity.

Also with (apparent) parallel incarnations we sometimes encounter mixing up and interchange. The arm test can then answer the question, "Is that your experience or an identification with somebody else?" Take first the statement, *This is my experience.* If the result is negative, take *It was identification with someone else.* If this answer is positive, we may find out with whom, if that question is relevant.

Sensitive people who have vivid imaginations can see images that are projections of fears or wishes or hearsay. Also images of films can sometimes play a role. The arm test is somatic and so works very well for intellectual-minded people with flattened emotions. Other situations for use are:
- *a fading self feeling*
- *feelings of insecurity and obscurity, especially after sessions that are not rightly consolidated*
- *confusion by persistently recurring feelings and thoughts*

If confusion remains, then a preceding aura exploration in combination with the arm test can resolve the issue. Also, the eight questions of LeCron can be answered very well by the arm test.

If we doubt the reality of some experience, we may check in two ways. The first way is to test all possible answers separately. For example:

This farm life was mine.
This farm life wasn't mine.

If the patient keeps an upright arm the first time, but not the second, the answer is clear. The advantage of this method is that four answers are possible. When the experienced life was partially true and partially fantasy, both tests can elicit positive answers. When both get negative answers, there might not have been a farm life at all; the experience may have been fantasy or a psychodrama.

The disadvantage of this method is that after a positive response on the first question, patients know that the second should be answered negatively. This fact may diminish their strength of resistance. Therefore, for most people the best method is to test each alternative only once, taking the positive statement. Keeping the arm upright should mean that something is real, belongs, is to be retained. If patients are almost sure that something is fantasy, still the statement to test is, *That farm life was mine.*

Start the test with simple questions about name and age and place of birth. Take one or two false statements to see and feel what happens. This pretest is helpful for you to feel the amount of resistance a true and a false statement elicits.

As the following example shows, the arm test can be used as an alternative to finger signals, without the need for hypnosis. The stretched, resisting arm and the down-going arm can also become strong somatic anchors. We can ask what patients felt after each single test.

In the example situation, a patient appeared to experience a Celtic life. He doubts if this life, a very real experience in itself, is the same as one he had been dreaming about ten years earlier. Or has his dream influenced his regression experience now? Is the association with the Celts and with Great Britain an intuition to be trusted? His older sister from that life reminds him of a girlfriend he had recently. Is this just an association, or a true identification?

I have lived the life I experienced in this regression. (This is a general test of truth. His arm remains stretched. He feels proud of that, and realizes that in that life he was a proud man also, that he is proud of this proud life, that this life is alive and kicking in his body now. He feels very happy.)

This was a Celtic life. (He resist pressure, but not quite. There is a weary feeling in the arm. Apparently this statement is not one hundred percent true. Why? He suddenly realizes that he travelled when he was young. Maybe he lived among Celts later.)

I lived my adult life among Celts. (Arm remains outstretched. Bingo!)

This was in the present Great Britain. (Arm falls flat, disappointed.)

This was in what now is France. (Arm remains outstretched, but not quite. He feels sudden weariness. Apparently the answer is about right. He feels that he should desist from further location testing now.)

Suzie was my sister in that life. (His arm falls flat. He feels a strange confusion. Maybe she was something else in that life? Maybe she was a sister in an other life?)

Suzie was my sister in another life. (His arm is strong, remains stretched. He feels satisfied. There is no need to explore that now. He realizes that he still cares about her. He wants to ponder this over later.)

Trust the arm, but only as part of the total person. This is not a mechanical oracle. Watch for other feelings, impressions, somatics. Feel the whole. We may instruct so at the beginning: "Trust your arm, but do not concentrate on it. Feel yourself calm and complete, curious, but relaxed. Be."

Choice of methods.
What follows are some arbitrary themes of patients. Seek in each case the most obvious bridge for regression and the most obvious supportive technique:

1. *Someone has suicide thoughts. "I might jump from a building."*
2. *Someone wants to stop smoking.*
3. *A rational person wants to get to her emotions.*
4. *Inability to enter a woman.*
5. *Fear of what people might think.*
6. *Fear of being discovered as a fraud.*
7. *Chronic insomnia.*
8. *Fifteen years not having been oneself.*
9. *Persistent worries.*
10. *"I feel that in fact I am emotionally bankrupt."*
11. *"Why did I come into this life?"*
12. *"I will die at 55."*
13. *"I know the solution already."*
(List your own responses before reading further.)

"I might jump from a building." Begin with the imaginative bridge: "You are about to jump. Just imagine. What is inside you?" *Despair.* Then despair is the basic emotion. We ask where that despair is in the body, and we have E+S.

If no emotion arises, "Imagine, you are up that building and you jump." The imagination then changes into a psychodramatic waking dream. For someone who dares to imagine that, we ask, "What do you see now?" *I see myself lying on the street, all dead. Oh, I have messed up the street!* A fundamental fear that we are bothering other people, troubling other people. Even in death we are bothering others, if only by creating problems with the insurance.

If someone does not dare to imagine this jump from a building, then we use aura exploration: "Where is that fear?" On that fear we zoom in through the emotional bridge. Egostate is also useful: talk with the part that intends to jump from that building, and afterward talk with the main part that opposes it. The verbal bridge is less adequate with suicidal tendencies.

Stop smoking. Difficult for regression, but if you want to try it, then use the verbal bridge. *Smoking is . . .* For example: *unhealthy, bad, nice.* The next harvest is then: *If I smoke, I feel . . . , If I don't smoke, I feel . . . .*
   An egostate would usually be the first choice. During intake discuss the reason someone wants to stop. *It annoys my husband,* or *I am afraid of cancer.* We can follow up these emotions. In egostate we may let the smoker and the non-smoker, the anti-smoker and the one who is scared about cancer, talk with each other.

Rational people want to feel emotions. Clearly, the emotional bridge is out. Then we try as input what we need as output. The reaching of feelings is a difficult goal. In a sense, the question is wrong. Probably we will find schizophrenic tendencies. But if people want that, what do we do? The easiest way to evoke feelings is through imagination. We can ask if they have a partner or children, what kind of feeling they have for these people. Still they may discount that response as unreal feelings. If we would ask: "What is your feeling now?" the reaction would also be, *What I do feel right now is not real feeling.* If someone consciously wants to feel, that person may encounter a taboo on feeling.
   Surely, anybody feels, but people may feel inhibited in allowing themselves to experience and express their emotions. Some feel irritated, but they cannot become really angry, or cry; they can't indulge fully in an emotion. There always remains some control, something dry, something parched. For once they want to be drenched by rain.
   Through the verbal bridge we may find the fundamental postulates. Then we do regressions to lifetimes in which those postulates originated. People may start to understand themselves, while emotional liberation still remains elusive.
   People who cannot indulge in emotions often carry perfection postulates. They may have been prominent clerics, perhaps high priests, bishops or cardinals. Apparently their feeling is locked away. Look to see if their feeling is in the body and where

it might be. We take the somatic bridge if any somatic offers itself. With aura exploration we can do that, too, but emotions may remain purely mental. The most fundamental approach to emotions is through pain. There are always pain experiences that are hidden and that cause tensions in the body. With inaccessible emotions, use the back door: the body. The best bet is acupressure. Find a sensitive spot and press it really hard.

Or talk with the insensitive egostate, and afterward with the locked-away sensitive egostate. The insensitive subpersonality is usually from a past life, a strong personality, prominent, civilized, competent, often cynical. As therapists we have to gain credibility with such a figure. We have to show that perfection blocks further development. "What has happened with you since?" *I was just irritated with all those toddlers around here.* "How much further did you come? How come?"

There are people who have themselves locked in so strongly with a perfection postulate that they rarely communicate. Usually the last emotions that they experienced were very painful, and they have seared up themselves.

Another shutoff command: We have dedicated ourselves unconditionally to another, we trusted that person completely and then we are betrayed. *Never again!* We start to distrust our own judgment. Our emotions may run amok with us and then something terrible may happen. *People are dangerous, people are unpredictable, people injure deeply, from these people I have to shut myself off.* Our self-image involves repression and so forgetfulness. Part of ourselves is locked away.

Acupressure pushes through the resistance. It provides the best access to such repressed material. My first choice is acupressure, my second choice egostate, and my third choice aura exploration.

For the remaining examples, see the list below.

We do not need to deal with postulates by using regression therapy. Regression makes clear how and when and why these postulates were born. With traumas, insight is the crown; with postulates insight is the beginning.

Through our methods, patients explore and heal themselves. Also, we use those supplementary methods in such a way that we leave much to the patient. The temptation to force the patient may thus be somewhat stronger, but we also can force in a regression.

CHOICE OF METHODS

	Bridge	ES	VE	AE	BP
1. Urge to jump off a building	I	2	-	1	-
2. Stop smoking	V	1	3	2	-
3. Rationalist wants emotions	S	-	-	2	1
4. Being unable to enter a woman	I	3	1	2	-
5. Fear what people think of you	E	1	-	2	3
6. Fear of being seen through	E	1	-	2	3
7. Chronic insomnia	V	2	1	3	-
8. Fifteen years not being oneself	V	1	3	2	-
9. Persistent worries	V	1	2	-	-
10. Hidden emotional bankruptcy	E	1	2	-	-
11. Why did I come into this life?	I	2	1	-	-
12. I will die at 55.	V	2	1	3	-
13. I know the solution already.	V	1	-	3	2

Regression itself remains the most fundamental technique, because it involves the fewest tricks. These other methods are tricks to get at something, but regression remains the most straightforward procedure imaginable: "Do you have trouble with something? Let us see how it came about."

Finally, I want to say something about general cleansing. I prefer directed cleansing; I prefer to deal with what is on top. However, if people have worked through their major problems, they may feel a sincere interest in a general check-up. How do we go about that?

First, remember or find out which methods work well with this patient. Start with the most congenial methods and finish with the least congenial methods. You could choose the methods by the arm test.

Generally, I would work from the body upward. We could start by back pressing without an entry point, just exploring the back again and again, until no more sensitive points can be found. Take any somatic as a somatic bridge.

Then use the imaginative trips from Chapter 11 to identify attachments and pseudo-obsessions, then traumas and then hangovers. Continue with open aura exploration.

Finish with verbal exploration. Explore loops and postulates or enter into regressions.

Then you may shift into a different gear altogether. Instruct the patient to go back to the earliest lifetime that is directly involved in the present life. Go to the death experience and from there to the next birth experience. Continue with snapshots from the consecutive lifetimes, concentrating always on birth and death, to gain an overall picture of the most recent incarnations. Find the *Gestalt*.

At the end go to the beginning by homing. The rest lies in being here.

CHAPTER 8. WORKING WITH SOULS

If we experience repercussions from previous lifetimes, and if we can access previous lifetimes, something continuous remains after death. Something goes on, even without a body. Let's call that something the "soul." For a large part of our work the precise nature of the soul, its non-physical reality, is not too important; regression therapy works.

We enter the non-physical reality when we find that for therapy it is essential to work with experiences that occurred after death and before birth. We have found that fact to be true with pseudo-obsessions. We find the same when, in working with egostates or with aura exploration, we encounter non-physical realities that appear to come from outside of the patient. The usual parlance is to speak about energies. A more precise indication would be to speak about etheric realities. The etheric body has partially been explored by Robert Crookall as "the vehicle of vitality." Other explorers have been Karl von Reichenbach, Wilhelm Reich, Nicola Tesla, and the modern investigators of meridians, bio-electric fields, etc. The classic Indian concepts of aura, chakras, kundalini and prana belong to the same area. This book speaks about charges, and my growing conviction is that those are etheric charges.

Often a distinction is made between mental processes that are free and noncommittal, and emotional processes that charge otherwise neutral thoughts. That distinction is a misconception. The real difference is not between intellectual and emotional reality, but between psychological and etheric reality.

Some thoughts are free, while others are charged. These charged thoughts are postulates. A charged thought is no longer flexible; it has some kind of independent reality. Why can affirmations change lives, while many thoughts, however repeated, remain idle? Positive thinking works; when thoughts become charged, they become an etheric reality.

Some feelings have no permanent reality, while others do. There is the difference between infatuation and love. Some emotions are fleeting realities, and other emotions have some kind of permanence. The angry reaction to some present frustration differs from anger that remains as a power.

Some people believe that symbols determine our life. For other people, symbols are shallow conventions that are of historical or cultural interest at most. The difference again is between charged, energized symbols that have etheric reality, and those symbols that are only conventions.

When during a session we encounter energies that appear to come from others those energetic realities have very different qualities. The simplest are those from people we know or have known: parents and siblings, husbands or wives, other family members. Sometimes we even find energies from strangers. One example would be the intense jealousy of someone who has been watching us in a sidewalk cafe.

Attached energies from a father may remain after the father's death. These energies may be so strong that they become almost a real presence. The presence reacts as a being with intelligence and volition. We can communicate with it. Some presences are deceased people whom we never met, people who have joined us without us (and sometimes without them) realizing it.

Once I considered all this energy business to be fairy-tale stuff. Now, however, I do not think one can do deep healing without also considering this subject.

Finally, some problems appear to stretch through lifetimes, into a person's first incarnation on this planet, and even earlier. Character problems, strengths and weaknesses, and interests between people, differ deeply. We find different patterns because of different soul histories. Those histories differ right from the beginning. Human souls apparently come in different kinds, in different families.

This chapter is about the least understood and most controversial aspects of our work. I include these subjects with some reservations, as they may prejudice the sensitive credibility of our craft. While I include them with some reservations, I do so without real doubts. Our reference group does not consist merely of colleagues but also of clients. We come across all of this material in practical therapy with real people.

Attachments. Obsessions. Releasing attached energies and attached spirits.

Attachments are energies and projected subpersonalities from living people or from presences of deceased people. Usually these attachments are disturbing, often parasitic. Aggressive attachments are those that we call obsessions. Obsessors we encounter often, especially in cases that are heavy or complicated or persistent, with problems of both mind and body.

But attachments are the rule. Let us start with obsessions as being the more aggressive. Strong indications for obsessions are:

- *SUDDEN PERSONALITY CHANGES: in intelligence, character, behavior or appearance*
- *PHYSICAL CHANGES: extreme strength, epileptic attacks, catatonic symptoms, voice difference and numbness to pain*
- *MENTAL CHANGES, such as sudden comprehension of and speaking in foreign languages*

The best short introduction on the subject is the article by William Baldwin (1983). He gives several symptoms to watch out for and several practical possibilities for diagnosis and therapy. He says, "Recurring or persistent body sensations with no medical cause are suspect, especially if the feeling or sensation changes or moves around within the body while the client is in altered state." I have found the same, although pseudo-obsessions exhibit similar symptoms.

Winafred Lucas gives the following indications for obsession: strong decrease of the energy level, chronic fatigue and general physical complaints. Often symptoms begin after the sudden death of someone the patient knew. Edith Fiore sometimes diagnoses an obsessor by anachronisms in a regression. Someone, for instance, looks at a black-and-white television set in a previous life, while the patient is already in his forties.

An intruder may even take over the driver's seat, in possession. Possession results in complete personality changes. The Brazilians, in particular Ferreira, offer spectacular examples of possession. Exorcism in the Middle Ages and the Renaissance present the same picture. The manifold statements by obsessors that they had lived before, were regarded as sowing doubt by the Devil himself. The clergy who tried to exorcise those "devils" often became possessed themselves.

At Loudon in the 17th century a young nun in the convent became possessed, and soon more nuns suffered the same symptoms. During fits they changed into screaming shrews who rolled frantically on the floor, banged their heads against the wall and swore like troopers. Several church authorities who concerned themselves with the problem ("Out with you Satan!") met with death. The French mystic Surin got the obsessors out

215

of the convent, but during twenty years the good man was ravaged by several entities.

According to Allan Kardec, the spiritual strength needed to deal with an aggressive and stubborn obsessor is usually too much for one person. He suggests that five or six dedicated spiritists should work in this type of problem together.

Calm and knowledgeable therapists can deal with every obsessor if patients are on their side. Whenever you feel any doubt, or when the patient is young, frightened or psychotic, call in a helper. If you cannot use the patient to perceive the obsessor and communicate with it, you need a sensitive.

Most obsessors are undead: they died but they lingered on. Why do souls remain earthbound? There are as many answers as there are emotions. Nearly all human emotions can make a soul earthbound. Many are tied to a particular desire, whether for sex or for peanut butter. They often incite living people to fulfill those desires. Piggybacking on living people gives these obsessors a fake satisfaction.

Obsessors are either maniacs or simply perplexed. For instance, a girl dies during a bombing raid. She doesn't realize she is dead and keeps calling for her mother.

Kardec mentions a miser who keeps an eye on his possessions. Often the obsessor is imprisoned in a "frozen" moment, an experience, or a state of mind that has frozen and become timeless. A dead farmer lingers on to see if his successor on the farm does well. The spirit of another farmer who had hanged himself bothered the family that later lived in his house. When he emerged during a session, he complained of the pain in his neck. The therapist's remark that now the rope could be taken away made him exclaim, *But then I will fall to pieces!* The farm had already been rebuilt and that particular beam no longer existed, but in his mind he still hung there.

Why should we bother? Why not leave it to guides? When the farmer who hanged himself was asked whether he had seen lights or figures, he reacted, *You don't mean those ghosts that flutter around me all the time, do you?* He saw these guides as creepy, shining ghosts. To earthbound souls such as the farmer, incarnate people are more credible.

In another example, a Brazilian physician meets resistance in an obsessor. The obsessor shows him the filthy prison where he had died of starvation with his family: *In his previous life your client did that to me and you want me to forgive him just like that?*

Attachments may be deceased beings who are attracted in a moment of weakness, strong emotion or strongly negative mood, by a similar disposition. Usually these emotions are charges that have been acquired from other people who carry undissolved emotions, negative thoughts and other diffuse charges.

The difference between obsession and pseudo-obsession is seldom clear all at once. The intensity of the patient's complaint is not decisive enough to make this difference clear. Active obsessors call up the most serious symptoms; from waking up exhausted to confusion and suicidal tendencies. Pseudo-obsessions, also, can lead to serious phobias or neuroses, while a passive obsessor may cause mild symptoms. A strong pseudo-obsessor can, just as an obsessor, attract other obsessors. This situation can be confusing.

Hearing voices or seeing faces are sometimes clues. Even smells can be clues. Someone, for instance, often smells something unpleasant, *like a shabby street bum.* One patient repeatedly saw a figure dressed in black who was trying to hide behind him. When the obsession symptoms lessened, he would see this figure with his wife or his children. Obsessors can switch. So, when treating obsession, we should know what we are doing. Removing an aggressive obsessor against its will may thwart us in therapy and in our life.

An investigation in Brazil concluded that sixty percent of the obsessors had karmic, personal reasons, and forty percent were driven by general hate for people. Talking with such obsessors we may hear, *I already got sixteen, and her I'll get as well.* They're at it for two hundred years, and they will persist until they have the next one. The best outcome is that the obsessor achieves catharsis, and then we treat two in one.

Often obsessors acquired a deep hate for people from some horrible experiences of their own. Perhaps they were abandoned, tortured and killed. That hate for people makes them grab blindly anyone they can get. There does not have to be anything karmic involved.

An obsessor can attract several others. The others are usually passive, attracted by accident, and often leave just like that when the leader leaves. Meanwhile they worsen the patient's complaints considerably.

There are pseudo-obsessors and obsessors who intend well but are still disturbing, for example, "sentimental hangers."

From an early age, a boy has a girl hanging around him, sadly in love with him. *Why did you do that to me, lover boy, to go down without me?* Because of that obsession, the boy develops slowly, and perhaps doesn't care for girls. The result can be homosexuality or pederasty. Such hangers-on (we meet those girls in the flesh, too), vague and wrung out, work like obsessors. Also a pseudo-obsessor can be a pathetic lingerer, an unintentional killjoy.

Treating obsessions is methodically simple, but is not for the weak of heart. Personal integrity of the therapist is essential. If there is one aspect of past-life therapy that requires learning from an experienced professional, this is it. Whatever follows here is mere introduction. Every therapist needs a basic understanding of this subject to be able to spot intruding energies and intruding minds in the microcosm of our patients.

When we doubt if a charge is from the patient himself, we dissociate the charge by using egostates. We let the patient imagine arrival of the carrier of the charge, and see that charge in the eyes. When the egostate does not want to show itself, when they avert their face or have an invisible face, it is usually an attachment, sometimes stronger - an obsessor.

Doing a regression with the obsessor (or the pseudo-obsessor) already produces a relief. Look for some pleasant episode in the last life of the obsessor. This approach breaks the lock, the self-hypnosis of the obsessor. What works well, also, is to ask them who they last loved, or with whom they felt at home. Then we ask, "Where is that person now?" That question also springs the locks of the negative emotion.

People are indestructible; they must be somewhere. Perhaps they are waiting right now; perhaps they live again elsewhere. *She died.* "Yes, I know, but where is she now?" When we say that with conviction, something starts to shift. Sometimes people nearly run away and may come back some weeks later. Suddenly we feel a radiant presence. *I found her. I have seen where she is, it is all right,* or, *Here she is.*

Finally, when obsessors refuse to talk to the patient, let them talk with you. When they refuse that too, Netherton says, "Right now you are part of the unconscious of the patient, and as long as you stay there, you do exactly as I tell you. You cannot shut yourself off from what I say to you. You hear me and you answer me." Netherton is a street fighter, and sometimes that is an excellent quality in a therapist.

Usually it is not promptly clear what the patient is facing. Therefore go calmly and methodically through the following steps:

1. Establish eye contact. When that does not work, ask the obsessor why it avoids this eye contact. Accepting the reason often helps, but if necessary force eye contact. We always have access to one who has access to us!
2. Let the patient say what the eyes express. What are the basic charges? What mood is that person in?
3. Ask the obsessor if it is happy. This is never the case. Acknowledging this truth makes communication with pitiful figures easier and diminishes fear of possibly evil figures.
4. Let the patient ask - keeping the eye contact - "When did you come to me?"
5. Let the patient ask then, "Why did you come to me?" Does the entity realize it died?
6. When the answers show that the obsessor is someone else, we let the patient feel where the charge of this other person got stuck in his or her body. Then we let the remaining charge from the whole body be sent back across that point to the carrier.
7. Ask the obsessor if on their own accord they can reach people with whom they feel at home. If not, ask, "Who was the last person you loved?" If necessary force a regression. "Where is that person now?" Call up that person, or someone who knows the way to that person. Take leave, and close the spot where the charge came out.

Suicidal people may have a pseudo-obsession, but more often they have an obsession. With a suicidal patient we do an egostate. Then often the subpersonality appears to be an intruder. With suicidal tendencies, a patient is already divided against himself, and that division always suggests egostate therapy.

It is a past personality, not the whole soul, that keeps lingering about. Now one part of the patient is shut off, cannot be reached. The patient comes back, but part of him stays in that black pit or in that tomb. Usually, the present personality may feel a strange passivity, but when the previous traumatic experience is restimulated, a psychotic episode can occur.

Why do people remain stuck after death? Often they hear a shutoff command, either from another or from themselves.

When this shutoff command is from themselves, it may relate to guilt or fear. But often it is from others. Priests may ritually kill people while indoctrinating them, threatening, "You will never find the way to the gates of heaven. You will be eternally doomed." With people who are out of their minds, that threat registers, so they will enter a dark, hell-like condition.

Or, in another example, a king is going to die. The thought that his beautiful young mistresses will go to other men is unbearable for him. So he lets the ladies be placed beside him in a tomb. Religion, reinforced with drugs or hypnosis, keeps them quiet, so they meet their destiny bravely. Similarly, hypnosis locks people in. Let's look at a further example:

> *In an Indian civilization in Central America, priests are training boys. During a selection ritual the boys are singing in a circle and one by one they are taken away. Now and then those who stay behind hear a boy screaming and yelling.*
>
> *The screaming comes from a nearby site where, one at a time, boys are held by their feet over a deep black pit, while the high priest (who plays God for a change), looks on behind a big mask. The priest looks to see whether each boy is frightened. Those who remain composed are selected and later may wear a mask themselves. Some boys are dropped, particularly those already found wanting or self-willed during training.*
>
> *One of those difficult boys is dropped and smashes into the bottom of the pit. Unfortunately he does not die straight away. For hours he hears moaning around him, and it takes him almost three days to die. In the regression it appears that it has taken him 700 years before he has drifted out of the mountain by accident and seen incredibly blinding green. Here catharsis became possible without renovation, because he drifted out by accident and no postulates were registered, postulates such as, "You belong in the underworld, you will never come out." When there had been shutoff commands, he might have lingered on even longer.*

Sometimes people have to use their frightening presence to guard something after their death. That practice is plain black magic. The worst occurs when people are tortured to death and are given posthypnotic suggestions. They are told that after death they must frighten other people and make them ill. That kind of suggestion ruins a soul. The soul becomes locked, and on top of that it is instructed to ruin others. People may make souls vicious, as they can make dogs vicious.

People who have pseudo-obsessors that are lying in tombs or graves are often dulled, as if they have a part they cannot reach. In a regression that part is also hard to reach, but once you succeed, then never let go. When you do get through, people bloom miraculously.

Ask the pseudo-obsessor to come out of the tomb. When they can do that, great. Often they cannot manage immediately: *When I leave the tomb, I arrive in an underworld with bloodthirsty crocodiles.* That notion is a hypnotic suggestion or self-made fear image. When there has been a curse, the fear of the people who did this to the pseudo-obsessor may return. Then our job is not yet finished.

Let the pseudo-obsessor see a light around them. When they cannot manage, ask, "What keeps you here?" *An influence holds me.* "Go to the cause of that influence." We ask clients to see who gave the command. Sometimes priests are obsessors, not through their presence but through their power. Maybe somehow these priests can wake up, wherever they are now. The confrontation that occurs next may be so intense that it feels like a real presence.

Do not let yourself be impressed when a furious god appears; it is the façade of high priests or other self-styled giants who do not dare to show their face. Always let them look you in the eyes. What do the eyes express? Drop the rest.

Usually those are human eyes, sometimes animal eyes, and occasionally these eyes become glassy or empty holes. Then the presence is purely a thought image. What first appeared to be a god often shows itself to be a priest, still strong, but now of human proportions. People who enlarge themselves obviously do not have enough self-confidence to go without imposing rigmarole. Make that clear.

Don't protect patients by putting a white light around them or anything of that nature. Encourage them, but don't relieve them. Help them to overcome and remove any foreign presence. If need be, call up their wrath as a cool white rage. In self-liberation the magic word is "enough!"

If patients cannot find their own strength, don't give them strength, but ask, "Where is your source?" *Somewhere above my head. It comes through, but it is feeble.* "See how it grows and nears." The return of strength and purpose and love of life is the most beautiful there is. When the patient is exhausted and cannot find the source, do not accept that answer. The source is there. Ever.

Negative attitudes. Evil.
Negative energy is often the corruption of positive energy. Many of us, and many people who come to us, suffer from the consequences of old lives of trying to do good and wielding power. Such people have compassion, but also contempt for the society around them. One day the world is beautiful, and the next day the world is exhausting, chaotic and treacherous. They love people in general, yet they despise many in particular.

People who wield power with good intentions, but with limited insight into why things around here are as they are, become frustrated. They want to ennoble the common people, but sometimes those people have enough of that. We may find regressions into priesthoods, often Egyptian or Mayan or Incan, ultimately Atlantean. Atlantean power combined spiritual authority, social status and political power. That combination corrupted people easily.

When we come to the moon, which has weaker gravity, and we move in the same way as we do here, we bounce to all sides at once. When powerful, evolved souls enter a world where frictions are lower because awareness is lower, they start bouncing around as if walking on a world of lower gravity.

Our constitution is adapted to this planet. When we are pulled along by our own powers, we lose our powers and we have to struggle to win them back. But we then find new qualities, with kinder wisdom. We have to learn to walk on the moon: be subtle, refined, calm, restrain ourselves.

We are not doomed to make serious mistakes, but there is no freedom and self-responsibility without our making at least small mistakes. When we live all-knowing in a world of harmony and safety, we have perfection and enlightenment, like fully aware zombies. Only by washing ashore on our own island, in our own confusing and painful territory, may we find ourselves back as free, creative, responsible people. If we know abandonment and hate, we know love for the first time. Making mistakes may be human, but it is the door to the divine.

The measure in which we err is a measure of stupidity, often self-chosen stupidity, but it is also a measure of inner courage. When we "turn black," when we follow the itch, we may feel intense strength, and we think that being good means being weak and soft. Executioners may despise their victims because they behave like trembling rabbits.

When we commit atrocities in a war, we transgress human nature, we trespass unwritten human laws. We make ourselves into beasts or devils. So we become outcasts, we enter the great darkness, and we will hate people who shuffle along in their petty bourgeois lives. We have one reason to keep our self-respect: at least we have guts. It take guts to become demonic.

Many "initiations" throughout history were aimed at steeling the will by doing or witnessing gruesome things. In one regression a woman finds herself as a man entombed in a small cave with a newborn baby. He had to stay there until the child had died, and to witness the decay of the baby's body. The choice is between going nuts and becoming hard. But this hardness results in loneliness and soon leads to hate toward those who did not or could not pass this test. Then, humiliating and mocking others comes easily, until one day we are accustomed to playing God, or rather the devil. Being hard is not the same as being demonic, but one thing may lead to another, especially when the test to become hard has a demonic inspiration. It is inhuman to sacrifice little children. When we want to steel ourselves, we can find more natural, even noble ways.

Deep down the problem reinforces itself. When we enjoy torturing other people, we build up a self-hate that makes us want to enjoy it ever more, to anaesthetize that hate. Once we have locked into the black spiral, there is no easy way out.

People may hate so intensely that they cannot enter a human body anymore. They can only animate, obsess and destroy living people. Often the cycle is broken long before that point, because their self-hate erupts in self-destruction and they collapse into dark, brooding, guilty states from which they may slowly regain their humanity.

We may feel that cruelty and terror are here to stay. I think that we as humans advance all the time, but slowly and haltingly. Also, we should not mistake historic progress or lack of progress with successful or failing human evolution. Maybe the people who have learned depart, and new immature people enter.

We learn our limitations by making mistakes. Some people are wiser than others. For some, small mistakes are enough, while others need big mistakes. We all have to meet with rebuffs, but we do not all have equally thick skins. Apparently, confrontation with evil has evolutionary value for lazy, sleepy and complacent souls. Don't judge the success of evolution by any actual balance between human and inhuman, but by the net harvest of humane people. And as long as you cannot judge that, don't judge.

We may understand evil not as inevitable, but as a natural consequence and condition of evolution. An evil individual we can always understand. Mengele did not come out of the blue, anti-semitism did not come out of the blue, nothing comes out of the blue. Still it is always necessary to interfere forcefully and in a businesslike way when evil appears.

Even when an average civilization would not have progressed in thousands of years, the evolutionary yield still can be gigantic. Yet, some day it will be enough. Then we really want to make a civilized planet for ourselves. We will have developed so far that we can stifle evil and we can prevent potential criminals and terrorists from coming back. Parents may get criminals for children because they are criminal themselves, or through karma, but mostly because they are unaware of what they attract to themselves. This may change. Eventually we may have a world in which violent crime and terrorism will belong to the past.

Meanwhile, evil is around. Some of it may be inside. Some may have found its way into our system and even if it isn't inside us, the propensity toward it is ever-present.

Various evolutionary patterns.
In past-life therapy we come across people who somehow resist being here. They feel trapped in the body, trapped in this world. They hope that this is their last life on earth. As regression therapists we ask them to go back to the origin of this feeling, and this exercise may lead to experiences about the first incarnation on earth. We usually talk about the primal trauma. Sometimes we also come across experiences that occurred before that first incarnation. Such experiences are very different and appear to be related to themes of further lives.

Apparently, different kinds of souls have different cares, different sensitivities, different self-images, different attitudes, and different primal traumas. That makes a difference for therapy. We can't lump all our clients together. Understanding the different origins of people helps us to accept strange or seemingly weird experiences, to place them and to respond to them. We'll discuss different soul species insofar as they emerge in regressions and insofar as they are therapeutically relevant.

Different origins of individuals as souls give people different lines of experience. I link that difference to the nature of the primal trauma. What is the basic problem of souls who have become human? That they have an I-consciousness? That they have a body with all its limitations? That they are present at only one place at a time? That they have to talk and listen when they are going to communicate, and that something always goes wrong?

If we become human for the first time, we are already accustomed to some aspects of humanity. Other aspects are new for us and again other aspects are a prison for us. Different kinds of souls have different primal problems. That walking is tiresome and that we bridge distances so slowly, or that communication through language is so clumsy and unreliable, are not primal traumas, but primal hangovers. It wasn't very painful to become human, but we can't get used to it.

There was a first time that we received human consciousness. There was a first time in a human body. Those moments can be far apart. There also has been a beginning of ourselves as individual souls. That moment can be much longer ago.

First I will give an overview of what I call main families and subspecies. Then I will characterize each kind, sometimes with examples from therapy sessions. For each family I will give the consequences of therapy. The divisions are into four groups, depending on one's state before the first human life on this Earth, on being self-conscious or not, and on being in a physical body or not.

SOUL FAMILIES

Family 1. Self-conscious, in a physical body: *extraterrestrials*
1.1 Human extraterrestrials
    1.1.1 Visitors
    - Contributors - free
    - Contributors - entangled since
    - For own development
    - With aggressive intentions
    1.1.2 Compulsory arrival: exiled, lost or wrecked
1.2 Non-human extraterrestrials (aliens)
    1.2.1 Visiting aliens
    1.2.2 Lost aliens

Family 2. Self-conscious, without a physical body: *spirits*
2.1 Living on this planet: nature spirits
    2.1.1 Living in and below the ground (dwarf-like)
    2.1.2 Living on the ground (brownish, also house-
        bound spirits)
    2.1.3 Lower nature spirits (above ground and water,
        elf-like)
    2.1.4 Air spirits (high above the ground)
    2.1.5 Site spirits (from below the ground to high in
        the air)
2.2 Living on non-physical planets elsewhere
2.3 Living in a spiritual cosmos
    2.3.1 Gradually waking up in a shining primal soup
        (hatched)
    2.3.2 Part of shining planes and structures (light
        people)
    2.3.3 Individually created (modeled)

Family 3. Not self-conscious, in a physical body: *higher mammals*
3.1 Through general evolution (wild animals)
3.2
    Through personal attachment to people (tame animals)

Family 4. Not self-conscious, without a physical body:
starters

FAMILY 1. *Self-conscious and physical before: extraterrestrial souls*
The first family consists of people who find themselves back in
a physical human body on another planet, in a spacecraft or in
a science-fiction civilization, but not here. They were people
elsewhere, normal people with a head and arms and legs. Sometimes they experience themselves in stranger bodies: heavier,
lighter, bigger or smaller, or with other proportions. Probably
all are related to us; we could mate with them. They resemble
us; perhaps they lack ears or teeth, perhaps they have fewer
toes, perhaps their proportions are different, but they have a
similar body structure.

Today, they are often people who are brilliant, scientifically
minded people who also are cultural, who have liberal arts interests. Or they are interested in science and technology on the
one side, and on the other side in hypnosis, altered states of
consciousness and paranormal things, without feeling any contradiction.

Some people came from elsewhere out of their own free will.
Some didn't come out of free will: they were wrecked, entangled or exiled, for punishment or for education. Others decided
freely to come to this planet. They arrived here in a spacecraft.
After they died here, they were reborn here. Sometimes they
first went back and died on their home planet and were reborn
here. Very rarely, souls from elsewhere are directly born here.

In a session somebody found herself in a dinosaur. She got into
it only temporarily; she could not sustain her presence there.
Then she saw people in silver suits who left a bunker. She be-
longed with them. Apparently she experimented how it felt to
be in a dinosaur. She did not live and evolve as a dinosaur. She
tried to enter, but she already had a human consciousness.

Some feel they have come to a primitive planet, with people
who need help and education. These people feel that they have
come with a sense of mission and are entangled here. They were
wise and could do much and stood so far above normal people
that they gained positions of power and influence. But power
on a primitive planet brings its own problems.

We can be very wise, but each planet presents its own complications. Things that from the outside look easy often appear
more difficult once we are inside. Today, those souls often feel a
great revulsion against this Earth. They see ordinary people as

dumb and dirty and cold and limited and unreliable, etc. Such souls carry no primal trauma, but rather a primal postulate.

Others have come here by accident. In a regression they may see themselves before their first incarnation on Earth, but they see an exploding spacecraft. They are shipwrecked. Still others are exiled here.

Sometimes people find themselves before the first earthly incarnation in a body that has a completely different build. These I call aliens, though that word carries weird associations. These people have no trouble with being in a body, but they have trouble being in a differently organized body. They feel their body to be wrong; they feel like strangers in their body. They are far from home, very far. They feel alienated.

The primal problem of many extraterrestrials is that they got stuck on this planet. What has been their first feeling? Have they arrived on a dirty planet, a dangerous planet, a staggeringly beautiful planet, a primitive planet or a heavy planet?

With people who come from elsewhere, their first story is almost never true. Even the third or the forth story is often not true. Often they are people who have a superiority complex, who still haven't swallowed the reality that they have arrived on such a primitive planet. Dealing with primal postulates is tough stuff.

Seek the emotion that is coupled with remaining on the Earth. That emotion can be impotent rage. The primal trauma is impotent rage that occurred when they were sent or got stuck. Confusion can be attached, as well as despair and incomprehension. Maybe, after a dark, forgotten period, the first they notice is that they are walking around here on Earth.

FAMILY 2. Self-conscious and without a body before: spirits
A second family of souls consists of people who experience themselves before their first incarnation without a physical body, but with an individual, rational consciousness. They know what it is to be oneself, to think about oneself, to feel oneself, to know others and to communicate. Their trauma is not getting stuck in an island-consciousness, but getting stuck in an island-body, in a well-defined animal organism.

Those people tend, if they arrive in the middle of great problems or are under heavy pressure, to leave their body. They dissociate easily. They feel themselves imprisoned in their body. If there is a primal problem, that primal trauma or that primal hangover is to be imprisoned in a human, material body. They perhaps still haven't accepted the need to eat, to defecate and urinate. These activities seem strange and dirty. Their body has other uneasy properties, such as sex. Often they see sex as animal. They find it difficult to make a proper relation with this aspect of being incarnate.

Nature spirits perceive the natural environment, orient themselves in it and perhaps influence it, but they are not material. They come in two kinds: figures who avoid people and figures who seek people, who find us interesting. They live anywhere from in the ground to high above the world. The higher they live, the larger they are, the less circumscribed they are, the more space they assume, the calmer they are and the more individual they are - and the more often we encounter them in past-life therapy.

In and below the ground they live very busily in whole groups. They give the impression of being about 12 to 16 inches high. They are interested in us only when we do something in the ground. Their transition to becoming people seems rare.

On the ground live humanoids who are somewhat bigger, about 20 to 30 inches high. Often these humanoids live in groups, sometimes with a few, and sometimes alone. They are not intelligent, but at most are curious. In human terms they are weakly gifted. If they have an interest in people, they imitate us. They can even become house spirits, and sometimes they appear as personal attachments, but rarely with adults.

Once I encountered a truck spirit, one who joined truck drivers, traveling through half of Europe because it couldn't find its land back. It had once left Ireland with a truck and had never found the way back.

These spirits don't know exactly if they have a sex. If they imitate people, they want that also and they project protuberances on the spot of the sexual parts. In imitating clothes they succeed better.

They often have a hate-love relationship with people. If they avoid people, they don't become born as humans and for us they are of little further interest. Yet, they can sometimes attach themselves on a human and later become human. If they ever become human, it is often out of admiration or personal attachment. They are souls who have inferiority feelings. Their primal postulate is that they are less.

The third species floats above living water, above plants and shrubs, lives in trees or flies over the treetops. We may call them elf-like. These nature spirits are also humanoid, but thinner, transparent and more drifting. They have arms and legs, but keep them vague.

They love living water, small animals, simple things like grass and flowers and insects and birds, and they dally deliciously among all these things. Wind and clouds are important, just as are rain and sunshine. Almost all those souls find it heavy to be in a human body. If they ever attach to people, we get the problem of Andersen's mermaid.

Still higher, we come among the eagles and among the clouds. Here live souls that feel themselves high and clear and imperturbable. They see over the world, and are all mind. If we ask if they are alone, they realize that there are others, but these others are distant. These beings feel related to birds such as eagles.

In therapy, a bird's-eye view is easy for them. They can easily watch events from above. Once I encountered someone who was very good at making maps and atlases - panoramic, spatially and structurally good. They are people who tend to look rather than talk, who are intelligent, but don't like books, and are not very social. Also they can overview histories well. They can be married quietly and be satisfied, and after 15 years discover to their surprise that their partner felt frustrated all those years. It never dawned on them.

All air spirits complain about their heavy body in their first life, and mainly about walking. It takes too long to get from A to B. Before physical life, movement was easier. They mainly have problems with their legs.

A woman had problems with people. To the question of whether she belonged to them, she answered, *Not really.* "Go back to the first time you met people." *Oh, what funny brown dolls!* She experienced herself as big and hardly circumscribed somewhere in the atmosphere over the Pacific:

Deep under her, she sees a beach with moving small dolls. Out of curiosity she comes closer. One doll looks upward, feels her presence and calls something to the others. They bow deeply and throw themselves on the ground, because they feel that she is some goddess. She is surprised; strange that she never saw those before! She comes yet closer and explores where those brown dolls live. Then suddenly - zap, and the next thing she notices is that she is caught in a belly - so small and so dark! Traumatic.

Her first experience with people was not negative, but the second was. Since that experience she has not gotten over the fact that she let herself be sucked in.

Devas are nature spirits who are wide and spacious and associate themselves with a part of the landscape, a valley or a rock. They stretch from deep in the earth to high in the sky. They experience everything that happens in their surroundings. They are slow and deep. There is tremendous power in these souls, but our fast modern life makes them nervous. We live in another frequency; we have another clock.

Many people experience themselves on other planets that are not real planets. Society and natural surroundings look as they do here, but on closer inspection the environment appears to be immaterial. They have no body, but are already accustomed to a human consciousness and a human society. They have few problems here, except that they have a body with all its limitations. It is awkward to have to live with such limited parapsychological functions. Power, influence and communication exist in such worlds, but money and food and drink do not. They are not good cooks. They cannot deal with money. In politics they can succeed and in the church, too. Also, in writing professions they feel at home.

Goldberg was the first to describe "light people." These souls live in a world of shining dots or planes or structures, in a world of geometry and music. They are self-conscious, but not sharply separated as entities. They feel themselves as parts of bigger wholes, of bigger structures that have a kind of collective consciousness.

Their primal trauma is that they have broken away from that bigger structure or become torn away and sent away by stronger beings they call Planners. Independent existence means that their original harmony and links have been broken. They became amputated, not as if their hand had been amputated, but as if they are the amputated hand.

They also find talking and listening awkward. Telepathy is much easier. Before, they were almost as one brain. They discerned themselves, but they did not separate themselves. The way they are isolated and have to communicate here is almost maddening for them.

Others seem to have arrived complete and ready out of the hands of a Creator, their Creator. Many others slowly grew and developed in a shining primal soup and gradually awakened. The first ones seem to have been made by Fathers, and the second ones to have been hatched by Mothers.

FAMILY 3. Not self-conscious and physical before: higher mammals
Some persons in regression see more primitive lives of hunters and gatherers, sometimes in the Stone Age. Several have found themselves in lifetimes before primitive people, in primates, and before that in higher mammals. Though genetically we are much closer to chimpanzees, until now I have encountered almost exclusively gorillas. Monkeys seem to have little affection for people; they seem rarely to cross the line. Regressions into lives as dolphins are rare, but they happen.

These souls had already experienced themselves as physical individuals before they had individual self-consciousness. These souls probably have progressed through the higher mammals, often toward primates, in the normal evolution.

Their primal trauma is that they became imprisoned in a sharp, intellectual, human consciousness. The higher mammals are conscious, but their self-consciousness is vague; they lack intellect. Our thinking self-consciousness is difficult and painful for them, sometimes even maddening.

The first bridge between animals and people is increased brain volume. The other bridge is company with people, as enjoyed by domesticated animals - horses, dogs, sometimes cats.

Why do we rarely get former animals on our couch? First because they have fewer problems with physical life. In the future that number may grow. We may feel at home in a body, but physical survival becomes less important in our society. We have the luxury of mental problems, at least in the western world. For simple souls, mental problems are a great burden. Many problems come from simple souls who do not yet have the required level of refinement, and so come from their strength in their weakness. Second, such souls probably tend to shirk from more mental games such as therapy, and from ideas about non-physical existence.

FAMILY 4. Not self-conscious and not physical before: starters
These are probably the most frequent species of souls, yet we rarely or never get them on our couch. If we get them in past lives at all, they have had but a few such lives. If we regress them to before their first incarnation, we get the same sensa-

tions as they had before birth or after death - only a faint feeling of being around. They somehow know that they exist, but that's all. Before their first incarnation they had no conscious individual existence. This fact gives one the impression that independence and individualism began with their first life as human.

Where do those souls come from? Apparently, they become separated from a general psychic mass, a kind of soul cake. Was this separation achieved by intervention or by natural process? Both might happen. I am far from sure about this. Somewhere a cake is available that can easily be sliced off. Probably many people who are now alive walk around for the first time here, with freshly individualized soul substance. The population explosion puts many immature souls on this world.

From where does that soul cake come? Perhaps it is created, but that is no answer. Probably it is also growing through the physical evolution in plants and animals. Don't ask me how. Almost surely, in part it comes from human souls who weakened or degenerated, who didn't make it. We can ourselves lose or hurt so much and for so long that our soul becomes subcritical, and it no longer survives. The remaining soul substance then goes back into the general fund. Therefore, soul cake is not homogeneous. People who have had no experiences before their first incarnation are still different. Just as marble cake has dark and light patches, soul cake can be mixed.

According to anthroposophists, everyone who has a problem is insufficiently incarnated. That is almost by definition true, but the idea behind it is that humans are spiritual beings. That idea is true only for people who already were self-conscious without a body. Such souls feel better between lives than in lives.

In *Exploring Reincarnation* I described that the function of our body, that living robot, is to develop our self-consciousness. Only after several incarnations do we retain that self-consciousness between death and birth. That fact is true only for the third and forth soul families. Their primal trauma is the shock of self-consciousness, an enormous burden indeed.

People who come from animals have to become accustomed to human life during the intermission. First they will just sleep, later they may remain hanging around after death. We can encounter a deceased who misses coffee, let alone other bodily pleasures. It depends on what we are accustomed to. The last two main families easily become musty during their incarnations, and the first two main families easily become wounded. This difference does not depend on personal responsibility and personal behavior.

These general considerations have concrete consequences. The consequences are not about theoretical anthropology, but about practical therapy.

What is important is to help people to place themselves, to understand themselves. Resolution of the primal trauma means returning one step further to where one is home, and then coupling that home feeling with the here and now. Although we are on this planet, although we are in a body, we feel a link with our origin. Energetically, we do that by finding out where that link is: on the top of our head, on our back or in our heart, and reinforce that link.

Some people feel that they don't belong with their parents. The liberating experience is then to relive what happened just before this life. Something similar can occur on an other level. Why did I become human? How did I get onto this world? Then we explore what feelings are involved, what charges are connected with being for the first time in a human body, or with coming for the first time to this planet.

Those are primal chords we touch. They are "the left hand" of what we do in normal sessions. This plays a heavier theme, resonating through all our lives. Sometimes we hit something that has a thread to the origin. I call that a soul sign.

We work with energies that easily addict. Each therapist who works like a guru and gives people home feelings, touches deep chords. Few people don't know loneliness.

On a different level we may wonder if half a planet, a lower or other civilization, can come here. Perhaps it can. Such a possibility would be demotion or a second change. I don't think there are planets that are much more primitive than ours, though perhaps many are simpler than ours. If you think about the bottom of our society, it is difficult to imagine that a society can be more primitive than ours without murdering itself. We are, I suspect, a mixed planet as there are but few. With divergent souls of divergent levels, everything is mixed. Here it is free-for-all.

People from Atlantis can feel that they came to a primitive planet, but where were they before? They were on other planets or in non-physical worlds. Many experiences are seen as occurring on another planet, while careful questions uncover that it is actually a non-physical reality. People experience themselves in marvelous houses in a beautiful environment, but they transport themselves by thought power.

Atlantis was not the first civilization on this Earth. I think that the first civilized people here were temporary visitors. A temporary colony, an observation post - is that a higher civilization? I have the impression that the first attempts at durable colonization were made in the time of the dinosaurs, but that they failed. I think that traumas are still present from that stage. The first civilization that was numerous, I think, was the Atlantean period. There was a Lemurian age before that, but in Lemuria civilization and barbarism were strangely and fitfully intertwined.

Exploring your origin is not the same as homing. Homing is less committal. With homing you can also just home in on a pleasant life, or even in a pleasant childhood memory. This choice involves going back behind the primal trauma. If the primal trauma is a feeling of being exiled, or being abandoned, being left behind, we treat that feeling therapeutically. We do more than just homing. Where a person comes from is then associated with treason or grief or confusion. There can be guilt feelings attached, etc. Primal regressions provide the deepest healing - that is, if we ground them in the here and now. Otherwise they offer the deepest escapism.

CHAPTER 9. PATIENTS AND THERAPISTS

In therapy two people work together at a contract. With a single and separate starting point, and with some luck and self-confidence, we may gain substantial results in one session. Even with a deep trauma we can achieve a complete catharsis in a session of two or three hours, as long as the problem is an isolated one.

When the problem is part of a bigger picture, try to resolve a definite part of it, even if such resolution is right now only relief or understanding. Get a harvest during each session.

Pacing sessions.
Working three to five sessions on the same theme is normal. Needing only one session is quite common, but seven sessions would be rare. When three sessions have resulted in no significant improvement, stop the therapy. A complex theme can last five sessions. With a general cleaning eight sessions seem to me to be the limit.

Then take a break. Sometimes people come for one problem, and after a session they feel how it helped them. Then the next time, they return with a whole list of things they want treated. They think it is such an "interesting method." *I want to work at this and that, and there are still some things with my father, with my ex-wife and with one of my children.* But when we have gone through something that meant a lot to us, we need to assimilate it, live with it for some time. When a baby has been born, we don't want another baby next week. Beware of repititions.

For example, one patient mentions three themes. One theme is obviously at the top of her list. The first session touches on and explores the problem, finds the main charges and outlines further work. Then we do the main work in a second session, and consolidate in a third. Then we take a month of rest, maybe two or three months. The patient walks around, pondering and assimilating. In that time something else can come up.

My usual interval is a fortnight. Effective sessions need that amount of time to be digested. Once the original contract is exhausted, when all immediate ramifications are explored and released, take a break of three months before a patient comes back for more.

After an interrupted session or with an unfinished verbal exploration, the next session may be the next day, but after a catharsis allow at least a week in between, at most a month. If you don't know, take a fortnight.

A session lasts at least an hour and a half, often two and a half hours, sometimes three hours. Quite often after an hour and a half we take a short break. Allow at least fifteen minutes for the patient to wind down. Those are reference values only. Don't follow rules, follow the energy.

Regression therapy is more intense than almost any other therapy. The time that you should allow between seeing two different patients depends on how quickly you recuperate. Just as do patients, therapists also have to wind down, to recover, to digest things. Often a therapy session touches feelings and thoughts that are also present within ourselves. This does not necessarily mean that we identify with the patient, but that we feel involved. As human beings we happen to have the same chords. These chords are often struck, and even if their striking does not tire us, they have to flutter out.

We work with complex charges that often reverberate for some time after the end of a session. These charges have to fade away. Sometimes a catharsis moves us so deeply that it would be a pity to start working at something else right afterward. Sometimes a problem or a sensitive part in ourselves is restimulated. Some patients affect us so much that we need time to recover from them.

Also, after an intense session with one patient, the next patient can pick up themes from the previous one. Then we get the reverse of de-mixing; we mix up things. Beware of this kind of contamination. Every patient has a right to our undivided attention, without echoes from another patient's session. Never schedule another appointment immediately after a two-and-a-half-hour session. Allow a break of half the length of the session before the next appointment.

Therapy takes more time than do the sessions alone. Preparing and assimilating takes time, just as do telephone conversations. Add fifty percent to your session time for your time budget. Altogether, limit yourself to two sessions per day if you can.

Keep in mind also that no trauma occurs by itself. A trauma that carries postulate charges will have involved a string of restimulating experiences. When we cure the original trauma and disarm the original postulate we have removed the comet, but we still have its tail. That collection of secondary strings usually does not need therapy sessions, but it needs processing between those sessions. Many people are instinctively afraid of solving a problem, for every solution opens a temporary Pandora's box of issues - not dangerous, but confusing. Every problem that we are accustomed to carrying is part of a balance, so resolving a problem means loss of that balance. Therefore, fear of losing control especially discourages problem-solving.

Advise people about after-session effects, and explain that these effects are a sign of getting better, though they can be confusing at first. In daily life we assimilate our thoughts constantly in dreams, in daydreams, in shifting moods. In our musings, our feelings, our body disposition, we create and de-create, our attention fades in and fades out on the repercussions of actions, decisions and experiences. A good closure can do much to ease these after-session effects. For example, ask the patient, "Check how the resolution of this trauma affects your life." In other words, do not wait until the tail emerges, but have patients call it up, list its effects, and see if they can discover a pattern.

The basic instruction to patients for their homework is, "Pay attention to how the session affects you afterward. You will notice that thoughts and feelings come up, things will fall into place, and you may become more sensitive to certain things." Make this statement before finishing the session, so that it retains the power of the natural trance of the session.

Homework often consists of listing things and sorting them out. This kind of follow-up work is especially effective with egostates and pseudo-obsessions. Let patients feel how the session reverberates, and let them sort out experiences, feelings, contacts, etc. as to subpersonality or previous life or karmic theme. For instance, if three subpersonalities came up: "Make a column for each subpersonality, a column for *I do not know*, and a column for *other*, and in those columns write down your own characteristics, interests, and abilities.

Some patients wander among their problems instead of solving them one by one. "How did the previous session affect you?"

I had little time for it, I haven't been busy with it, but I think it was okay. That kind of response is bad news.

Therapists have homework to do as well. Some therapists visualize that they mentally clean their working space after a session with a patient. The following is a suggestion by "Gildas." Visualize a wave or a wall of white light, that moves from one side of the room to the other, washing everything clear in its course. For possible leftovers of "heavier" energy, visualize many little purple flames that digest these leftovers. Then let the wave of white light wash through again, to leave a fresh room ready for the next patient.

Usually I limit myself to some fresh air. I dislike using cleansing visualizations, because using them implies that patients are dirty or therapy is dirty. Therapy is more like giving birth. It may have dirty or revolting and painful details, but the process is clean, endearing and joyful, because the results are.

Visualize something only if you really feel like it. If you feel heavy after a session, think of light and dancing energy; if you feel exhausted, think of strength flowing back; if you feel nervous, think of calm. Whatever you visualize, see yourself as the source.

If you want a standard visualization, think of an open space with a secluded, lush spot that has fresh water, and surround yourself with your favorite animals. Tell nobody.

Suitable and unsuitable patients.

For regression therapy we need verbal communication. Evidently we cannot do regression therapy with the mentally handicapped, the drugged or sedated, or the autistic. Only medicine, physiotherapy and spiritual healing are possible with such patients.

For regression therapy with adults we need self-responsible people. We cannot work with dependent people. Therefore, do not accept people who are sent by others. Always let patients call personally.

For many people, reincarnation therapy has something sensational and so it attracts "professional patients" who want only to add us to their collection of "failures," or rather, "near-successes." Besides, past-life therapy is oriented to the alternative, spiritual community that is usually better at entertaining elusive beliefs than at resolving elusive problems. Many people may have heard from sensitives that they have a hole in their aura, or that they had practiced black magic in a previous life. Bad starts, those.

People who have already consulted several others just to hear about themselves will also expect this same treatment from a therapist. They have no intention of working, but would rather have spiritual surgery: *You make me fall asleep (you do hypnosis, don't you?) and when I come around my problem will be gone.*

Or they want to hear that they are a particularly difficult case. That is why I usually start with the question, "What do *you* want to work at?" When people say, *I do not know, I suppose you will know that,* I say, "Yes, I know what I want to work at, but that is none of your business at the moment."

Beware of patients who bind you, unless you do anti-therapy: *You have to help me, you are my last chance; I heard so many good things about you,* or *The first time I heard your name I knew: he is going to cure me. A clairvoyant saw your name in my aura.* These are not expressions of trust, but manipulation or exaggeration. When people trust themselves, they may come expectantly, curious and with hope, but quietly.

For regression therapy we need people who can explore thoughts and feelings and know the difference between fact and fantasy. Few psychotics do qualify.

Netherton treats schizophrenics, but only within an institution. He starts with visualizations and gradually moves on to real regressions. This approach works, but it is not very efficient. With autistic children he has had no success so far. Alcoholics have to be free of alcohol for about three days before treatment. People who use barbiturates or other tranquillizers have to undergo an addiction cure before they begin regression therapy. Woolger feels that for some clients, past-life work is too intense. He believes that some people do not need to have the raw areas of their psyche be exposed again, but that they need a personal therapeutic relationship to rebuild their trust and confidence in life. Others find it difficult to image and work inwardly:

Schizophrenic patients easily become enamored by subpersonalities. Such clients turn theories of reincarnation and metaphysics into grist for their personal philosophical mills. Their wonderful theories often are just a defense against being alive and present on this earth. Since a chief symptom of many schizophrenics is a denial of being fully present, with a poor reality sense, there is often impor-

tant work to be done around their birth traumas. Their deficient ego sense is often, in my experience, bound up with not having ever been fully born into this world. With the few schizophrenics with whom I have worked, I have encountered enormous resistance to doing birth work. My hunch here is that these clients were still stuck in utero, caught up in a disembodied or partially embodied state. Other clients with whom I have had limited success have all kinds of theories about their past lives, possibly derived from Cayce, Seth, Theosophy, or a psychic they have consulted. It is not the origin of the client's belief of which I find myself suspicious, but their obsessive attachment to these beliefs. The theories or doctrines to which they subscribe, have a "saving" quality, and I suspect that these people require me to put a stamp of approval on what they seem already to know. As is the schizophrenic, this kind of client is already intoxicated by secret and glamorous fantasies about his or her past lives.

Do not do regressions with people who must avoid any stress, such as epileptics or people who have heart trouble. Further, avoid pregnant patients, because the fetus may register regression experiences as its own. If therapy is necessary, address the fetus and protect it first.

Patients can be neurotic as hell, they may be shaking with fear, they may hear voices, they may have multiple personalities, they may be depressed, suicidal or murderous. As long as they want to work, as long as they assume their responsibility, we can work with them.

The most common conditions that will abort any insight-oriented therapy are the refusal to be a patient and the need to remain one. In both cases, people involve themselves in games, not in therapy. Decline as patients people who know better than the therapist and people who define themselves as sufferers. Or refer them to colleagues you don't like.

Therapists who do not want to be therapists are unsuitable also, as are therapists who want to remain therapists and who create dependencies. Beginning therapists want to prove themselves and are easily tricked into those games: *I do not know whether you can cure me, but I would like to try. You think you can try it with me?* When we respond "Yes," we make it our problem.

We further narrow down our pool of suitable patients by stressing the need for mutual trust. Think of the square of trust.

The first enemy of trust is an energy leak. Do not for whatever reason take people who affect your energy level, making you feel empty or blocked. Patients who drain your energy will prejudice your self-confidence and lessen your confidence in them. Maybe this lowered self-confidence is more your problem than that of the patient. Still, it won't work. Likewise, if patients strongly repel you physically, or strongly attract you physically, refer them to a colleague. Avoid patients who make you switch off a part of yourself.

A common problem is recursive lack of self-confidence. People carry such a problem into the therapeutic relationship. This situation creates a two-sided expectation: great hope for success and a strong fear of failure. High-strung expectation can easily turn into deep doubt. Such patients ask much of our capability and our self-confidence. Also, well-known or prominent patients often display a self-image and self-confidence that complicates therapy.

If your self-confidence is still vulnerable, avoid heavy cases and start with patients who have sufficient self-confidence. There are plenty of active, reasonable people who happen to have a strange, serious problem and who really want to know why they have it and how they can get rid of it. Start with those people. You may even remain with them; there are enough of them around.

Keep it simple. Do not analyze in a complicated way whether you can handle something; notice how you feel about it! When you feel nervous with someone, then don't do it, or at least tell them you are nervous. Avoid cases wherein you feel tense.

Start simple. Start with where you are, how you feel, where you feel confident. The square of trust is the womb of the session, and the entry point is the ovum. Establishment of a contract is fertilizing that egg. With a wise and relaxed therapist, nature takes over. Nothing works more quickly than the natural flow. Become a master of the natural flow. Remember, striking gold may occur in a matter of seconds.

Still, becoming simple is complex, and becoming natural requires training. It takes time before we manage to handle a canoe. The faster the river, the more difficult the task, until everything comes easily. Go with the flow, and learn to go with the fast flow and with the deep flow.

Regressions with children.

Just as a triangular relationship is more complicated than a pair, working with children is more difficult because parents are involved. Have a short talk first with the parents and child together. Then conduct the actual intake with the child alone, and do the sessions as much as possible without the parents present. Let the children decide for themselves what they want to tell their parents after the session. Make clear to the parents that they have to respect the child's opinion in this.

In sessions with children we need to use more intuition and, above all, more tact. As the square of trust is more vulnerable, we may have to create a safe space first.

The square of trust has two weak links when work involves children. First, just as with many adults, many children lack self-confidence. This lack of self-confidence depends mainly on the duration of the problem and the reaction of the parents. Second, a child may lack confidence in the therapist, for therapists are grownups as well (at least they look like grownups!) and grownups have already criticized the child too often. Respond to the child's need for safety, and do not resemble other adults too much. Show that you trust the child. Let the child itself tell you why it thinks it came to see you.

Use imaginative bridges. With an angry child who throws things about, we may ask, "If you had lived before, what would be the reason for your anger then?" or, "Suppose you lived in another country, in another time, what would have made you angry there?"

Have them complete their dreams or daydreams. Often this approach leads to a regression. Use dissociation to add safety. With children who read, ask them to bring their favorite book along. Talk about the main figures in the book. Choose the figure with whom the child identifies most, and let this figure relive dream situations, for example. Or let children place themselves in the surroundings of their favorite story. Then let them look for the cause of their problem in this story world, with or without the aid of the main character of the story.

Or have them draw a hero or a victim. Ask frightened children to draw their tormentor and then let them look for something or someone who is not scared of that tormentor. When such a courageous hero or heroine is drawn also, we meet the cause of the fear. Drawings often supply material for a subpersonality approach. Whole cartoon books sometimes appear, while the fear lessens and eventually disappears.

Perhaps you may have them bring their favorite pet toy or doll with them and have them visualize around that object. In a case of stammering:

T: *Imagine that your bear wants to tell you something and it can't say it. How do you think it would feel?*
P: *Angry and sad.*
T: *This anger, can you point out where the bear feels it?*
P: *In its feet and in its belly.*
T: *In its feet and in its belly. Imagine that you feel what the bear feels when it wants to say something and it has angry feet and an angry belly.*
P: *I want to kick, but I can't. There are ropes around my feet and they hold my belly tight.*

If this approach does not work, we let the child operate on the bear to see what is the cause of the stammering. All this is regular E+S and aura exploration, but with an imaginative dissociation to add safety.

We can use a pet animal as a helper also, or as someone who has all the qualities needed to get through the problem.

With an unclear starting point the verbal bridge may help: *When I was big, I was . . . , I was allowed to . . . , I didn't have to . . . , I could . . . , I felt . . . , I knew . . . , I thought . . . , I came . . .*, etc.

When I'm grown up later . . . , I will be . . . , I will be allowed . . . , I do not have to . . . , I can . . . , I feel . . . , I know . . . , I think . . . , I come . . ., etc.

How much they will rely on us depends more on the character of the child and the nature of the problem than on the child's age. When children notice that we trust them, they often come with solutions themselves. Children are surprisingly flexible in assimilating of strong emotions or physical symptoms and are capable of wonderful renovations. Usually we get good results in only a few sessions. Don't underestimate children.

Profile of efficient past-life therapists.
You may use the following as a checklist to evaluate where you are yourself at the moment:

245

1. Attitude
    - *Self-confident, but knowing your limitations.*
    - *Interested and compassionate, but not infatuated with people.*
    - *No inner need to be Helper, Rescuer, Savior or Messiah.*
    - *Professional, balanced between involvement and distance; doesn't get enmeshed, doesn't create dependency.*

2. Repertoire
    - *Communicates effectively, fostering trance.*
    - *Uses the four bridges.*
    - *Gives regression instructions.*
    - *Conducts present-life and past-life relivings.*
    - *Conducts prenatal and post-mortem relivings.*
    - *Uses psychosomatic explorations and test procedures.*
    - *Works with subpersonalities.*
    - *Diagnoses and treats attachments and obsessions.*
    - *Dissociates.*
    - *Renovates.*
    - *Anchors.*
    - *Conducts catharsis.*
    - *Uses rational and emotional closure techniques.*

3. Judgment and guidance
    - *Decides the desirability and feasibility of past-life therapy in individual cases.*
    - *Selects the starting point.*
    - *Selects the bridge.*
    - *Selects the appropriate reliving procedure.*
    - *Keeps track of the starting point.*
    - *Resolves blocks, barriers and disturbances.*

4. General insights in
    - *Individual developments and development problems.*
    - *Reincarnation patterns.*
    - *Traumas, hangovers, character neuroses, pseudo-obsessions and obsessions.*
    - *Therapeutic relations.*
    - *Trance.*

The role of the therapist.
Adler says it straight: "The first commandment for therapists is to win the confidence of their patients; the second is never to

worry about success." Patients have to feel free in relation to the treatment. They can do it or leave it as they please.

Many therapists play Savior. They want so much to help people. Often they do not accept a patient's lack of results. Instead of realizing that all of us sometimes meet our limits, these therapists blame the patient for failure of therapy. They often express this blame subtly, but sometimes openly. With their colleagues they talk about difficult patients who don't want to solve their own problems.

I talk, though this is unusual, about the patient, not about the client. I do not want to gloss over the asymmetry in the relationship, I want to manage it.

People come to see us because of *their* problems, not because of *our* problems. We are giving; they are receiving. They are hurt, but we are not. Naturally we have wounds, too, but this is not what patients come to hear. The therapeutic relationship is asymmetric. Accept the asymmetry, but restrict it. Respect the freedom of patients. Remember the square of trust.

If we use regressions to awaken hidden talents, if we deal with dharma instead of karma, we do not have a therapeutic asymmetry, but rather an educational asymmetry. Then we have a parent-child relationship.

Also, we have experienced more sessions than have our patients. We are more familiar with the procedure. We are in our own field. So playing father or mother, or at least an older brother or sister, is easy.

Few people have enjoyed a perfect relationship with their parents. Patients like to relate to a mummy or daddy when a childish part of themselves emerges. It is all right to respond to that childish part as would a father or mother; such a response is natural. We conduct sessions about traumatic child experiences, and we as therapists act fatherly or motherly, and in the session's closure we offer stronger positive suggestions than we normally would. But in other sessions we restrain ourselves in taking over any responsibility from the patient. We do not get enmeshed with patients. We respect their and our boundaries. So we do not accept gifts or small services during treatment, and we do not exchange mutual invitations or visits.

When we are new at this game we need to become confident; we need strokes. And so we may remain too close to the patient, too personal. Or we may need too much the smell of success. Please, do not overinvolve yourself either in the process or in the result. Therapy involves *their* process, *their* happiness, *their* understanding. Success and recognition and personal growth for us are just extras, a premium. Freud would call it a "lust premium," and Adler would say "a success premium." Be grateful for this extra, but don't seek it.

So work at your self-confidence as a therapist. Find your sources of self-confidence and self-doubt. You may do a verbal exploration. Start with "I have no confidence in myself" or "I have no confidence in myself as a therapist." Repeat this sentence five times, then complete, "I don't trust myself as a therapist, because . . ." Thus you will assemble a list with sources of doubt.

You do the same with "I trust myself as a therapist, because . . ." What images, sensations and emotions come up with that completion? You may do your own regressions whenever necessary to explore your own issues.

Exploring past lives, life preparations and life reviews gives people a new and richer perspective on life. We are working in a field that before now was speculation or superstition or religion, and which now becomes a field of experience. Whether we like it or not, we are associated with priests. Some even say that we should be, as ours is a spiritual calling.

I see the point, but I still have doubts. Ultimately, it is not so important if healers should be priests, but rather if priests are healers. A healer who is not a priest is still a healer. A priest who is not a healer is no priest at all. What is a priest anyway? A teacher, a healer, and a keeper of the flame.

Why is the priest role difficult for therapists? Because it increases the asymmetry. Before we know it we have become gurus. In their regressions people discover that the world is richer, wider, deeper and larger. Then there is the past-life therapist, as one who opened the curtains and the doors.

Likewise, if a patient goes through hell in a session, the closure is a coming into heaven. If a patient goes through loneliness, the closure of that loneliness is meeting people again. If a patient comes in from the cold, the closure is to feel warmth.

Let's consider a patient who came out of the cold and lost part of that coldness. She had a good catharsis, and now she experiences the opposite. Therefore she feels warmth all around her. And there is contact with another person because there happens to be a therapist present, one who is friendly and understanding (at least my patients usually think so). This warmth she associates with us. We went with her through the cold, and now there is this warmth. This warmth may linger on. The patient may feel friendship, may even fall in love, depending on her circumstances, on whether or not she is happily married with children. But if she is alone, the therapy gains a special aura.

The wrong type of reverberation from a successful session is the patient feeling personal affection for the therapist. A good closure may prevent that reverberation, not by the therapist acting distant or disagreeable, but by the therapist directing positive feelings toward others or toward the future in general.

A careful closure anchors positive feelings to future actions and meetings of the patient. During closure, we let the patient assimilate the after-image so that we play no part in it. When patients come back after a successful session and look at the therapist, they should feel trust. Even when sympathy is present, trust has to remain the basic emotion. As one example of a careful closure:

A woman finds herself earlier in her present life, as a girl in a Japanese internment camp. Her father has died. She constantly feels what her mother feels. "I am hardly there anymore. My mother continues to vibrate in me. I float half above it."
In that floating hides a choice. "I do not want to go back. Daddy is dead, so I want to die, I want to go with him." She is half out of her body, so the vacuum she has created is now filled by her mother, who may hold similar feelings.
First she must relive that choice. Here renovation provides catharsis: we let her follow Daddy. After the session we ask again about the father. "Where is your father now?" She sees her father. "Bring him with you to the here-and-now. Imagine he is here with you in the room. Feel it." We may even ask her to give him our regards.

Fear of rejection is widespread. Many people even reject others to prevent being rejected. A woman afraid of rejection comes to us and goes into regression, and now understands where that fear origniated. Her therapist has not rejected her, and now for the first time she can handle that original feeling of rejection. Do not let this experience of rejection be attached to you as therapist. Before she comes back, ask, "What are you going to do with your new understanding?" *I'm going to put an ad in the paper to find a husband,* or whatever. Then it is all right for her to embrace her therapist, but only when she says goodbye at the doorstep.

When sessions have dealt with loneliness, and when experiences of abandonment, isolation or mourning have been traversed, understood and resolved, ask patients to direct their joy and love toward the people they have loved or still love. Or make them aware of their new-found strength and warmth inside, and have them feel how this new energy will help them to love future partners or children or friends, how it will help them to find friends or partners. During closure we anchor positive feelings anywhere but with ourselves.

"What do you want to do with this?" *I feel great, I could embrace the world.* Then step back, for as therapists we are part of that world. "What will you do when you arrive home?" *Well, I'm going to give William a good hug!*

Or, "Imagine the near future. What are you going to do with that positive feeling?" *I will go to the zoo with my son.* In this case the charge is anchored in an intention. Thus we link a past catharsis to a future action. And by the way, if you think that hugging William or going to the zoo are anti-climactic, you don't know what these choices may mean for the patient.

What if we ourselves are desperately in need of affection, of warmth, of friendship and love? Then we address these needs outside of the sessions and outside of our clients. We may not be very good at doing that. Finding intimacy inside our work may be easier than finding it outside. Worse, our need for intimacy may be one reason that we do this work. We might find it easier to do therapy than to establish personal relationships in the free market.

The problem may be worse: we like relationships of intimacy in which we dominate. We may like to have relationships of dependency. Then we are not healers, despite any methodical brilliance. We become part of the problem instead of the solution.

Sexual intimacies between patients and therapists are common. Sometimes such intimacy is blatant abuse by a dominating or even manipulating therapist. If people are suspicious about hypnosis, this possibility of intimacy is, apart from the whimsical nature of stage hypnosis, the main reason.

More often, sexual relations between patients and therapists grow from the needs of both persons, facilitated by the private nature, the intimacy and the frequency of sessions. Whenever intimacy grows and becomes personal, whenever appreciation and admiration and friendship come into play, therapy is tainted.

When John Cleese goes into therapy and becomes the main selling point of his psychiatrist - when they go into business together - that psychiatrist is a fraud. Cured people should discover life, not psychiatry. And if they develop an interest in psychology, they should discover an interesting field, not the interesting person at the entrance.

Whenever the therapeutic relationship becomes personal, end the therapy. Take a break and resume contact outside the framework of therapy sessions or even outside a counseling relationship. Rarely do emerging friendships or infatuations survive the transfer from the hothouse of the therapy sessions to the cold and windy fields of ordinary life. If they do, okay, great. People may find each other in the strangest places, so why not in the therapy room? But such a relationship should be the exception that proves the rule, and it should be divorced from therapy at the earliest moment.

Some therapists worsen the problem. During regression they ask patients, "Have you ever met me there? Did I mean something to you?"

This line of questioning may lead to "ingathering," groups of people who feel they have known one another before. "These patients do not come to me by accident," a therapist may argue. Perhaps they don't, but it doesn't mean you know them all from former lives. And if you need this kind of thing, you should sell yourself openly as a guru, not as a therapist.

Netherton keeps it simple. If patients say that they identify him in their previous life, he responds, "This has no meaning for me at all; please continue with the session."

Sometimes we get enmeshed with the partners of patients. A good regression has a measure of intimacy. We touch deep levels, feelings and experiences that often surface for the first time. That partner back home suddenly becomes an outsider, but hears or feels that something intimate has happened. When, in addition to that fact, the patient and therapist are of opposite gender, the subject easily becomes sensitive.

Susan comes home with a dreamy look in her eyes and says, "I've never experienced anything like this before, Bill! It was fantastic with that man. Amazing what came out! You and I have talked so many times about it and nothing ever came out of it, but there it did." Now Bill will feel that something is going on between Susan and the therapist. Maybe the guy even uses hypnosis! And as everyone watching TV knows, untrustworthy therapists are a dime a dozen.

Sometimes a suspicious spouse phones us. Never say anything about a patient to somebody else, not even if that person is a parent. Never comment by telephone or otherwise on the contents or results of the session, unless the patient has introduced that person, has approved of our sharing information, and we feel it makes sense. Usually it doesn't. Let patients do their own explaining. Kids are the exception.

When partners want sessions because they feel left out, fine, but recommend that they go to a different therapist. What if a partner wants to watch a session? That's okay for exploration, but not for therapy. I make exceptions only for the first session. Sometimes we are counting back, and the onlooker enters a regression.

People should go into therapy without any fear (or hope) of personal entanglements. The same holds for partners of both patients and therapists. The game of healing has its own beauty, its own intimacy, its own rewards. The games of friendship, love, romance and sex have their own turf - elsewhere. Don't mix the two worlds.

How do we avoid such complications? Patients are sensitive and vulnerable, both before and after successful sessions. We have our own sensitivities and vulnerabilities. Our first defense is a professional attitude; our second is avoidance of the endless therapy business. The life of our patients does not revolve around a weekly march to the couch. Thirdly, we have our way with closures. Finally, we live what we preach, and so we lead full and rewarding lives outside the therapy room. We have wonderful partners, wonderful kids, wonderful friends and an exciting, meaningful and challenging life outside therapy.

I think you have gotten my point by now.

CHAPTER 10. EXAMPLES OF GROUP SESSIONS

Group sessions use imaginative bridges, possibly enriched by elements from egostates or aura exploration. I use them to evoke material for individual therapy. Only group sessions that focus on finding past lives and finding strengths and weaknesses are acceptable outside a therapy intensive or a course for therapists.

FINDING PAST LIVES

Relax in any way you are accustomed to doing. While you relax, you seek in your mind a place somewhere outdoors, where you can lie down undisturbed and completely relaxed. Your spot may be a place in your garden, a place that you know from a vacation, or a fantasy place.

Seek a place that is pleasant, where you may lie down undisturbed and imagine that you lie there in the same way as you now lie here. You feel yourself lie down here and you see yourself lie down there. Seek that place. See to it that it is not too cold, but that it has an agreeable temperature, maybe in a summer landscape somewhere.

You lie down and grow quiet and relaxed on that spot that is completely yours for now. You see the landscape around you, you feel okay and you feel that you are becoming more yourself. You are relaxed on a pleasant spot.

Maybe there is a light breeze. Occasionally you feel the wind pass. It is silent, but far away are some noises. Perhaps occasionally you hear a sound close by, the rustling of the trees, or a bird. The more you hear those sounds, the more you notice how silent it really is. Very relaxed, very silent.

You see the air above you, you feel the space of the sky above you and that feels very pleasant. While you lie there, you become more relaxed. You become ever more relaxed until you fall asleep. You fall asleep and every burden disappears, every burden disappears as you fall a sleep.

Once you have fallen asleep, the first thing that you now notice is that you are drifting in the air, just above your body, completely relaxed. You feel so light now that you automatically rise somewhat further, and while you rise you turn around and you look down to your body. Now you see your body lying on that spot, completely relaxed and undisturbed.

Now you feel the space around you, you feel that enormous space and you become freer and lighter. While you become freer and lighter, you become higher, lighter, more free, higher, more yourself. Everything that does not belong to you, you let go. You become more yourself; you feel lighter, more spacious, more free, and you go higher and higher, becoming more free and more spacious, lighter. You go as high as you want. You may go as high as you like and you notice now that you become higher and more free, higher, always lighter.

The world is now very deep below you and yet you go always higher if you want. You just go as high as you want to go, until you are so high above the world that you feel completely free now. You rise to a height where you are completely free, a height where you are completely light, a height where you are completely yourself, completely spacious, light and free. You see the world below and you look around and you notice how quiet and spacious you feel.

If you absorb the space, if you feel absorbed into the enormous space around you, if you feel the freedom and calm it gives to you, then you become curious about yourself. You think about the world down there and you ask yourself what business you have with that world, what that world means for you.

Then a thought comes up. There comes a thought that somewhere on that world below is a spot that is yours, but that you forgot. While that thought emerges, you notice that you begin to descend slowly and gradually and you feel that you are on your way to that spot. You are on your way to a spot on the world you had almost forgotten. It's a garden.

While you descend, you see below a thin layer of clouds. You descend to those clouds and pleasantly and quietly you descend through the clouds. The clouds are around you. Suddenly you come out of them and you see a landscape below you, a new landscape. While you descend, you feel a light wind, so that in descending you go forward and you see the landscape below you begin to move.

Somewhere far away, in front of you, down below, you start to see a spot. Your attention becomes drawn to a spot. It is the spot where your garden is, your forgotten, yet familiar garden. See what the landscape looks like. While you descend in a calm flight, you see the landscape more clearly, you distinguish more now. It is clearer and you see that spot where that garden is also clearer. It is now so clear, you are now so close that in a few moments you will land. You are about to land just before the entrance to the garden. You are landing right now.

With a small shock you feel the ground under your feet. Now you stand on your feet, just before the entrance of your garden. What kind of entrance is it? Is it a gate or a door or just an opening? If it is a gate or a door, is it open or closed?

Walk to the entrance, and if it is closed, you open it now. You now pass the entrance and you have your first glimpse of your garden. What is the first impression you get? What kind of garden is it? What grows there? You look to the left and to the right and you now see also the partition around the garden. Look at what you see, a gate or a wall or a hedge. You see the borders of your garden at the left and at the right.

You cross the border and you now enter your garden. There is a path that leads to the middle of the garden and that path you now take. What grows at the sides? Plants, shrubs, grass? Look. Any special colors? Any animals? Birds or butterflies or animals on the ground? Feel and hear how you walk there. Is it earth or sand or gravel?

You walk now further to the middle of the garden. Somewhere near the middle you see a big tree. Look at that tree. What does it look like? What kind of feeling do you get when you look at that tree? Does that tree have blossoms or fruit? Any birds? See the form of the tree. You come closer until you can touch the leaves or needles, whatever it has. Now can you put your hands on the trunk.

Put your hands on the trunk and feel the life within the tree. When you feel that life, you look upward along the trunk, so you feel and see the life of the tree. Let that feeling go through you completely. How does this tree feel? What does the tree mean to you? How does that trunk feel? Now you take your hand from the tree and then you walk back to the path. You walk the last part of the path to the center of your garden.

There, in the center, is a pool with water, and in the middle of the water is a small fountain. You hear the water run, you hear the fountain now. Hear the water. You come closer and now you come to the border of the pool and you put your hands in the water. Feel the water on your hands and wash them. Drink of the water.

Is it cold or warm or lukewarm? How does it taste? You now taste the water of your pool in your garden and you take as much as you want. Now that you have drunk, you feel the urge to enter the water, so you undress.

When you have pulled off everything, you enter the water slowly. Feel how the water comes around your legs, how it comes above your knees. Slowly enter it. You sink further in or you walk in, so that the water rises around you. It now comes above your knees and it still rises. You feel the water now at your waist and it goes still higher, it goes along your chest, along your shoulders. Your arms are already submerged and only your head is still above water. Now you let yourself completely submerge so that also your head is below water.

The water appears deeper than you had thought. Now you dive to the bottom. When you touch the bottom, you look up and you see the light at the surface up there. Then you swim across the bottom to the other side. When you arrive at the other side of the basin, you look up again and while you look up, you notice that you are rising again. You come out of the water.

While you emerge, dripping wet, you feel that you have another body. This is surprising, but also very familiar. Feel how that body feels. Get out of the water. Look at it. Are you a man or a woman or a child? Is your body big or small? Slim or firm? About what age are you? While you shake off the water, you look in front of you. There lies a towel and next to it are some clothes. You dry yourself and you dress yourself in those clothes. Feel how it is to dress in those other clothes. What do you wear?

You feel and you see yourself now in another body and in another dress. Now you continue the path. Perhaps there is somebody waiting for you. Perhaps is it someone you know, someone who belongs to this life. What kind of person is it? How does that person look like? What kind of destination does that person have? What does that person feel for you and what do you think of that person?

Now you go across a narrow ridge and you arrive with that person in an important situation. You are suddenly in an important situation of that life. See around you what happens and understand why this is important to you. What do you do? What do you see? What do you feel? What do you think? What kinds of sounds can you hear? Absorb all the impressions of that situation. Understand what happens, understand what you are doing there and understand why this is important to you.

You see now a certain detail of the situation. You see a detail that you didn't notice before, and that detail is important to you. Where is your attention drawn now?

Now let go of this situation. You let go of this situation and you go to another situation in that same life, in the same body, a situation that explains what kind of life you have lived. You have now arrived in that other situation, a whole other situation. It explains what kind of life you have lived there.

What do you do here? Is anything expected of you? What kind of role do you have there? Look at what you do, look at what happens. If there are other people around, how do they react to you? Why do they react in this way? What do they think of you? Feel how it is to live there. Feel how it is to be busy in this way. It gives you a clear impression of how things were then. It gives you a clear impression of how you were then.

Now you feel that you want to see something else of this life. You don't know what it is, but you are curious about it. I count from one to three and at three you gain a new impression, a completely new impression from the same life. One . . . , two . . . , three . . . .. What is your first impression? Where are you? What happens? What do you do? Who else is there? What goes through you? What do you feel and think? What here is important for you?

Now you let go of this situation as well. You let go of this situation and you now go to the moment when you made your most important decision in that life. You now go to the moment of decision, to the moment of your most important decision. There you are now. Where are you making that decision? How do you feel at this moment? What kind of decision is it? What is it about? Do you find it easy or difficult to make this decision? Do you make that decision all alone or is there somebody who tries to influence it? This is the moment of your most important decision and you again experience making that decision. What passes through you when you make this decision?

If the moment of that decision has become completely clear again, you get a quick impression. You now see a situation that shows the consequence of that decision. You now see a situation that shows the main consequence of your decision. What do you see now? What kind of consequence do you now see? What do you think of this consequence? Now you understand the main consequence of your decision.

At last you go to the moment of your death. You arrive there now. You are now in the situation in which you are about to die. Where are you and what happens there? What is the cause of your death? You see and you feel and you understand the precise cause of death. You understand why you will die now. Are you alone or are there people around you? Do they attend you or are you surrounded by enemies? Now you feel what you felt at the moment of dying. Your last feelings and thoughts now emerge. You feel, you realize now what went through you at the moment of dying. You feel and realize that again. Then you go to the moment of dying itself. This is the moment you die, this is the moment you leave the body. After you have left your body, what is the first thing you notice, the first thing you experience? Now your situation changes, you now see or feel something different. What happens? When you have seen and felt this, you go further. You go further to a place of overview. You now go so much further and so much higher that you arrive at a place where you have overview over the life you just lived. You now arrive at that place.

Are you there alone or are there people with you? How do you feel on this place of overview? Now you look back on your life. You look over the whole life and suddenly you realize what the main goal of this life was. Some words are now emerging. You realize the main goal and you ask yourself to which extent you have accomplished that goal. It becomes clear right away, it becomes clear right away to what extent you have accomplished that goal, to what extent you can feel satisfied.

If you did not accomplish this goal completely, then it now becomes clear how that occurred. You realize the main reason that you did not completely accomplish your goal. What was that main reason? Again you see it happen in that life and you understand why it happened.

Now you go to the other side of that same place. You look in the opposite direction and now you think about your present life here and now and suddenly you see a connection between those two lives. You see the main connection between the life you lived then and the life you are living now. You see and understand the main connection. If in that former life there was somebody you knew well, whom you also know well in your present life, then you suddenly see that connection. You suddenly realize that who you know now, you also knew then, if there is such a connection. If it is there, you suddenly see that connection and you understand who it is now and who it was then.

If you have seen all that, you are suddenly back in your garden, in front of the pool. You stand at the pool, you undress and enter the water again. You enter the water at the same spot where you came out. Feel the water again surrounding you. It surrounds you until only your head is yet above water. Now your head is under water and you dive to the bottom. When you are at the bottom, you look up and you see the air through the water.

Now you ascend and you rise out of the water without a body. You go very high above the world, very high above the world until you come back to the spot you began. On that high spot where you again are completely free and spacious. If you have arrived there, you think about the body you left behind, that body that lies there. Slowly you begin to descend now, you descend to the body you left behind.

Always further you descend, and the world below comes closer. You distinguish more, until you see as a dot the spot where your body lies. It comes closer. You now see a small figure lying down, a figure that is still unrecognizable. It becomes clearer and ultimately you are low enough to see yourself.

Now you descend very quietly, and just above your body you stop for one moment, as if you stretch your arms to touch your body. Where do you touch your body? The moment you touch that body, you say something to yourself. You say something to that body. Now hear what you say to your body. If you have said that, you enter the body. You feel yourself lying down, you occupy your body again. Feel your body. Feel yourself lying down. Thus you come back to here and now. You come back to here and now, at your own speed and in your own way and with everything you have experienced. Everything that you have seen, stays clearly with you. You return to the here and now, at your own speed and in your own way.

FINDING HANGOVERS

Close your eyes and direct your attention to your body. Feel your body as a whole, as if you are finely divided and fill your whole body. You don't concentrate. You fill your body as evenly as possible with a calm attention that is divided as evenly as possible. Feel all parts of your body just as strongly or just as little. No part is dominant.

You see that equanimity as a sparkling mist, like tiny drops of pearl that fill your whole body. You are completely penetrated by a pearl glow. Feel how calm that makes you. A calm, sparkling mist. You are a calm, sparkling mist.

Now you see that mist become lighter, as if the sun shines through the mist. That shine, very light and pure, rises in your body until it is in your head. Now it rises further and a marvellously brilliant white ball is above your head.

If you now look at your body, if you feel your body, there is something in your body left behind, something that cannot come to that white sparkling ball, something that could not come with the light. Now you remark that there is something dark, something drab in your body, a dark figure. You see yourself from the outside. Your body is transparent and you see that dark figure in it. See that figure emerge from your body and stand next to it.

Is that figure bigger or smaller than your body? Now you get an impression of what kind of person it is. It is a drab figure, as if all the drabness of yourself is in that figure. Look quietly at it. Note it for yourself without any reaction and enter your body again.

Now you feel that white radiating light that is above, and for one moment it streams completely from the top of your head to your feet and of from your feet you take it completely up again.

While you draw it upward, there appears another figure, a heavy figure. All of the heaviness from inside yourself is in that figure, and that heavy figure sinks out of your body now. It is so heavy that it sinks out of your body. You step backward, light and transparent. You see that heavy figure now in front of you. You get an impression of what kind of person it is. It seems that it has all your heaviness. You just note it and again you let the white light move from above to below, let it rinse through you, sparkling to your fingertips and to your feet.

Then you let that white light withdraw again and for the third time you see something. Now you see something that looks weak and ill, something weak and ill. It is as if all weakness and illness in yourself is in this figure. That figure is so weak and ill that it slips out of you and you lay it down in front of you. You get an impression of this figure as well, a weak and ill figure. You now see three figures, one drab, one heavy and one ill and weak.

Now you return to the body for the last time. For the last time you let that white light go down through your body, to your fingertips and your feet. For the last time you withdraw very slowly until a fourth figure remains.

Feel what the quality of this figure is. What is the main nature of the negative energy of this figure? What kind of feeling does this figure carry? Let this figure step out of you as well, so you can see him in front of you and you see and feel what kind of person it is.

Now you have seen four and you again let the white light go through you until again you are filled completely with white sparkling light. From that white sparkling light you now see four figures in front of you. The drab, the heavy, the weak and ill and the fourth. The light dims slowly until there is just a sparkling mist that fills your whole body evenly. In that calm and rest you come back to the here and now, in your own way and at your own speed.

FINDING PSEUDO-OBSESSIONS

You are in a small valley. In that valley is a house and that house is yours. It is a pleasant house, pleasantly situated, where you feel at home. You see that house surrounded by nature. There is a big yard all around, there is a garden, there are some woods, there is some water and there are also fields and bushes. See the landscape. It is a small valley, there are some fields, some woods, some shrubs, some water, a stretch of swamp maybe, perhaps some rocks. Just see what you see. It is a nice and interesting valley and a nice and interesting house.

Now you stand at the front door. You have the key in your hand, and you feel that you are the owner of this house. You put the key in the lock and you open the door. You see a hall and at the far end the door to the living room is half open. It is light there. You close the door behind you and you walk through the hall into the living room. See what it looks like. This is the living room of your house. Perhaps it is a study as well, perhaps it has books. You can study here, but you can relax here also. Look at what you see.

Now imagine that you sit there completely relaxed and you see that the evening comes. You see how the evening falls until it is so dark that you light a lamp, perhaps light a fire in the fireplace. You draw the curtains or you pull blinds for the windows, until the darkness is shut out. There is a pleasant light and a pleasant warmth in the room and you return to your seat. You know that you'll have visitors. One or two past lives of yourself are about to visit you. They are past lives that you know. They are familiar to you.

There is a knock on the door. You see the first one enter. You welcome him or her and you let him or her take a seat. Feel what it means to you to sit there together. Feel what you mean for each other.

Again there is a knock on the door and a second past life enters, one that you already know, one of which you know something. Recognize and feel what this entrance means to you. You welcome him or her and let him or her sit down. How is it that the three of you are together?

If you want, you can see more past lives enter, past lives that you already know now. If there are more familiar persons and if you wish, you can see one or several enter. Do it one at a time. First have each one sit down, and recognize them, before the next one enters. Go on until you feel a kind of circle. When it becomes a circle for you, that will do. If you feel a circle, look them all in the face. Now you make that circle a little wider. Everyone is standing up and pulling their chairs back, widening the circle. Now you see a few empty chairs between the others. Count them.

Now you realize that the people who belong on these empty seats are still outside, nearby on the veranda or farther away in the valley, perhaps in the bush or in the woods, perhaps hiding or wandering.

You leave the house and start seeking. You feel that you are drawn to a spot where there is the nearest of those who should come inside. You walk outside into the dusk.

You encounter the first now, the first one who stayed outside, the first one who was not able or did not want or didn't dare to come. You see yourself with the other person, enter the room and you offer him or her an empty chair. Look at what happens.

See what that person looks like. How does that person itself feel? You don't need to do anything with that person at this moment. Just explain that you reserved this seat for him or her. Have that person relax itself. If you don't succeed and he or she leaves quickly again, send the thought: "This chair will stay here for you. I know now that you are there." What is the strongest feeling that person has? What is the dominant feeling or the dominant power? Note that.

If there are yet more empty chairs, then you go outside again and you do the same. Your attention becomes drawn somewhere. You go somewhere and you find somebody. You bring that person with you. You see what she or he looks like and you feel the dominant thought or dominant feeling. Do it all again if there is yet a chair.

If there are still several chairs, then you repeat this action several times. You fill the circle. Fill the empty places. If one or more people need something, you give it to them. You continue until the circle is complete. When the circle is full, you come back to the here and now with all your impressions. You continue until the circle is complete and then you can return to the here and now and you can record your impressions. Continue quietly until you are ready. You are not in a hurry.

FINDING STRENGTHS AND WEAKNESSES

Relax. Breathe quietly and deeply and perceive your body. Feel the weight of your body on the floor. Feel the weight of your body. Your body is important. It is as if you are a finely divided mist that evenly fills your whole body, a sparkling mist that is evenly present in your whole body.

You feel yourself as quiet, even and calm. With each breath you become calmer and more yourself. Let the unrest flow from you. Everything in you finds its own place now. When everything finds its own place, it gives rest, a relaxed, natural power.

If you now think about yourself, you think about yourself as a therapist. Here lies a healer. Think about yourself as a therapist. You now feel curious to explore yourself. What kind of therapist are you really? What is your ability really? With what do you work really? While you think about all of that, some-where in your body a point awakens.

That point starts to glow, surrounded by that sparkling mist and becomes always stronger. This is your main source of power as a therapist. Now go to your main source of power where you feel yourself most strongly as therapist, a source from where the power emanates through you and radiates outward, a source from where you may work with others. It may be that you use your own energies, it may be that you attract energies, but this is the point from where you work, your strongest therapeutic power source. Feel the place and let it become stronger.

You feel it, perhaps as vibration, perhaps as warmth, per-haps as color. Let that color become clearer. You see the color of that point and you feel the living energy and vibration it has. It even might have a tone. Perhaps you hear something with it. Now you feel your strongest point as therapist, and while you are centered there and everything else within you is subordi-nate to that, you go back in time.

You go back to a place and a time long ago, when you worked with this power. You go back to a place and a time when you worked from this point. I count back from five to one and while I count back, you go further back in time. At one you arrive at the apex of your power as therapist, the strongest moment at which you work from this power source. Five . . . , four . . . , back through time . . . , three to the origin . . . , two . . . of this power as therapist, one.

Where are you now and what do you do? Feel and see your-self busy. Which people are around you? Or are you alone? See and feel and understand what you do. With what kind of hu-man problems do you work? How do you do that?

Insofar as it is a question of knowledge, parts of that knowl-edge now appear. Insofar as it is a question of ability, now you feel and see how you apply that ability. Insofar as it is a ques-tion of perception, you see and feel how you perceive and what you perceive. Feel and see and understand what you are doing there.

Now you see the consequences. You now see the conse-quences of being successfully busy with people in this way. What happened to those people? Do they feel changed in any way?

You now get an impression of how you began. You go back in time to the moment when you first came in contact with this work, when you first felt or knew that you would do this work one day. What did you experience at that moment? What were your motives? Did you seek it? Who selected you? Was there someone who advised you? You now see your first step in that work. How does it feel to take that first step?

You now go to a moment in that life, a situation that gives you an impression of the place and the time where you lived. You now get an impression of the place and the time where you lived. You see something that shows it. See where and when you lived.

Now you go to the end. You go to the last moment when you were busy as a therapist. You go to the end of your activities. How do you feel at the end of your activities? How did that end arrive? Is it exhaustion or age? Is it an outside event, or did you stop for personal reasons? You see now why you stopped.

At last you go to the moment you died. You now see and feel and experience that you are dying there. You have come to the end of your life and you understand how you die and from what you die. What is the last you feel and think and see before you leave your body?

Now you are free of your body and you feel how it is to have to leave that life behind you. You feel how it is to end it and look back at it. You feel to what extent you have succeeded in what you set out to do and if you are satisfied with that. If you are not completely satisfied, then it now becomes clear why not, where you fell short perhaps. If you are satisfied, you now get an impression how you have been helped, what supported you, who supported you and why.

Slowly you release yourself from that life. You feel it again in your present body. That strong source slowly dims. It remains, but you don't need it right now. It dims, until it returns to its usual strength.

Now you divide your attention again all over your body as a sparkling mist that penetrates everything. You think again about yourself as therapist. There now comes another thought or another feeling. You wonder what your main handicap is, your main block, your main leak that keeps you from being a good therapist.

Now your attention is slowly drawn to another spot, where you feel a different energy. Which spot is it and what is it? Let that feeling now become clearer and stronger. Is it a block or a deformity? Or is it a hole? Feel where it is, feel how it feels, see how it looks.

Does it give sensations like warmth or coldness, heaviness or lightness? Any sound, or silence? You now experience your main block, your main handicap or leak as a therapist and you feel how it works out in your body, what feeling it gives you.

Now you go back. You go back to a place and a time in which this block was formed. I will count back from five to one and at one you are at the origin of this problem, this weakness. Five . . . , four . . . , always further back, three . . . , through time, two . . . , to the origin, one.

Where are you and what happens? What causes this block on this spot? How do you feel? What happens to you? What do you do or what do you try? See and feel and understand what happens here. See and feel and understand the origin of this block.

Are you a man or a woman? About how old are you? If other people play an important role in this block and if there is anything personal connected with it, then you get a sharp impression of the main perpetrator. If there is anybody, then you get a clear impression of that person.

If in this moment something important was on your mind, a thought or something you heard, then you remember the words now. What words do you hear, if any? What do you say to yourself or what do others say? Hear and understand those words.

Now you go to the moment of death in the past life where this block originated. You now relive the death experience, until you are completely free of your body, until you find complete rest, until you find the rest to do an overview of this life and to realize what you leave behind.

From there you go further. You return to your body here and now. Feel the repercussions in your present life, how certain people or certain circumstances trigger this block and wake it up. You now get an impression of the person in your present life who is most strongly connected with this block. You see and you understand how that happened. You feel that spot again in your body. It slowly dims, until it returns to its usual power.

Now you feel yourself simultaneously in the center of your power and in your center of your block, as if you are just those two dots. Feel your greatest power and your greatest weakness as well.

Now you link the center of your power with the center of your weakness. You draw a line of energy. Begin with a thin shining line. Make that line stronger and thicker, until it can transmit any energy inside you.

If you have done that, you make a short circuit between the two dots. You don't need to do anything, to try anything, you don't need to be afraid of anything. You only feel that you are making a short circuit. If you don't succeed in that, then you touch one point with one hand and the other point with the other hand, and you link them that way. Feel the whirling, feel what happens. Watch while you feel calm and relaxed. Let the energies run and whirl until they come to rest.

If you have found rest, go again to the point of your power. If it is more faint than it had been, you remember how clear it was. You boost it until it is again as it should be. Notice how those two spots feel and how the link between them feels. Feel if perhaps anything remained in that weak spot. You realize what you have to do about that. You know where it comes from and you know if it will wear out, will disappear, or if you should do something about it.

You feel whether you can do that yourself or whether you need help. It is clear to you. Your whole body is completely quiet again, as quiet as can be.

At last we go to the future. You are about one year further and you are about to receive patients. The patient who is about to enter is for you an ideal patient, someone you can help very well and who will leave feeling very satisfied. The door opens and someone enters. Is it a man or a woman? About what age? He or she sits down and tells you his or her main complaints. What kinds of complaints or problems does your ideal patient have? You feel calm and strong. You feel you are the right person for this kind of person with this kind of problem. Now you see the moment after the session when the patient leaves and you see how he or she is changed.

Now there is a new patient at the door. This is the kind of patient and the kind of problem that is completely outside your line of work, the kind that you really cannot handle, the kind that makes you miserable. What kind of patient now enters? What kind of person with what kind of problem? The patient sits down and talks and you feel that this is not for you and you see yourself saying that calmly and convincingly. That patient leaves, perhaps disappointed but completely accepting that he or she should go elsewhere.

It is now completely clear to you what kind of patient fits you and what kind does not. You feel your body again in the here and now. You return to here and now, at your own speed and in your own way.

CHAPTER 11. EXAMPLES OF INDIVIDUAL SESSIONS

Most of the individual sessions that follow are demonstration sessions conducted by the author, while some are exercise sessions handled by students. In each case, E stands for *emotional charge*, S stands for *somatic charge*, and M stands for *mental charge*.

EMOTIONAL AND SOMATIC BRIDGE TO TRAUMA

This patient experienced in a former session that she had lost her basic trust while still in the womb. Now she would like to learn why. Other emotional charges that are present at the entry point are fear and anger. During this session there emerged rebelliousness, loneliness and longing, with clusters of anger and grief.

The original somatic charge was one of pressure. The somatic charges that emerged later were pain, coldness, paralysis and exhaustion. Somatics experienced during this session were nausea, coughing, trembling, shivering, leg weakness, pressure on the breast and throat and involuntarily assuming the fetus position. Mental charges were panic, vulnerability, disbelief, compassion, obstinacy and resolution.

The therapist allowed this patient to go back to the womb, where she feels oppressed, with a sense of alarm in the legs. She sees a compassionate figure next to her. This figure is her own soul. This patient does not like to see that her soul attaches itself to the green and yellow embryo.

The therapist has this patient feel the body of the embryo. The therapist encourages the patient, who does not dare to make a decision. "Let it happen. Feel the fear . . . ," the therapist urges, but the patient reacts with pain, fear and longing.

Then the patient appears to be in shock. She feels blank, nothing. She does not dare to continue. The therapist asks the patient if she can see from above what happens, but this attempt is in vain. Then the therapist asks this patient if her soul can see from above what happens, but this effort also proves to be in vain. Then when the therapist says, "Let your body tell it," all kinds of emotions and somatics begin to surge.

The patient feels disbelief, grief and anger when she sees that her mother tries to induce an abortion. The mother experiences this pregnancy as a tumor, a black flower, a morbid growth, with a lack of attention from her husband and others. The mother feels anger and revulsion toward the unborn child. The therapist asks if the patient wants to go back to when the mother did not yet feel this way. The patient reacts with irritation and anger; she does not want to know right now.

When patient moves to the moment when delivery begins, she panics. She suffers weak legs. The mother does not cooperate in any way. The patient collects new energy, now encouraged by the therapist. The therapist tells the patient that she has much more energy than her mother: "Feel that energy growing." This helps.

The patient feels lonely and chilly, but she firmly decides to make it in this world. She is proud that she has done it herself. At birth she distances herself mentally from her mother. When the mother finally touches her and lifts her, the infant has built a brick wall against the mother and the rest of the world. This child feels very lonely.

The patient suddenly sees a girl six or seven years old, cheerful, roguish and with willpower. She realizes that she is the girl. The girl is standing on white stairs and taking away bricks with her bare hands. She is hurriedly pulling down that defensive wall. She does not like walls, she says.

P: *I get weak legs again.*
T: *Go to that girl and talk with her.*
P: *She wants to pull down that wall with me. I feel marvelous now. As long as it doesn't go too quickly, but at my own speed. That girl waits for me when I get frightened again.*
T: *Can you take the responsibility of pulling down that wall? After all, that girl is just six or seven years old.*
P: *Instinctively she feels what fits and what doesn't fit. She has complete confidence. I want to stay with that girl. That feels good.*
T: *Are there any other children?*
P: *No. I am that playful child. But the embryo remains sad. It needs much fostering, like a wounded animal.*

T: Go to a moment of deep, unconditional love. Breathe this several times through your whole body. Transmit that feeling to the embryo.

P: The embryo is now rosy purple, less afraid, less vulnerable. I put it in a flower where it lies protected. It goes to sleep. It would be a burden for me right now. I entrust the newborn baby to a woman guide. She is wise and has much positive energy. With her this baby can regain its balance.

T: Who is this woman?

P: She's me in a former life.

T: Is it okay now, or is there anything else?

P: It is okay.

This patient achieved an important moment of catharsis when she realized that she had been born by her own power. Despite every opposition of the mother, she firmly decided to be born.

After the regression, this patient felt relieved, surprised, sad and angry toward her mother. Now she understood how she had lost her basic trust and why she had always been in conflict with her mother. She expressed surprise at her own inner force.

Strikingly, the patient did not want to go back to the moment of overview that would have occurred before the mother was pregnant. She still has much to work out with her mother.

At the close of the session anger, grief and disbelief were still present. This patient said in the evaluation that she could deal with these emotions herself, later.

EMOTIONAL BRIDGE TO A PSEUDO-OBSESSION
(Extensive session)

P: I strongly got the feeling of being left behind.

T: Lie down, and when you feel you are ready, say "Yes."

P: Yes.

T: You feel you are left behind. Do you feel that now? (Checks emotion.)

P: Yes.

T: You feel that you are left behind. Let this feeling grow. Feel where it is in your body. In your head, your chest, your arms and legs? Where is this feeling? (Confirms emotion, looks for somatic.)

P: I feel my left wrist.

271

T: *What kind of feeling?*
P: *Twitching.*
T: *Are there other feelings in your body related to being left behind?*
P: *No, not now.*
T: *All right, concentrate on that twitching feeling in your left wrist. What kind of feeling is it? Is someone pulling at you, or are there twitches from inside? What does it look like?*
P: *As if I am pulling myself.*

Now there is an E and an S that is not emotionally charged as such, but has the beginning of an image, so S with M; together ESM.

T: *Okay, I'm going to count back now from five to one. At one you arrive in a situation in which you are pulling with your left hand and you have the overwhelming feeling of being left behind. You feel that you are being abandoned and you pull with your left hand; five . . . , four . . . , ever more back, three . . . , ever closer to the original happening, two . . . , ever closer to the source of these feelings, one . . . . What is the first thing that comes to mind? What are you doing?*
P: *A deep well and I am pulling at that rope.*
T: *How do you feel?*
P: *Neutral.*
T: *Why are you there?*
P: *I see very dry earth, with big cracks in it, where I walk on it. There is simply a need for water.*
T: *What, in particular, is that water needed for? ("In particular" = specificator.)*
P: *I am a little girl. I think for drinking.*
T: *Is it heavy? Is the well big for you?*
P: *Yes.*
T: *Do you manage? Is there water inside? Can you get it up?*
P: *It is very deep. There is only a little water inside.*
T: *Nearly dried up. Is there still water coming into your bucket?*
P: *The rope is all frayed. This bucket does not come up either.*
T: *Does it go stiffly? Is something stuck? It is hard, isn't it?*
P: *Nothing happens, I can't get it moving.*
T: *Are you thirsty? (Checks charge.)*
P: *No.*
T: *Did you go yourself or were you sent?*

P: *I am panicky. (First charge.) Yes, I think I was sent. I am afraid that it will all go wrong.*

T: *What will go wrong, when you don't get water?*

P: *Then nothing can be done; you can't cook, you can't drink.*

T: *Are there no grown-up people who can get water? Or are they ill?*

P: *There is only an old woman, who is waiting. She can't do anything anymore.*

T: *And you are so young, you can't do anything yet. Where are the others?*

P: *There is a very poor wooden hut, all weather-beaten, and the others are gone.*

T: *Why did they leave? Didn't they want to stay?*

P: *Maybe they are also looking for water.*

T: *Did they abandon you?*

P: *Perhaps.*

T: *Now you have to look after an old woman as well and the rope is frayed and the well is deep and there is hardly any water and you're all by yourself; it won't work. Do you feel panic?*

P: *Yes.*

T: *What else do you feel?*

This question, "What else do you feel?" is a search for other charges.

P: *I feel angry, furious. (Second charge.)*

T: *At those people?*

P: *Yes.*

T: *What else do you feel?*

Should have asked: "Toward whom in particular?"

P: *It's unfair; it's unfair.*

T: *You feel panic, but also anger. You think it is unfair they left you behind. Do you feel anything else? Is there yet another feeling?*

P: *I am scared.*

T: *You are scared. Scared of what?*

P: *It is related to the panic of having nothing, of being unable to survive.*

T: *You are scared of dying.*

P: *Yes.*

T: *You are all by yourself, with that old woman. Is that your grandmother or just any old woman?*

P: *A relative, I think.*
T: *Do you have a father or mother? A father or mother who moved away? If so, you get an impression from that.*
P: *I don't see him.*

This answer, "I don't see *him*," will prove to be important, as we will see later.

T: *Are you an orphan?*
: *Now I can see a leaf, lying on the ground, a dry leaf.*
T: *That is you, that dry leaf. You feel like a dry leaf, fallen to the ground.*

We now have a traumatic situation with charges of *abandonment*, *panic* (fear + desperation) and *anger* because of unfairness. So we have an *anger-grief knot*, probably embedded in *fear* and childish *incomprehension*.

T: *Now leave this situation for a moment. Let it go completely. You go back in time, back to the time when everything was still all right and now you are going to get an impression from that. What is the first thing that comes up?*
P: *I think I am three years old.*
T: *How do you feel?*
P: *I am brown and lively, little curls. I think I am black.*
T: *That's nice, isn't it?*
P: *Yes.*
T: *Do you feel good?*
P: *I wear a pretty dress.*
T: *Are you proud of it?*
P: *Yes, I think it is very pretty.*
T: *Who do you love most there?*
P: *Granny, she looks after me.*
T: *Aren't your father and mother there?*
P: *I only see chickens. I can't see any father or mother. Granny and the chickens. My granny can still walk, with difficulty. There are no other people.*
T: *Do you have to look after the chickens?*
P: *Yes.*
T: *Is that going well?*
P: *Yes.*

T: *You are lively, you wear a pretty dress. What do you think of the chickens?*

P: *I like them, sometimes I chase them and they flap their wings, I'm not afraid of them.*

T: *Are you yourself a flapping little chicken too?*

P: *Yes, I enjoy chasing them.*

T: *What do you think of yourself, there?*

P: *I feel very free. There is no obligation; very simple.*

T: *Now you let this situation go. Slowly you move forward through time. You get a little older and now we go to the first moment that has to do with the feelings that still live in you now of being abandoned. We go to the first moment that starts to become difficult. You get an impression from that. What is the first thing that comes up in you?*

P: *My granny fell down with awkwardly crossed legs. Perhaps a broken leg.*

T: *What do you feel when you notice that?*

P: *First I think "Where are the others?" I cannot do it.*

T: *How old are you there? Let some age come up in you.*

P: *Four or five.*

T: *Go to the next moment the situation changes. What happened now? Did you find other people?*

P: *No, it is very lonely, no other houses even. It is very dry.*

T: *What happens now with your granny?*

P: *She can only sit. She sits in a corner near the door post.*

T: *Is she in pain?*

P: *Yes. She is also a little angry with me.*

T: *How come?*

P: *She gets very weak.*

T: *What are you going to do?*

P: *Get water.*

T: *Now you go to the well to get water. You stand near the well. Can you get water, do you manage?*

P: *No.*

T: *You feel panic, you are angry at the people who left, you think it is not fair and you are only five years old. What happens now?*

P: *I don't understand it at all.*

This response, "I don't understand it at all," reinforces the main mental charge, a complicator: *incomprehension*.

T: *Do you return to your granny without water?*
P: *I don't dare.*
T: *What are you afraid of? That she will get angry or that she won't wake up anymore?*
P: *I only see gray wood, dried up trunks, branches, twigs.*
T: *Everything is dried up and you feel like a dry leaf on the ground. Did you see your granny again? If you still did see her, go back to that moment.*
P: *I don't think so.*
T: *Now you see the situation changes again. What do you see happening now?*
P: *I see the contours of a tree in the distance. Behind a branch there is light shining.*

This image of light shining looks like an after-death experience.

T: *Is it pleasant light?*
P: *It's not dark, just a bit dusky.*
T: *Evening or morning?*
P: *Evening.*
T: *Where are you? How do you feel? Do you sit, lie, stand?*

These questions check on the apparent impression of a discarnate experience.

P: *I can't see it.*
T: *Go up and look at yourself somewhere down below. You descend to yourself and you see yourself. What kind of impression do you get now?*
P: *I lie on a slope, on the way to that tree with my pretty little dress on.*
T: *What does the dress look like?*
P: *White with little flowers.*
T: *There you are. A little dead brown curly head. What did you die of, of the drought, of desperation? What did that little girl die of?*

The question, "What did you die of?" checks what charge is on the dying itself. But there is no response to this question.

T: *We go through it again, you go back to the moment your granny broke her leg. When you can see that again, you say "Yes."*
P: *Yes.*

T: *Now you feel that the others are gone. You go to the moment you felt strongest, deepest, that you were abandoned. Go to that moment.*

P: *At the well.*

T: *At the well, with that frayed rope.*

P: *It was so weather-beaten, it just fell into pieces.*

T: *Let this feeling of abandonment go through you completely, without keeping anything back. Go right through it. You feel totally abandoned. Feel it until that feeling starts to diminish. Don't hold onto it. When you feel anger, then let the anger go through you. Go right through the anger and the injustice. Let it go through you. Can you feel it?*

P: *(Nods.)*

T: *Very good.*

P: *I am thirsty.*

Only now the physical charge emerges!

T: *When was this thirst the worst?*

P: *As I walked away from that well and didn't know what to do.*

T: *You didn't know what to do, you only felt thirst and despair. Go to that moment, to the moment of greatest despair, the moment you gave up completely.*

P: *Then I fall in a dry river bed, it seems, a dry river bed.*

T: *Can you see yourself, from a distance?*

P: *I pick up a stone. The stone I hold in my hand, my left hand. I hold onto it. The stone is greenish.*

T: *There was a bit of moisture on it, the remembrance of water. Is it still moist?*

P: *No. An old hunch-backed woman passes by.*

T: *Is that granny?*

P: *No.*

T: *Does she see the girl?*

P: *Yes. She is very weak herself.*

T: *Do they meet each other?*

P: *No, that girl is gone. Unconscious or dead. The woman walks past. She looks at it. She walks away again.*

T: *She just walks on. She cannot do anything about it. Did the girl still feel that? She is abandoned again. She is dying, they leave her to her own devices. Do you feel that?*

P: *Yes.*

T: *Let this feeling go right through you. The fear of dying, the anger, the loneliness and the abandonment, the thirst and the drought. Go through the dying. In your little white dress with flowers, a green stone clutched in your hand. Feel the sadness, the pain, the hopelessness, the incomprehension. Go to the moment of dying. What is the last feeling that passes your mind? What is the last feeling?*

P: *I cannot reach granny anymore.*

T: *What feeling does this give, this "being unable," not being able to reach anymore?*

P: *Powerlessness.*

Right at the end of her experience we find another charge.

T: *Is that the last feeling of the little girl, powerlessness?*

P: *Yes, I can't do anything anymore.*

This remark, "I can't do anything anymore," may be a postulate.

T: *Let this go through you, that feeling.*

P: *I give up.*

T: *Feel how you can't do anything anymore, feel how you give up. You know the feeling of giving up, don't you? Let it go through you and keep nothing back, go right through it. Give it up, give it up completely, you can go on no longer, for you are abandoned. When you have gone right through, and you are free of fear, despair, anger, abandonment, when you are free of it all, you see the branch of the tree again with the light behind it. That to you is the sign you have gone right through it. Can you go right through it or is there still something holding you back?*

P: *I cannot get at the anger. Still, I feel I am furious.*

T: *It is difficult for a little girl of four, five years old, to get at her anger. That anger that you still hold onto, where is this anger situated?*

This question represents a shift to aura exploration because the present person has to digest this anger.

P: *It feels like a belt around my waist. It can't get out.*

T: *Do you want to loosen that belt?*

P: *Yes.*

T: *Can you imagine you are lying on your bed at home with that belt of anger around you?*

P: *Yes.*

T: *Imagine that everything is getting darker and that now you are asleep. The first thing you see is that you stand beside your bed, you can see your body very vaguely lying in the dark. When you can see that, say "Yes."*

P: *Yes.*

T: *Then it gets so dark you can't see at all and in that darkness a glow appears around your body on the bed. When you can see that, tell me what color the glow has.*

P: *Turquoise with spots. Around the waist it is lighter.*

T: *Go with your attention to the waist. What color does the light have there? What is in the light? What can you see around your waist? What is that belt? Make it visible in that light.*

P: *Golden yellow. It looks like a solid belt. Very hard. Looks steel, gold colored steel. Anyhow metal.*

T: *Metal. Cold or warm?*

P: *Cold.*

T: *Can you untie it? Can you find something to untie it with, or is it in one piece?*

P: *At the other side it is tied to a chain. There is no lock.*

T: *What does the chain mean, what comes up in you?*

P: *Stuck.*

T: *Has it to do with slavery or being stuck in a situation?*

P: *In a situation.*

T: *Now you start cutting through this chain.*

P: *They are very solid links.*

T: *Then you need a very strong pair of cutters. Do you have such strong cutters?*

P: *No, I just use a laser beam.*

T: *What color does that laser beam have?*

P: *White.*

T: *With what hand you will do this?*

P: *Left.*

T: *There is a silver white laser beam coming from your left hand. While you pull the chain from your body you cut through the links as through cake. It is loose in no time. You put the laser beam aside, pull the chain from under your back. Is there something on the steel, outside or inside, or is it just plain?*

P: *Just plain.*

T: *What shall we do with that steel chain?*

P: Burn it, throw it in the fire.

T: Can you imagine a fire with the same color as the laser beam?

P: Yes.

T: White, silver white, that chain simply melts away in it. Can you see that? A silver white flame, it goes through it and it is gone. Can you see that?

P: It completely melts away.

T: Okay, shift your attention now to the body on the bed. Is there still something around the waist or is it now completely free?

P: Free.

T: Then you go back to the little girl and you see if there is still something that keeps her stuck. We go back to the dying girl. Do you still want to know why she got so stuck in that situation? Or is it no longer important? Did your granny tell you why there were just the two of you?

P: She did tell stories sometimes, in the rocking chair. Why we were there by ourselves

T: Did you ever ask her or did she tell you?

P: At first I cried sometimes when they had just left.

T: Who had just left?

P: I think my father. My mother, too.

T: Go to the moment your father and mother are leaving. You see that now. You cry. Feel what you felt then. Let it go through you. Can you see them leave?

P: I don't think so. They were suddenly gone.

T: What was the first moment you noticed that they were gone, when you felt it?

P: When I came home from playing and asked, "Where is daddy, where is mummy?" Then granny said something like, "They're gone, but they will come back someday."

T: Did she believe that herself?

P: I don't think so.

T: What did she feel about your father and mother that they had left?

P: She had no ill feelings.

T: She knew life. Did she understand it?

P: Yes. She thought it would be all right with me.

T: Did she think she could look after you better than your parents?

P: Yes.

T: Who were you actually angry about? Who did you think was mean?

P: My father.

T: Did you love your father more than your mother?

P: Yes.

T: Can you still feel how you loved him?
P: Yes.
T: Can you also feel the sadness and the anger and the love?
P: Yes.
T: All mixed, hard for a little girl. Can you now really feel how it was?
P: Yes.
T: Can you die now?
P: Yes.
T: Can you now see that little girl lie there, that little body?
P: Yes.
T: Has something happened to that little body, that hurt you?
P: No.
T: You are gone. And now you go very high up, take yourself away, very high, very light and very fresh. So fresh, so cool and you hear the water murmur and you are near a brook and you stand in it and you drink the water of the murmuring brook. Clear, cool water, can you see that?
P: I feel as if my hands are still limp.
T: Are they still limp?
P: Yes.
T: Can you hold those hands in the water? Do you still feel power-less?
P: Especially the right one is very limp.
T: Can you cure that yourself in that cool water? Drink it, let the strength of that cool water go through you. Let it go through your neck and your shoulders and your arms and your wrists down to your hands. The strength of that water, let it go through you, healing. Can you manage to do that?
P: Yes.
T: You feel better, and while you are feeling better you grow, and while you grow up, you get older until you are a young woman, until you are grown up. When you feel that, say yes.
P: Yes.
T: How do you look now, are you still brown with curls or are you different?
P: I think of accepting, but I don't see myself.
T: Go to a place where you have a survey over your life. You come to that place, you see it before you as if you walk over, on or in something to a place where you have a view of that life as a girl. What comes up in you now?
P: It was only short.

T: *Why this short life? Why did the girl have to die in that way? Let it come up in you, the survey is obvious and clear, why? Is it getting clear to you?*

P: *No.*

T: *Then you go back to the time before you were born. You go back to the time of the decision for that life. The time of the moment you were going to take that decision. I will count back from three to one and then you are there. Three . . . , two . . . , one. You stand now before your life and you see the life that is coming. What goes through your mind? Why do you go?*

P: *It looks as if I have an appointment.*

T: *An appointment with whom?*

P: *With my father.*

T: *What did you arrange together?*

P: *That we were going to meet each other.*

T: *Were you looking forward to that?*

P: *Yes.*

T: *You loved him.*

P: *Yes.*

T: *Was it the intention that you were dying so young, or did he abandon you? Feel it. You may express it. Let it go through you, dive into it. When you keep this feeling back, it hurts, it hurts badly. Can you feel being stuck in this deep pain? Can you feel where you carried this along?*

P: *In my pelvis.*

T: *You are angry with him, aren't you? You loved him and he let you down. That went very deep. Can you free yourself from what is in your pelvis?*

P: *It looks as if I want to take revenge myself.*

T: *Can you understand that?*

P: *Yes.*

T: *Did you take revenge or did you keep that inside yourself in your pelvis?*

P: *I only hurt myself with it.*

T: *Yes. It's hard, isn't it? What do you want now with this revenge? Do you want to do something with it?*

P: *No.*

T: *What do you want to do then?*

P: *Get rid of it.*

T: *You want to get rid of it. Let it go through you. You also have to clean your pelvis and your hands. Revenge is also in your hands. Those hands want to do it, but the source is in the pelvis. See your-*

self as a spiteful bitch with vengeance coming from your pelvis to your hands, go right through this. It makes you ugly, this vengeance. Feel the ugliness of that vengeance. It makes you twitch. Is it humane to hold on to that vengeance?

P: No.

T: *The longer you hold on to it, the less human it becomes.*

P: Yes.

T: *Did you do something wrong in that life when you entered it? Would you do it differently now? Is it wrong to love someone?*

P: I was too late.

T: *Did you want to marry him?*

P: Yes.

T: *Did your father recognize you then? Did he feel it was you?*

P: I think he did.

T: *So he betrayed you. It is very stuck in you, isn't it? It will come out, but layer after layer. It is hard, almost horn-like, it has been with you that long. Do you understand now why it is in your pelvis? You wanted him as a woman.*

P: Yes.

T: *Did this vengeance play a role in your present life?*

P: Yes. I had to go through it.

T: *When you come through it, where do you end then?*

P: I don't know.

T: *What is the beginning? Go back to the beginning. What is the original feeling?*

P: That I love him.

T: *That you love him. All beginnings are simple. So where do you end, when you've been through everything?*

P: That I love him.

T: *That you love him. The end is simple too, but still it isn't the same. You can solve that vengeance only in the feeling from which it originated. Where has this feeling been? Surely, you tucked that away very deeply?*

P: Yes.

T: *Where is this deeply tucked away feeling? What is it in?*

P: I see a little ball with light around it. Maybe it's a lump of ice. It's in my belly.

T: *In your pelvis too?*

P: Yes.

T: *Is it underneath and in that vengeance?*

P: Yes.

T: *What should we do with that little ball?*

P: Free it.

T: Who does that little ball belong to?

P: To me.

T: It's yours. You are that little ball. Now you are going to free your-self, for you have been imprisoned long enough. Would you like to do that?

P: Yes.

T: Where does a little girl who plays with laser beams get the energy from?

P: My heart.

T: From your heart. Now you go from the source of energy to that little ball until there is a connection and when there is a connection you say yes. It starts to come, doesn't it? Do you have to go through a lot?

P: Yes, it goes very slowly.

T: But surely.

P: I have contact.

T: Now this little ball starts growing, swelling. What kind of feeling is in that little ball, apart from love?

P: Exuberance.

T: Exuberance, pleasure and joy. What is stronger: the vengeance or the exuberance?

P: It completely swells up.

T: Look at what happens, just see what happens, it can't break anymore now, it is that strong. Now you had almost let yourself down, but this did not happen.

P: It looks like a bean that is swelling up.

T: Is your belly full of it yet? Does it come out? Where does it come out?

P: It is all bulging, around me or something.

T: Does it come out from all sides, or doesn't it? Don't you dare to trust yourself to it?

P: Two half balls. I think it is much. It can't be true.

T: Maybe you just think that.

P: It could be gone again.

T: Why would it go away and where to?

P: A habit of "I'll get him." Power struggle, too.

T: Does it still pull?

P: Yes.

T: How can you free that left wrist?

P: Just free it.

T: Of what?

P: *Fear of losing face or something. Accepting that I was wrong, that I didn't see it right.*

T: *Is it human to see something wrong?*

P: *Yes.*

T: *Is it human to go on seeing something wrong?*

P: *That is stupid.*

T: *That is stupid. Not inhuman, but not very intelligent either. For whom you are afraid to lose face? For him?*

P: *Yes.*

T: *Do you know who he is?*

P: *Yes.*

T: *Can you still feel that love?*

P: *Yes.*

T: *When you feel that love, can you lose face? Who has to be afraid of losing face? Was there a competition going on between you?*

P: *I think so.*

T: *Would you like to bring a present for him?*

P: *Yes.*

T: *You have a nice present for him: a brown curlyhead with a little white dress with flowers. Go and get that present, for it still lies there in the dry river bed. Wake her up to life, with your left hand. You need all your love and all your acceptance, otherwise it won't work. Do you see her lie there?*

P: *Yes.*

T: *What do you feel when you see her?*

P: *Tenderness.*

T: *Let this tenderness flow through your hands and shine through your eyes. Do something nice for her. What is the first thing she needs?*

P: *Water.*

T: *Where will you get it from?*

P: *I carry it with me.*

T: *How long did you carry that with you?*

P: *For a very long time.*

T: *Go back, ever more back, to the moment you got water. This is the time you got water. It's difficult to get there, isn't it?*

P: *Yes.*

T: *It is so long ago, the channel has nearly dried up. That well has nearly dried out. Look in that well and let the water come up. Can you let that water come up? Can you let it come bubbling up?*

P: *Yes.*

T: *It is a well, the water comes up, and now you feel what you felt long ago when you first got water. It flows through the channel of time to the present. Make contact between now and the first moment you got water. Can you immerse yourself in the water?*

P: *Yes.*

T: *How did you feel on the first moment you got the water, long ago?*

P: *Sparkling and clear.*

T: *Have you ever been without water since then? For now you have water to give to that little girl?*

P: *I didn't know where it was. I'd forgotten where it was.*

T: *Why did you lead that life then? You had to look in the dry well, feel panic and pain and despair, be abandoned, because your well had nearly dried up. Can you feel that?*

P: *Yes.*

T: *You looked inside yourself. But because the little girl in the white dress dried out then, you just didn't reach it. Now you see the water coming up in the well and now you give water to the little girl as you got water in that ancient past. That water is clear and sparkling. Let her drink in tenderness and sparkling. Feel how she leans against you. Watch her face as she drinks the water. Like a mother gives milk, so you give water. Can you see that? Can you drink from it yourself?*

P: *There is plenty.*

T: *Will you drink of it yourself?*

P: *I will do that.*

T: *Why do you stay dry? Everything you can learn from staying dry, you have learned now, haven't you? What does vengeance have to do with water?*

P: *Hide it.*

T: *There is vengeance in that well. Everything died out until you could only see the contours of a dead tree against the light. That girl remained faithful to the water. The stone with the memory of water she clutched in her hand. This is why you can give water now to the girl, for that water was inside that girl. Give water to her now like your father and mother once gave water to you in the ancient past. You lost the habit. It takes long before the dryness is gone from you. Are you afraid of losing something, when you let the water in, afraid of losing yourself?*

P: *No, I don't think so anymore.*

The words "I think" suggest distance, so this is not a complete catharsis.

T: *How does the little girl feel now?*
P: *She is tired and she is comfortably leaning against me.*
T: *On which side of you does she lie?*
P: *In my right arm.*
T: *Now you take her with you and she stays with you, yes? Feel her next to you. You are lying here as a little brown curlyhead and you like it too. You believe it, but with difficulty. You are afraid it will slip away again. Drink lots of water. You notice that part of yourself only half comes along. Those are the masculine sides of yourself, they obviously ask for different things. Accept that, but let the fear go that it will dry up again. Now is the time for the girl in the little white dress. Okay? Come back in your own way and in your own time until you are here and now again.*

EVALUATION

Why did you say, "Go back to the little girl and give her water"?
That is dissociation. I treat the girl as a pseudo-obsession, a previous life that is still with her unresolved. I tried to reach catharsis by letting her go through that experience of the little girl. Also, I tried to let her feel the girl outside her to take her along later. I did that because I felt a great resistance from the masculine sides. I felt this didn't help them much. She had to realize she always carried that water with her, that she had never been without it. Such a notion provides a breakthrough, a liberation.

With her that wasn't so. So I pushed on a bit further, back to the source, to the beginning. The stone in her hand was a strong image to me. Moses struck water from the rocks. This image is an even stronger symbol, it is deeper - the dry river bed with the dried-out stone. The little body is lying there and conquers, for it remains lying there in her soul for these long years until a session as this one comes along, wherever and whenever.

Would it have been possible to arrange a meeting with that father after the dying?
Then first the vengeance should be gone. Vengeance in a person's hands is one of the most stubborn things I have ever come across and prevents catharsis after death. After her death she stayed lingering on up to this moment, until she received the water she always carried hidden with her.

287

The twitching hand was also powerless, for the twitching was in vain. Later it appeared that the hand was powerless, because there was vengeance in it that couldn't come out. It was locked up as an internal armor available to become firm in the power struggle. When a power struggle starts happening, you need armor, for when you get weak, you get wounded. I nearly said it wrong at first, *"being* abandoned," but it was *"feeling* abandoned." An important difference. She had really been abandoned, but under her own direction. Her "bigger sister" directed this all and chose that life, and on top of that prevented her from seeing him leave.

What about that metal plate?
I only now realize that. The chain was, *I am stuck to something.* That was the foreplay. In her belly was vengeance, but it was gold colored, so it had to be good. It was gold colored, because that life was chosen, it was the rescue operation. So they were self-chosen bonds. Afterward I made a mistake that I will now put right:

We burned the stuff, but it was something of yourself that you burned. So now it melts into something else that you must keep. *Imagine that you make an ornament for the little girl, using the gold from the oven. What would you give her?* "A ring." *Where will she wear it?* "On her left hand." *What finger?* "The ring finger." *When that dryness, that hardness becomes too strong in yourself, you simply show the ring and then you drink a glass of water. Okay.*

Because it was gold you felt no urge to look for what was underneath the belt in the body?
I asked, "Is there still something else that doesn't belong there." *No.* Then it is all right. Only later it appeared that there still was something.

What about that laser beam?
That is a basic tool in aura exploration. The patient imagines a silver white force going through his hands and coming out of his fingertips. From the left hand this light comes as a thin, intense beam that can be focused. With that beam you can examine, untie, work open, cut open. With the right hand you make from the light a silver white glove to take hold of unpleasant things and take them away. Perhaps it is reversed with left-

handed people. I let people make that beam of light, but when someone comes up with that himself, it is a good sign.

She obviously felt resistance against the heavy pair of cutters I suggested. She needed something more civilized. That laser beam was a spontaneous idea? *Yes.*

It sounded very matter of fact, as if it was most natural.
If she couldn't have seen the water in the well, I could have made her open the well with her laser. Another possibility would have been to let the little girl with her green stone descend into the well. You have to improvise with what you have, and sometimes you have it all there in front of you. The best is when you let the patient work with whatever he or she suggests on their own. It is an almost aesthetic challenge to compose like that.

I was rather surprised when you made that diversion, "Did you want to marry him?" Then she answered, "I was too late," and I thought, "What made him ask that?"
She as abandoned by her father with whom she had an appointment. Her resentment about that was in her pelvis. How is the pelvis of a woman related to a man? So I suspected they had been lovers before.

You asked her to go back to the previous life. She then said she had an appointment with that father. Why did you ask that?
I had the feeling that it was going well, but not well enough. She also had to understand why he left her. Therefore I wanted to know if she had chosen that life In a karmic relationship you can feel unfree in the entanglements, but you are never forced without cooperating yourself; it is always your responsibility, too. She mentioned an appointment. Therefore she is, apart from being a pitiful little girl, also engaged in a retaliation against her father. She didn't keep her part of the appointment, for she came too late. Besides that, she didn't realize that he, too, would fail to keep his appointment.

You tried a couple of times to take her through the death experience of the girl to the point of oversight. In between you chose another form by saying, "You grow until you are older," after death, obviously as an alternative way to get to the point of oversight, but it didn't work.
A girl of five can go to a place of overview, but has to have a situation of overview too, so she has to grow up. It did work,

but it felt muddled and uneasy. Perhaps "being grown-up" wasn't well put. Here that attempt is a renovation, for she lingered on in the experience of that light in the distance with that dead branch. The dead branch is the branch from which the dead leaf has fallen. The ancient image is that you are a branch of a tree. The sap channel has dried up, the branch dries out, the leaf falls off.

Can this overview come via the higher self? When you have died, you are the complete spirit, and no longer in a child's body, aren't you?

That five-year-old girl remained a five-year-old girl until today and the higher self sees it and surveys it but cannot come near the girl. How did it go exactly? First there was a misunderstanding about the place of survey and being grown up.

She said, "When I think of being grown up I think of accepting, but I cannot see myself." Then you said, "Go to a place where you get an overview. What do you experience?" Then she said, "It was only a short life." "Why? Now you have to go back to the time before you were born, the time you took the decision for this life."

This, by the way, is easy on the "place of overview," for there you look back on your life, including the start. You go with a deceased child usually first back to the last situation of adulthood. I wanted to know what she experienced just before birth. Did she feel pushed from behind or did she choose herself? She was enthusiastic, for she had an appointment with her lover.

I am still thinking about your question. I dislike the term "higher self." I don't know what I evoke then. I would rather leave it an open question. I ask her to "go to the place of overview." I do not have a contract with her higher self, but rather with her.

Then you stay put in your limitations.

Better than roam about in your limitations. I distrust short circuits. Those subpersonalities are stubborn and they have to change. The higher self does not have to change, that is all right as it is.

We can ask the higher self things that are connected with those personalities.

As long as I can ask *her*, why should I?

Because it is less cumbersome.
Therapy is not a matter of getting information efficiently and solving a puzzle. It's a matter of changing someone. I work with those areas of resistance precisely because they have to change. Now, as a therapist you can lose sight of things. Probably you have done something wrong somewhere, and you try to link with that big computer up there. I would only do so as a last resort.

The road to catharsis was pregnant with symbols here. Nearly every concrete event - the stone, the water well, the water, a fallen leaf - everything you used as symbols of ancient data to prepare for the catharsis, and in the end you wrapped it together.
That may all be fine, but only for lack of better means. The normal procedure is to let someone go through his emotions, so that those emotions let go and he can be free. Here this failed, everything had to be done within very narrow margins.
Then it is important to know how to use such instruments. I think this is farfetched for us.
Possibly, but have some confidence in yourself, too, and in Our Good Lord. Maybe you get peole with symbols that appeal to you. Maybe something else emerges within you. The main thing is that you make do with what you are offered. Talk in the other person's language; that deepens the experience. With her that deepening was important, because, although she was well into her experience, there was a strong upward pressure to get out. When you talk in terms that are not connected with the situation, you increase the upward pressure.

I often work suggestively, but I stick to the story and I leave open ways to escape, such as, "Or is it something else?" and "Or something like that."

The last part I experienced as healing. Where do you draw the line? When does the patient delegate responsibility and self-reliance, and ask the therapist for help?
There is a transition between craftsmanship and priesthood. This to me has to do with a sudden insight that goes further than the incarnation as such. For me it was the flash that she already carried this water with her always. I open that and work it out, but I don't contribute anything myself. I want to let her feel in her bones that she always had the water within her. In this kind of situation I interfere, but in such a way that she can

291

stop any moment. That is healing, that is no longer a regression therapy.

We have to avoid forcing, though. I wanted to help that girl. But we have to be careful in playing Our Good Lord. I would rather train craftsmen than priests.

A woman returned to several male and female lives and every time she died, she stayed lingering on by herself. In that session I made a strong intervention: "When you die after this life, and you leave your body, you think of me and in a flash you are with the people where you belong." She told me afterward she was shaking then, and felt, *Now he got me after all*, yet without being bothered by it.

If the higher self always worked, we wouldn't be sitting here, I think. No. It is there of course, and it does work, but only to a certain degree. The higher self remains dependent. Whatever they plot at the general staff, we are at the front, we have to carry it out. The best is when the general staff and the front communicate well.

You said that the source had dried out a long time before that. Is this then the manifestation of the awareness of the self, with that stone and that wrist?
It is more than awareness. It is an attempt to create a balance. The girl corrected something, but the seed didn't sprout, it mummified and has only partially sprouted now. Partially. The main work did not happen this evening, but in the years that the little girl walked on this earth. Now she gathers the fruit, but then she did the work. The girl died in that life of the consequences, the drying up of the well.

There was a beginning with water and lasers. Then there was a series of probably hard and dry lifetimes. Then there was the life of this girl with before that at least one life in which the man-woman relationship with the father played a role. That girl lingered on, traveled along like a constant pseudo-obsession. So she stopped those harder lives.

Where is that turn, the choosing of that life of the little girl? You say it was a mistake. I don't believe that, for the short life of that little girl has been incredibly important.
Again, the awareness she had before she incarnated, that personality that was not the higher self made two serious mistakes.

Only, these mistakes were planned, directed by the higher self. Some mistakes are divine.

EMOTIONAL BRIDGE TO HANGOVER THAT APPEARS TO BE AN ATTACHMENT

In an inventory of hangover charges, this patient felt in the left part of her body a drab old woman who did not want to show herself. The patient felt *revulsion*, but also curiosity. She did not recognize the woman. Patient acknowledged that she can feel tired herself, but not drab.

The therapist asks if the woman is a part of this patient. The patient does not think so, but *unrest* remains and she does not know what to do with it. When she rests after hard work, she feels the unrest of that woman, unrest and revulsion. Also *anger* and *rage* are present, especially in the hands. She cannot do anything with these feelings; she feels powerless herself. There is some *guilt* attached. Unrest is the strongest charge.

T: Go to the moment this unrest was strongest.
P: Through a stream of messages I got.

This patient lived as young girl in a castle, free and careless, until she becomes imprisoned at the time of a power struggle. Patient feels beating heart, fear in the throat, a cramp in the shoulders, and shivers. Everything beautiful became drab. The therapist lets this patient experience these sensations until she feels better, and then asks the patient to move to the end of this misery. The patient becomes liberated through many people.

P: But it remains with me. That dungeon, not really understanding, the injustice, wanting to do something, but not being able.
T: The old woman has that feeling?
P: Yes, but she never did something about it, she couldn't.
T: Go to the end of the unrest.
P: I have died. I have had a simple life. The unrest has broken much of me. That simplicity feels pleasant, otherwise I could not have coped with it. Stupid. I would now get angry about it. For me it is unrecognizable. I have no affinity for it. The revulsion comes back. Perhaps I don't want it. I see myself not as this old woman. I see only pictures.

293

T: *Ask this woman when she came to you.*
P: *She has to do something with my mother. I think that she is my mother.*
T: *Go to a moment when it becomes clear to you.*

The patient finds herself in the womb, where she has a drab, dark, suffocating feeling. She cannot do anything. She loses her temper when the mother does not respond to problems and argues with the father. She pushes everything away, keeps her face straight. Patient loses her temper and would like to hit the father from her position in the belly. The arguments, and the way the mother deals with those arguments have hit this patient pretty hard. So drabness has crept in. She feels the greatest temper and sense of suffocation during delivery. The baby cries in temper. Her leg hurts. It is twisted.

Therapist asks patient to go to the moment when the drabness definitively entered in her life. There emerges an incident with an ironing board that scared the patient. She sees again the high chair where she had to sit for hours in front of the window. She found it maddening, but her mother impassively went on cleaning the room. Patient felt locked in, angry, with no way out. She could not do anything. One day she finally resigned, but never really.

T: *Were there ever moments of choice?*
P: *Yes, throw down the indoor plants before the windows. I don't know. I just lost my temper. Later I fled to the streets. I never realized this. I have picked up much more of that sealing up than I thought; I never discuss things. It makes me slow, I withdraw.*
T: *Is the old woman still around? Do you want to say or do anything with this old woman?*
P: *Yes, and I want to get rid of her.*
T: *Has there ever been a time when she felt good?*
P: *When she was young.*
T: *What should happen?*
P: *She must realize that she doesn't need to feel guilty. Now she laughs. That guilt feeling, that responsibility feeling, are nonsense. The old woman leaves. The drabness lifts. I feel that in my body. Also from my chin and shoulders the tension lifts, it leaves space. I send the woman to the light and I feel glad.*

Patient discovers that for a long time she has been burdened with those feelings. She couldn't deal with people who could not handle their feelings. She lost her temper or felt depressed. She even had to learn to talk about herself.

To make sure, therapist checks every charge, but patient feels good and chuckles like a four-year old girl.

IMAGINATIVE BRIDGE TO PSEUDO OBSESSION

This individual session is a follow-up to a group session (see previous chapter) in which this patient saw a boy and felt gloomy.

T: *Tell me something about the boy you saw.*
P: *He was the third who entered. He had a set face, about ten years old, and took the chair next to the fireplace.*
T: *How does he feel himself?*
P: *Insensitive, a hard expression on his face, shrugging shoulders, cynical and gloomy. A heavy feeling of gloom and hardness.*
T: *Leave the images of that house and that room and go to wherever that boy usually is. Find him in his own environment.*
P: *A street with dilapidated wooden houses. The sun is shining. It is dirty and muddy.*
T: *And where does he live?*
P: *In some shed. It is open at the front.*
T: *It doesn't have a front at all?*
P: *Yes, there is a doorway without a door and the windows are open holes. These have been beautiful houses, but they are run down. This is in the twelfth century or something. It has been a well-to-do neighborhood, but it is now all weathered and bleached wood.*
T: *How come? What is the reason?*
P: *I see now very many people lying down exhausted by illness and indifference. A combination of despair, revulsion, poverty. It gives a sense of meaninglessness, giving up.*
T: *Has this happened during his lifetime?*
P: *Each effort is meaningless.*
T: *We begin with the moment of the dying. Find where and how he died.*

This suggestion illustrates a standard intervention when a pseudo-obsessor is likely involved.

P: *He lies on some rags, he just gives up.*
T: *How old is he there?*
P: *Ten.*

T: *Ten. Hungry?*

P: *A bit.*

T: *He just doesn't want to go on. Being ill, giving up, how does he feel that?*

P: *Everything is dead inside.*

T: *The people he loved, are they also dead?*

P: *He doesn't know anymore. He doesn't care anymore.*

T: *He doesn't?*

P: *No.*

T: *Okay. Everything is dead inside. Is there no other feeling? Any thought or decision crossing his mind when he dies?*

P: *"I don't want no more."*

T: *Look how he leaves his body.*

P: *He doesn't. He sticks around. He is half out, half above his body.*

T: *What does he perceive?*

P: *Nothing.*

T: *So he doesn't see his body.*

This answer, that the boy perceives "nothing," is important and suggests that he never realized he died.

P: *Not really. He looks up. He doesn't look to the body.*

T: *And what does he see looking up?*

P: *Drab. Brown planks.*

T: *He even can't leave the shed?*

P: *He has no more energy.*

T: *Okay. Now see yourself, as you are today, entering the shed. You project yourself there. Try now to contact him. Describe what happens and how you get him moving.*

P: *He stretches his arms and I pull him out and now he suddenly shoots all the way up.*

T: *Join him, shoot up with him. See where he arrives.*

P: *It is light, and all green and lush. (Deep sigh.)*

T: *What happens to him there?*

P: *He begins to cry. He lies on grass and there are shining figures around him.*

T: *What do you do with him?*

P: *I sit next to him, I put my hand on his head. He lies now with his head in my lap. I stroke his hair. He just cries.*

T: *Stay with him until he stops crying. (Deep sigh, nods.) What has to happen with him now?*

P: *He doesn't understand what happened.*

T: Can you explain to him that he died?

P: Yes.

T: Does he get it?

P: No, he doesn't understand it. He can't.

T: Does he trust you?

P: He does.

T: Okay, take him back with you to the shed and show him his dead body.

P: Yes.

T: Now point at that. He should recognize it.

P: Yes, it dawns upon him.

T: He remembers now also how that came about. He remembers how he had given up.

P: Things simply were too much for him.

T: Do you want to do something with that body or can you just leave it or do you prefer to bury it?

P: I want to cover it with something.

T: Okay, see how you both cover the body. (Deep sigh, confirms.) Now you look at him and you ask him where he wants to go. He may stay with you or he may go up.

P: Up. But he wants us to go together.

T: Okay, then go up with him, to the spot where those light figures are. There transfer him, hand him over to somebody.

P: Mmm.

T: Okay, is this a past life of yourself or not?

P: Yes.

T: Then you say to him: "Always if you want to, at each moment, you may join me."

P: That feels better. Not for him, but for me.

T: He may stay there as long as he wants. Say to him, if you don't come back to me, I want you to wait for me until I get there. If you want to join me beforehand, you know where you can find me.

P: Yes.

T: He may also just visit to see how you are doing. They can help him further there, can't they? Is he now in good hands?

P: Yes, we have made a deal that I return at times, to maintain contact.

T: Okay. Now for one moment you again see your house with that room and those chairs. Is that chair near the fireplace now empty?

P: Yes. (Surprised.)

T: Reserve that chair for him.

P: Yes.

T: *Is there still something what you have to see or do right now?*
P: *No.*
T: *Then come back to the here and the now.*
P: *Say, that feels good. A lot of his gloom has been starting to go. Thanks.*

VERBAL BRIDGE TO FEARS

This session addresses traumatic moments that occurred in the present life, coupled with a traumatic death in previous life. It includes *dissociation and renovation* of an experience that occurred to the patient as a small child.

Therapist invites this woman to participate in the demonstration session, because he saw a glimpse of fear in her eyes. The woman accepts.

T: *Do you feel anything or are you blank?*
P: *I am blank.*
T: *Repeat this sentence and complete it: "I am scared of . . . ."*
P: *. . . anger.*
  . . . violence.
  . . . power.
  . . . what I don't understand.
  . . . violence.

Repetition is evident, so the list is stopped. Therapist starts at the top, as always with a small list:

T: *"I am scared of anger." Say that five times. (Patient does that.) What do you feel?*
P: *I'm trembling, in my arms and legs, I feel scared.*

Both an emotion and a somatic (E + S) are present, so regression can begin.

T: *You are trembling in your arms and legs, you are afraid of your anger. Go back to the situation in which you felt this for the first time. (Counts back). What do you experience?*
P: *A train, I sit in a train. There are people on the platform, soldiers.*

This is the German occupation. So it is in her present life.

P: *The train is on the point of leaving the station.*
T: *Do you know this situation?*
P: *Yes.*
T: *Go to the anger.*
P: *I was angry.*

Note this patient's use of the past tense! She is still angry, and very much so, but fear represses this anger.

P: *A soldier has taken my food, I wasn't to have it. I don't understand. Soldiers have found the food and taken it away when I wanted to get on the train.*
T: *Go to the precise moment. Look at that soldier. What does he express?*
P: *He enjoys his power, he laughs. He sees my fear, he laughs at his comrade. I am angry.*

Now the patient speaks in the present tense!

P: *I can't express it; I am frightened. The fear checks my anger. They walk away with my basket; the train will go soon now. I shout, "Wait!" I leave the train and grab the basket with my food. The soldier comes after me. I kick him off the footboard and the train departs.*
T: *Are you lying on the platform?*
P: *No, he is. I'm sitting in the train.*
T: *How do you feel now?*

When the action stops, you ask patients how they feel.

P: *I feel shame. (New charge.) Because I kicked him off the train. I shouldn't have done that. I don't feel good. I took back that basket by violence. I am scared of my own violence. I don't think I have eaten the food.*
T: *Go to the next important moment.*
P: *I am at home, feeling sick.*
T: *Where do you feel that?*
P: *In my throat. I feel a tremble in my throat. I have to eat from my parents, but I can't.*
T: *Go back to the beginning of this trembling.*
P: *I'm sitting in the train; I tremble from tension, from anger, hate, guilt. Not fear, but shame.*

T: *That shame is connected with that guilt. Feel the trembling and nauseous feeling in your throat. What comes to mind?*

P: *I am so lonely. They don't understand me, my father and mother. They don't understand that I don't want to eat. I feel angry, alone, sad.*

At home with the parents a new wave of emotion comes up, one that expresses itself somatically, at her throat. She cannot eat. The feeling of "They don't understand me" is the opposite feeling of "I am scared of what I don't understand." Being alone is an important *original charge*. The basic emotion - the feeling of that feeling - is sadness.

T: *What else do you feel in your throat except anger and grief?*

P: *That's it.*

T: *What prevents you from letting go of this anger, sadness, hate, guilt?*

P: *It is not allowed.*

T: *Where is this situated, this not allowing yourself to let go?*

P: *In my head. It feels heavy at my forehead.*

Therapist next does *aura exploration*.

T: *What color light do you see around you?*

P: *Almost white.*

T: *Concentrate on the spot near your forehead.*

P: *I see a ball pressed against my forehead. It is a large ball, not really round, with prickles.*

T: *Is it a thing or something alive? (Checks whether it is a sea urchin.)*

P: *A thing.*

T: *Dark or light?*

P: *Dark and cold.*

T: *What do you want to do with it?*

P: *Push it away.*

T: *You can, but first you should understand what this ball is. Go to the moment the ball arrived. (Counts back.)*

P: *I am at the foot of a mountain. A ball rolls on top of me. I feel fear; I can't go away; I am rigid with fear; the ball rolls on my head. I lie there, I am crushed. That ball is crushing.*

T: *Check to see if this ball is symbolic or an experience from a past life. You are at the foot of a mountain. What do you see?*

P: *There are people under the mountain edge. They kick me. They have fun, they are drunk. I am scared, I hurt a lot. I am a woman of about twenty years old. They enjoy kicking me. They are just men. They drag me down, into the ravine.*

T: *Did they rape you?*

P: *No, just kicked me to death.*

What does this kicking to death have to do with the starting point, which was *fear of anger*? The kicking is done by drunken men. The patient interprets this connection as follows: *When I get angry . . . I get fuddled . . . I start kicking . . . I destroy someone.*

T: *Go back to the moment just before this all happened, to understand it.*

P: *I had to look after the sheep or something. I went to sleep. I woke up when I heard a group of men. They assaulted me. Mostly they were drunk. They wanted to make fun. They kicked me; I don't understand why; I didn't do anything to them.*

T: *Go back to the most crushing moment.*

P: *I couldn't hold onto anything when they kicked me down. I fell very hard, I couldn't grab anything to hold onto.*

T: *Let this go through you very deeply, this crushing, this having nothing to hold onto.*

Always ask for the worst, here feeling crushed. She has to go all the way through the deepest agony - once the question about sexual abuse was asked. Here the most shattering experience was literally being smashed to death, and having nothing to hold onto. To her, being crushed and having nothing to hold onto have become knotted together.

T: *What feelings do you get with it?*

P: *Fear. Of pain, dying, being alone.*

T: *Before that you were on your own, too, with nobody to defend you. Go to the moment of dying. What do you experience?*

P: *I feel thirst, I see blood.*

T: *Have you been lying there for a long time?*

P: *No.*

T: *You are thirsty, you see blood. What is the worst feeling?*

P: *Being alone.*

T: *Go to the moment of death, what happens?*

P: *Now it is fine. I feel light, liberated, dissolved. I am in the light, I don't have to anymore.*

301

T: Go to a next, slightly changed situation.
P: I see flowers, it is all right now, I am surrounded by flowers.
T: Can you look back on your life. Do you want that?
P: Rather not. It is all right like this.

Not wanting to look back is a bad sign. It suggests incomplete dying, despite the beautiful surroundings. Some karmic theme is present there.

T: Are you alone among those flowers?
P: Yes, there is peace.

"Peace" is a word that suggests a pseudo-catharsis; an evasion of a confrontation, successful for the time being.

T: Go back to the moment of being kicked. Can you see that? Look from a distance at the meaning of that situation.

This suggestion forces some kind of retrospective after all.

P: Strange, but it is all right.
T: Do you understand why it is all right?
P: I wanted it this way.
T: Go back to the moment when you wanted this to happen.
P: I don't want to go on living. I was alone. That's why I went to sleep.
T: That is the root of everything, the feeling of being alone; can you evoke this feeling in yourself now?
P: It does not matter anymore now, now I feel peaceful.
T: You want to leave it that way?
P: Yes.

Whether there has been real catharsis or not, the patient decides!

T: Now go back to the moment when you are with your parents; you feel sick and they don't understand why. You feel angry and alone.
P: It is difficult to feel that.
T: Did something interfere, or did these feelings slip away?
P: I am still amidst the flowers.
T: What is nicest there?
P: Peace.

T: *Can you feel the source of that peace? Where is the source in or around your body?*
P: *In my head. It is all in my head. Quiet, warmth.*
T: *Concentrate on your forehead; is the ball still there?*
P: *No, it is gone.*
T: *Touch it with your hands to feel it.*
P: *I still feel a little pressure on my ears.*
T: *Go back to the moment with the train; the soldier lies on the platform. Do you still feel shame and guilt because you used violence?*
P: *No, pride rather. Because I dared to do it.*
T: *Is there still something trembling in you now that you feel proud?*
P: *No.*
T: *Do you still have that nauseous feeling?*
P: *No.*
T: *Then open your basket and start eating; can you do that?*

This suggestion begins the renovation.

P: *Yes.*
T: *Are you still scared of your anger?*
P: *Not anymore.*
T: *What's the difference?*
P: *I achieved something, and I feel that anger is sometimes good, justified.*

Note this patient's use of the word "sometimes!" So there is no generalization anymore; the program is dissolved.

T: *Say three times, "I am not afraid of my anger." (Does so.) What do you feel now?*
P: *Somewhat proud.*
T: *Why just somewhat and not completely?*
P: *Should not completely.*
T: *Why?*
P: *I don't know.*
T: *Does it have something to do with the pressure on your ears?*
P: *Yes.*
T: *Would you like to take that away?*
P: *Yes.*

Aura exploration is done on her ears.

P: *I hear the deep voice of a man. It is some kind of monk. He talks to me.*

T: *Let it become clearer. This is the source of the pressure on your ears.*

P: *I am very small, three or four years old. It is this life. I sit on his lap.*

T: *What does his voice say?*

P: *"It is nice, it is nice, it is nice." He fiddles with me, under my skirt, between my legs. Nice, but creepy. The pressure on my ears is from his voice. It has something hypnotic.*

T: *Shall we take that pressure away?*

P: *Yes.*

T: *How can we do that?*

P: *That man has to go.*

T: *Look at the situation as you are now. What do you think of what's happening there?*

This change in perspective achieves dissociation.

P: *Dirty, I think.*

T: *What would you like to do about it?*

P: *Take that child away from that man.*

T: *Do so. Take that child away. Where will you bring her?*

P: *I put her on my lap. I leave the man behind.*

T: *Feel how you leave his voice behind. In what kind of place are you now with the child?*

P: *It is clear daylight, outside.*

T: *See that it has just been raining; see how the world is washed clean.*

P: *Yes, I can see it.*

T: *Take this child up into yourself; it fuses with you. Do you hear the sounds of nature? What do you hear?*

This suggestion is offered as an alternative to the hypnotic man's voice.

P: *Birds.*

T: *Listen to those birds. The sound is liberating and takes away the remaining pressure. From now on you will, whenever you hear the chirping of birds, feel freer, liberated. Is the pressure on your ears gone now?*

P: Yes.
T: *Go back again to the situation with the train. How do you feel then?*
P: *Fine.*
T: *Are you still scared of your anger?*
P: *No.*
T: *Repeat and complete: "I am no longer scared of anger, because . . . ."*
P: *. . . I can handle it, . . . I am allowed to, . . . I allow myself to, . . . because I know what I'm doing.*
T: *Say three times, "I know what I'm doing," and feel it going through you. (She does this.) Go back to the flowers again; is that sufficient for you to stay peaceful?*
P: *I now bring her with me to the here and now.*

The patient dissociates spontaneously, and in so doing treats that previous life as a mild pseudo-obsession.

T: *You appreciate the peace she brings along; but you have a lot to give to her. Do you realize that?*
P: *Yes.*
T: *Listen to the sounds of the birds, smell the flowers, open fully to the peaceful feeling: you know what you are doing. You can now come back in your own time, when you are ready for it.*

The therapist lets the patient "taste" three more sentences:

T: *"I am scared of violence."*
P: *I don't feel that anymore.*
T: *"I am scared of power."*
P: *I still feel that.*
T: *"I am scared of what I don't understand."*
P: *No, I don't feel that anymore.*

So the fear of power is still there. This is work for a next session. Also the root experience of loneliness could still be explored.

VERBAL BRIDGE TO HANGOVER

The following is an exercise session that illustrates problems that occur with weak guidance and a difficult client. The entry

305

point was a general feeling of *revulsion*. This emotion is easily recursive - revulsion may be directed to the session and to the therapist. Also, revulsion may be directed back to the patient. The dangerous word in all this is "general." Nothing is done in the session to make the feeling of revulsion more specific.

T: *Try to catch this feeling of revulsion in sentences.*
P: *I cannot get going. I don't get the locomotive going. I walk in circles. I never break out. Adrift. No end to it. It goes on and on. It is never enough. I am fed up.*
T: *Say a few times, "I am fed up."*
P: *I am fed up. I want to run away, I am not in the mood, I don't do it, I refuse to do it. As if a big "must" is behind all this somewhere. I am fed up with "have to."*
T: *What do you feel with that?*
P: *Anger, especially at myself.*

The charges *anger* and *grief* come quickly. After that emerge *powerlessness* and *impotence*.

P: *It is so much. I'll never finish. I never ever will be ready.*
T: *Never ready with what?*
P: *With duties, with "musts." An alternative is do nothing, but then you belong nowhere anymore.*
T: *Who requests those duties?*
p: *I do. What I put on is never enough, it is never enough, it is never enough.*
T: *Go back to the moment when you had that feeling for the first time.*
P: *Strange, "It is never enough" is the same as "It is too much."*

At this point the patient begins to talk about camp experiences.

T: *Choose either "It is too much" or "It is never enough."*

The patient repeats five times:

P: *It is never enough.*
T: *What do you feel with that?*
P: *Weariness. As a donkey in the treadmill: always the same, never enough, never rest, just going on. I feel heavy and tired. It feels almost like a rhythm. One foot before the other, nothing else.*
T: *Do you feel your legs?*

P: *From my calves to my ankles. As if everything is kept upright there. The rest doesn't count.*
T: *Do you see your feet?*
P: *Bare feet. Sand. A kind of living chain at a rope. I can't see that chain, but it feels like that.*
T: *You now go back to the beginning of this situation. You are now at the beginning.*

Then this patient sees herself as a boy of five or six years old, who takes leave of his mother. The mother squats. Patient sees that men take the boy on a camel, apparently as a slave. Then patient feels her feet in the sand, as boy of 12 or 14. She sees little else.

T: *Go to the moment when "It goes on and on, there is no end to it" was the strongest.*
P: *I get the idea that I fall, that I am exhausted. I lie, but my feet keep walking. Such a strange feeling in my feet. They lead their own life. I can't stop them.*
T: *Did you collapse?*
P: *I feel that I lie in the dark, rejected. I get no more food. I starve, gone to pieces. They just let me die.*
T: *Now go to the end of that life. Can you leave your body, are you out of it?*
P: *Yes.*
T: *Can you look back?*
P: *I am still busy nursing the body a bit. I am afraid that animals will eat him. I want to cover him with sand.*
T: *Just do that. Just say when you are ready.*
P: *Yes.*
T: *As you look back on that life, is there any moment when you could have made an important choice?*
P: *I didn't make any. I hadn't the willpower to choose. I had my head completely switched off, I just hoped there would come an end to it.*
T: *Could you have prevented something?*
P: *No, I was just low level. Perhaps I was without brains.*
T: *Can you accept that now?*

Why accept such an ordeal without understanding?

P: *It takes away the blame.*
T: *How is your anger right now?*

P: *Stands apart, is a different thing . . . I believe I couldn't get out.*
The anger is repressed. I am angry at myself.
T: *Is the life you relived related to that treadmill feeling?*

Anger at oneself should always be elaborated.

P: *Yes. I have made a decision. I don't want that ever again, I will*
prevent that. That is no life, it's worse than a beast.
T: *How does it feel now when you say, "It's never enough?"*
P: *Feels now completely as if it's never enough. Sorry, it's my prob-*
lem.

This is not catharsis, but rather the reverse: confirmation of the problem.

T: *Say with increasing attention, "It's never enough."*

The patient repeats this sentence, then feels tension on her throat, and it becomes dark. When the therapist asks her to increase the tension, that tension suddenly goes away. The darkness remains. Somewhat later:

P: *I get an association. I crawl through a soft tunnel, groping along.*
Not hard, cold, wet, but soft and dry.
T: *Go to the moment just before you entered that tunnel. Can you see*
how you entered that tunnel?
P: *I want to stop.*

Note the magic word: "stop."

T: *Is there yet something you must do before you stop?*
P: *Thank my feet for being with me.*
T: *Take your time. Okay for now?*
P: *Yes. How are you?*

During the evaluation of this session the atmosphere is heavy. The patient says that at a certain moment she felt that the therapist sounded distant, less interested. Before the session, this patient had negatively perceived a remark of the therapist. Perhaps this negative perception had affected the square of trust. The patient also often played co-therapist. She felt responsible for the process. She wanted to take care of the therapist. She felt guilty when she could not satisfy a request of the therapist.

The therapist says that the process took energy from her. Suddenly the patient said she wanted it to be enough, she wanted to feel a choice in this, to go from victim to activist. She felt she had only feet and could think no longer, and that appealed to her willpower, made her active. This perception is rubbish. Rather, the reverse is true. The atmosphere grew still heavier and tougher, like bubble gum. This heavy atmosphere is very understandable!

VERBAL EXPLORATION OF FEARS

The following session illustrates a verbal exploration of *fears* in which, apart from emotions, postulates can emerge. When someone wants to work at fears in general, we first map out what fears there are, and then, often in several sessions, work them off one by one. The verbal bridge rakes up charges "in dilution." Listing fears easily triggers reliving, sometimes spontaneously, but a shopping list should be made first. The evaluation that follows the session discusses the method employed.

T: *Say "Yes" when you have the feeling you are ready to start.*
P: *Yes.*
T: *Now you feel that you want all the fears that are inside you to come to the surface. Say five times as calmly, attentively and deeply as possible, "I am scared." (Patient repeats it five times.) Now I'm going to say a sentence and you repeat that and when you have repeated it, you complete it with the first thing that comes to mind and then we will go for new completions. "I am scared of . . . ," repeat it.*
P: *I am scared of . . .*
   . . . being alone.
   . . . black magic.
   . . . crowds.
   . . . stupid people.
   . . . incomprehension.
   . . . being locked up.
   . . . being alone in the dark.
   . . . coldness.
   . . . pain.
   . . . crowds of people.
T: *Okay, let us stop here.*

Crowds of people are probably the same as crowds, which was one of the first items on this patient's list. Such repetition is a sign to stop.

T: *Repeat three times attentively, "I am scared to be alone." (Does so.)*
P: *I feel sadness.*
T: *Did you feel anything in your body while you say this?*
P: *No.*
T: *"I am scared to be alone because . . . "*
P: *. . . because then I am locked up, locked out.*
T: *Can you feel this sadness now?*
P: *Yes.*
T: *Where is this sadness?*
P: *In my stomach.*
T: This will do. You are afraid to be alone, you feel sadness in your stomach and you feel especially scared to be locked up, locked out. This is what it's all about. You know now, you can let it go completely for the time being. Let it go right out of you, breathe it through.

We don't want to enter reliving yet.

T: *Then we go to the next. Say three times attentively, ever deeper, "I am scared of black magic." (Does this.) What is the first thing that springs to mind?*
P: *That no contact is possible then, no communication. It hurts somewhere.*
T: *Where?*
P: *Not a physical pain, more in my heart.*
T: *"I am scared of black magic, because . . . "*
P: *. . . it makes everything so ugly.*
T: *What makes it ugly in particular, is . . .*
P: *. . . people. When I see this ugliness I feel pain and sorrow.*
T: *That pain is in your heart, and where is the sorrow?*
P: *In my shoulders.*
T: *You are scared of black magic, you feel pain in your heart with it and sorrow in your shoulders. There is no contact, no communication and everything becomes ugly, people become ugly. This will do for now, let it go completely now. Would you like to do another?*
P: *Yes.*

T: Say three times with growing attention and depth, "I am scared of crowds."

P: I would rather say, "I am scared of a crowd of people."

T: Okay.

P: I have the feeling that it is all about the same again, that I am locked out again.

T: "I am scared of a crowd of people, because . .. "

P: . . . they don't know what they are doing anymore.

T: When they don't know what they are doing, then . . .

P: . . . they start having fun.

T: When they start having fun, then . . .

P: . . . they are cruel.

T: When they are cruel, then . . .

P: . . . they are no longer themselves.

T: Shall we leave it at that? (For it looks like a circle.)

P: Okay.

T: Now we get "I am scared of stupid people." Is that the same?

P: Yes.

T: "I am scared of incomprehension." Is that about the same thing, too?

P: Yes.

T: I am scared to be locked up, is that about the same, too?

P: That is more literal, I think.

T: Then we repeat this one three times: "I am scared to be locked up." (Does this.) What do you feel with that? (Silence.) "I am scared to be locked up, because . . . "

P: . . . I run into walls.

T: I run into walls, because . . .

P: . . . I want to get out.

T: I want to get out, because . . .

P: . . . I want to go to the light.

T: I want to go to the light, because . . .

P: . . . I do not like the dark, cold and clammy.

T: I am locked up, because . . .

P: . . . I am locked out, I don't fit in.

T: Can you feel that in your body?

P: Rather dizzy, floating. Now I also have a heavy feeling in my arms.

T: You were once locked up in a place where it was cold, dark and clammy, that is one thing. Another thing is that it has become a symbol of how you can feel yourself in your body. That's why the dizzy and heavy feeling.

311

P: *Very heavy.*

T: *You were locked out somewhere because you were locked up in the body. And because you are now locked up in your body, you feel locked out from something where you belonged, but where you still did not fit in. Can you sense that?*

P: *I can feel this being locked up in my body, but not where I didn't fit in, I think that had to do with something else.*

T: *I suggest that we leave it for now. What you can keep is, "I am scared to be locked up." That is a specific experience and a fundamental one, too, a postulate. "I am locked up, because I am locked out, because I did not fit in." Can you let that go now? I think the others are all the same. "I am scared to be alone in the dark," does that have to do with being locked up?*

P: *That being locked up is more in a confined space, while "dark" can be big, but you cannot get out. "I am scared of cold" also has to do with this incomprehension. I am scared of pain - I think that is all pain.*

T: *We touched on a stupid, ugly crowd with cruel things, eventually inspired by black magic. You feel locked out there, incomprehension, you have no contact with that, you cannot communicate with that. Secondly there is a fear of imprisonment, possibly generalized into a fear of being incarnated. So these two complexes are connected.*

Repeat what the patient has said, as a complete sentence. This repetition provides a quiet rhythm and it tells the patient, "I am with you, I heard you, it is registered, it is taken in, it is okay. We can go on to the next now." In this way we create a carrier wave of calm, attention and clarity.

Continue with the list until you reach a repetition or a blank. Don't permit long silences. People may pause only after they have spoken the first part of the sentence. People may complete a sentence immediately when you say, "I am scared of . . . ." Accept their completion, but try again to have them repeat the entire sentence.

The list of completions we work through in the original order, unless we take only one or two items. Select the sentences that immediately evoked emotions or somatics or images, or take the most emotional or the most specific. "A crowd" is a more specific item than is "being alone."

Have the selected sentence repeated five times. More than five times requires conscious counting. Avoid that complication. Sometimes we may ask the patient to repeat a sentence until an image, an emotion or somatic emerges. Then we go for E + S.

In this example we have heard, "I want to get out, I'm clawing against the walls, I want to get to the light, I don't want to go to the dark, it is cold here and clammy." From the start of the listing her hands have been busy. They have been crawling over these walls.

P: Yes, I really felt I was scratching with my hands against a brick wall.

At some point came, "I am locked up because I am locked out." Being locked up is being locked in, so here is a paradox, an indication of a fundamental postulate. Together they are fatal. Inside I am locked up, because outside they don't want me. The outside world locks me out by locking me in. So there is nowhere to go. There is no safe territory, so there is no home.

I noticed from her bodily reactions that being locked up corresponded with being in the body. She felt she was getting dizzy, also; that is excarnation, withdrawal from the body. After that she became heavy. So we have the whole problem of incarnating: the soul in the body.

Let's assume that it is a fundamental incarnation problem: Up there I am locked out and down here I am locked in. The resulting problem will manifest itself lifetime after lifetime. Therapy should not merely involve moving through the traumas of these different lifetimes, but should focus on solving the original problem. When that problem has been solved, you get rid of the resulting traumas in no time.

Usually I suggest that someone first work out the traumas, first clean the emotional charges. Then there is room for insight and oversight. But sometimes we may have to open a deeper lock first. This deeper approach is also indicated when a patient moves through traumas well, but still the catharsis remains subdued. There is relief, but no liberation. Then there is something more fundamental to go after.

VERBAL EXPLORATION OF A HANGOVER

T: I have three sentences that came up in a previous session: "I want to forgive." "I don't care." "I can't get away with it." With what shall we start?

313

P: *With the second.*
T: *Sit so that you feel as relaxed as possible so that you can realize the feelings and physical phenomena that come up when you say something. Say something when you have a clear feeling, or when an image comes up spontaneously. Now you say five times, calmly, tasting, but with growing attention: "I don't care." (Patient does this.) Now I am going to ask you to complete that sentence, repeatedly, in a different way. Repeat my words and then look only at what comes up in you. "I don't care, that..."*
P: *. . . I am alone.*
    . . . it is black.
    . . . there is famine.
    . . . there is no way.
    . . . it is big.
    . . . there is pain.
    . . . it is no accident.
    . . . (a floating impression of a green coat.)
    . . . it is a disaster.
    . . . it is all gone.
    . . . there is violence.
    . . . (nothing comes.)
T: *Then we go back to the first: "I don't care that I am alone." Say three times calm and tasting, "I am alone." (Does this.)*

The session continues: I am alone because . . . *the others are gone.* The others are gone to . . . *the field.* The others are gone to the field because . . . *the work has to be done.* I am here because . . . *I am ill.* I am ill because . . . *I am old.*

Now say three times, tasting the words: "I don't care it is black." (Does this.) I don't care it is black because . . . *it has always been black.* It has always been black because . . . *nobody took any notice of it.* The blackness I see, is . . . *me.* I am black, because . . . *it is the color of my skin.* Because I am black, I feel . . . *unfree.* Because I feel unfree, I feel . . . *small.* Because I feel small, I feel . . . *worthless.* Repeat: "I am black and worthless." (Does this. Anchors.)

Say attentively: "I don't care there is famine." (Does this.) I notice there is famine, because . . . *I am hungry.* I don't care that I'm hungry, because . . . *there are so many who are hungry.* These people are hungry, because . . . *the food is kept from them.* The food is kept from them by . . . *landlords.* The landlords keep their food because . . . *it gives them power.* They want that power, because . . . *they can keep us down.*

Attentively repeat: "I don't care there is no way." There is no way because . . . *I cannot walk it anyway.* I cannot walk it because . . . *my body doesn't want to anymore.*

Repeat: "I don't care it is big." What is big, is . . . *the barn.* I don't care the barn is big, because . . . *it is empty, anyway.* It is empty because . . . *there is no more food.*

Repeat attentively: "I don't care there is pain." I don't care there is pain, because . . . *it has always been there.* It is especially the pain of . . . *working.* Working causes pain, because . . . *it is so beastly.* The most beastly of the work is . . . *that you have to work on hands and feet.* You have to work on hands and feet because . . . *everything has to be planted and weeded.*

Repeat attentively: "I don't care it is an accident." It is an accident that . . . *I am black.* I don't care that I am black, because . . . *I think I do care!* (Important!) I care because . . . *otherwise I would have had a better life.*

Repeat: "I don't care about that green coat." I don't care about that green coat because . . . *it is red.* It is the red coat of . . . *a soldier.* I don't care about that soldier, because . . . *they can't see me anyway.* They can't see me anyway, because . . . *I am in the bushes.* I am in the bushes, because . . . *I hide myself.* I hide myself for . . . *the war.* After I hid myself . . . *a shadow fell on the road.* It was the shadow of . . . *many men.* After those men I came . . . *to my senses again.* My age was then . . . *53.*

Repeat: "I don't care it is a disaster." I don't care it is a disaster because . . . *it can't be helped.* The worst of the disaster is . . . *that we are so helpless.* We are helpless because . . . *we are negroes.* (First full acknowledgment!)

I don't care it is all gone, because . . . *it wasn't ours anyway.* What is gone, is . . . *the barn.* The barn is gone because . . . *it was burned down.* It was burned down by . . . soldiers. They burned it down because . . . *they felt like it.*

315

I don't care there is violence, because . . . *there is so much.* There is so much because . . . *people are like that.* People are like that because . . . *they always want more.* People always want more because . . . *they do not understand that enough is enough.* They do not understand that enough is enough, because . . . *they do not know when to stop.* They do not know when to stop because . . . *they never lived like us.* (Important!)

T: *Okay, how do you feel now?*
P: *Heavy.*
T: *Do you think that will sink away or do you want to get rid of it now? Or don't you care?*

This is an ambiguous remark of therapist evoking possible recursiveness.

P: *(No clear reaction.)*
T: *Repeat and complete: "What I care most about now is . . ."*
P: *. . . have peace.*
T: *Say, "Now I have peace." (Patient does this.) Feel that a source of peace is entering you. Feel where it enters you and where it goes to. Let the peace go through you. Afterward you come back in your own time and in your own way.*

EVALUATION

Those men in the shadow. What happens after those men? Why are these men there? Did you skip that on purpose?
I do not want to make a rupture by going over to different words or ending up in a television interview.

She says, "The others are gone to the field because work has to be done," and then you say, "I am here, because . . . ."
Better would have been, "I do not need to go to the field, because . . . " I couldn't find it so quickly.

You could have said, "Those men are there, because . . . ."
Yes. I had the feeling it was all to do with the same life. I just wanted to show you can get a real regression by just completing sentences.

Then there are no emotions.
Here the emotion is indifference, and I think she did feel it, that mood.

Yes, well, I felt heavier all the time. That indifference seemed to me like a spell.
Indifference often is. Of course it is a spell. You can hardly keep it up, especially the beastly part. *I don't care* is a survival answer. *I don't care* means literally that it makes no difference to me, it can't hurt me, because I can't change it. If everything is equally bad, you can mind it, but it doesn't matter. This is a typical hangover life. When you treat this further in a regression you can ask, "When did you feel this indifference for the first time? Go to that situation. When did this indifference got so stuck that you couldn't change it anymore?" You also can ask, "What makes the most impression within that indifference? When did the indifference stop?" Maybe never, not even after death. Maybe she still carries this gray veil of indifference with her. When the indifference was not resolved in the death experience, you change to aura exploration. Then you take it up in the form of its current consequences. You work them through one by one, wash them clean and with special changes you go back to where and when they arose, just until she is completely vital.

The fact that she wants peace is natural, but it is also a loser's strategy: *There is no more in it for me, you can just as well leave me in peace.* With this type of problem you also can do bio-energetic things, for she had to crawl like a beast. Let her crawl over the floor like a beast, and press her back so that she starts screaming. Then you rebuild that strength until she starts walking. She should not just find peace, she has also to learn to walk again, she has to become human again, upright, not having to crawl through the bushes or on the fields.

VERBAL EXPLORATION OF CHARACTER PROBLEM

To the question of what he wanted, this patient answered: *Overcome certain shortcomings.* Besides that, he said his eyes always started to hurt during regressions. The therapist takes this last somatic, since it is more concrete.

317

T: *Repeat and complete: "My eyes are . . ."*
P: *My eyes are . . .*
    . . . burning.
    . . . weak.
    . . . piercing.
    . . . sharp.
    . . . friendly.
    . . . hard.
    . . . clear.
    . . . distant.
    . . . attentive.
    . . . watchful.
    . . . attentive.

Repetition has begun, so the therapist stops. He begins with the first sentence, partly because it is the first, but secondly because it probably carries a somatic charge, and thirdly because it is directly connected to the starting point.

T: *My eyes are burning, because . . .*
P: *. . . when I concentrate, they start to hurt.*
T: *They start to hurt, because . . .*
P: *. . . I concentrate so hard.*

A circle is evident, so it is time to stop. But now the therapist blunders by going back to a *somatic* without asking for an *emotion*. He remains consistent in this omission during the entire session:

T: *You are over-concentrating and your eyes hurt. Go back to the cause of this pain. (Counts back.) What do you feel, what comes up in you, what do you think about?*
P: *There isn't even a thought.*

At this point the therapist switches to aura exploration, but the image remains vague.

T: *What is there with your eyes?*
P: *A big white-yellow iron book end, to the right of my eyes.*
T: *Can you put it aside?*
P: *Yes. Damn it, I lost myself completely.*

The patient losing himself is the consequence of bad guidance on the part of the therapist. Next, the therapist just tries something:

T: *Go to the bathroom and look in the mirror.*
P: *I have something sly in my eyes. Now the burning lessens.*

But this burning is what it is all about, and all the rest is not important. The therapist again gives instructions to go back, but without result:

T: *Repeat and complete: "My eyes are burning, because . . ."*
P: *(No clear answer.)*
T: *Repeat and complete: "People have burning eyes, when they . . ."*
P: *stand in the smoke.*
   . . . stare into the night.
   . . . cry a lot.
   . . . did not have enough sleep.
   . . . have much sorrow.
   . . . cannot see it.
   I stood in the smoke once when I made a bonfire.
T: *Go back to when you first had burning eyes because you stood in the smoke, stared into the night, cried a lot, couldn't sleep, had much sorrow and did not see it.*
P: *Now it flows through me.*

Bingo! The patient experiences a strong somatic. What is flowing through him? An emotion, of course. The therapist also stares into the night and does not see it. From a strong charge he moves to lesser charges. Besides, he was successful in interpreting all the completed sentences as belonging to one situation, and now he is taking them separately again. He is obviously insecure. And this therapist wants to be a trainer and even write books about it!

T: *I now take up the sentences again and you tell me whether the burning lessens or grows worse. "I stand in the smoke."*
P: *The same. There is a change in color though, indigo.*
T: *"I stare into the night."*
P: *Gets stronger.*
T: *"I cry a lot."*
P: *Color gets darker, feeling remains.*
T: *"I haven't slept."*

P: *It gets lighter, pain stays.*
T: *"I have much sorrow."*
P: *I see a shape that I cannot place, the pain stays the same.*
T: *"I can't see anything."*
P: *More pressure.*
T: *Say a couple of times, "I stare into the night, but I can't see anything."*

The therapist thus combines sentences that carry strongest charge. Patient repeats these statements:

P: *I see a big blue dome above me. It is the sky. It is beautiful. Blue with a shutter. Behind that is a tunnel. (Spontaneous imagination.)*
T: *Go through that shutter into the tunnel.*
P: *The pain is going. (So this was an escape.)*
T: *Can you imagine that you are staring into the night?*
P: *Yes.*
T: *Are you standing there alone?*
P: *I think so.*
T: *Outside or inside?*
P: *There is a wall where I lean on with my arms, a kind of parapet. I think I cannot sleep. I am worried. About something very awful, I don't know how to say it. I have to do something, something to do with bad news, a hard act.*
T: *With what is it connected - execution, sacrifice, pierce out someone's eyes?*
P: *Something to do with punishment or sacrifice. The verdict has already been pronounced. I think I can still do something about it.*
T: *Did you do this before?*
P: *It was never necessary before, to punish. They can make an appeal to me. When they don't, execution will follow. After sunrise ten or twelve people will be burned. They are heretics, they do things that are not allowed by the church.*
T: *Go to the moment of execution.*
P: *I have little to do with this. It is somewhere down below me. The smoke drifts toward me.*
T: *Does it smell?*
P: *That is of no consequence.*
T: *Why don't you go away from the smoke?*
P: *It is my duty.*
T: *What do you think?*

P: *It wasn't necessary. They are stupid.*

T: *Is that a reason to burn them?*

P: *No, yes, it was impossible what they were doing. It was forbidden. By the church. By God.*

T: *Why didn't you leave their punishment to God?*

P: *It is my job.*

T: *What made the most impression on you?*

P: *That they did not ask for mercy.*

T: *Would you have given them mercy then?*

P: *Perhaps I would have, but they didn't ask.*

T: *Maybe they did not care much for your mercy? Now they burn there. Do you understand those people?*

P: *No, I cannot understand them.*

T: *What is stinging most in that smoke?*

P: *I don't understand them. I look at it and I don't see it. But I have no regrets. I am proud. It is the work of God. Not very nice. I hoped it wouldn't be necessary. I was wrong.*

T: *Such things come from not understanding.*

P: *I don't mean that they misjudged, I mean that they did not ask for mercy. It is my job to pardon.*

T: *How do you get the smoke out of your eyes?*

P: *By not thinking about it any more, about those people.*

T: *The best way not to have to think about those people any longer, is understanding. When there is understanding, there is also a solution.*

P: *Now I am two personalities: the other has very different standards. They are heretics. They go against the church. If I don't burn them, there will be ever more then.*

Note that all attempts by the therapist to change incomprehension to understanding fail every time.

T: *Obviously you are not very well suited to teach God's words to disbelievers. How would Jesus have done that?*

P: *People have to obey the church.*

The patient's avoidance shows that this statement has struck him.

T: *Then you should not complain of your burning eyes.*

P: *I am the church, whether my eyes hurt or not is not the question. I am called for this vocation, whether I am happy is not important.*

T: *What happens when you die?*
P: *Then I will go to God.*
T: *Have you been there?*
P: *I don't know this time. I was with Maria. She smiled very friendly. Afterward I went back to something like this and again.*
T: *Does this Maria know what it is like to suffer?*
P: *She smiles in spite of that grief.*
T: *Does she have smoke in her eyes?*
P: *Being a heretic is the worst there is.*

The patient again avoids the subject, so obviously he was touched again.

T: *Isn't it already a punishment not to see Maria?*
P: *I don't know.*
T: *Can't you bring the heretics to Maria?*
P: *No, they don't want her, nor me.*
T: *Why wouldn't they want you, do you think? Because you haven't got Maria in you?*
P: *They did not ask for mercy. (This goes on for some time.)*
T: *Why don't you let go of the smoke?*
P: *Then there will be no church anymore.*
T: *Would you yourself go into the fire with the heretics?*
P: *Perhaps, when the church would ask that.*
T: *I ask it in name of the church built on Peter's rock.*
P: *They are so stupid!*
T: *When you can go into the fire from your free will, you will rise into the sky like the smoke.*
P: *I cannot free him; he turns away from me. (The patient shrugs his shoulders.)*
T: *These thoughts will not leave him! This will go on working.*

Therapist tries to score after all.

P: *I don't think he believes they are doomed, but the question is what does the church believe? This mercy means, by the way, being strangled before being burned. (Shrugs his shoulders again.) Now it is gone.*
T: *So this bishop is still stuck, though he cannot hide any longer.*

AURA EXPLORATION OF TRAUMA
WITH A CHARACTER POSTULATE

T: *I do not know which way this demonstration of aura exploration will go, induction or therapy. I start with the psychosomatic. For example, you have trouble with a part of your body. This keeps coming back without an apparent cause, in the form of pain or cold spots, or a part of your body that you always fall upon or hit. I remember I often hit my head until I was ten or twelve, so often that at the moment I felt the pain of the shock, I experience an echo effect. Others will always hurt their knees or pinch their fingers between doors.*

P: *What often bothers me is a bruised spot on the side of my left knee. When I go to sleep, I do not keep my legs together but shove them apart. For the rest of my body no trouble.*

T: *So no trouble, but there is something funny, chronic. Do you feel that spot now?*

P: *No. I know where it is, though.*

T: *When did it last bother you?*

P: *Some four or five nights ago.*

T: *Were you awake?*

P: *Before going to sleep.*

T: *Can you recall that memory? Was it the same as usual, or was it stronger or less strong or different?*

P: *Same as usual.*

T: *It comes back the same. Try again to describe it. How big is the spot?*

P: *When I lie on my right side my left knee presses on my right knee, and it seems as if there is a bruise. Underneath the knee cap there seems to be a nerve, a sensitive spot. It nags. I cannot bear to keep my knees on each other.*

T: *You want to know where it comes from?*

P: *Yes, I have no idea.*

The therapist then follows the standard starting procedure, including the question after the color of the light:

P: *White yellow, a yellowish white.*

T: *Then you come closer, you go to yourself and let the light become stronger, so you can see more. Now you perceive your left knee, you go with your attention to the spot on the inside of your left*

323

> *knee and there you will see something. You are going to see some-*
> *thing that causes that bruised spot. What is the first impression*
> *you get?*

P: *It looks like an inflammation.*

T: *An inflammation. You come closer and you see what causes the*
inflammation. What is that? You are like a doctor, you inspect it
from close by. When you cannot see it well, it is as if you turn a
lamp on it, or if you put it under a microscope and then you will
see it. If necessary, the tissues are transparent and you can look
inside. Something is there that causes the inflammation.

P: *It looks as if a nerve is wedged between the bones.*

T: *How did that happen? Go back to the moment this happened.*

This therapist has made an error at this point, by giving a regression instruction without asking for emotion.

P: *It looks as if my leg was crushed there, recovering from an acci-*
dent.

T: *Okay, I count back from three to one and at one you are at the*
moment of the accident. Three . . . , two . . . , one. Where are you
and what happens?

Because the therapist has forgotten to include an *emotion*, this
attempt to enter regression does not work.

T: *Can you feel the spot on your leg now?*

P: *Very vaguely.*

T: *Can you make that stronger? Look at it while you are going to feel*
the spot more strongly. Is it getting clearer, or does it stay that
way? When you imagine that nerve wedged between the bo::es,
and the leg is crushed, is there something else you haven't seen,
that makes you linger with that image.

The therapist appears to blame patient for this stagnation, instead of blaming himself.

P: *It looks as if the leg pulls a little to the left. My foot stands turned*
out.

T: *You are still a doctor examining your own body. Now you walk to*
your left foot. Is there something special with the left foot?

P: *It seems to turn outward.*

T: *By what? Is it twisted?*

P: *Yes.*

T: Can you go back to the where and when this twist occurred? I now
    count back from five to one. We go ever more back to the moment,
    place and time where this twist occurred. Five . . . , four . . . , three
    . . . , two . . . , one. What is the first thing that comes up in you?
    Are you inside or out?

Naturally this therapist continues with exploration techniques
because he still forgets the emotion.

P: Out.
T: Where are you, how does it look?
P: I have the impression I fell off a horse.
T: Are you on the ground?
P: I lie on my right knee.
T: Get an impression of yourself. How you look, who you are?
P: I wear a coat of mail.
T: Do you also wear something on your legs?
P: Looks like some sort of trousers with rope around it.
T: Now you go further back when nothing was the matter. You sat on
    a horse. What happens, where are you?
P: I ride very hastily.
T: Are you alone there?
P: I am in a hurry!

The therapist has already forgotten the emotion, and now misses
the word "haste,", which also carries an emotional charge. If
the patient stubbornly repeats himself, as has this patient, the
therapist has usually missed something.

T: Do you have to go somewhere quickly, or are you trying to run
    away from something?

The therapist keeps messing about as in an exploration, instead
of doing therapy.

P: I think I have to bring a message. I have to warn them of a great
    army that is advancing. (Tears, strong emotion, choked voice, shakes
    with his whole body. He does not wait until the therapist asks for
    an emotion. He is right.)
T: Let it go right through you. It was a terrible experience. The pain
    in your leg and foot, let all feelings of despair go through you. You
    won't make it. How did you come to fall from your horse?

P: *Stupid haste. Now I can only hobble along. My knee and my foot are damaged.*

So haste also carries the charge of *guilt* and *stupidity*. But here the therapist stubbornly goes on exploring. Obviously this is not one of the therapist's better days.

T: *Where is the horse?*
P: *A little further on.*
T: *Feel what goes through you as you stumble along.*
P: *I am in great pain, but I do come to the horse. (Pain: a third charge.)*
T: *Can you get on the horse?*
P: *I stand on the other side. (A sentence that could be a postulate.)*
T: *Are you on the wrong side of the horse?*
P: *Yes.*
T: *Can you come to the right side of the horse?*
P: *No, that I cannot manage.*
T: *Do you get any further?*
P: *I hang over it.*
T: *But you go on. How do you feel now?*
P: *Desperate. (Fourth charge.)*
T: *Is the enemy close?*
P: *Right behind me.*
T: *What is the first thing that happens now? See and experience what happens.*
P: *I am being trampled.*
T: *Who is doing that and what do they feel? Go to the moment you are being crushed. Let the feelings go through you.*
P: *Despair, bitterness. I didn't make it. (Fifth charge: bitterness.)*
T: *You didn't make it. Whom did you want to warn?*
P: *I was told to warn the towns as quickly as possible.*
T: *Did you get this instruction in time?*
P: *I heard it very late and I had to hurry. There had been a break-through. The resistance was broken. (But the fact remains that he was sent away too late.)*
T: *What do you feel about yourself that you didn't make it?*
P: *It is a shame, but I did what I could.*
T: *Go to the moment of dying, move through it. What goes through you while you're dying?*
P: *They put a stone on top of me because I went on crawling.*

So therapist moved too quickly here.

T: *What happens when you have died? Did you see yourself lie there?*
P: *Yes.*
T: *When you see that, what goes through you?*
P: *I still feel that stone.*
T: *When you are there above your body, do you still feel powerless?*
P: *I feel sadness. (Sixth charge.)*
T: *What is the saddest of everything?*
P: *It is so terrible what is happening. I felt so powerless. I shouldn't have stumbled.*
T: *How did you come to stumble?*
P: *My disbelief that things could be prevented. It is already too late.*
T: *How come?*
P: *We resisted until the very last. We leave the village. Many have been already killed. We are on horseback to warn people, exhausted as we are.*
T: *Then you were already past saving. You could no longer lead your horse well. The horses are so scared, they go on running. You know you won't make it. Go to the moment that the despair fastened itself on you. On what moment and through what did the despair fasten itself?*
P: *They are with more; and they are still fresh. I see how fresh the enemy is and how close they are.*
T: *You are dead now and you go to a place of overview. When you've arrived there you say "Yes."*
P: *Something is in the way. My hands tremble and I feel pressure on my belly.*
T: *We go to the cause of that. You get an impression of the cause of the trembling of your hands and the pressure on your belly. What happens? What impression do you get?*
P: *Just a strong physical sensation.*
T: *What is strongest? The pressure on your belly or the trembling of your hands?*
P: *They're equally strong.*
T: *Now you imagine you're home in your bed and you see yourself standing next to it and you look at yourself in the vague yellow white light. When you can see that you say "Yes."*
P: *Yes.*
T: *Then you come closer and the light gets stronger. In the stronger growing light you look at your hands and your belly and you are*

going to see what's the matter there. What is the pressure on your belly, what is the trembling of your hands?

P: *My hands want to go up. My left hand is light.*

T: *And your right hand?*

P: *Slightly darker, a bit vaguer. It is especially the left hand that glows up.*

T: *Look at your right arm and go with your glance up your arm and look for something that blocks the light in your right hand. What stops it?*

P: *Where the index finger is well lit, there is a line, a division.*

T: *Look at what causes this division, you see something.*

P: *A clot of blood that blocks the passage.*

T: *If it had something to do with the dying, you go and see that now.*

P: *It is trampled. A hoof stood on it. My fingers are not crushed, but my thumb is.*

T: *Now you stand next to yourself and you see that right hand and with your left hand you stroke that other hand. A strength comes from that hand.*

The therapist works with renovation, for the injury is still in the way after death.

P: *With my left hand I go over my right hand.*

T: *Just as long as it glows through. Keep your hands in front of you and look at them until both flame up. Continue calmly until it is healed again. Are both equally strong now?*

P: *Yes.*

T: *Then you go to your belly, stomach. It was a pressure, you said. Look at what causes this pressure.*

P: *It seems as if there is a stone on it.*

T: *Feel how heavy it is.*

P: *Quite heavy, very solid.*

T: *Then you go back to that life, to that situation in which the stone came on top of you. So you know what this stone is before you take it away. I count back from three to one, and at one you get an impression of that moment. Three..., two..., one..., what comes up in you?*

P: *They threw it on top of me.*

T: *When you lay down there?*

P: *Yes.*

T: *Why?*

P: *Teasing.*

T: You cannot even crawl anymore now and you have to die on the spot.

P: I am at my last breath.

T: Shall we take the stone away?

P: I want to breathe.

T: That is all right, but the stone will not be a help. Feel the strength in your hands and arms. What will we do with the stone?

P: I take it off.

T: Imagine there is a slope from where you throw it off.

P: I see a ravine.

T: You see it fall and you hear it bouncing and falling. Go now then to the place of overview. Can you get there?

P: No.

T: Is there anything else on your belly or stomach?

P: I have the feeling something is still pressing on me. A doctor's arm, an arm with the sleeve half rolled up. A rough way to apply artificial respiration.

T: Look at the face of the one who does this. How does it look? Is it a man or a woman?

P: A man.

T: You now get a clear impression of the situation. Where are you?

P: In an operating theatre.

T: What is going through you?

P: It is finished.

T: Do you feel despair?

P: Yes.

T: What can you do to stop the pressure on your stomach?

P: Accepting and just breathing quietly, breathing through.

T: Do you want to know when and where this situation was?

P: No, there is no need.

T: You can keep the image as a memory, so that later you can go back to it. Now breathe through quietly. You do not feel a trace of despair, just peace. Calm acceptance. You breathe quietly through it and while you breathe calmly, you feel yourself going higher until you arrive at the place of overview. Can you let the peace go through you?

P: I still have a tendency to interfere.

T: You do not need to interfere now. Breathe through, until you have arrived at the place of overview, and then you say yes. How do you feel now?

P: I'm going.

T: Do you sink away deeper or do you come back?

P: *I come back.*
T: *Come back then in your own way and in your own time.*

EVALUATION

I was lying there dead and felt despair. That man kept pressing my stomach to get the breathing going again. while he didn't need to do this for me.
It seems to me that he had a pattern of always going on, that had to be corrected once. The second short image is about the moment of utmost despair, where he doesn't feel the despair himself anymore, but sees it in someone else.

I had wanted to say, "Stop it."
That can mean that with that a cycle was finished, the learning effect is there, only there still was a bruised spot on his leg.

I had the feeling that I had the strength to let my blood start flowing again through breathing and through my hands, to bring life into my-self.
You seem to have a natural strength in your hands, and breathing is a magnificent way to get energy. To a certain extent this applies to us all, but here there was a specific clue. Interesting that such little things can have such charges.

Stones often appear in aura explorations. When you dive in deeper, for instance in the solar plexus, it appears that there is a lot more. You did not dive in.
Not now, but often I do. I had the feeling that it lasted too long. As an explanation he says they put a stone on him. Now that is enough. It can well be that they really put a stone on top of him. Often a stone in an aura is a symbolic stone, a symbolic weight. He found himself in a situation with a real stone. When you arrive in a situation with a metaphorical stone, such as stone on a stomach, you ask, for instance, "Open that stone. Is something inside?" Usually there is something in it or under it. I presumed it was a real stone, and that there didn't have to be other charges on it. But it could have been possible.

It surprised me you didn't ask, "Do you want to get rid of the stone?"
That would have been better.

They even smirked. They saw that I wanted to go on. They teased me with it. Because they put a stone on me, I couldn't even use my last sign of life to save what could be saved. Their faces expressed, "You want to go on, don't you? But you're finished."
In a situation like that you can only surrender, but the machine keeps on muttering through until the end.

I recognize that of myself. I cannot easily give up.
Often a question in such cases is, "Does that stone belong there?" Some say then, *I rather like it.* "Okay, then we go on to the next." Then they say a little later, *It's heavy, after all.* Here the stone meant he couldn't move to the place of overview. So I assumed there was a block that had to go anyway, but I should have asked.
The starting point - that bruised spot on the left knee - got lost a bit. That was the moment he stumbled and so failed. His leg was twisted and so he remained paralyzed in his legs. Then the emotions came as, *I won't make it, I am too late.*

You did not finish with the point at which you had started.
You're right. I should have asked, "Do you still feel that spot?" The entire session isn't finished. I wanted to go to the place of overview to check the charges, but he came back before that.

The moment I accepted that I couldn't crawl from under that stone to warn the people after all, I felt my strength growing in my hands and in my whole body. I felt myself vitalize. I did not need any more instructions. I knew how to heal my hands and how to breathe. When you said, "Now we go a little further," it wasn't necessary for me anymore. I could easily get rid of it, because I accepted that I couldn't go on, that I had reached the end. The stone finally made clear to me that I couldn't avoid it; I had to surrender. Then I got strength. I felt it flowing into my hands just after my breathing got light.

BACK PRESSING FINDING A HANGOVER

This is an exercise session that succeeds only partially. The therapist searches the back for a spot, and the patient shows where he feels pain.

331

P: *This is a good one.*
T: *Am I right here?*
P: *Yes.*
T: *What feeling emerges? What do you see?*
P: *A traumatic feeling.*
T: *Where do you feel it?*
P: *In my throat.*
T: *Okay, breathe through it.*

This is a wrong instruction. The suggestion to "breathe through it" is for digesting material afterward, not for starting.

P: *(Seems about to throw up. Wants to spit.)*
T: *Let the feeling become stronger, just breathe through it, very quiet, very wide, let it become stronger.*

The therapist here gives contradictory instructions.

P: *It disappears.*

The feeling has disappeared because of the therapist's wrong instruction.

T: *What do you feel now? (Presses harder.)*
P: *I feel dizzy, drifting, nauseous.*
T: *Where are you and what happens?*
P: *I see a young woman, about sixteen years old. She lies on her belly, with her head in her arms.*
T: *What do you feel with that?*
P: *A beautiful body.*
T: *What kind of life this has been?*
P: *Cheerful. She dressed herself beautifully.*

At this point the therapist, instead of focusing on the experience, jumps away from it. He gives wrong and excessive instructions, and any relationship between pain and the instructions remains completely unclear:

T: *Go back to the moment of death. See what happened. I count from five to one. Look at it; you are in the body; you feel that you are once again in the body. What happens? Any emotion? What emotion emerges?*

P: *Dirty. I see this woman lying down in a long gown. It is a bedroom. Dirty things happen here. I see she undresses. Probably prostitution. On top of her lies something black, something magic.*

This point is important!

T: *Enter your body and look at it. You see who or what is on top of her. What emotion does it give?*
P: *Revulsion. (Throwing up.)*

The therapist has given a double instruction. With magic, move to insight and not to emotion.

T: *What happens?*
P: *He forces me.*
T: *You go further in time, you let go of this, you breathe through it. Again the same thing occurs: the patient enters but is pulled out again. Of course there is no reaction, so the therapist has to go back.*
T: *You are in the body, you feel the emotion.*
P: *Dirty.*
T: *Is that man yet in the room?*
P: *He is undressing.*
T: *Does he say something? (It would have been better to ask, "What was dirty?")*
P: *He looks over his shoulder.*
T: *Do you get paid for it? (Nonsensical question.)*
P: *No.*
T: *Go to your death. (Nonsensical instruction.)*
P: *I am not dead. (Sensible response.)*
T: *Then go to the moment when you decide to do this kind of thing. (Better, but still jumping around. What is dirty? What is black and magic?)*
P: *I am twelve years old. Ordinary clothes, I see cauldrons and casseroles or so. It resembles gypsies.*
T: *Can you see your feet?*
P: *Callus, worn-out, rope-like shoes.*
T: *Are you happy? (Nonsensical question; this was about a decision.)*
P: *Something exciting happens behind the bushes. A man takes me with him. He caresses me between my legs, at the inside.*
T: *Did this make you decide to go for more?*
P: *Yes. It is very pleasant.*

T: *Okay, go to moment of dying. (Why, for Heaven's sake?)*

P: *Old woman with a stick, slumped together, in a house.*

T: *How does she look back on her life?*

P: *Bitter.*

T: *Why?*

P: *It looked so good, but it was so dirty.*

T: *Go to the moment of death.*

P: *She is stiff, oh goodness, shriveled and crumpled. Yet I still feel revulsion. (This revulsion has indeed not yet been explored.)*

T: *What did you learn from it?*

P: *Real beauty and money don't go together.*

T: *Go to the moment the revulsion is strongest.*

P: *The prick of that man. I should clean it. (Vomits.)*

T: *Just let go. (Is this reliving or a flea circus?) Have you made any decision?*

P: *I don't want this any more. I'd rather be poor.*

T: *Go to the moment you died. Do you want to do or say something to her?*

P: *I want to stroke her.*

T: *How does that make you feel?*

P: *Close.*

T: *Go to feeling of revulsion. Can you get there? (Again a flea jump back.)*

P: *Much more difficult. (Of course: first get out and then get in again. Maddening.)*

T: *Go back, you come again in the situation.*

P: *If necessary, I will bite it off!*

T: *Do you want to change the situation? Do you want to do something like that?*

P: *Mess in my mouth. I feel that I can't handle it. Yes, change. I can do it. He doesn't dare to push through. He is angry, surprised; he leaves. (A prickly renovation.)*

T: *How are you left behind?*

P: *Angry. What the hell do they think they can do?*

T: *Go to moment of death. (Again?)*

P: *I drift above the body.*

T: *Go to the feeling of revulsion, can you feel it yet?*

P: *More an echo.*

T: *Okay, breathe through it, let it go. (Worthless catharsis: decision unclear, blackness unclear, revulsion tucked away. Patient breathes quietly.) What happens with the woman? How does she feel?*

P: *Revulsion, she is in shame.*

T: *When was that feeling of shame the worst?*
P: *Her whole life afterward. (!)*
T: *There must have been a worst moment.*
P: *That prick.*
T: *What can she do to help herself? (Why was that serious? First time? Dirty man? Unwashed? Spectators? Was something said? How did he force her? And so on.)*
P: *She turns around and around in her grief. (After shame a new charge.)*
T: *Go to a moment she could have handled differently.*
P: *Bite hard I think.*
T: *Okay, do it. Bite it off.*
P: *(Is clearly doing it.) It is no solution.*
T: *What should be the solution?*
P: *Not withdraw from everything and everybody, stop feeling disgust and shame about myself. I think back about the girl of twelve, a pure, open-minded, attractive girl, but confused, with a feeling that something was wrong.*
T: *What have you learned? (Leaves the innocent twelve-year-old girl in the cold.)*
P: *That I must n't shut myself off. I feel ambivalence between withdrawal and excitement. Revulsion. (Breathes heavily.) I have the idea that it fits in with what is going on. Somehow she is framed. (The black!)*
T: *But she knew what to expect, she could have chosen otherwise. (Moralizing therapist.)*
P: *No reaction. (Rightly so; therapist consults with colleagues.)*
T: *What happens with that woman?*
P: *I tell her to have patience. She wants to get love. I can look her in the eyes.*
T: *What do those eyes say?*
P: *Grief.*
T: *What held her?*
P: *It had become a habit.*
T: *What happens with her?*
P: *I see a spot of light. She goes through a whirl or tunnel, a new birth as it were.*
T: *Do you come in a womb? (Suggestive.)*
P: *Could. Yes. (Coils himself, becomes nauseous.)*
T: *What happens?*
P: *It doesn't set through really. I feel pressured. Birth pangs. (Vomits, utters dry cries, then rest.)*

T: *What happens now? Are you born?*

P: *I see nothing further, as if I have closed my eyes. I feel cramped, dirty.*

T: *You found it dirty, to be born? Is that the same feeling as that woman had? (Good connection.)*

P: *Yes, the same, totally. That same dirt. (The same dirt means the same blackness.)*

T: *Go to the origin of the revulsion. (Good again.)*

P: *A black face that looks angry, an idol. (Bingo! Again black!)*

T: *What does it look like?*

P: *A male figure, bigger than I first thought. I have made a whole collection of magical statues. This is really scary.*

T: *Why did you make those?*

P: *Something about being exciting. As if it would make me something special.*

T: *Are other people there?*

P: *Yes, I am a priest, sitting. I feel I have power. People are awed by me, I am awed by myself.*

T: *How did this cause the revulsion?*

P: *Out of fear. I see disgusting statues. That revulsion comes from the statutes. I want to erase them.*

T: *Go to the most disgusting statue.*

P: *A skull with a black hole. Disgusting green and yellowish hot energy comes out of it. It is also fear that I would lose control.*

T: *Can you release that now? (Very fast; no relation with black curse on girl.)*

P: *Yes.*

T: *What about your revulsion?*

P: *I now think the situation ridiculous. I started to believe it myself, that hocus pocus. (Good, but too easy.)*

T: *Do you still feel revulsion?*

P: *No.*

T: *Do you still feel fear?*

P: *No.*

T: *Can you release everything? (Dangerous suggestion.)*

P: *Yes.*

T: *Come back to the here and now.*

P: *This spot on my back remains a bit sensitive.*

Of course, that spot has not been cleaned yet. Why was there pain on this spot? We still don't know.

BACK PRESSING FINDING A CHARACTER POSTULATE

P: *I have pain in my back, deep. A pain as big as a nickel. I have already had it for about ten years. The pain comes and goes, as if a bullet enters. I can show it clearly. (Below the right shoulder.)*

Therapist determines the spot via more or less pain. When the therapist presses on the proper place patient screams.

T: *What happens here?*
P: *Much grief. (Begins to cry, clearly has much pain; becomes also angry.) Always pain, I am ill, I always have pain.*
T: *Go back to the moment this pain began.*
P: *I am ill. (Voice changes. Cries. Has much pain, screams now and then. Kicks with her legs, moves much with her right hand.) I am six years old. I am a girl. I am in a big house, a big garden. Many people around me, servants. I sit in a little chair, I can't walk. I wear a checkered dress and I have a ribbon in my hair. They drive me around. I have crooked hands.*
T: *Go back to a time when you could still walk.*
P: *I am four years old. I am playing in the garden. I play with my skipping-rope. I have a ribbon in my hair, as always. I am glad. I have no brothers and sisters, only a mother. Father is far away, I see him rarely. We are rich.*
T: *Go to the moment just before the pain began.*
P: *I am tired, I sink through my legs. The doctor comes. It pulls through my whole body. My hands are crooked. My arms hurt, my back hurts, everything hurts. (Cries vehemently.)*
T: *What happens?*
P: *My back hurts so much. That spot hurts terribly; it seems that something stabs in my back. (Suggests an older pain from an earlier life.) I don't want this pain. (She repeats this four times; becomes angry.)*
T: *Go through it, through this pain, through this period.*
P: *(Clearly is in terribly pain, asks for mercy.) I can bear it no longer. (Repeats this at least five times; cries, becomes angry. The pain seems unbearable.) I can bear it no longer. Pull it out. It seems I am tortured! Stop stabbing in my back! I sit tied down. (Enormous pain, then she suddenly becomes quiet. Looks like a torture in an earlier life, restimulated through an injection.)*
T: *What happens now?*
P: *I go up. (Blows her nose, lies down again and is silent.)*

T: What happens now?

P: I am again in the garden, six years old. I am allowed to sit nicely in my little chair. Now they are all sweet to me. The pain now feels like a bruise, a scar. It is not too bad in my little chair.

T: Go ahead in time.

P: I feel sad again. I am now twelve years old. I am always in pain. I live in that big house, big garden. My mother is rich. I am fed up with sitting in that chair. The pain gets worse again. I can't stand it anymore. I want to get rid of this terrible pain. I want to die.

T: Go to the moment of death.

P: I couldn't do it. (Cries.) I wanted to marry, to have children. I want to leave.

T: Where are you now?

P: I am old, 70 years. All is crooked.

T: Go to the moment of death.

P: I don't want to, I can't release the body. The pain comes back. (Undigested charges.)

T: Go through it. When you are ready say "Yes."

P: It becomes hot. I am dead. I look back at my life in that body.

T: Now leave your body.

P: I don't want to. I was mean. I've had nothing, only sitting in a chair. (Goes through much pain and fight.) She is angry, also at herself. (Spontaneous dissociation.)

T: Who did this to you?

P: I did. I wanted love and care. Through sitting in my chair, I got this care. I didn't want to do a lot, because I wanted care.

T: Can you forgive yourself? (Better: ask how come.)

P: I have to do it over. I do it over and then I'll do it differently. (She dies.) I see my mother. She says she is also to blame. She says she always left me to my devices. She should have been more strict with me. She left me to the servants. I should have exercised. She will help me to go back. I don't feel much for her.

T: Go to a place of overview.

P: If you want something, you must exercise and leave the chair. Stupid oaf, spoiled child. If you want something, you must put in an effort. My anger is gone. The pain spot feels like a bruise now. I can still feel where the pain has been. I make a plan with my mother. She knows how to do it. She is a professional. Then I go back, to live again. It's okay now.

T: Come back to the here and now, in your own way, at your own speed.

P: Wow, that hurt! It went right through my back. Below the thera-

pist's hand some muscle rolled, and that really hurt. I wanted to kick, to hit. You can't do that to your therapist, can you? I am very tired.
In the regression I didn't accept that this happened to me. Yes woman, but then do something! Yet not do it. I could give nothing, just sat in that chair. It feels exaggerated. I had come to that lifetime to get love and care. I got confused because I got stuck in my feelings. I had the tendency to kick the therapist, but still a story emerged. I recognize my complacency and my obstinacy as a kind of collision. Thus I had much to do in the next life.

This has been a pretty effective session, but still it has missed an essential part of the problem. Behind this life as a paralyzed, spoiled girl is a life in which she was apparently tortured to death. Probably the life as that girl came right after the life of torture. The physical problems probably are a straight repercussion of the torture, and the psychological problems probably are an inversion of the tortured life.

For example, a man, independent, poor, revolts and is caught and tortured to death. His response: *I want to be a girl, I want to be rich, I don't want to be independent, I want to be cared for. I deserve that. They owe it to me,* etc. Exploring this line of reasoning would have released the physical pain, and would have released the remaining confusion and ambivalence. It also would have put the relationship with the therapist less in jeopardy. By causing pain instead of releasing it, the therapist has become associated with one of the henchmen.

Beware of pain experiences that are complicated by confusion. Torture unhinges the mind.

EGOSTATES USED FOR FINDING A PSEUDO-OBSESSION

In a group session, this patient invited several persons into her imaginary room, while outside two others roamed about and did not show themselves. She wanted to find out about them.

T: *Imagine again the room with the circle. Now invite one of the two who remained outside.*
P: *One enters. He is invisible. He smiles. No further contact.*
T: *You'll see now the cause of the invisibility.*

P: It has to do with fleeing, making himself invisible. (Fear and a somatic in the throat.)

T: Go to the moment that he became invisible.

P: He lies dying on the battlefield. The spirit is half out. The body doesn't want to release it. I see it from the outside. I don't know if it's me. Now I feel grief.

T: Where do you feel that grief in your body?

P: In my heart and throat. Now my eyes flicker. I can't see well.

The therapist instructs this patient to go back in time, on that grief and fear. Two images appear: a child who just sees the table top, and a battlefield just before a battle. The therapist suggests that this patient take the last image.

P: We must leave for the battlefield. We are afraid and we feel tense. "Let's go anyway." I lead a group. I am in the front line. It is night, but unfortunately there is a moon. We are targets. It is a shame. I am angry that we must fight this way. (Feels throat and breast). Then the battle begins. This cannot be; we are like sitting ducks; this is madness! I want to be invisible.

T: What happens then?

P: I am hit in the heart. I lie on the ground. I feel despair. I am still angry. I resent the people in charge. I feel powerless. I had to obey—what could I do? I am still angry at myself because I accepted the command. I feel guilty toward my men.

T: Go back to the moment of choice.

P: Now I am with the general, who says, "It is an order, you have to go." I am mad as hell. I am so angry and sad! I can't do anything. What an asshole!

The patient becomes emotional and therapist lets her experience her emotions completely.

P: Now I become apathetic, after the cursing and shouting. Then I just go and tell the men nothing. They are like sheep going to the slaughter house! Would that I was away.

Then many emotions come. The therapist encourages patient to experience them completely.

T: Do you want to find out why that general decided as he did?

P: Yes, I do. The general explains that we must help other men. It *isn't doable, but we have to. They need more force there. Now my feeling changes. I let him convince me. I see the why of the operation. We are as ants that sacrifice themselves to help other ants across the ditch. Now the general and I understand each other.*

T: *Go again to the moment of the shot on the battlefield.*

P: *I feel the shot. I am in pain. I am almost dead. Most emotions are gone. My left leg hurts. After death I hover over the body. I am very sad. I cherish the body and take leave. I straighten its leg. Can you do that as a spirit? Good body, so strong! I want to leave now. I still want to know what happened to my comrades.*

Patient feels happy when she discovers that many have survived. Then patient notices the soldier she once was, sitting in the circle in uniform.

P: *He is in my home. He makes a fine soldier's gesture to me. We are together again.*

Therapist checks to see if the situation is still charged, but all is right now.

T: *Now concentrate on the image of the child who could just see the table top.*

Patient experiences herself now as a four-year old child, with paralysis in the left leg. With great persistence the child pulls itself upright at the table. What a power! In the end, the child gains complete control over the leg and can even become a soldier. This soldier is the one who dies on the battlefield.

T: *Go through the death again. (Sensible.)*

P: *Leaving was so difficult. He had fought his body together. Therefore I straightened that leg. (Impressive detail!)*

T: *Look from a place of overview at what was most important in that life.*

P: *In that life I developed persistence, power. I feel that power in my pelvis and breast. When the soldier went into battle, the body went on with that power, while the brain said "No." Also in this life now my body often just persists, while the brain is afraid. This power I can often put to good use.*

341

Therapist asks patient to move to the prenatal period. There the power is restimulated by an incident where her mother was in bad shape (and she, too). The pregnancy took much of the mother's energy. She had polio. She really didn't want the pregnancy, but had to be strong. Patient recognizes this contradiction (not wanting, yet persisting) in herself. Also the birth began before the mother wanted it. During the birth, patient feels her power and brings that power with her to the here and now. She feels good and strong.

RELEASING ATTACHMENTS THROUGH EGOSTATES

T: *Find a spot where you can be wholly undisturbed, a place that is wholly yours. When you are there, say "Yes."*

P: *Yes.*

T: *You concentrate on the thought that you want to become clean and that you can clean everything that is in you or is with you, that is not yours. With that thought you now call up everything that does not belong to you, and you begin with what most disturbs you, what gives you the most trouble. Now somebody enters.*

P: *My mother.*

T: *Your mother. What impression does she give?*

P: *She is relaxed, but she is not really present.*

T: *How is she troubling you?*

P: *Because sometimes I am the same as she is, and I cannot stand that. It works the wrong way.*

T: *As she is now standing there, does she see you? (Nods.) Since when did she come with you this way? She says something and you get an impression. When did she invade your space for the first time?*

P: *When my father died. I was twelve then.*

T: *Do you understand why she invaded you?*

P: *Yes, I had to be that way.*

T: *Can she now go on herself?*

P: *Yes.*

T: *Can you now wish her simply the best?*

P: *Yes indeed.*

T: *Can you see her leave?*

P: *Yes, she is all right now.*

T: *Does she feel the same?*

P: *Yes. She was always insecure, but she can do it now on her own.*

T: *Okay, you see how she leaves the house, leaves the door. There you*

make a radiant silvery white shield, or you make around the door
an intensely silvery white frame, so that only people who are completely themselves can enter. If your mother wants to return too
soon through this door, she will see only a mirror. From now on, all
contacts between you and your mother go through the front door.
Does that feel good?

P: Yes, that feels good.

T: Okay, now you let a second presence enter. Who is the next one
who is troubling you?

P: My brother.

T: What does he project?

P: He always needs help and I just cannot give that anymore.

T: How come he cannot help himself? What is he missing?

P: He lacks an ego.

T: Ask him, "Where and when did you lose your ego?" Now you see
an image; together you'll see an image.

P: Yes, before his army. He kept hanging around. He got stuck there.

T: How come?

P: I see all fragments, as if he blew up. I see no core. I will look to see
if I can find things.

T: Go to the moment immediately before that explosion, that frag-
mentation. You now see the cause.

P: He steps on a mine or something. Yes, those were mines. It explodes, he goes to pieces, he lost himself.

T: Okay, go through that death and look at how he wakes up on the
other side. Apparently he didn't die well.

P: No, he is completely in pieces.

T: Yes, his body is in pieces, but how about his soul?

P: Dead. Gone.

T: He thinks so?

P: Yes.

T: You see him now in the same life in which he steps on that mine,
but you see him now in a situation where he was yet vital and
happy.

P: Yes.

T: Now you take that image to the room where you are and you ask
your brother if he can see that. Can he now see how vital and happy
he was?

P: Hum, yes. (Hesitates.) This makes me cry. It's beautiful.

T: Can he absorb that image?

P: Yes, they now become one. It's special, it's beautiful.

T: Just say to him: This was what you lost and what you needed back.

P: *I don't need to say anything, they do it themselves. (Therapist bothered unnecessarily.) They are now again complete.*

T: *Where is he going now?*

P: *Both go - it's so special - sort of: I am here again. He leaves through the same door. He doesn't need others anymore.*

T: *Good. This was the help he needed.*

T: *Now you see the third intruder who troubles you. The third now enters. Who is it?*

P: *(Laughing.) A little dog enters.*

T: *All right. What kind of dog?*

P: *A little bastard, somewhat of a sheepdog. A very nice little dog.*

T: *Do you know that dog?*

P: *No.*

T: *Okay, if this is a dog who died, you now see the moment when it died.*

P: *Hmm. Now a man comes out of the dog. A man without a home, something like that.*

T: *He feels himself like a bastard?*

P: *Yes. God almighty, he has been treated like a dog. He really is a kind person, only somewhat dependent.*

T: *Now you see something of his life. Go to a moment when he was happy, with others around him, a moment when he wasn't yet treated like a dog. Help him to see that.*

P: *Now is he a little boy. He is sitting in the kitchen with other children and a mother. I see no father.*

T: *Is it good between him and his mother?*

P: *Yes, yes, she is a very kind mother. But it has nothing to do with me.*

T: *Apparently not. Ask him, just as he stands there in your room, if he knows where his mother is now? (Forgets to ask when and why this man joined her.)*

P: *No. I fetch that little boy. I have that little boy fetched. (Better than what the therapist suggested!) The little boy now sees that man.*

T: *He had forgotten that little boy?*

P: *Yes. He didn't know anymore that he once was that little boy.*

T: *That little boy can also bring him back to his mother.*

P: *Yes, they go. That little boy shows him the way.*

T: *Ask him if he knows the way?*

P: *Yes!*

T: *And that dog, has it gone too? (Always check; leave nothing and nobody behind!)*

P: *Yes, it's gone.*

T: *How does that feel now?*

P: *Nice.*

T: *Okay.*

P: *Wow, that went really well! (Deep sighs.)*

T: *If there is a fourth troubling you, it now enters.*

P: *Oh my God, eh, a girl. God, she doesn't mean anything to me. The word "orphan" comes to me, an orphan girl.*

T: *An orphan girl, okay. What does she project? How are her eyes?*

P: *She is so pitiful, oh, how pitiful! She is dirty.*

T: *Ask her, while you look her in the eyes, "When did you join me?" You get an impression of your age and the specific situation.*

P: *When my father died I got scarlet fever, with high fevers. Then she came.*

T: *When you were weak. (Premature assumption.)*

P: *When I was also alone.*

T: *So when you were weak and alone and pitiful. (Premature assumption again.)*

P: *Yes, and she was also alone and pitiful.*

T: *So she entered on similar emotions.*

P: *Yes. I had lost my father.*

T: *And she had lost both her parents.*

P: *Yes.*

T: *Okay. Ask her, "Can you remember your parents?"*

P: *No, she can't.*

T: *Her father or her mother or both now enter, or somebody who knows where they are.*

P: *A man and a woman enter, young people, I think they are farmers.*

T: *How did they die?*

P: *I think through a disease, but they look healthy. Maybe a disaster. They are not from here. Gee.*

T: *You get an image of the environment.*

P: *Snow, an avalanche. That's why they still look so good.*

T: *How does the girl react to those two people who enter?*

P: *She doesn't understand a thing.*

T: *Did she know she was dead? (Therapist should have checked before.)*

P: *No.*

T: *Can you explain that to her?*

P: *Not easy.*

T: *You see the moment when she died and she is seeing it with you.*

P: *She became ill and died. She starved or something.*

T: Tell her, "When you die, you go to the same place your parents went and so you can find both of them again."

P: Yes, now she accepts it.

T: What happens now among those three?

P: She realizes who they are and starts to radiate. They recognize one another, they are together again.

T: What do they do?

P: Like this. (Makes gesture of embrace.) It all comes together now. How sweet! They now have one another.

T: Just wish them luck. They are glad that they have found one another again. When they have left the room, say "Yes."

P: Yes.

T: If there is still somebody troubling you, then you see that person enter the door now.

P: There is no end to it! There comes a man, let me look, a terribly dull man.

T: A man who has no clue at all of what to do after dying.

P: Absolutely. And not a shred of humor. Terrible. He is heavy as lead.

T: Ask, "When did you first join to me?" You now get an impression of your age and of the specific situation.

P: He came to me when my stepfather died.

T: Was that also a heavy time for you?

P: Yes, it was difficult.

T: Why did he join you?

P: He found me strong.

T: He wasn't strong himself?

P: No.

T: Ask him, "What have you done with your strength? Where have you lost your strength?"

P: In his life, he says.

T: You now get an image of the situation where he lost his strength.

P: A car accident. He loses his wife and children. Only he survives. He is terribly bitter, terribly alone.

T: Does he know that he died meanwhile?

P: No, he roams about.

T: Let him now see. Force him to look to the moment of his death. He sees now how he died and he sees his dead body. Look back at it with him.

P: He dies in bed, from tuberculosis.

T: Tell him, "Your bitterness has become so strong that you didn't want to realize that you died. But if you died, you are in the same

346

reality as the ones you lost before." Does he understand that?

P: He doesn't believe it. He asks, "How do I know that I will find them again?"

T: He first must be sure before he begins anything?

P: Yes.

T: Why? Is he lazy or does he think he's got privileges?

P: He is somebody who doesn't dare to take any risk at all.

T: And now he runs the biggest risk of all: standstill.

P: Well yes, he has done that for a long time.

T: Yes. (Waits, gives it time - very good.)

P: (Sighs.) No smile, nothing.

T: What must be done with him?

P: A kick in the butt, maybe.

T: Well, we don't need to kick him. Show him the door and say, "Now you go through that door and you see who is there on the other side."

P: He looks at me and hesitates. I tell him with my eyes that it is okay. (Silence.) He is going now. He stands on the threshold and he just looks and smiles. Well, he is gone. (Deep sighs.)

T: Can you understand such a man?

P: I do indeed.

T: Have you wished him the best?

P: Yes.

T: Really?

P: Yes, really.

T: Then the next one who is troubling you enters.

P: No, there is nobody left.

T: Then we get to the dessert. There enters a dessert. Now enters a part of yourself that you had forgotten.

P: (Starts grinning and moaning.) Little five-year-old Carla (her own name), with those pigtails I hated so much! What an attractive child, how she comes running to me!

T: What do you do with her?

P: We just hug. She really runs into my arms. Unbelievable. So full of life!

T: Well, feel her as well as you can. Feel the shock when she bumps into you. Feel it reverberating from your head to your toes.

P: Hum, yes.

T: Can you feel her inside yourself? Can you absorb her?

P: Yes indeed.

T: Where she is most present?

P: Everywhere!

T: *Return with her to the here and now, in your own way and at your own speed.*
P: *Well, that was fast going! God almighty! (Laughs.)*

This session offers a good example of attachment release. Family members are often attachments. Others are lost souls, entering at critical moments of weakness, often with similar emotions. Many of them don't know what they are doing. Some don't even know they are dead. Most are sad or gloomy, for all sorts of reasons.

There were no virulent, aggressive attachments here who knew what they were doing. Still, it is amazing how quickly such a process may go. This session took under 40 minutes. Afterward, the patient has the usual response after attachment release: feeling many pounds lighter.

PERSONAL INTEGRATION USING EGOSTATES

This session took place during a training seminar in Brazil for practicing psychotherapists. The patient had done some regressions and from dreams had a few impressions of probable past lives. She offered herself after I had said that I wanted to work with someone who felt different sides within himself or herself. The client lay down and then began the session that took about an hour.

T: *Say "Yes" when you feel you are ready to begin.*
P: *Yes.*
T: *Imagine a pleasant place, a spot that is yours, where you feel at home. When you are there, say "Yes."*
P: *Yes.*
T: *What place is it?*
P: *I walk in a meadow with trees.*
T: *Do you have your own place in that field? Is there a spot that is yours?*
P: *I sit on a few stones, near a small fountain.*
T: *Now you will see that a few people will appear at that spot. Each of those people will be a part of you, but you'll see them as separate people. Now concentrate and see the first person coming to you. Who is it?*

P: *A woman, a mother with big skirts. A real Mummy.*
T: *How she is called?*
P: *Mama.*
T: *Okay, Mama. How is Mama doing? Is she all right? What does she love? What does she hold important? (Too many questions.)*
P: *(Mama:) My children. (Her voice changes and becomes purring.) They are so cute and lovely. I love to be with them and care for them.*
T: *Do you want to say something to Anna Regina? (Name of client.)*
P: *(Mama:) Yes, that I am satisfied with her right now.*
T: *Very good, Mama. Please be seated for now.*

T: *Now you see a second person entering. How does this one look?*
P: *This one is long, dry, objective.*
T: *Is it a woman again? (Better: Is it a man or a woman?)*
P: *Yes, it is a woman again.*
T: *What are her main qualities?*
P: *Objectivity and rationalism.*
T: *How does she want to be called?*
P: *She doesn't give her name. She doesn't say her name. She just stands there being intellectual.*
T: *How is this intellectual dressed?*
P: *Very formally and old-fashioned. She is not very likeable.*
T: *Why is that?*
P: *Because she is so cold, because she puts people off.*
T: *Good, then now ask this intellectual lady why she is cold.*
P: *Because she has work to do.*
T: *What kind of intellectual work do you like? Do you have a special subject?*
P: *(Intellectual:) No. About life, about people. (She wants to write about what she keeps at bay!)*
T: *I would like to know, intellectual, when did you enter the life of Anna Regina?*
P: *(Intellectual:) Early, when she was small, before . . .*
T: *Before what? Before birth?*
P: *(Intellectual:) It has been much more I than she, but since she has taken much space.*
T: *So she had a smaller place, but you were already with her before birth?*
P: *(Intellectual:) Yes.*
T: *Now we would like to know from the intellectual when she entered before that in the life of Anna Regina. You'll now see the intellec-*

349

tual as she looked in a previous life. Intellectual, show how you looked originally.

P: I see an aristocratic lady, alone in a castle, yes, with the same clothes I have seen her in already.

T: Is this a life of which you have seen something already?

P: Only in dreams.

T: When you want to explore this life further, to understand how this intellectual side formed or how this intellectual side transformed herself into a cold side..., oh, wait a minute, my apologies, Mama, I forgot to ask when you entered Anna Regina's life.

P: (Mama:) Only a short while ago. She was afraid of me. Only now she gives me space.

T: But now is it all right?

P: (Mama:) All is right and I love her.

T: And you, Anna Regina, how do you feel about Mama?

P: This Mama is new. I have seen her already once before. She was completely deformed then. I feared her much then. She was terrible. Now I have accepted her.

T: The intellectual doesn't seem to like that this mother has taken so much space and let her work less.

T: Now the third subpersonality enters. What does this one look like? (Forgets the opening to the past life of the intellectual.)

P: Oh, how beautiful! A sweet girl aged six or seven, playing in the sunlight.

T: What does she want to be called?

P: Bijou.

T: Welcome, Bijou. Do you like this mother?

P: (Bijou:) Yes.

T: Do you like the intellectual?

P: (Bijou:) I am afraid of her. (But see what happens later!)

T: What quality does Bijou have?

P: Energy.

T: Tell me, Bijou, when did you enter Anna Regina's life?

P: (Bijou:) I have always been there, only I am imprisoned because that other (She points apparently to the intellectual.) never has given me freedom.

T: Were you already there before six years? Beforebirth?

P: It was a life that I already know from a regression in which I died as adolescent. Now Bijou shows herself younger, but I feel the same energy. Remarkably, her dress is now modern. (Suggests spontaneously progressing integration.)

T: Thanks, Bijou. Just sit for a moment.

T: Let us see who enters next. Is there anybody?
P: A man.
T: What kind of man?
P: Quiet, friendly, loving, full of energy.
T: Do you like him?
P: Yes, he looks like my father.
T: What does he want to be called?
P: Louis.
T: Is that the name of your father?
P: Yes.
T: This personality is thus a copy of your father inside yourself, but it is a part of your soul. Louis, sit and be welcome. What do you think of the other three?
P: He is attracted to Bijou, he thinks the mother wonderful and he respects the intellectual.
T: Even while the intellectual is so cold?
P: Yes, even so.

T: We now look for the next personality that enters.
P: It is a grown boy who observes everything.
T: And what does he want to be called?
P: José.
T: When did you enter Anna Regina's life, José?
P: (José:) In a former life.
T: Can you see when that was? Which life formed José?
P: It was a life that I have also seen already once in regression. He was a prisoner of the Romans, a slave. A servant of a magistrate. He succeeded in making himself respected.
T: Do you think that he also is a part of you in this life?
P: No.
T: But he is here. He entered. How do you explain that?
P: He observes all, he reconciles all.
T: Thanks, José. Be welcome and take a seat.

T: Is there anybody else?
P: A woman, half savage. She is dangerous.
T: Can you talk with her? What does she want to be called?
P: She remains in a defensive position, ready to attack. She is difficult to approach. She is an aggressive savage.
T: Aggressive savage, when did you enter the life of Anna Regina?

351

P: (*Savage:*) *When she had to fight to survive.*

T: *When was the first time?*

P: (*Savage:*) *When she had to defend herself against her mother. She needed strength.*

T: *Were you born then or before?*

P: *She woke up then.*

T: *What is her aim?*

P: *Conquest, and defending my space. She succeeds in that.*

T: *Thus she has a positive aim?*

P: *Yes, but her appearance deters others. She is terrible. She was a witch, a sorceress.*

T: *Do you know that life?*

P: *Not this way, but I can feel the energy of the witch.*

T: *What do you want to do with her?*

P: *I need her. When I didn't have her, I had to cry a lot. She cannot leave, I cannot do without her, she is strong.*

T: *The intellectual has a positive aim, but is cold; the aggressive savage looks fearful, but is strong. They brought these characteristics with them from other lives. I suggest that you give a name to the aggressive savage. What will you call her?*

P: *I call her Anna. (Patient's first Christian name.)*

T: *Now she enters with the name of Anna. Take your place and sit down, Anna.*

P: *The intellectual scolds her that she is a witch. She feels disturbed, she is very tense. She is angry now, but she has somewhat lost her coldness.*

T: *Now I will talk with you, intellectual. Now we no longer accept the term "intellectual." Now we want your real name.*

P: (*Intellectual:*) *I am Regina. It was clear that I am the queen, wasn't it? (Her voice changes completely, her upper lip becomes thin and a cool, dominating lady is talking down to us mortals who are present.)*

T: *Welcome, Regina. How come, Regina, that Anna troubles you?*

P: (*Regina:*) *At first I was alone, but now with all those others that she let in, around me, I have no more space. I cannot write anymore.*

T: *How can we solve that, Regina?*

P: (*Regina:*) *I need more space for myself. I want all space. (Very demanding.)*

T: *'All' is much. What can we do? Who could help you?*

P: *But it has been always like this. She never had friends. The biggest part of her life was this way. She dominated in everything.*

T: *Is somebody there who can help to solve this?*

P: *Her father. She needs a safe person, a sure person. She needs some-body who takes care of her, on whom she can depend.*

T: *Can Louis help her?*

P: *I think that it is possible for all of them, that there is time, that there is space. She has to transmit much, what she must write. She has so much that she can do, that she can bring. She must transmit things, but she doesn't allow herself to do it. She keeps people at such a distance. She has burdened herself by a very big guilt and therefore she must serve, serve and serve. Become a warm being, human, friendly, understanding. All that she must do, also be mother.*

T: *Do you want to set yourself free? Do you want to come out?*

P: *(Regina:) Yes.*

T: *Who stands in the doorway?*

P: *Bijou.*

T: *Now let go of every coldness, every pressure. Leave the prison and enter the sunlight with Bijou. Go through every coldness and re-lease it. (Very strong physical reactions, her whole body begins to tremble.)*

P: *My feet are so cold. (Two colleagues massage her feet.) All my muscles, my whole body is cold. I see now that she was mainly paralyzed in her right leg, her arms and her hands.*

T: *What else can we do now?*

P: *(Regina:) Let somebody touch it and warm it, from her elbow down-ward and the legs from the knees downward. Her hands are also rigid. (She lists her complaints as a queen. Regina now calls the patient "she"!)*

T: *(After patient has been touched and massaged.) How do you feel now?*

P: *I am less cold.*

T: *Now you feel an integration in your whole body. Now you are redeeming, aren't you?*

P: *(Regina:) I must redeem my guilt, but I must write and I don't succeed in that.*

T: *Do you have to resolve that now?*

P: *(Regina:) Yes, much has to happen and fast.*

T: *Is there somebody who stops that? Who blocks it?*

P: *(Regina:) The people I feel guilty about. There are many of them. Through my fault so many people died. Then I died and they came to bury me. I was so great. Everybody feared me. I am yet strong. They couldn't kill me. Despite everything I am here. I am so afraid, I am so sorry. (Cries, wrings, swallows, turns one way and an other until relief and catharsis come. Moans, sighs and begins slowly to come back.) I was never less of a queen. I was never so humiliated. I was so great, so powerful.*

T: Does Anna Regina yet have a chance?

P: (Regina:) Yes, I have a chance. I will do no more wrong things and cause suffering and I know how I must do that. I know that I really want that. I am of good will now, yet I feel nothing in my body. I see Bijou dancing in the sun, but I cannot feel the sun yet. I can only see it.

T: Is there somebody who can advise and help you?

P: There is an ancient priest.

T: Does he have power?

P: Yes. He has great power.

T: Is he an old part of you? Or is he related to you?

P: Yes, he looks at me and he says that I need him.

T: And what do you say to him?

P: That he finally can see the light.

T: He now shows you what he has done. You now see what he has to show you.

P: He served the God. He threw children in the mouth of the God. There were hot stones, a furnace, a roaring fire. He did what he had to do, because he thought that it was the right thing to do. Oh, those terrible screams of the children. It scares me so! (She begins to scream in horror and misery, it goes to the bone. She puts her hands before her eyes and she enters completely the terror of that earlier time.)

T: Let the mother enter the fire and get the children back out. Feel that this mother is older and stronger than the fire. The mother is true, this fire is a lie. (Sobs and moans and twists. She is clearly working.) Let the mother embrace the priest, as if he is a child now. (A long silence, but obviously big things happen inside her.) How are you now?

P: Good.

T: Now you see them together. How is mama?

P: She smiles at me.

T: How is Louis?

P: He is the priest. They became one. Now he wears a white-golden robe.

T: And the boy?

P: He now wears a Roman tunic and carries a lance.

T: How is Anna?

P: The witch now blended with the mother.

T: *Is the mother also a witch?*
P: *Oh yes, she can do everything with that smile of hers!*
T: *And is Anna Regina ready to write? Is she now less under pressure?*
P: *Yes, she is ready.*
T: *Do you want to talk with somebody else?*
P: *No, they are happy now and they are strong.*
T: *Do they still need anything?*
P: *The light of the sun. (At least Regina still was in the shadow.)*
T: *Okay, together go into the light of the sun. Go into the original fire and be one.*

What has happened in this session? The first subpersonality who came was new for her, and this "Mama" served mainly to calm her. The patient experiences this subpersonality as a restored, normalized form of a former experience. The original, wild form later enters as a separate personality and at the end integrates with the first, the mother role. Apparently, in this session she is redoing consciously what has already happened subconsciously.

The second personality who enters is the "intellectual," whom she recognizes from dreams, but whom she speaks about in a strongly associated way. She feels this association clearly as an aspect of her present personality.

The third personality, the young child Bijou, she knew already from a regression, but this personality now shows itself as younger and modern, which means that she had started to integrate this personality already.

The fourth, her father, is a "screen personality," in which hides one of her earlier lifetimes. She has repressed that lifetime for reasons that became clear during the session. This was the priest who sacrificed young children.

The fifth personality, the grown boy José, she also recognizes, but she sees him at first not as a part of her present personality. After the therapist's question, however, José appears to have an essential function. At the end of the session he is also consciously integrated.

What is beautiful is also how a personality from a former life becomes directly associated with this patient's second Christian name, while the savage and the mother unite into her first Christian name.

The first catharsis occurs when the cold, prominent intellectual is liberated from her coldness and stiffness by the young and sunny girl. Usually, reliving the original traumatic experience leads to a catharsis. Here the catharsis leads to a liberation of the original traumatic experiences. In that partial healing the former personality, already strongly present in the here and now, takes over the driver's seat for a moment. But the resolution halts and then the key figure of the ancient priest enters.

Apparently, the trauma and especially the heavy guilt of that earlier lifetime are directly related to the coldness and rigidity and the hiding of emotions in the later life as the aristocratic lady. As so often happens, there is great force present in a life in which somebody seriously went over the line and has silenced his humanity. That force lies repressed below the guilt feeling, the self-reproach, and with that also the fear of assuming power again. But the moment is right and the original misery expresses itself intensively. No written text does justice to the screaming that erupts when a fountain of old pain and terror finally bursts forth.

Until then, the session almost runs itself, but now the therapist takes his role as healer and lets one personality liberate the other. Once that happens, the only thing to do is to wrap up. What is beautiful is the realization that a mother is also a witch. At the end comes the simplest question: if the client needs anything else.

GLOSSARY

AFTERLIFE. The experiences of people following their physical death. In therapy, two essential events during the afterlife period are meeting companions and having a life panorama or life retrospect. This life retrospect occurs at a place of overview, or *panorama platform*. During the afterlife people experience debriefing, restoration, often learning, and finally preparation for the next round.

Patients may be guided back in memory to this place of overview in the afterlife, to see how their lifetimes are connected to one another, or how they prepared for or previewed a next life.

ASSOCIATION and DISSOCIATION. The sense of connectedness (*association*) or disconnectedness (*dissociation*) that people may feel in relation to an experience or event. These processes of connecting and disconnecting are important in the recording and digestion of experiences, the exploration and resolution of problems, and the relationship between patient and therapist.

For any experience, all impressions that are recorded at the same time become connected, or *associated*. Similarly, any impression becomes *associated* with like impressions.

Restimulation is an *association* of the second degree. A house fire may become associated with feelings of guilt for failure to prevent the fire. The fire may also become associated with smells and sounds of the fire and the firefighting. The sound of a siren may later trigger, or *restimulate*, guilt feelings.

During a regression, a patient is guided to identify with whatever had happened at the earlier time and place. The therapist addresses that former person as "you" and speaks in the present tense. The therapist invites the patient to identify with the earlier body, feeling it from the inside. Regression thus is an *associative* procedure, as is back-pressing.

One specific association technique is *anchoring*, the association of a problem charge or a solution charge with a specific somatic or a specific action. Anchoring reinforces the charge and makes it easier to access it, to trigger it at will.

The triggering of opposite charges at the same time is a cathartic technique called *collapsing anchors*. The patient experiences the resulting catharsis as a short circuit, an explosion, an implosion, or a whirling or turbulence.

By contrast, *dissociation* may happen when a therapist asks the patient to take a bird's-eye view or other similar disconnecting step. Dissociation may also be achieved by employing *egostates* or *aura exploration*. In these two approaches, the patient projects part of himself outside of himself to look at that part, understand it, treat it and finally re-integrate it.

Reliving the past means association, dissociation means storytelling. With association a patient enters an experience fully, feeling its emotions and bodily sensations. With dissociation a patient looks at himself from a distance and is less involved, as if he is observing somebody else. In dissociation a therapist speaks in the past tense, refers to the patient's former self as "he" or "she," and invites the patient to see his former self from the outside. Dissociation means disconnecting from experiences that may be too heavy, too intense, or too confusing. It means regaining clarity and overview. Basic techniques for dissociation include the bird's-eye view, aura exploration and use of egostates. Following such dissociation, association then involves the patient's re-entering the former person or absorbing that former person.

In regression therapy, many problems of over-association may be solved by dissociation. Likewise many problems that involve over-dissociation may be solved by association. When too many charges have become interconnected, the therapist must try to disentangle those charges.

Therapeutic dissociation happens when a therapist is too aloof and distant. The reverse is more common, when a therapist becomes too personally involved. In such cases, bonding, enmeshment and transference may become issues.

Successful therapy alternates between and combines associative and dissociative episodes. Patients who tend to be overly dissociated may especially need associative approaches, while those patients who are overly associated may especially need dissociative approaches.

ATLANTIS. A legendary continent, which may have existed more than ten thousand years ago in the Atlantic Ocean. In regressions, patients commonly describe Atlantis as having a highly developed, stratified culture. Within that culture, priesthoods held religious, political, scientific and educational influence. Technology and parapsychology appear to have been intertwined.

Regression experiences that seem to involve Atlantis give the impression that Atlantis was a totalitarian culture, and a hotbed of elitism, jealousy, contempt, and religious warfare. An even older civilization that is sometimes seen in regression is that of Lemuria. Lemuria appears to have been barbaric, a hotbed of brutality and racial warfare.

Regressions show us former times mainly in their traumatic aspects, so the picture we get from those prehistoric times is rather bleak. Unresolved business from those ancient times is surprisingly alive. At the other hand, some people tend to have exalted and glamorized memories of ancient times, especially about Atlantis.

ATTACHMENTS. Energies or presences from others. These energies may become attached to a person's body or aura. *Inserts* appear to be inert objects, while *parasites* appear as animals or vermin that eat energy. *Holes* are dark places that may be perceived in the body or aura, places that appear empty and indicate previous losses of energy.

Hikers are deceased persons who have attached themselves to living people without wishing to interfere. Hikers may strengthen passive or depressive moods. *Intruders* are those deceased persons who have entered consciously, for their own ends. Persistent intruders may be referred to as *squatters*.

If attached presences harbor aggressive intentions toward their host or toward others, they are *obsessors*. Such entities often intensify a mania that may already be present in a person. Suicidal tendencies that arise for no apparent reason often come from obsessors. *Karmic obsessors* are those attached beings who hold a personal grudge. *Possession* occurs when a squatter takes over the driver's seat.

Most obsessors became aggressive in the distant past. Some, however, appear to have been aggressive from the start; they may never have been born. Such beings appear bent on obstructing or destroying people, they are evil. If they are also intelligent, we call them *demonic*. *Exorcism* is the removal of such non-human, destructive energies. It might be best to forget this term altogether, as classical and romanticized exorcism is disgusting and ineffective. It confirms a patient's own weakness and may even be evil in itself.

Egostates and *aura exploration* are the most helpful methods to find and resolve attachments. Often, attachments need to be disentangled before regression therapy can be effective. When attachments are human precences, they can be regressed to their own death experience and to their last positive memories. When attachments are animal presences, they can be sent back to their natural habitats. Demonic energies may be sent back to their (rare) subterranean origin or their (common) outer space origin. Vermin, dirt or negative thought images may simply be eliminated. Inserts and unwanted gifts may be returned to their sender.

AUTOPSYCHODRAMA. Self-pity complex.

BOIL-OFF. A period of drowsiness, yawning and sometimes dizziness that may occur during a therapy session. A boil-off releases any remaining somatic and mental charges left from past experiences that had involved loss of consciousness.

CATHARSIS. Purification, cleansing, chastening, from the Greek term "katharsis." The mental, emotional and physical liberation from a problem, yielding lasting relief and understanding. The most intense experience of catharsis is similar to that of dying and being reborn.

CHARGES. The mental, emotional or somatic qualities that carry (etheric) energy and thus have some reality of their own. *Karmic charges* are those mental, emotional or somatic effects that remain from a wounding or overburdening experience and from a person's response to that experience. Karmic charges may especially involve decisions that have carried lasting consequences. *Cathartic charges* are the mental, emotional or somatic aspects of healing experiences. Charges may be single (grief, joy, envy, headache, heaviness) or clustered.

CLUSTERS. Charges that are connected with one another, so that a triggering of one charge will also trigger others. *Coverers* are charges that cover up other charges. Guilt and shame are examples of coverers. *Complicators* are mental charges such as

perplexity and confusion, which hinder processing of associated emotional and somatic charges. *Boosters* are charges that
reinforce each other. Impotent rage is a cluster that includes
anger, powerlessness and feeling beside oneself. Desperation
is a cluster of fear, despair and perplexity. *Knots* are clusters of
counteracting charges, one of which is likely to be expansive
and the other contractive. Examples are anger-grief knots and
anger-guilt knots.

CRUCIAL MOMENTS. Moments of deepest energy that may
mark a *karmic event*, the *crux* of a problem. Contrary to what is
usually assumed, the crucial moment is not the moment of initial decision, but the moment of ultimate test. In Christian terms
the karmic event is not the decision in the garden of Gethsemane,
but the crucifixion on Golgotha. Why? Because any problem
that is faced by an individual is anchored at the moment of
deepest energy. A crux is a crucifying experience, the most crushing moment. In metaphoric terms, first a drawing is done in
pencil, then in ink. But the crucial moment is that of engraving,
when acid eats into the metal. Thus, at the moment of deepest
energy an event is engraved in a person's experience. A *catharsis* is the crux of a solution. This catharsis is the dharmic event.
Its positive energy can be just as intense as that of a crucifying
moment. Ascension is so intense that it may be painful.

DOUBLE BIND. A manipulative judgment or response that
binds a positive appraisal with a negative one, so that it becomes difficult to reject the negative appraisal. A remark such
as, "You are even more beautiful when you are angry" says that
your anger is not taken seriously (thus *you* are not taken seriously), while something positive is said about you. Double binds
commonly occur in relationships of domination. They may be
explicit: "He is an old soul, but momentarily confused." They
may also be implicit: "She still has beautiful potential."

EGOSTATE THERAPY. Therapy that guides patients to look
separately at certain aspects of themselves and consider those
aspects, or *egostates*, as separate individuals. Egostates are parts
of ourselves that more or less lead their own lives. Examples of
egostates may include the sulking infant, the shameful teen-
ager, or the romantic adolescent in ourselves. Egostates may
also consist of a recurrent rage, a dark hole of depression into

which we stumble now and then, or a fantasy of the future that remains exciting.

In egostate therapy, such parts of a person are visualized as separate persons, and a communication is established with those personalities. Each problem and each resource of a patient may thus be evoked as a subpersonality. Similarly, in past-life therapy previous lives may be encountered and treated as separate personalities.

ETHERIC BODY. An energy body that penetrates and envelops our physical body. This energy envelop is called *aura*, a globe or an egg around us. It has nerve centers or *chakras*, and strands of energy that include the upward stream called *kundalini*. The energy itself is called *prana*.

Outside the body, people experience themselves according to their mood or self-image; the discarnate reality is psychoplastic. But the *etheric body* is a more objective, energetic reality.

We discard part of our etheric body after death, but keep the remainder as a permanent vehicle. No matter how many different previous personalities we may have had, only one permanent etheric body remains with us. This etheric body is the carrier of karma and dharma.

The etheric body's basic color is silvery white. Further colors appear to depend on our moods and mental states. Brilliant colors suggest full vitality and full awareness, while transparent colors suggest natural states. Opaque colors suggest low energy, holes suggest energy loss, and metallic colors may indicate inhumanely durable qualities.

In therapy, perception of the aura and its concomitants such as light rays and gloves provide powerful and effective imagery. Use of this imagery greatly speeds up the therapeutic process, also without pretensions of reality. Yet if perception of an etheric body is mere fantasy, why is this perception so effective?

EVIL. Negative or wicked. Evil charges may result from evil experiences or evil acts. Such charges often appear to have entered from outside of a person. When egostate therapy or aura exploration are used, a patient may detect evil or demonic presences in more or less human shape. These perceptions may be the products of fear and guilt, and may dissolve when the fear and guilt are resolved. Such perceptions may also represent a person's own evil tendencies, or confrontation with or infection from evil in the past. Occasionally, evil charges represent obsessive energies that need to be removed.

FUNKTIONLUST. A German psychological term that denotes the pleasure in acting smoothly in doing things, even without regard for results or rewards.

GESTALT. A German psychological term that denotes a meaningful, configured and interconnected whole. When such a whole is broken into parts, this *Gestalt* no longer exists. A mountain of bricks can be split in two smaller mountains of bricks. It isn't a Gestalt. A marriage, a whale, an impressive painting cannot be split and remain what they are. They are Gestalts.

Gestalt psychology investigates how we recognize and produce Gestalts in our cognition. Gestalt therapy treats experiences, dreams, and events as wholes in which all elements belong and are interconnected. If a person dreams about being chased across a cold prairie by two wolves, then the prairie and the wolves are parts of the entirety of this experience, and are therefore parts of this person. Similarly, any relationship between two or more people is a Gestalt. Whatever one person means to another is a part of that person, too.

HANGOVER. In regression therapy, the repercussions of long periods of low energy, of depression or oppression, of bondage, of weakness or illness, of insignificance or meaninglessness, or of boredom. The result of such periods of low energy is not a psychic wound, but rather a psychic *dirt skirt*, a chronic heavy, gloomy, musty feeling.

HEALING. Helping a person to return to a state of wellness and wholeness, mentally, emotionally, physically and spiritually. Healing may refer in general to the awareness, the attitude and the aims of the therapist. More specifically, *healing* often refers to the use of spiritual means from the outside. Such means may include the transmission of energies, the invocation of presences, or the evocation of spiritual parts of a person's subconscious.

HIGHER SELF. A theosophical term meaning the eternal, superconscious part of the human mind. A transpersonal therapy term that denotes a point of view, knowledge, or energy that transcends the ego and the usual self. A higher-self intervention asks the assumed higher self to advise, to support, or to provide an explanation to a patient (and therapist) who may be in dire straits.

HYPNOSIS. A state of trance in which consciousness is shifted. When we are under hypnosis we may feel drawn inward or drawn into a subject that has captured our attention. We are temporarily less alert and less aware of surroundings. Our perception of time changes, and we may become either more aware or less aware of our physical body. Imaginative ability increases. Our body state changes too: skin resistance increases, brain waves slow, and we become more sluggish and silent.

Hypnotism is the induction and use of such a trance, usually by others (*hypnotists*) and sometimes by oneself (self-hypnosis). *Hypnotherapy* is therapy that is conducted while the patient (and probably the therapist) is in trance. In such a state, one may more easily explore past experiences or more effectively receive suggestions.

KARMA and DHARMA. *Karma* is any liability that remains from prior lifetimes, while *dharma* is any asset that remains from such lifetimes. Both karma and dharma are etheric realities. Karma includes the troubling repercussions from everything that we have either done or avoided, especially from prior lifetimes.

While most experiences, decisions and acts leave few recognizable traces, some events are so momentous in their consequences that they are described as *karmic events*. Usually a karmic event, while already a very intense experience in itself, involved a decision of great future consequence - to give up, to seek revenge, or to persevere despite the obstacles.

Group karma results from a group of people who share a single karmic event, a common experience, or a common responsibility.

MAGIC. The supposed ability to do something through the help of supernatural powers or secrets. Much magic of former times probably consisted of post-hypnotic suggestions, which may have been perceived as magic words or spells. All other magic that is not fraud, deception or illusionism seems related to etheric powers.

NEUROSIS and PSYCHOSIS. Neurosis is emotional inhibition and instability, while psychosis is a loss of reality. *Neurotic* people suffer from impaired learning. Rather than learning from experience, they use a program and then become stuck in a loop, usually from discouragement. Their feeling of self-worth is sensitive. Common neurotic roles are those of the Victim, the Helper (or Rescuer or Savior), the Prosecutor, the Perpetrator and the Spectator (or Observer or Witness).

Psychotic people, by contrast, suffer from an impaired sense of reality. Usually such people confuse inner realities with outer realities. Common psychotic roles include assuming a non-human identity such as that of the Angel, the Devil, the Robot, the Thing (e.g., the Channel), the Stone, or the Plant. Also possible is a scattered psychotic identity as the Group or the Multitude.

PERSONALITY. The particular way that a person presents himself or herself. In the case of a discarnate, the personality is the manner in which a discarnate manifests itself.

In past-life therapy the present personality is seen as different from personalities of previous lifetimes, and also different from attached personalities. *Subpersonalities* are parts of a person's present personality that manifest themselves semi-permanently.

Egostates are aspects of personality that, because of instructions given during therapy, are configured as separate personalities. *Egostate therapy* is the method by which a patient is guided to view his or her own psychological aspects as separate entities. For example, a therapist may tell a patient, "Now you see your timidity enter," or "Now the most timid part of you enters." This patient may then see himself at a younger age, may see a caricature of himself nearly crawling with timidity, or may see his own father as a boy. He may likewise see a former lifetime or an attached personality.

Sometimes a personality enters that appears to be more inclusive and may encompass the present person. This personality may be that of a former lifetime when the patient was stronger and wiser. It may also be the forever discarnate part of the soul, also known as the *higher self*. This higher self may hold the "seed personality," the original source. In any case it is the "fruit personality," a synthesis of the harvest of all lifetimes experienced thus far.

POSTULATE. A mental engram in the form of a charged, recurring sentence that acts as a program line in the evaluations and actions of our mind. Postulates are program lines, while programs are interrelated sets of postulates that determine how we will respond to a situation. Postulates are essentially fixed ideas, mind-closers that result in ritual responses (induration), wrong responses (falsification) and abstract responses (generalization).

Postulates that do define us are called *character postulates*. Most such postulates begin with the word "I." Other postulates consist of indirect statements of character, such as statements about people in general or about reality in general.

All postulates are *generalizations* in that they are no longer connected to the original experience that triggered them. The conclusion, "It is no use to go on trying" may have been valid in a death struggle or a futile escape attempt. But once this statement has become disconnected from the original experience it becomes a postulate.

Antithetical postulates such as "Never again!" trigger strong behavior alternations. Hubbard calls such postulates *bouncers*. *Perfection postulates* such as, "Nothing can touch me, "or "My life belongs to God," work in reverse by implying that further change is unwanted and unnecessary. Such postulates belong to the group that we call *perpetuators*. Another type of perpetuator often results from drawn-out suffering such as long torture, slow death, or endless toil. Such a postulate may claim, "This will never stop." *Repetitors* are related to perpetuators, and may conclude, "I run around in circles," or "It always comes back to the same thing."

Postulates that have been engraved by others are known as *commands*. *Shut-off commands* told us to keep a matter secret or to forget something. These shut-off commands may be *silencers* such as, "Don't talk about it," or *deniers* such as, "It never happened." Many other silencers and deniers are self-imposed. Extreme deniers are *erasers*, such as, "I wasn't there," or "It didn't happen."

Postulates known as *groupers*, such as a statement that everything happened at once or at the same time, or with the same intention, blur distinctions. Similarly, *misdirectors* indicate an erroneous time or place for a given event.

Repetition of postulates serves as an excellent verbal bridge and effective focusing technique. Repetitors and even *inversions* of a postulate may also be helpful during closure of a therapy session. Such repetition or inversion may anchor the cathartic results of therapy, proving to the patient's mind that an earlier program line has now been erased or exploded.

Postulates may be released through *specification*, through an understanding of when and how a postulate originated. A postulate may have resulted from specific circumstances, or it may have formed from undue indoctrination and wrong interpretation.

Postulates may also be defused through either *inversion* or *explosion*. A postulate that states, "People have no taste" may be inverted and changed to, "I have no taste," or "People have taste." A double inversion would be, "I have taste." An *explosion* of this postulate may be achieved by overdoing it with the statement, "Nobody ever had taste and nobody ever will have taste."

PRESENCE and ABSENCE. *Presence* is the state of being grounded, of being in the here and now, fully in the body. Lack of this grounded state is *absence*. Long-term problems with presence and absence may come from birth problems, or from pregnancy problems before birth. *Rebirthing* is a powerful means of resolving problems of presence and absence.

Effective therapy requires a patient to be grounded in the present, while at the same time being anchored in the earlier experience. This simultaneous awareness of two separate foci is a form of elliptic consciousness.

PROCESSING. Resolving of a patient's issues through any of a variety of therapeutic techniques. Such *processing* techniques include assimilation, digestion and transformation of charges during the therapy session; strengthening of impressions by anchoring and focusing them; avoidance and removal of recursive blocks by use of dissociation; resolution of confusion and contamination; or assisting in a patient's catharsis through abreaction, collapsing anchors, reframing and renovation, or integration and progression.

PSEUDO-OBSESSOR. The personality of an earlier lifetime that may remain stuck in a self-limiting after-death state. This pseudo-obsessor may now reside in or around our physical body as would an attachment.

PSYCHOSIS. A disturbed perception of reality. A patient who suffers from psychosis may perceive himself, other people, or the environment as unreal. He may also perceive unreal things or presences as real. He may see symbols as reality, or regard real things as symbols.

PSYCHOSOMATIC. Any problem of the physical body that originates in a psychological problem. Psychosomatic problems may include low energy and stamina, tension, hypersensitivity, hyperactivity, or physical complaints that have no medical explanation.

REALITY FIRST. The idea that concrete experience comes before any lesson or conclusion drawn from that experience. A concrete experience, or *reality*, includes what we see, hear, touch, smell, or taste. Reality means feeling the body, the cool grass, the emotions. Reality means location in place and time. If the patient encounters a door that will not open, the therapist would be wise to ask what that door looks like, rather than ask (or even worse: tell) what a closed door means. Experiences and stories are concrete, while lessons and symbols are abstractions that must wait until after reality is examined.

A patient may feel abandoned and may feel that in the chest, behind the eyes and in the belly. She sees that this feeling originated in a hut in winter. In regression she wakes up alone, in the dark, and finds that everyone else is gone. She moves toward the door, where a freezincold enters. Does she hear a wolf howling in the distance? She feels perplexed, afraid. Her mind stops.

Perhaps this experience also carries a deeper, more general sense. It could be a metaphor for a soul who discovers that it is alone in a cold world. But meanings come later. First comes the specific, concrete experience. Abstractions and analogies must wait.

Concrete experience is the only anchor for the abstract. Symbolism and abstraction are the refuge of the weak and the arrogant, as well as of some swindlers.

RECURSION. A looped reality. A shortcut between levels of abstraction or levels of condition. The most common recursion arises when content works back on its form, or a product works back on the process. For example, a person who is fearful in general will be afraid to deal with his fearfulness. This looped reality forms an *emotional recursion*. Similarly, if someone had once been locked up and knew that she would not get out, the repercussions of this experience tell her that she cannot get out of these repercussions. Thus, she experiences a *mental recursion*. Finally, if a patient is either too dependent or too independent, these dependency problems will hamper a good working relationship with the therapist. This situation forms a *therapeutic recursion*.

REMIGRATION. In general, a neutral term that means a reliving of the past. Its three modes are exploration from curiosity, for therapy, and to awaken old, hidden talents so that these talents may be mobilized.

REPERCUSSION. The karma from a previous experience. For instance, a trauma is a wound that made the ego collapse. A hangover is a chronic frustration that made the ego pinch off. Alienation is a loss of the sense of belonging and feeling at home somewhere. A pseudo-obsession is a previous ego that died incompletely and still roams about. A character postulate is a robotization of the ego.

RESCRIPTING. Rewriting of the memory of a past experience. A good rescripting rewrites only the interpretation of the experience, and thus changes the way that experience is filed in the memory. Memory of the facts of the experience remains intact. *Renovation*, however, is an actual rewriting of the record, an altering of the description of the facts. Renovation is acceptable only as a temporary expedient to break a deadlock, except when that renovation alters memory of the immediate after-death experience.

SESSION. A meeting between patient and therapist. The first such meeting usually begins with an *intake*, and subsequent sessions begin with debriefing the patient about results of the previous session. Possible "homework" is discussed, along with developments since the last session.

The meeting continues with the *contract*, defining the issues to be addressed in the session, and identifying the *entry point*. An *induction* follows, using the verbal, imaginative, emotional or somatic *bridge* or combination of bridges. Alternative methods of focusing the patient on one issue may include the use of egostates, aura exploration or back pressing.

During the session proper, a patient is guided into a reliving or exploration through the use of open questions, open suggestions and open instructions. Important principles are the location of experiences in place and time, the anchoring of weak impressions and the resolving of blocks.

The session proper ends with *catharsis*. During *closure*, the cathartic results are confirmed, anchored, elaborated and connected to the present life of the patient. During *exit*, the patient is brought back to normal consciousness. Finally, a *review* is made in normal conversational mode. This review mirrors the intake and includes suggestions for homework.

SOMATIC. A bodily action or bodily sensation that signals a mental or emotional charge just before or during a session. A typical somatic might be a stomach that is tense with fear, cheeks that feel hot from shame, shoulders heavy from a mental burden, or head or back pain for which there is no medical cause.

SOUL. The entity that reincarnates. Some souls appear to have begun their individual lives as humans, and may be thought of as *starters*. Other souls appear to have evolved from higher mammals. Still others have been *spirits*, aware but not in physical bodies. Finally, some souls appear to have come from other planets. Aliens, extraterrestrials who once had non-human bodies, are rare. Starters and those who may have evolved from higher mammals are probably the most numerous by far, but they rarely seek past-life therapy.

SUBCONSCIOUS. Everything that we have forgotten or repressed, but also everything within us we have not yet discovered or realized.

TAO. In Chinese philosophy, a perfectly natural state involving the perception and acceptance of everything with tranquillity. A state of being centered and grounded, but also free and selfless.

TRANSACTIONAL ANALYSIS. A psychological theory developed by Eric Berne and Thomas Harris. Harris distinguishes three general egostates, the Adult, the Parent, and the Child.

Berne identified the TA-triangle with its three roles in neurotic games played between people: the Helper (also Rescuer or Savior), Prosecutor and Victim. Recognizing these roles is important in past-life work. Two more roles are included. First is what Morris Netherton identified as the angry or guilty Perpetrator, and the other is the avoiding or ignoring Witness.

TRAUMA. A mental and emotional wound that has not healed. The experience that caused this wound is referred to as traumatic or traumatizing. Emotions that are common with trauma are fear, grief, anger and despair. Mental responses to trauma are often confusion, perplexity and shock.

VOICE DIALOGUE. A psychotherapeutic method that evokes subpersonalities. With voice dialogue the patient assumes a different voice and a different position, and often a different location in the room, for each subpersonality. Conversation with and between subpersonalities involves a patient's shifting of position and voice.

BIBLIOGRAPHY

Albertson et al. - Post Traumatic Stress Disorders of Vietnam Veterans: A Proposal for Research and Therapeutic Healing Utilizing Depossession.
The Journal of Regression Therapy, Vol.3, No.1, 1988.

Ansbacher, Heinz L. & Rowena R. Ansbacher - The Individual Psychology of Alfred Adler. A Systematic Presentation in Selections from his Writings.
New York: Basic Books, 1981.

Baldwin, William - Healing the Unseen.
APRT Bulletin-5, Summer 1983.

Baldwin, William J. - Regression Therapy. Spirit Releasement Therapy.
A Technique Manual.
Carmel, CA: Center for Human Relations, 1991.

Banerjee, H.N. - Lesson in Past Life Regression.
San Diego: Metaphysical Book Club, 1981.

Caetano, Trisha - The Interview Technique in Past-Life Therapy.
APRT Newsletter, Winter 1985.

Cerminara, Gina (1950) - Many Mansions.
New York: Sloane, 1970.

Cerminara, Gina - Many Lives, Many Loves.
New York, Sloane, 1963.

Cerminara, Gina (1967) - The World Within.
London: Daniel, 1973.

Cladder, Joahnnes M. - Past-Life Therapy with Difficult Phobics.
The Journal of Regression Therapy, Vol.1, No.2., 1986.

Denning, Hazel - Restoration of Health Through Hypnosis.
The Journal of Regression Therapy, Vol.3, No. 1, 1987.

Dethlefsen, Thorvald - Voices from Other Lives.
New York: M. Evans and Company, 1977.

Edelstein, M. Gerald - Trauma, Trance and Transformation.
New York: Brunner/Mazel, 1981.

Findlay, Steven - Birth Trauma: A Factor in Teen Suicide?
USA Today, March 20, 1985.

Finkelstein, Adrian - Your Past Lives and the Healing Process:
A psychiatrist looks at reincarnation and spiritual healing.
Farmingdale: Coleman, 1985.

Fiore, Edith - You Have Been Here Before.
New York: Ballantine, 1978.

Fiore, Edith - The Unquiet Dead. A Psychologist Treats Spirit
Possession. Detecting and Removing Earth Bound Spirits.
Garden City, NJ: Doubleday & Co., 1987.

Fiore, Edith - Freeing Stalemates in Relationships by the Resolution of Entity Attachments
The Journal of Regression Therapy, Vol.3, No.1, 1988.

Fisher, Joe (1985) - The Case for Reincarnation
London: Grafton Books, 1986.

Glaskin, G.M. - Windows of the Mind.
London: Arron Books, 1974.

Glaskin, G.M. - Worlds Within.
London: Arron Books, 1978.

Glaskin, G.M. - A Door to Eternity.
Wildwood: Book Wise, 1979.

Goldberg, Bruce - Past Lives, Future Lives
North Hollywood: Newcastle, 1982

Hansen, Paul - Post-Accident Trauma Release: Release of Body Trauma from Current and Past-Life Traumas The Journal of Regression Therapy, Vol.3, No.1, 1987

Holzer, Hans - Life Beyond Life: The evidence for reincarnation.
West Nyack: Parker, 1985.

Hubbard, L. Ron - Dianetics: The modern science of mental health.
Copenhagen: New Era, 1982.

Ireland-Frey, Louise - Clinical Depossession: Releasement of attached entities from unsuspecting hosts.
The Journal of Regression Therapy, Vol.1, No.2, 1986.

Kardec, Allan (1857) - The Spirit's Book
London: Psychic Press, 1975

Kelsey, Denys & Joan Grant (1967) - Many Lifetimes.
London: Corgi, 1976.

Lenz, Frederick (1979) - Lifetimes: True accounts of reincarnation.
New York: Ballantine, 1986.

Lucas, Winafred B. - Mind Mirror Research on the Retrieval of Past Lives.
The Journal of Regression Therapy, Vol.4, No.2, 1989.

Lucas, Winafred B. - Regression Therapy: The Handbook for Professionals. Two Volumes.
Crest Park, C.A.: Deep Forest Press, 1993

McClain, Florence Wa ner - A Practical Guide to Past Life Regression.
St. Paul: Llewellyn, 1926.

Moss, Peter and Keeton, Joe - Encounters with the Past:
How man can experience and relive history
London: Sidgwick & Jackson, 1979.

Muller, Karl E.- Reincarnation based on facts.
Psychic Pockets, 1967.

Netherton, Morris & Nancy Shiffrin - Past Lives Therapy.
New York: Morrow, 1978.

Schlotterbeck, Karl - Living Your Past Lives.
New York: Ballantine, 1987.

Schubot, Erroll - Creative Source Therapy.
The Journal of Regression Therapy, Vol.2, No.2, 1987.

Shubow, Robert - The Return of the Soul:
A Transpersonal Model of the Disease and Healing Process.
APRT-Newsletter, Vol.9, No.3, Summer 1989

Siemons, J. L. - Revivre nos Vies Anterieurs.
Paris: Albin-Michel, 1984.

Sutphen, Dick and Trenna Sutphen - The Master of Life Manual.
Scottsdale, AZ: Valley of the Sun, 1980.

Sutphen, Dick and Taylor, Lauren - Past-life Therapy in Action.
Malibu: Valley of the Sun, 1983.

Ten Dam, Hans - Exploring Reincarnation.
London: Penguin, 1990.

Wambach, Helen - Reliving Past Lives.
New York: Bantam, 1978.

Wambach, Helen - Life before Life.
New York: Bantam, 1979.

Wambach, Helen - Past-Life Therapy: The Experience of Twenty-six Therapists.
The Journal of Regression Therapy, Vol.1, No.2, 1986.

Wambach, Helen S. & Leona L. Lee (1978) - The Wambach Method. A Manual for PastLife Recall.
APRT-Publication, 1986.

Weissman, Alan - We, Immortals.
New York: Pocket Books, 1977.

Whitton, Joel L. & Joe Fisher - Life between Life: Scientific explorations into the void separating one incarnation from the next.
Garden City: Doubleday, 1986.

Williston, Glen & Judith Johnstone - Soul Search. Spiritual Growth through a Knowledge of Past Lifetimes.
Wellingborough: Turnstone Press, 1983.

Woolger, Roger J. - Aspects of Past-Life Bodywork: Understanding Subtle Energy Fields. Part I: Theory. The Journal of Regression Therapy, Vol.2, No.1, 1987.

Woolger, Roger J. - Aspects of Past-Life Bodywork: Understanding Subtle Energy Fields. Part II: Practical Aspects. The Journal of Regression Therapy, Vol.2, No.2, 1987.

Woolger, Roger J. - Other Lives, Other Selves:
A Jungian psychotherapist discovers past lives.
New York: Doubleday, 1987.

INDEX